Informal Finance
in Low-Income Countries

Informal Finance
in Low-Income Countries

EDITED BY
Dale W Adams
and Delbert A. Fitchett

Westview Press

BOULDER • SAN FRANCISCO • OXFORD

This Westview softcover edition is printed on acid-free paper and bound in library-quality, coated covers that carry the highest rating of the National Association of State Textbook Administrators, in consultation with the Association of American Publishers and the Book Manufacturers' Institute.

Published in 1992 in the United States of America by Westview Press, Inc., 5500 Central Avenue, Boulder, Colorado 80301-2847, and in the United Kingdom by Westview Press, 36 Lonsdale Road, Summertown, Oxford OX2 7EW

A CIP catalog record for this book is available from the Library of Congress
ISBN 0-8133-1504-2

Printed and bound in the United States of America

The paper used in this publication meets the requirements
of the American National Standard for Permanence of Paper
for Printed Library Materials Z39.48-1984.

10   9   8   7   6   5   4   3   2   1

We dedicate this book to the much maligned moneylender because of her ability to walk barefoot where bankers fear to tread.

Contents

Preface

This book is a continuation of a line of inquiry into financial markets in low income countries begun in the early 1970s by the Agency for International Development (A.I.D.). Under the leadership of E. B. Rice, A.I.D. conducted a worldwide review of small farmer credit programs in 1972-73 that uncovered substantial and widespread problems. A summary of this review was published in Gordon Donald, *Credit for Small Farmers in Developing Countries* (Boulder, Colorado: Westview Press, 1976). Later, prescriptions for dealing with these problems were discussed in a Colloquium on Rural Finance in Low-Income Countries held in Washington, D.C., in September 1981. The meeting was sponsored by A.I.D., the Economic Development Institute (EDI) of the World Bank, and The Ohio State University. Most authors of papers presented in the Colloquium argued for major changes in donor funded finance projects. These papers were later published in Dale W Adams, Douglas H. Graham and J. D. Von Pischke, *Undermining Rural Development with Cheap Credit* (Boulder, Colorado: Westview Press, 1984). A companion book of readings was edited by J. D. Von Pischke, Dale W Adams, and Gordon Donald, *Rural Financial Markets in Developing Countries* (Baltimore, Maryland: Johns Hopkins University Press, 1983). These books outlined a new approach for developing financial markets in low income countries that was further elaborate upon in the World Bank's *World Development Report 1989* that focused on the importance of financial market development.

Until the early 1980s most attention focused on formal finance (that portion of the financial system regulated by a central monetary authority); only occasional mention was made of financial activities that were not regulated—informal finance. During the 1980s, however, research increasingly showed that informal finance played an important developmental role, especially for poor people: small farmers, landless people, operators of microenterprises, and women. It also became apparent in a number of countries that the informal system operated more efficiently and equitably than did formal finance.

These findings stimulated the organization of a state-of-the-arts Seminar on Informal Financial Markets in Development in Washington, D.C., October 18-20, 1989. The meeting was sponsored by several Bureaus within A.I.D, the EDI, the Agricultural Policies Division of the World Bank, and The Ohio State University. It brought together about 150 researchers, employees of donor agencies, consultants, and employees of non-governmental organization. This volume is made up of revised versions of papers presented at the Seminar along with several supplemental papers that cover topics or geographic regions not treated extensively in the Seminar.

We acknowledge the financial support given to the Seminar and to the preparation of this volume by the World Bank, A.I.D., and The Ohio State University. Melissa Brinkerhoff, Mike Caughlin, Eric Chetwynd, William Douglas, Antonio Gayoso, and Gloria Steele from A.I.D. were most helpful in assisting with arrangements for the Seminar. Avishay Braverman, Gershon Feder, Jacob Yaron, and Nicholas Wallis gave similar support from the World Bank.

The Seminar would not have been possible without the hard work behind the scenes of Barbara Lee and Sandy Krulikoski-Walden of The Ohio State University who typed, handled budgets, mailed, called, arranged, and, above all, had patience with the Seminar organizers. Sheri A. Jackson and Patrick Lavey of EDI efficiently and cheerfully handled the final preparations of the manuscript for publication. The individual authors of the various papers performed admirably in preparing their papers and acquiescing to revisions.

We especially wish to acknowledge the contribution of Professor F. J. A. Bouman, an authority on informal finance, who played a key role in reviewing chapters in this volume. While he was not able to attend the Seminar, he did prepare two valuable chapters that are included in the collection.

Finally, it should be pointed out that the views expressed in this publication do not represent the official views or policies of the Agency for International Development or the World Bank.

Dale W Adams
Delbert A. Fitchett

1

Introduction

Dale W Adams and Delbert A. Fitchett

Until recently few students of development concerned themselves with the financial activities occurring beyond the fringe of formal financial markets. Conventional wisdom held that these endeavors were comprised of exploitive loans from usurious moneylenders and of benign consumption credits lent by friends—neither of which promoted development. Moralists, politicians and policy makers occasionally fretted about informal lending, and these concerns usually had a negative tone: preaching against its evils, trying to regulate it, or developing credit programs aimed at substituting for it. Recently, however, increased interest in the private sector and a clearer perception of the difficulties in many formal credit programs have prompted many individuals to reevaluate old views about informal finance. Most of the chapters in this volume were written by researchers who are involved in this reassessment. The tone of their reports differs from conventional opinions about this topic and many authors conclude that informal finance makes important contributions to development, partly because formal financial systems often perform poorly.

What Is Informal Finance?

Various labels have been attached to the activities discussed in this book. A few decades ago the simple term moneylender was commonly used to categorize lending outside the purview of governments. As more was learned about this topic it became increasingly obvious that this term inadequately described the variety of financial arrangements involved. New terms such as unorganized, non-institutional, and even curb market were used to label these activities. As still more information became available these terms were also found wanting. The label unorganized did not adequately describe informal finance activities that persisted for long periods of time, that occasionally involved large transactions, and that were sometimes similar to bank functions. For example, a system that transfers funds earned by guest workers in the Middle-East to relatives living in the Philippines—guaranteeing to do so in only a couple of days—is hardly unorganized or non-institutional. Also, it seemed inappropriate to apply the term curb market to activities such as small savings and credit groups that are often found operating openly in government offices and even in central banks, or to pawnshops licensed by government.

In the past few years the expression informal finance has increasingly replaced these earlier terms. In this volume it is applied to all financial transactions, loans and deposits, occurring outside the regulation of a central monetary or financial market authority—the regulated activities being labeled as formal finance.

Instead of a simple dichotomous definition, it may be more useful to think of financial transactions as lying along a continuum that ranges from casual loans among friends and relatives, through loans made by merchants and traders, through loans and deposits handled by various types of informal credit and savings groups, through pawnshops that may operate with government license, through finance companies that have a corporate charter but are not regulated, through credit unions that in some countries are regulated and in other countries are not, and to banks that are closely regulated by a central bank. The middle part of this continuum is a grey area in many countries that does not lend itself to dichotomous categorization. These activities may be partially regulated by a government agency through licensing or supervision; Hans Dieter Seibel has suggested applying the term semi-formal finance to these transactions. In the rest of the chapters most of the discussion focuses on informal financial markets, but a handful of the authors also deal with semi-formal arrangements.

What Follows?

The chapters that follow are grouped by geographic area starting with Africa, followed by Asia, and then moving on to Latin America. Several general and summary chapters conclude the collection. The 31 authors provide insights into informal financial markets that can only be fully appreciated by reading each chapter. However, some useful insights come from looking across several chapters. From this cross-chapter comparison we came away with a number of new impressions; other readers may find it useful to compare their impressions with our list:

- Informal finance is ubiquitous in low income countries and it is concentrated wherever there are substantial amounts of commercial transactions—especially in urban areas—regardless of the state of development of formal financial markets.

- Although a large proportion of poor people participates in informal finance, informal loans and informal deposits are common among and between all economic classes. Informal financial markets are much more complex than just rich people lending to poor people.

- Informal financial markets often include a collage of dynamic, innovative, and flexible arrangements that are adapted to the local economic and social environment. These arrangements are resilient and many of them are sustained efforts. Although some forms of informal finance are contracting or disappearing, other forms are emerging or evolving into semi-formal or formal institutional forms. It is particularly surprising to see so many forms of informal finance thriving in countries where formal financial markets are severely stressed and also in countries where formal finance is operating efficiently. Clearly, informal finance does not simply wither away as formal financial markets expand.

- Informal finance provides other important services to participants besides loans; the most important of these being deposit opportunities. Someone must save to provide each unit of money circulating in informal finance. Large amounts of informal loans mirror an equally large amount of informal financial savings and many people who participate in these activities do so because of the opportunities it offers to save.

- Contrary to popular opinion, there is surprisingly little evidence of exploitation or monopoly profits in recent studies of informal financial markets. High opportunity costs of funds, important transaction costs, substantial lending risks, and lack of creditworthiness among borrowers appear to explain the high interest rates associated with a small proportion of informal lending.

- Traditionally, informal finance has been viewed as a plague on poor people. In contrast, most of the authors of the following chapters argue that large numbers of poor people benefit from their participation in informal financial markets. Although a few borrowers of informal loans may encounter problems in repaying their debts, a much large number realizes a net benefit from borrowing and repaying their loans without difficulty. Besides, for many poor people informal arrangements are a major saving technique and some poor people earn a major part of their income from lending.

- Informal finance also enhances the efficiency of resource allocation. It allows millions of individuals, firms, and households in low income countries who have surplus funds to redeploy them as loans to other individuals and firms who have better economic opportunities. This results in an increase in output and in capital formation over what would occur if informal financial markets did not, or could not operate.

- Some traditional discussions involve the assumption that informal and formal financial markets seldom touch. Recent programs aimed at linking formal and informal finance are predicated on this assumption. The following chapters show that major elements of informal finance are intertwined with formal finance. Informal deposits often move to banks, and funds from formal loans, when spent, often circulate through informal channels. It appears that formal and informal finance may be complements instead of substitutes in many cases.

We hope readers will come away with a more positive view of informal finance, more appreciation of its strengths, and find new ideas that might be used to improve the performance of formal finance projects: especially those aimed at small farmers, operators of microenterprises, and women. Simultaneously, we hope that readers will understand that this volume is not intended as a paean to informal finance. We must not lose sight of its limitations and the fundamental importance of efficient and undistorted formal financial markets to support economic development. Only an efficient formal financial system can provide the numerous large and long-term loans needed to promote major investments. Only formal finance can provide the security and liquidity that are needed to mobilize the large volumes of deposits required to make low income countries self sufficient in their capital formation efforts.

2

Taking a Fresh Look at Informal Finance

Dale W Adams[1]

Occasionally I have been asked to identify sustainable agricultural credit programs in low-income countries (LICs), but answering these requests causes me embarrassment, disappointment, surprise, amazement, and puzzlement. My embarrassment comes from being able to name so few sustainable programs, despite the tens of billions of dollars committed to hundreds of these efforts. At the same time, I painfully remember large numbers of transitory credit activities that have been plagued by loan recovery problems, chronic dependency on outside funds, and excessive transaction costs. My disappointment stems from seeing little improvement in the performance of these efforts since the mid-1960s when a number of us began working on problems of rural financial markets (RFMs).[2] Although our understanding of how financial markets function and what causes them to misfire has expanded substantially in the past two decades, only in a handful of cases has this new knowledge been used to treat these problems. I have

1. Many of the ideas in this paper have been gleaned from others. F. J. A. Bouman and Clifton Barton gave me lectures years ago about the importance of informal finance that I only now appreciate fully. J. D. Von Pischke, Robert Vogel, and colleagues at The Ohio State University have done much of the research and original thinking on which I base my chapter. Two anthropologists, Marie Canavesi and Virginia Sandoval, also exposed me to informal finance in Bolivia and the Philippines. In addition, I learned a great deal about informal finance while attending an excellent seminar on informal finance in the Philippines in early 1989 sponsored by the Asian Development Bank and organized by P. B. Ghate.
2. This work has been funded mostly by the Agency for International Development and has involved research in more than three dozen low-income countries.

grudgingly concluded that creating sustainable rural credit programs is far more difficult to do than most of us had heretofore thought.

My embarrassment and disappointment are tempered by surprise. In doing research in Bolivia and the Philippines—two countries suffering substantial economic stress—I encountered informal finance thriving amidst the rubble of formal financial markets. I was surprised to see informal lenders recovering most of their loans while nearby formal lenders were awash in defaults, and I marveled at the ability of informal finance to mobilize and allocate large amounts of voluntary savings, while banks had trouble attracting deposits.

My amazement arises from the contrast in the types of people served by formal and informal finance along with the differences in types of services provided. Formal finance typically involves large loans and deposits, secure collateral, relatively long-term financial instruments, and legal support. Formal finance also services mostly individuals who are the crème de la crème but who are required to come to the financial institution to transact their business. In contrast, informal finance frequently involves small loans and deposits, commonly operates without collateral, typically deals with short-term transactions, and often works in the legal shadows. Many participants in the informal system are poor people, women, operators of small businesses, small farmers, and the landless—people who are often unable to obtain formal financial services. Unlike formal finance, transactions in informal finance usually occur at the doorstep of clients, at their place of work, or in popular markets. I am amazed that informal finance can provide these services to the people it does without choking on expenses and drowning in defaults. Like the aeronautical engineers who have analyzed bees and concluded they should not be able to fly, I am convinced that informal finance defies the laws of financial gravity.

Further, I am puzzled by the ability of informal finance to provide sustained financial services to large numbers of individuals who have been targets of transitory formal credit programs. These formal efforts are usually staffed by educated people who receive extensive assistance from donors and governments along with ample access to both subsidies and concessionary funds. Even with these advantages, formal rural credit efforts often founder, while informal finance typically flourishes. Success in financial transactions appears to be inversely related to years of education of the participants, technical assistance received, access to concessionary funds, and extent of regulation. This raises several important questions: Why do formal agricultural credit programs so often fail? And, why do informal financial activities so often succeed? I deal mainly with the latter question in the following discussion.

Traditional Views About Informal Finance

Informal forms of lending—particularly moneylenders—are stereotyped as being evil in many cultures. Poets, prophets, playwrights, and politicians have pointed accusing fingers at informal lenders and questioned the comfort of their after-life since the beginning of recorded history. Individuals as diverse as Cicero, Shelley, Shakespeare, Marx, the Prophet Mohammed, and authors of the *Old Testament* have vented their spleens on the supposed evils of money lending. Pejorative and emotive terms such as *monopolist, usurer, shylock, loan shark,* and *exploiter* color discussions of this subject. I know of no other topic in development where anecdotal horror stories are told and retold so often to nurture traditional views. For my tastes, too many discussions of informal lending include racial and ethnic undertones reflecting the dark side of human nature: for example, biases against Jews in Europe, overseas Chinese in East Asia, Indians in East Africa, Ibos in West Africa, and people from the Middle East in Latin America. These biases also stem from the natural tendency to fear and dislike an activity, such as financial intermediation, that is poorly understood and, to some observers, is mysterious.

Until relatively recently, much of the research on informal finance was done in what was Colonial India or by sociologists and anthropologists. Studies by Darling (1925) and others in India in the early 1900s showed that informal lending provided most of the loans in rural areas and that the interest rates applied were often higher than those charged by banks in either India or the United Kingdom. Subsequent studies in India—especially the All-India-Rural Credit Surveys carried out each decade since the early 1950—set the agenda for much of the later research and policy dialogue on informal finance in other regions. This agenda was generally negative in tone and stressed documenting the relative importance of informal finance, the extent of monopoly profits in these transactions, how loans linked to other marketing activities boosted profits, and the extent to which informal lending was used to appropriate land pledged as collateral.

I am uneasy with this stereotyping and with the associated negative research. I feel there are important lessons to be learned from more objective study of informal finance—lessons that are overlooked as long as we insist on chasing bogeymen in research on informal finance. Taking a fresh look at informal finance should involve studying the services provided along with the associated techniques, practices, and technologies used. Careful analysis of informal finance may also provide clearer insights into the types of financial services individuals and firms find to be most useful.

Types of Informal Finance

Finance exists because of heterogeneity among firms and individuals and because of the specialization and trade that ensues from these differences. This, in turn, results in a variety of financial needs that are partly met by a multiplicity of informal arrangements. Although the stereotyped moneylender receives most of the publicity, a large variety of other arrangements handle most informal financial transaction in LICs. Some of these arrangements are centuries old, while other systems of informal finance are constantly evolving as the contours of the society and the economy change. The kaleidoscope of arrangements defies simple classification, and it is unusual to find a substantial number of these arrangements that are identical—a testimony to the flexibility and creativity involved in informal finance. For purposes of illustrating the variety found in these systems I briefly describe ten types of informal finance. Although I treat these ten types separately, it is common for them to overlap and also to be intertwined with other production or marketing activities.

Sophisticated but Unregulated Institutions

In many countries various types of organizations provide loans or accept deposits that are only regulated slightly by a government entity. Regulation may be as simple as a license to operate with little subsequent supervision. Credit unions, indigenous banks, pawnshops, and finance companies are examples of institutions that receive only cursory regulation in certain countries. In addition, nongovernmental organizations (NGOs) may be providing financial services with tacit government approval but with only slight regulation.

In several countries, including the Dominican Republic, Guatemala, Pakistan, and India, sophisticated financial institutions have emerged that are informal only in the sense that they are not regulated. These institutions act like commercial banks and are often located in bank-like offices that appeal to middle- and upper-class clients. They exist primarily to avoid taxes or regulations. In some cases they may be affiliated with banks through joint ownership or holding companies.

Several studies suggest that these unregulated organizations charge reasonable interest rates and operate with modest transaction costs (Vogel 1988; Zinzer and others 1986; and Nayar 1982).

Moneylenders

Individuals who spend most of their time lending money—moneylenders—are significant sources of loans, mainly in Asia. Typically, their loans are granted for short periods, are unsecured by collateral, and are extended to long-term clients. Most moneylenders operate on a small scale, extend loans mainly out of their own funds, and restrict lending to less than fifty or so individuals. Moneylenders typically charge interest rates that are high relative to other lenders but extend loans quickly and impose few transaction costs on borrowers. These lenders operate in localized markets and often have highly personalized relationships with borrowers.

The main advantage moneylenders have over formal lenders is the comprehensive information they accumulate about their clients through day-to-day contact which limits the number of clients they can assemble. Timberg and Aiyar (1984) found an extreme example of this when they asked an Indian moneylender how he decided to take on additional clients; he responded that he had never had a new client. Understandably, the proprietary nature of this information causes moneylenders to be leery about sharing candid information about their operations with researchers.

Merchants

A closely related and much more common form of informal credit is provided by individuals who are primarily merchants but who also extend loans linked to the sale or purchase of commodities (Floro 1987; Harriss 1983; and Bardhan 1980). Typically, lending is only a minor part of the merchant's activities, loans are repaid in relatively short periods of time, many of the loans carry no explicit interest charge, and the lender may adjust the price of the commodity involved in credit transactions as compensation for the loan. Economies of scope are the main advantage that a merchant realizes in providing loans. Merchants can generally sell more fertilizer or purchase more rice, for example, if they also offer loans to their customers. Like the moneylender, merchants have the advantage of possessing inexpensive information about the borrower that is accumulated through purchases and sales of commodities. Under normal conditions the volume of loans provided by merchants increases as commercialization expands.

Some itinerant peddlers also provide small, short-term loans to customers. In the Philippines, peddlers—often called Bombays—sell items as diverse as umbrellas, electric fans, cosmetics, and clothing door-to-door in rural areas. They often make their village rounds on a daily or weekly basis to sell goods, take orders, and collect installment payments on previous purchases. Fruin (1937) reported similar services provided in rural areas of Indonesia during the 1930s by "installment chinamen."

Pawnbrokers

Still another form of informal finance is pawning, one of the oldest forms of lending. Some pawnbrokers work full-time at this occupation, whereas others pursue it as a sideline to money lending or marketing. In several countries, Indonesia and Sri Lanka, for example, pawnshops are affiliated with some banks.

Distinctive features of pawnshops are that they typically make small loans for short periods and resolve the loan collateralization problem inexpensively by requiring borrowers to exchange collateral physically for loans. Unlike banks, moneylenders, and traders, pawnbrokers need almost no information about their borrowers unless they are wary about receiving stolen goods. The pawnbroker realizes revenue from interest on loans and from the difference between loan amounts and sales receipts from items received as security on defaulted loans. Contrary to conventional wisdom, Bouman and Houtman (1988) argue that most pawnbrokers prefer to have individuals redeem the items they pawn, as this improves the chances of their continuing as clients.

Some individuals in the Philippines make their living primarily by conducting informal pawning operations combined with peddling items door-to-door that are not redeemed. These individuals may have loose working relationships with formal pawnshops or with relatively wealthy people who occasionally provide them operating funds. They may also combine their pawning activities with selling nonpawned goods door-to-door and offering installment arrangements on these sales (Adams and Sandoval 1989).

Loan Brokers

Another type of informal finance is carried out by loan brokers who facilitate contacts among people with money to lend and borrowers by trading on inside information about potential clients. Typically, loans handled by brokers are relatively large and for a longer term than are most informal loans. Virtually anyone can enter the business who is able to assemble information about potential clients. Because borrowers of these brokered loans usually do not qualify for additional bank credit, interest rates applied to these loans may be relatively high. As Larson and Urquidi (1987) point out, some lenders in Bolivia insist on collateral such as real estate before making a brokered loan. The broker is usually not a principal in the transaction but merely arranges contacts between lenders and borrowers. Some brokers may also provide collection or guarantee services and thus become more like principals than agents.

A different form of loan broker operates widely in rural areas of Bangladesh. These brokers obtain loan application forms from banks, help illiterate people fill them out, obtain necessary signatures and guarantees, and also allocate bribes necessary to overcome barriers to borrowing (Maloney and Ahmed 1988). The broker is commonly rewarded through a share of the bribe or a share of the loan and acts as a legal buffer between the payer and receiver of the bribe.

Landlords

Although the practice is less common now than previously, some landowners still provide their tenants with loans. The main reason for this is scope economies. These loans facilitate access to labor and entrepreneurial skills that might otherwise be difficult to employ or manage. Typically, landlord lending declines in relative importance with land reform and with the expansion of other types of formal and informal finance (Sacay and others 1985).

A variant of this occurs when landowners who borrow money transfer to a lender usufruct rights over land, orchards, or fishing facilities for a time until loans are repaid. This arrangement is common in the highlands of Ecuador and among cacao farmers in Ghana (Adegboye 1969). It is also increasingly found in the Philippines, where farmers may pawn the title to some of their land and transfer use rights to the lender for a time to obtain relatively large loans to finance employment abroad by a family member.

Friends and Relatives

Perhaps the most common form of informal finance, both in terms of number and value of transactions, is loans from friends and relatives. In some countries these credits make up half or more of all informal loans. Many of these loans involve no interest or collateral, they may be large or small, and many have open-ended repayment arrangements. The most important feature of many of these loans is reciprocity: the expectation that the borrower is willing to provide a loan to the lender sometime in the future. In cases where the individuals involved have scant access to other forms of finance, the reciprocity may be an important way of managing uncertainty and risk through establishing and strengthening interpersonal ties. In many parts of Africa loans between father and sons and between wife and husband are common.

Money Guards

Another form of informal finance is the money guard, a responsible person who agrees to safeguard cash for individuals. Graham and others (1988) report finding money guards in Niger, Maloney and Ahmed (1988) also found them in Bangladesh, and Bouman and Houtman (1988) report similar arrangements in India. Almost the entire reason for money guards is that they offer a secure place to deposit funds. In most cases these deposits earn no interest, although money guards may give depositors token favors or gifts. There are no restrictions on the uses money guards may make of deposited funds. In some cases depositors feel guards are doing them a favor by holding their money, and the amount of money deposited by each individual is usually small.

Savings Groups

Another important form of informal finance is done through savings groups. These consist of individuals who either regularly or irregularly, deposit funds with a group leader (Maloney and Ahmed 1988; Begashaw 1978). In most cases these groups are formed spontaneously, but in Thailand a government agency—the Community Development Department—plays a role in organizing such groups. The main problem these groups resolve is the pooling of savings, and it is not uncommon for mobilized funds to be deposited in banks. While groups may collect funds regularly, they do not distribute them among members through any systematic rotation. These groups are part of a larger class of informal groups that pursue a variety of purposes ranging from conducting financial intermediation to taxing group members in order to improve public facilities.

Some groups periodically collect funds from members and then return the amounts deposited to savers at the end of a given period; these are essentially contractual savings programs. Instead of returning contributions to members, other groups use money collected as emergency loan funds. Group members are essentially building reciprocal credit possibilities through their deposits. In other cases, the funds collected may be used to invest in enterprises that are administered by the group. Some groups are managed by commission agents, while others are run by volunteer leaders. Various forms of these groups can be found in most low-income nations, but they are especially important in Africa and in Islamic countries.

ROSCAs

A more complicated form of group finance is called rotating savings and credit associations (ROSCAs). They are found in many LICs and have been extensively studied, especially by sociologists and anthropologists (Bouman 1977). In a number of areas more individuals participate in ROSCAs than have dealings with formal financial institutions, and large amounts of money may be involved. Recent research by Schrieder (1989) in Cameroon suggested the volume of deposits moving through ROSCAs there may be larger than the amounts held in banks. In some countries, especially among ethnic minorities, ROSCAs are a primary way of raising funds to make large business investments (Barton 1977; and Wu 1974).

These associations are particularly interesting because they explicitly pool savings and tie loans to deposits. ROSCAs also resolve the loan collateral and borrower information problems by enrolling only members who have mutual confidence in each other or by having organizers who guarantee the performance of individuals they enroll. Loan recovery is seldom a problem in ROSCAs because a defaulting member not only loses the opportunity to remain in the association but may also be shunned and experience the loss of social and business ties that accompany membership.

It is surprising how often ROSCAs are found among employees of formal financial intermediaries: in the National Credit Union

Federation in Chocabamba, Bolivia; people working for the Development Finance Corporations in both Belize and St. Kitts/Nevis; numerous employees of commercial banks and central banks in Belize, Papua New Guinea, Bolivia, the Dominican Republic, and the Philippines; and in 1987 there was even a ROSCA operating among employees of the International Monetary Fund in Washington, D.C., all of whom had doctoral degrees in economics or finance!

The Case Against Exploitation

Critics often cite exorbitant interest rates as the main justification for condemning informal finance. Cases of lenders charging 10 percent per day on loans, for example, are cited and then generalized as being representative of exploitation and proof of monopoly power. Also cited and generalized are horror stories about evil moneylenders or merchants who, in order to capture the borrower's collateral, extend loans to individuals whom lenders know will be unable to repay, debts that are inherited by the borrower's children, landlords who tie their tenants to land through debt at the company store, and merchants who link loans to repayment in kind and force borrowers to repay with products that are grossly underpriced (Basu 1984; and Bhaduri 1977). These horror stories illustrate situations that are only possible when the lender exercises a large measure of monopoly power. Also, they report one-time operations that normally do not make economic sense for lenders who benefit from sustained relationships with their clients.

These blanket indictments, moreover, ignore the large number of informal loans made at modest interest rates, the multitude of loans made and repaid without the lender foreclosing on collateral, and the complexities involved in loans tied to marketing and production. They also ignore the extensive deposit mobilization that occurs in these markets, the multitude of informal loans made with no collateral involved, and the large number of people who pay high interest rates on their loans but realize even higher rates of return on investments made with borrowed funds. Critics also fail to mention that moneylenders may make only a few loans at extremely high interest rates, that these credits are often unsecured, and that borrowers paying the highest rates have weak credit ratings. Critics also ignore inflation. In the mid-1980s informal lenders in Bolivia would have lost purchasing power on their loans if they had only charged 10 percent per week while inflation roared along at a rate of several thousand percent per year.

It is also important to remember that many of the loans with so called usurious interest rates are small and are for very short periods. It is common in Latin America, for example, for street vendors to borrow occasionally in the morning enough funds to cover their sales for the day and then to repay loans in the evening. A typical loan may be for only $10 and require repayment of $11, an annual interest rate of over 3,000 percent. At the same time, the loan may allow the vendor to realize daily earnings that are several times the value of the loan. It is unlikely that moralists would be upset with a merchant who each day sold merchandise to a vendor but added a markup of 10 percent to the price of the good, a transaction that did not involve a loan.

At least three questions must be answered to establish whether lenders are taking undue advantage of borrowers: (1) What are a lender's opportunity costs of funds, transaction costs, and the risks involved in lending? (2) Are most informal lenders in a position to extract monopoly profits? And (3) are credit transactions tied with marketing and production to enhance exploitation?

Opportunity Costs and Risk

Much has been asserted about the ubiquitous monopoly power of moneylenders, but little proof has been presented to support this allegation. Several recent studies show that moneylenders' interest rates are high because the opportunity costs of funds together with lending risks are high (Von Pischke and others 1983). It is unreasonable to expect moneylenders to charge borrowers less than the rate of return lenders could realize on alternative investments and many moneylenders have business alternatives that yield high marginal returns. The high interest rates in informal markets may largely indicate that funds are scarce and that at least some people realize high rates of return from using borrowed funds.

In chapter 20, Christen makes the same point from the perspective of borrowers in Latin America. He argues that many managers of microenterprises borrow from moneylenders at high rates of interest because of the low transaction costs involved and the high quality and dependability of the informal financial services and also because high rates of return result from the use of borrowed funds. Many of these high return activities are also available to lenders and are further indications of high opportunity costs of lending.

In addition, because of the seasonality of agricultural production, informal lenders may find it impossible to keep all of their money lent

during the year. This forces them to charge higher interest rates during
the time their money is lent to make up for periods when some of their
funds are idle.

Monopoly Profits

Because of the lack of barriers to entry, the large number of forms of
finance, and the large number of people who are willing to enter
markets where high rates of return are realized, it is difficult to see
how informal lenders can regularly extract substantial monopoly
profits. All of the many forms of informal finance, as well as formal
lenders, partially compete with each other. In addition, anyone with
money or easily transferable resources can become a lender. Effectively,
there are few barriers to entry into informal finance. Likewise,
borrowers can compete with informal lenders through substitution of
equity for debt, barter, and sale and repurchase of assets. For example,
if farmers have been borrowing funds from moneylenders to pay cash
rent on farm land, they can instead rent land on a share basis from
landowners. Also, the reason people invented money is that it will
substitute for so many other things, but the reverse is also true: many
things are partial substitutes for money through barter. The conditions
necessary to realize monopoly profits exist only with barriers to entry
and a highly differentiated product, conditions seldom encountered in
informal financial markets.

If traces of monopoly power exist in informal financial markets they
can be moderated by expanding formal lending. To be fully effective,
however, the expansion in formal finance must compete with those
elements of the informal system that have too little competition. An
expansion of cheap formal loans that goes largely to well-to-do
individuals does not compete with informal lenders who are largely
serving the poor (Gonzalez-Vega 1984).

Loans Linked with Marketing

It is often difficult to establish clearly the charges that are applied
to loans when the loan or the repayment are in kind, as is often the case
with loans linked to marketing. For example, a merchant in Sudan may
agree to lend a farmer two sacks of millet and require the repayment of
three sacks at harvest time in only two months. On a commodity basis,
this amounts to a monthly interest rate of 25 percent or an annual rate of

300 percent. On a financial basis, however, the rate is much lower, even ignoring inflation. Usually, the market price of millet between harvests is significantly higher than the price during harvest. If the interharvest price ranged from 25 to 50 percent higher than harvest prices, the interest rate on the loan would range from 0 to 120 percent on an annual basis. When loan repayment is in kind, the merchant assumes all of the price risk, something that is of additional value to the borrower. If a merchant, in fact, consistently realizes a monopoly profit on his millet-credit transactions, the cause may be imperfections in the millet market rather than monopoly power exercised in credit transactions. The merchant may own the only truck in town that is needed to haul millet to central markets, but it is less likely that the merchant will be the only person in the area who has funds or resources to lend. If monopoly power lies in other markets linked to informal finance, that power will not be directly affected by finance activities or their regulation.

Although I have not systematically studied linked credit transactions, I have talked with a large number of merchants in various countries who provide loans to some of their customers to facilitate purchases or sales of goods. I have yet to find a merchant who would not prefer cash transactions over those involving credit. This suggests to me that most merchants view lending as a necessary nuisance rather than as a way to sweat additional profits out of their clients.

Moneylenders as Hospitals

Some so-called malignant informal lenders are mainly involved in providing small, short-term loans that are seldom backed by collateral and that are made to individuals who often suffer economic reverses. It is this part of informal finance that is a lightning rod for criticism of informal finance in general.

Instead of stereotyping as evil the informal lenders who serve this difficult set of clients, it may be more useful to think of them metaphorically as hospitals. Many of the patients who go there are physically (financially) stressed. They lack sufficient knowledge (funds) to heal themselves. As a result of their visit, some of these patients are cured and never return to the hospital. The health of others is improved by their visit, but some of them must return periodically for additional treatments (loans) to sustain their well-being. A few patients may perish (default) after coming to the hospital because their illnesses were too far advanced, they had afflictions that could not be treated by medicine (loans), or they refused to follow prudent health practices (were inefficient or unlucky managers).

Continuing the metaphor, hospitals are the most expensive form of medical treatment (charge the highest interest rates) because they mostly handle patients who are seriously ill (have the lowest credit ratings). In times of plague or natural disaster, a higher proportion of the patients (borrowers) coming to the hospitals may expire (default) because the hospital staff cannot give them sufficient attention (loans) or because they cannot extend the treatment over a long enough period of time (roll over the debt). More of the patients may also pass away (default) because they arrive at the hospital in worse shape than is true in normal times. In addition, doctors (informal lenders) will make more mistakes in their treatments (loans) because they are also stressed by the disaster. Because hospital employees are susceptible to many of the ills suffered by their patients, some of the employees (informal lenders) contact diseases from their patients and become seriously ill and even expire (go bankrupt).

Blaming moneylenders for the financial difficulties encountered by a few of their borrowers is as illogical as condemning hospitals because they treat people who are ill and because some of their patients pass away.

Lessons from Informal Finance

Informal finance persists and often flourishes because it resolves important problems that are handled poorly or not at all by most formal financial systems. I see at least six important lessons in this.

Types of Services Provided

The variety of informal financial arrangements is evidence of the broad range of financial services demanded by people in low-income countries. It is surprising how different these services are from those emphasized in traditional formal credit programs. Deposits, small loans, and short-term loans make up a large majority of informal financial transactions—services that are almost always absent in formal credit programs for poor people. I conclude that many traditional credit programs may be providing the wrong mix of financial services.

Process Based on Discipline

Informal finance almost always involves participants in orderly processes that result in increasingly disciplined behavior. Informal lenders must discipline themselves to save funds for lending. They must further discipline themselves to collect sufficient information about prospective borrowers so their loans can be made on the basis of creditworthiness. Informal lenders typically learn to judge creditworthiness and mobilize deposits over many years and only survive in the business if they are successful in developing these skills. Because most informal lenders have equity interest in their loans, they look at credit as a privilege, not an entitlement, and view lending as a serious transaction rather than as a game of passing out favors.

Informal borrowers also learn discipline as they attempt to establish and expand their creditworthiness in the eyes of informal lenders or group members. Borrowers of informal loans must earn the privilege of borrowing through disciplined steps that may include saving before borrowing, repaying small loans before receiving larger loans, and always repaying obligations to sustain access to informal finance. The products of increased discipline are strong and dependable working relationships between lenders and borrowers. These working relationships are the foundation of stable, reliable, and sustainable financial markets.

All too often, traditional development lending is a hurried event that ignores this important process of learning, testing, and discipline building. I conclude that formal lenders ought to spend more time learning how to make loans on the basis of creditworthiness and that more attention must be given to helping borrowers systematically build their creditworthiness before flooding them with loans.

Savings

The large amounts of savings that surface in informal financial markets are an indication of substantial propensities to save voluntarily and also show the failure of most formal financial systems to provide attractive deposit services. Rural banks and cooperatives that do not accept deposits, negative real rates of interest on many deposits, and cheap rediscounting facilities in most central banks have resulted in few formal deposits being mobilized. Although formal financial systems should have a comparative advantage in mobilizing voluntary deposits, they have been largely designed to dispense cheap funds provided by government and donors. I conclude that informal finance works well because it depends on voluntary savings (local money), while formal finance often fails because it heavily relies on governments or donors for funds (foreign money).

Reciprocity

Many forms of informal finance involve reciprocity: the direct tying of loans to deposits or one person lending to another with the understanding—often implied rather than explicitly stated—that the lender may someday need to reverse roles. These unutilized credit reserves are especially important for low-income people. Seldom do traditional formal credit programs provide lines of credit or more than just a single loan during a given period—they do not provide emergency credit. I conclude that formal finance would be much more useful to many people in LICs if credit reserves were more readily available.

Financial Innovation

Informal finance is laced with innovations that reduce transaction costs, especially for depositors and borrowers. It is surprising how quickly informal finance can innovate to accommodate changing conditions such as inflation, economic prosperity, or economic downturns. Flexibility and suppleness are hallmarks of informal finance. In contrast, much of the innovative energy in formal financial markets is directed at regulation avoidance, and formal finance is often too brittle and rigid to respond effectively when economic conditions change.

I conclude from this that managers of formal financial institutions ought to be more observant of innovations and changes in informal finance and try to emulate some of these innovations.

Transaction Costs

A major achievement of informal finance is keeping the transaction costs of borrowers and savers low by bringing financial services to places and at times that are convenient to clients. In contrast, formal finance focuses mainly on reducing the transaction costs of the financial intermediary with little concern given to how this affects depositors and borrowers. With rare exceptions, clients of formal financial intermediaries must make deposits and seek loans on the premises of the intermediary, at times that may or may not be convenient to clients.

The sharp differences in the distribution of transaction costs among participants in formal and informal financial markets are excellent proxies for the basic orientation of principal actors in these two markets. Formal intermediaries are mainly concerned with cultivating their major sources of funds: government officials, central bank employees, and donor employees; borrowers or depositors of small amounts are often treated with disdain. Informal intermediaries, in contrast, are almost entirely concerned about sustaining quality relationships with their borrowers or depositors.

I conclude from this that formal lenders must pay much more attention to reducing the transaction costs of borrowers and depositors and that they will likely not do this until large amounts of external funds are no longer available to them.

Concluding Remarks

Sustainable financial markets that operate efficiently and equitably are vital ingredients in rural development. The results of many formal agricultural credit programs in LICs over the past 30 years have been disappointing, and informal finance appears to be doing a better job of servicing the financial needs of many people in these countries than do these formal efforts. I do not want to be misinterpreted as arguing that formal financial arrangements are unnecessary and that informal finance is sufficient to support development; informal lenders are not the equivalent of the "noble savage." An efficient formal system is clearly necessary to intermediate over large distances, to efficiently manage large amounts of deposits, to make large loans, and to make long-term loans.

My contention is that instead of trying to abolish informal financial arrangements, policymakers would be better advised to learn from them. Studying these markets will help to clarify the financial services that informal finance is providing more efficiently than formal intermediaries and may also uncover practices that could be adopted by banks and cooperative that are providing financial services. Giving three cheers for the informal lender may be more in order than trying to drive them out of business.

References

Adams, Dale W and Virginia Nazarea-Sandoval. 1989. "Informal Finance in the Philippines." Economics and Sociology Occasional Paper No. 1570. Department of Agricultural Economics and Rural Sociology. Columbus, Ohio: Ohio State University.

Adegboye, R. O. 1969. "Procuring Loans by Pledging Cocoa Trees." *Journal of the Geographical Association of Nigeria* 12.

Bardhan, Prahab K. 1980. "Interlocked Factor Markets and Agrarian Development: A Review of Issues." *Oxford Economic Papers* 32: 82-98.

Barton, Clifton G. 1977. "Credit and Commercial Control: Strategies and Methods of Chinese Businessmen in South Vietnam." Unpublished Ph.D. dissertation, Department of Anthropology. Ithaca, New York: Cornell University.

Basu, K. 1984. *The Less Developed Economy.* Oxford: Blackwell.

Begashaw, Girma. 1978. "The Economic Role of Traditional Savings and Credit Institutions in Ethiopia." *Savings and Development* 4 :249-262.

Bhaduri, Amit. 1977. "On The Formation of Usurious Interest Rates in Backward Agriculture." *Cambridge Journal of Economics* 1: 341-352.

Bouman, F. J. A. 1977. "Indigenous Savings and Credit Societies in the Third World: A Message." *Savings and Development* 1: 181-220.

Bouman, F. J. A. and R. Houtman. 1988. "Pawnbroking as an Instrument of Rural Banking in the Third World." *Economic Development and Cultural Change* 37: 69-89.

Darling, M. L. 1925. *The Punjab Peasant in Prosperity and Debt.* London: Oxford University Press.

Floro, Sagrario Lim. 1987. "Credit Relations and Market Interlinkage in Philippine Agriculture." Unpublished Ph.D. dissertation, Stanford, California: Stanford University.

Fruin, Th. A. 1937. "Popular and Rural Credit in the Netherlands Indies." *Bulletin of The Colonial Institute of Amsterdam* 1: 106-115.

Gonzalez-Vega, Claudio. 1984. "Cheap Agricultural Credit: Redistribution in Reverse." In Dale W Adams and others, eds., *Undermining Rural Development with Cheap Credit*, pp. 120-132. Boulder, Colorado: Westview Press.

Graham, Douglas H. and others. 1988. "Informal Finance in Rural Niger: Scope, Magnitude and Organization." Economics and Sociology Occasional Paper No. 1472. Department of Agricultural Economics and Rural Sociology. Columbus, Ohio: The Ohio State University.

Harriss, Barbara. 1983. "Money and Commodities: Their Interaction in a Rural Indian Setting." In J. D. Von Pischke and others, eds., *Rural Financial Markets in Developing Countries.* pp. 233-241. Baltimore and London: The Johns Hopkins University Press.

Larson, Donald W. and Rene Urquidi 1987. "Competitiveness of Informal Financial Markets in Bolivia." *Economics and Sociology Occasional Paper No. 1426.* Department of Agricultural Economics and Rural Sociology. Columbus, Ohio: Ohio State University.

Maloney, Clarence, and A. B. Sharfuddin Ahmed. 1988. *Rural Savings and Credit in Bangladesh.* Dhaka: The University Press Ltd.

Nayar, C. P. S. 1982. "Finance Corporations: An Informal Financial Intermediary in India." *Savings and Development* 6: 15-52.

Sacay, Orlando J., Meliza H. Agabin, and Chita Irene Tonchoco. 1985. *Small Farmer Credit Dilemma.* Manila: Technical Board on Agricultural Credit.

Schrieder, Gertrud. 1989. "Informal Financial Groups in Cameroon: Motivation, Organization and Linkages." Unpublished Masters thesis, Department of Agricultural Economics and Rural Sociology. Columbus, Ohio: Ohio State University.

Timberg, Thomas A., and C. V. Aiyar. 1984. "Informal Credit Markets in India." *Economic Development and Cultural Change* 33: 43-59.

Vogel, Robert C. 1988. "Guatemala: Informal Finance" Unpublished study prepared for the World Bank in Washington, D.C.

Von Pischke, J. D. and others. 1983. *Rural Financial Markets in Developing Countries: Their Use and Abuse.* Baltimore, Maryland: Johns Hopkins University Press.

Wu, David Y. 1974. "To Kill Three Birds with One Stone: The Rotating Credit Associations of the Papua New Guinea Chinese." *American Ethnologist* 1: 565-583.

Zinzer, James and others. 1986. *Mercado Financiero No Regulado.* Santo Domingo, Dominican Republic: Centro de Estudios Monetarios y Bancarios.

3

The Rope and the Box:
Group Savings in The Gambia

Parker Shipton[1]

Juloo, "rope" to a Mandinko, means several things. It can refer to a small-scale trader, or to credit and debt. Every Mandinko knows the meanings are related. Traders are also lenders, and their loans, although sometimes useful like a rope ladder, also tie down a borrower like a rope around the neck. When rural people in The Gambia speak of juloo, in any of these uses, they consciously or unconsciously connote slavery. The Mandinko and other peoples of this small and impoverished West African river nation have had occasion in history to learn about ropes and involuntary servitude and about debt.

In recent decades, international interventions in Gambian agriculture have been based mainly on credit. Each year, with mixed motives, new committees in public and private agencies convene in Banjul, the capital, to seek new ways of extending loans into the countryside. The composite record of the lending projects has been disappointing for farmers and nearly all others concerned. Particularly unimpressive have been the records of the government cooperatives, which now dominate the rural credit picture with their inefficient yet now rather indispensable operations, and the commercial banks, which deal with almost no rural Gambians (Demissie and others 1989; Shipton 1987; Rmamurthy 1986; and Wing 1983).

1. The research on which this paper is based was funded by the Agency for International Development (AID), in association with the Harvard Institute for International Development (HIID) and the Ministry of Finance and Trade in The Gambia. The staffs of the Ministry and the AID Banjul Mission, and my colleagues at the HIID provided valuable assistance.

In the following discussion I suggest that the country's financial development strategies, formulated with outside assistance, have been unbalanced. Farmers need not just loans, but also more and better opportunities for savings, partly to reduce their dependency on borrowing. A policy based on only loans without savings is not only ethically dubious, but also impractical; it is like walking on one leg.

The informal rural financial mechanisms that work in The Gambia, as elsewhere in Africa, link loans and deposits, and they combine elements of individualism and collective responsibility. They take account of both achievement incentives and social risks for savers. Where farmers are involved with financiers, not just capital but also information must flow two ways between them if rural people are to benefit.

The findings presented here are part of a larger study of rural financial systems, both formal and informal, in The Gambia. The research methods, too, have included both formal and informal kinds. Participant-observation and intensive, open-ended interviewing with key informants—usually the best ways of learning about rural African societies and economies—have been supplemented by structured surveys in a small sample of villages. In these, we interviewed 138 farmers (April and May 1987) and an expanded sample of 167 (July through October 1988).[2] Their ethnic distribution roughly resembled that of the country as a whole.[3] Equal numbers of men and women were interviewed in the surveys, each visited repeatedly.

Credit as Debt

"Saving" is definable as any conservation of movable property by an individual or group for future use or disposal. Usually most of a family's savings are held in nonmonetary forms such as livestock, grain, machinery, or jewelry; and further wealth lies in obligations owed by

---

2. Counted after disqualification.
3. In the expanded 1988 survey, our informants identified themselves as Mandinko (36 percent), Fula (or Peulh) (28 percent), Wolof (21 percent), Jola (Diola) (8 percent), Serahuli (4 percent), and others (3 percent). The 1983 national census, sometimes questioned, gives this distribution: Mandinko (40 percent), Fula (19 percent), Wolof (15 percent), Jola (10 percent), Serahuli (8 percent), and others (8 percent), including Arabic-speaking Mauritanians (Gambia 1986: 8). The Gambia's ethnic groups are somewhat mixed around geographically and have much intercontact. I hope elsewhere to examine some differences in their financial customs.

kin or neighbors (some even define savings quite defensibly, as including immovable resources like trees or even land). Saving in rural Africa is often not clearly distinguishable from investment or consumption, particularly where it involves animals or consumer durables.

"Credit" or a "loan" is defined here as any transfer of goods or services by one person or group to another, or to any of its members, with the expectation of compensation at a later time. The loan and the compensation may take the same form or different forms. In The Gambia, virtually everything is lendable, including land, labor, livestock, seeds, fertilizer, pesticides, and farm tools. Craft tools, vehicles, and household goods are also lent. The local arrangements are infinitely varied, and deals mutate from one season to the next. No single translation of "credit" or "loan" into any Gambian language suits all these arrangements, hence some wildly discrepant figures are collected in statistical surveys.

"Credit" to anglophones has a cleaner ring than *juloo* to Mandinka-speakers. Its connotations are positive: confidence, trust (it comes from Latin *credere*, to believe or entrust), and helpfulness. This may be one reason why the term appears so often in development plans, and why planning committee recommendations so often boil down to credit. But credit, of course, is only a nicer way of saying debt. Credit is debt: it matters only whether one takes the lender's or borrower's viewpoint. If "credit" is replaced with "debt" wherever the word appears in project documents, the image changes: "The main impediment to farming is lack of debt"... " In project year one, 2,500 farmers will be issued debt..." *Juloo* contains something of this disturbing truth, something of a warning.

Just as there is no credit without debt, there is none without patronage. At all levels—international, national, and local—cheap loans can be a way of securing supporters, clients, or voters. Yet the language of international lending agency reports conveys subtle but clear assumptions of condescension. Lenders are misidentified as "donors." Borrowers are called not borrowers but "target groups," as though they were merely passive recipients of something grandly provided. Agency officers normally write of "supervising" borrowers, and of "discipline," rather as though borrowers were not adults. "Moral hazard" seems to refer always to borrowers, never to lenders. Credit, or debt, is an unequal tie.

Cultural differences between international lenders and borrowers in The Gambia make their partnerships hard to manage. Assumptions about interest charges, for instance, differ profoundly between northern and West African peoples. Whereas the former conventionally distinguish fair lending from usury in terms of "interest rates" (that is, increments per unit of time), the latter tend to draw the distinctions more in terms of interest ratios (that is, of interest to principal, as the amounts are finally paid), the amount of time elapsed being less important. Differences between Judeo-Christian, Islamic, and local religious concepts concerning interest multiply the misunderstandings.[4]

Farmers unassisted by governments, cooperatives, or banks are neither without credit (as some reports would have it) nor entirely at the mercy of "moneylenders" (as others would have it). Many and varied loans occur within and between villages, including, for instance, seasonal crop loans, share contracting arrangements, delayed marriage payments, contributions for schooling or labor migrations with remittances expected later in return, and seed capital loans between small entrepreneurs (see Shipton 1991a, 1991b). Some loans last only hours, others up to several generations. Gambian farmers live in a credit economy already, and most are perpetually involved in a complex web of debts and credits to relatives, neighbors, friends, and merchants. Anyone planning to lend to smallholding farmers should understand, then, that farmers have their own personal hierarchies of creditors, and that the newest, most distant, and least familiar lenders rank at the bottom. This understanding puts into perspective pejorative judgments about "moral hazards" and "delinquency" where farmers fall into arrears or default on formal loans.

Personal Saving Strategies

Individual saving strategies in The Gambia, described more fully elsewhere (Shipton 1989b), are many, and saving is often not clearly distinguishable from investment or consumption. Most saving takes forms other than money: livestock, jewelry, resaleable farm machinery, individually and collectively stored crops, household furniture, and radios. Some forms, notably large livestock (for men) and large gold earrings (for women) and other jewelry, are gender-specific, and they can be used to shelter wealth from the daily demands of one's kin and neighbors. Spouses are a particular concern, especially when it comes to cash: there is less free sharing of wealth in Gambian marriages than in some countries outside Africa. Rural Gambians who can afford them keep locked boxes within their houses, partly to safeguard their valuables against spouses, but many also hire carpenters to build them

---

4. The clash of cultures in the area of interest rates and ratios is discussed more fully in Shipton (1991a).

small wooden saving boxes, with slots, that even they cannot open themselves without breaking them. Other common strategies for defending one's money against oneself include handing it over to a money-keeper: a trusted friend or neighbor, who is expected to return the cash interest-free upon demand. Seasonal share contractors and wage workers often request infrequent payments as a similar saving strategy. Some of these mechanisms are convenient but expensive in lost interest opportunities or inflationary costs. In effect, Gambians are paying to remove cash from their own hands. All these patterns suggest not a liquidity preference, as many economists have assumed to exist, but at least as much the opposite, an illiquidity preference. Gambian farmers like their savings to be accessible when they need them, but not when they merely want them.

Other Gambian saving methods, with counterparts across Africa and elsewhere, involve local groups, and they combine the functions of saving and credit. I discuss some of these groups next. These are by no means the only group financial mechanisms. They and others not yet fully described in cultural-economic terms for The Gambia may incorporate bonds based upon ethnicity, on patrilineages (a nearly universal organizing principle in Gambian societies) or on cross-cutting matrilateral (mother's side) or affinal (in-law) kinship ties; on membership in castes or classes, or local productive or trading corporations; on school or worship group ties; or on other criss-crossing affiliations.[5] A Gambian's "friends and relatives," lumped together in some studies as a kind of residual category, are often a diverse group.

Group Finance

Villagers with debts believe there are some people they should, or must, repay before others. To this extent, at least, credit and debt are socially constructed and controlled. Any lending institution, formal or informal, faces competition from other formal and informal creditors when it comes time for collection.[6] This section examines some indigenous local financial mechanisms that suggest how this can be

---

5. For a few ethnographic descriptions of social divisions variously relevant to Gambian financial life, see Colvin (1981); Diop (1981), Haswell (1975), Hopkins (1971), Weil (1971), and Linores de Sapir (1970). Most of the larger Gambian societies, including the Mandinko, Fula, and Wolof, have patrilineages, age grades, and castes.

6. I use the term "institution" here in the narrow sense of a particular organization of persons, rather than in the broader sense of behavior patterns, mores, etc.

done. Some are not strictly financial in that they may deal at times not just with money but also with other goods and services—as well as serving important noneconomic functions—but one can observe some of the same principles operating in groups exchanging labor, for instance, as in those exchanging cash. One key principle is the use of peer-group pressures to guarantee repayments; another is the linkage of credit with deposits or investing.

Village Women's and Men's Associations

Every Gambian village normally has one or more groups of the kinds known in Mandinka as *kafo* (or *kafoo*).[7] Although the term referred in the past to men's or women's age-grade organizations, and usually still does, it can refer more generically to various interest groups in a village. Today they may be organized around a specific activity such as a sport or dancing, or loyalty to a political party; and they often have multiple functions.

Membership in kafo groups is voluntary, but commonly it includes most persons of the eligible gender and age range in a village. As few as under 10 or, in a sizeable town, as many as over 300 members may belong. Nearly always, in a village, women's associations have a more comprehensive coverage than men's. Occasionally an individual belongs to kafo groups in more than one village.[8]

Kafo groups are commonly unnamed, or their names shift by activity. But the larger ones usually have a number of elected officers, are organized in hierarchies sometimes modeled after governments of larger polities, often with presidents, secretaries, treasurers, messengers, and sometimes even have "police." Women's groups are not always wholly autonomous as such; commonly a group has a trusted male patron in its village who may hold the group's money or, with an advantage of literacy in English or Arabic, keep the accounts as a favor. Although the head of a men's kafo usually plays a subordinate role to the village headman, the head of a women's kafo may be, by virtue of this position, the most powerful woman in her village.

---

7. The Mandinka term kafo (corresponding roughly to *yirde* in Fula, *morom* in Wolof) is sometimes used by non-Mandinko. In Fula, *kafo* groups are more commonly called *compin* from "company." The Mandinka term is used here for convenience.

8. Some women who have married near their natal homes belong to the kafos of their parents' and husbands' villages.

Having functioned in the past to mobilize labor for free use by members, for hire to other villagers, or for community projects, kafo groups today also serve other diverse economic purposes. Some have collective fields for cash or food crops, and collective crop stores; others have fields with collective infrastructure but individuated plot and crop ownership. Some have small restaurants, hotels, or milling machines. Kafo groups save money from members' dues (often less than a dalasi per member, per week) and fines, from group labor hired out, or from dances, concerts, wrestling meets, or market stall sales they organize, among other means.[9]

Kafo groups handle money in various fiduciary ways. Commonly they lend their group labor. Strong kafos save money in group bank accounts; they may use several senior officers as joint signatories to ensure no individual has private access to the deposits. A kafo may lend or give money, food, seeds, or tools to members and their families, or to other villagers, members obtaining preferential terms. Cash loans from kafo groups to individual villagers in 1988 usually ranged from about 10 to 100 dalasis, and more often than not they carried interest that varied between about 10 percent and 60 percent (nominal rates) over six months.

A common purpose of kafos is to help members with events such as emergencies. Such groups can mobilize contributions quickly for hospital trips, court bails, or house rebuildings after storms. In an impoverished country, kafo group savings have an advantage over "formal" insurance or deposits in banks for emergencies, in that they keep the money in local circulation rather than draining it to cities.

Kafo groups vary substantially in organizational strength and command over funds. Some save thousands of dalasis and make substantial investments in community agricultural projects and purchases, build community centers, or finance political campaigns, while others seem hamstrung by problems including factionalism and graft and are unable to mobilize any funds. Women's kafo groups are more vigorous and economically more important than the men's, but any kafo is only as strong as its leaders.

Recently some private voluntary organizations in The Gambia have experimented with kafo groups as conduits for loans for various purposes, including small enterprises and market gardens. (Some of the kafo groups are new ones of the international organizations' own creation.) The Department of Agriculture has also used kafo groups as channels for seed and fertilizer loans for group farming ventures. Some kinds of kafo seem to hold promise as a link for connecting poorer

9. Currency Exchange Rate (1987/1988): 6.9 dalasis=US $1.

farmers with formal financial institutions. A kafo's strength is its multifunctional nature. Because no one wants to be ostracized from a main village kafo—this can mean becoming a pariah—the group can sanction its members (by fines of a few dalasis) for not participating in its work gatherings; and it may similarly be able to sanction loan defaulters. As yet, however, little is known about what kinds of kafo groups can do these things effectively.[10]

Indigenous Contribution Clubs

Contribution clubs for money are a newer idea in rural parts of The Gambia than kafo groups for labor. But they are based on the same idea. A form that seems to be spreading outward from the cities and towns is the *osusu* (*susu, esusu*), or rotating savings and credit association. In The Gambia it is usually organized by women.

The basic principle is simple. All members of the osusu make fixed contributions of money at regular intervals. Each time, one member takes it all. Each member takes a turn until the cycle is completed; then it may recommence. For an individual whose turn comes early in the cycle, the groups are a credit mechanism; for a person whose turn falls late, they are a savings mechanism. Since Gambian osusu groups usually involve no interest payments, a member who draws early in the cycle gains an interest free loan, and indeed, if inflation is taken into account, realizes a real net gain. One who draws late in the cycle has given an interest free loan and incurs a net loss; but osusu members appear to feel that the function of enforced savings is valuable enough to offset this loss.

Gambian osusu groups are especially important among market women in towns, and for junior-grade civil servants in Banjul and in the province, but they also appear in farm villages. Osusus operated in four of five villages studied during the time of research (the exception being a Fula village in Upper River Division), though some villagers everywhere knew the idea and some had belonged to other osusu groups when living outside their villages.[11] In our 1987 survey, 17 percent of the women interviewed currently belonged to osusu groups, and only 1 percent of the men. In our 1988 survey, farmers were asked whether

---

10. See March and Taqqu (1986) for insights gained in other countries.
11. Tuck reports that in her sample of 54 Senegalese households in 11 rural villages, 34 percent of the households had members in rotating savings and credit associations. She finds that "only women belong."(p. 68).

anyone in their compounds had ever belonged to one; 19 percent said one or more women had belonged; 4 percent said one or more men had belonged.

Nearly all the groups in the villages were female-only, and many of these included only persons of comparable ages. The groups in the towns and cities were more likely to include mixed sexes. Each women's osusu group represented in the sample existed within a single village, town, or city; and in the largest village they were composed of members of the same neighborhoods. Some consisted entirely of kin, others not. One group was based on ethnic identity, its members representing a minority in their village. The overlaying ties of neighborhood, gender, age, kinship, and ethnicity all seemed to give the groups the capacity for peer-group pressure that may have been needed to ensure members' regular participation. Each group had a recognized leader or organizer.

The osusus in which informants had participated (1988) contained between 7 and 31 members, with a mean of 13.4, in the osusus within informants' own village; between 7 and 50, with a mean of 24.8, in the town osusus; and 17 and 30 in two urban osusus of Banjul and Serrakunda.

Individual contributions in the osusus ranged from one to 20 dalasis weekly, or equivalent; but in 91 percent of the groups each member paid between one dalasi and five dalasis weekly or equivalent, that is, less than one U.S. dollar a week. A number of the women who belonged to osusus in the villages had some small sources of cash income in addition to seasonal crops, for instance small-scale fried food vending or palm-oil processing. The women in osusus used their earnings for a variety of purposes, including ceremonies, clothing, livestock purchases, and seeds for mango trees. A male informant who had recently belonged to an osusu described it as being composed of 12 civil servants, living in three villages, who each contributed 75 dalasis monthly. Another had belonged to an osusu of young men in an army camp, each contributing 7.5 dalasis monthly.

Little is known about how long osusu groups last in The Gambia. The oldest group within the sample was said to have functioned continuously for ten years, and others had worked for five or six. Many operated only during the dry season each year, suspending operation during the rains when members were short of money; some others simply reduced the amounts of contributions during the rainy season. In one group that suspended its main function seasonally, members continued contributing (a dalasi each) to each others' ceremonies during the rainy season, reflecting the valued social and symbolic roles of both the osusu and the ceremonies.

Osusu groups in The Gambia are characteristic of the West African forms in that they do not involve variable individual contributions.

The order of rotation is variously preset as the cycle begins—in one case, by members' ages—or determined by lottery upon each collection. In either case, the order may be broken when particular members encounter special cash needs. Members also make their own personal arrangements with each other to swap turns.

Pros and Cons of Contribution Clubs

The advantages of the osusu as a way of mobilizing funds are several; some of these are also enjoyed by the kafo group:

1. The osusu controls the "squawk factor" for savers, because it gives them a socially acceptable excuse to deny loans or handouts to nonmembers.
2. The osusu provides financial services to people who may be ineligible for banking, for lack of initial deposit capital and other problems.
3. It normally requires no collateral.
4. It is not intimidating, as formal financial institutions can be. It need not involve language barriers.
5. It requires little or no paperwork or travel: it minimizes some kinds of transaction costs.
6. It provides an occasion for social gatherings.
7. Because transactions usually take place in group meetings, thefts and cheating are reduced.
8. If the group wishes, it can supervise its members' expenditures of the funds.
9. The osusu can serve as a form of insurance.
10. Because it arises from members' initiative, the osusu commonly benefits from a high level of commitment. Groups that gather to make their contributions may also benefit from the social occasion.
11. Where members belong to several osusu groups, these help to circulate money throughout a population in significant sums.
12. Savings in an osusu are not subject to government scrutiny, control, or taxation.

There are, however, disadvantages:

1. The year-round osusu is not ideally suited to communities depending on rainfed agriculture, because many of the members' needs for funds are likely to come at the same season: the "seasonal covari-

ance" problem. By the same token, osusu groups are seldom useful for financing agricultural inputs.

2. Even in the easy season, one cannot always get the money when one wants it. Most osusus have flexible orders of rotation, but someone else's needs may be deemed greater than one's own at the time.

3. The group depends heavily on all members' continued participation.

4. The group cannot easily accommodate members who migrate in and out of a community.

5. Deposits and borrowings in an osusu are not kept secret locally.

Size Considerations

The optimum size, and the range of acceptable sizes, may vary with the task, and with the characters of the members or leaders. It might also vary by gender, by ethnic group, and by age: little is yet known about these issues.

If the group is too small, several problems arise. The larger benefits of joint savings or cooperation are too small to repay the efforts of joining. Each member can simply avoid the other(s) when he or she has not been cooperating. The smaller the group, the easier the avoidance, and the less likely that the members also belong to other organizations in common, for example, sport groups and age-sets, through which to apply pressure. Also, in a small group, the potential damage of a member's quitting or moving away is greater than if it were a large group.

If the group is too big, on the other hand, different problems occur. Each member will lose only a very small fraction of his or her investment by the noncooperation of one other member. There is little incentive to pursue him or her, or to work to enlist another person to apply pressure. A large group rotates to a given individual only infrequently. Communication between members becomes difficult and it becomes likely that some members will move away.

Contribution Clubs as Conduits

Development agencies have shown much interest in finding ways of "plugging in" external funding to rotating credit and savings associations. Certainly, the largely female composition of these groups and the peer-pressure elements are features attractive to larger lenders or donors. The incorporation of deposits with loans is something many lenders are now striving for, and this principle is already woven into the fabric of the osusu. It is not clear, however, that men would not take the groups over if substantial amounts of cash were infused from outside. It is likely, too, that new groups would spring up overnight to receive funds, without the overlapping bonds of kinship and other social ties that make osusu groups work.

The osusu has features worth emulating, however, in the design of institutional formal credit schemes. The social pressure within a group of about a dozen people to repay (and even to use loans wisely. is clearly a desirable feature. At the primary level, at least, the number of farmers who have collective responsibility for repayment should be limited: the members of the group should know each other and have other kinds of influence to bear upon each other. Second, the small group should probably have a single leader, chosen by the members, as the osusu has. Third, the integration of deposits and loans—they are the same transactions in the osusu—gives members the pride of accomplishment: they earn what they borrow. They have an investment in the group's success.

Other Lessons from Informal Finance

Kafo and osusu groups are found among both men and women, but in the rural areas they seem more important to women; and the associations that succeed in rural financial matters usually are single-sex. There are lessons in this. Gender and age specificity of rural kafo and osusu groups cut down the chances of great disparities between members' solvency or financial abilities. A rough comparability, in turn, helps prevent some members from domineering or exploiting other members. Gender and age specificity also make it more likely that members will have other kinds of contacts with each other, and thus ways of devising their own sanctions for noncooperation.

In external interventions, dividing projects for women and men into separate but parallel projects helps keep the control over gender distribution in an agency's hands, and helps to prevent men from monopolizing funds. A similar principle may apply to age groups. Dividing project funds between younger and older people's kafos can help ensure a more balanced distribution. (Leaving out one group or another, however, may induce it to try to sabotage a project). The experiences of private voluntary organizations in The Gambia, as elsewhere in Africa, suggest that loans to women are not necessarily harder to collect than loans to men. Provided women's borrowing groups are appropriately constituted, it may even be easier.

For leadership and group membership, insiders can choose each other on character better than outsiders can choose them. They are also, of course, more aware of interpersonal "chemistry" in the groups: potential harmonies or clashes between the personalities. This may take a lifetime of mutual acquaintance to recognize. Local leaders such as an *alkalo* (village headman, or a women's kafo head are usually chosen with much deliberation; it generally makes sense for projects to use these local leaders as contact points, or as pressure points if necessary.

The local-level groups most likely to succeed in mobilizing or managing finances are those that exist already for other purposes, such as farm-work groups, youth activity groups, and sport groups. The groups' having more than one function ensures that members have ways to exert pressure on each other when needed. They will usually be bounded in membership, for instance by residence in a single village. Simplicity also seems to be a main key to success in local financial organizations. They tend to have clearly delimited membership, and to use strict and regular meeting schedules, standard contributions, and standard fines for nonparticipation.

Probably nothing should be issued on credit without some contribution from the borrowers themselves, whether in the form of funds, labor, or local materials. Such a rule is important for several reasons: (1) screens out borrowers who are not serious, capable, or organized. (2) gives borrowers an investment in the enterprise or development, and thus (3) it adds their scrutiny to the financial management of local project organizers, an important factor in remote areas hard to monitor or supervise regularly from the capital city; and (4) demanding a contribution also helps to accustom farmers not to expect handouts in the future. Projects will succeed only when rural people consider them as substantially their own.

A subtle advantage of the osusu and other contribution clubs is that they cannot easily overburden their members with debts, because the amounts of loans are regulated by the amounts that farmers in similar circumstances can deposit. Amounts are automatically tailored to repayable levels. Formal programs should follow the example, if not by making loans dependent on others' contributions, then at least by starting borrowers with only small amounts until they have proved their capacities to repay.

A general observation emerging from studies like ours on rural financial systems in The Gambia and other West African countries is that group-based saving and credit systems tend to work more smoothly than individual-based ones among the rural poor, and particularly among women. One reason, as seen earlier, is that they allow individuals to save without seeming selfish to their neighbors and kin, an important point in most of rural West Africa. Another is that the groups and their leaders can serve as conduits to institutions such as banks, which ordinary rural people may perceive as inaccessible, and may reassure the members who feel that approaching institutions is risky.

An Untried Strategy for the Adventurous

Although the issue of interest rates on bank deposits cannot be treated in detail here, some possibilities must be noted. If interest rates on commercial bank loans are raised from their present rates (27 to 28 percent per annum in October 1989), interest on savings deposits (12 percent, should also be raised. The low or negative real interest rate (inflation measured 12.5 percent in 1987/8 may help explain why bank deposits have been unattractive for potential rural savers.

Subsidized credit has been the norm for financial institutions in The Gambia, as in other poor countries. Consistently, staffers of large aid agencies have sought in this way to dispose of large amounts of money; and statespersons and local politicians, to dispense patronage and win supporters. The approach has brought about familiar institutional problems (Adams and others 1984, Shipton 1991b). Some analysts believe as a conclusion, or as an ideological principle, that subsidies generally should be reduced or eliminated, as has gradually been happening in The Gambia. This "pro-market" approach has indeed become a new orthodoxy in financial agencies, and there is some practical sense in it, but credit subsidies persist across Africa.

Apparently no institution in The Gambia (or perhaps even in Africa) has yet been documented to have tried a radical reversal, subsidizing deposits rather than loans, as a rural development strategy. Very low ceilings on the size of such deposits might discourage abuse by the rich. The farmers and rural poor would become the "moneylenders." The approach would probably require some cooperation between large agencies, banks, and private voluntary organizations (PVOs). There would be pitfalls, of course, and transaction costs would be high. These might be minimized by group-based participation.

It should be remembered, in establishing more banking opportunities, that not all rural people want them. Many are satisfied with indigenous forms of saving. These preferences should be respected. If it does not pay substantial interest to depositors, savings banking does little more than drain wealth from rural communities to towns and cities. And interest, even if relabeled as "profit," itself involves religious and moral quandaries in a mainly Muslim country. Rural Gambians are not of a single voice in demanding deposit facilities. What they want is more options.

Conclusions

Credit is not the answer to all problems in development. The most obvious fact about credit ironically is often overlooked: credit indebts. People who have borrowed feel behind; the English phrase "in the hole" expresses a position rural Gambians know too well. As some farmers explained it, one who has a loan to repay is working for someone else, and this weakens incentives to work.[12] That Gambians borrow less from local traders after the good years than after the bad, and that few of the richest farmers interviewed borrowed from these at all, suggest again that rural Gambians basically do not like to be in debt to strangers. They know the "debt ratchet" principle, the vicious circle whereby interest charges can progressively impoverish farmers and make them increasingly dependent on credit. That the co-operatives have witnessed strong demand for credit seems to be largely due to the easy lending terms offered, and to a history of lax collection. Cooperatives, banks, and foreign funding agencies rank low in farmers' priorities for repayments: rural people always have more pressing personal debts. And as seen by the "target group," even big guns, far enough away, look small.

If institutional interest rates are raised to reflect real costs on formal loans, in the interests of financial viability, it may be worthwhile at the same time to reassess critically the role of credit in general. Where interest rates are based on real costs, borrowing is more expensive than

---

12. This is doubtless what Shakespeare meant by "borrowing dulls the edge of hus-bandry." (Hamlet I 3: 75).

saving.[13] Farmers who cannot afford to save can even less afford to borrow.

The rural financial mechanisms working least well are those designed for credit only. It has been the habit of most large and small development agencies with funds to place, to look for ways to lend, rather than to seek local funds that might be mobilized, or to do both. Rural people consider most of the resulting credit projects to belong to someone else: the capital city, the government, the whites.

By contrast, in The Gambia as elsewhere in Africa, the financial systems that appear to work most smoothly, like the informal osusu groups, appear to be those that link deposits with lending. Savings in the osusu are the same as credit. The groups embody several other sound principles: local initiative and funds, character screening by members, lending linked to repayment capacity, and peer-group pressure as the main means of enforcing cooperation and repayment. Osusus spring up by voluntary initiative in rural towns and villages, as in cities. Although some suspend operation seasonally, some last well over a decade, and as they dissolve, new ones form. They have their limits, but at least rural people consider these systems to be their own.

These observations suggest an incorporation of deposit components in credit programs wherever the institution in question is financially sound enough to merit farmers' trust, and wherever it can build upon existing social networks. Much remains to be learned about how, and whether, financial institutions can emulate the financial principles observed already working in the rural areas. Whether savings and credit are linked or not, however, farmers clearly feel they need both. In the long run, the rope of credit and debt without the box of saving can scarcely serve farmers' interests.

References

Adams, Dale W, Douglas H. Graham, and J. D. Von Pischke, eds. 1984. *Undermining Rural Development with Cheap Credit*. Boulder, Colorado: Westview Press.

Colvin, Lucie, Cheick Ba, Boubacar Barry, Jacques Faye, Alice Hamer, Moussa Soumah, and Fatou Sow. 1981. *The Uprooted of the Western Sahel: Migrants' Quest for Cash in the Senegambia*. New York: Praeger.

---

13. Except, of course, where loans are not collected. Some of these factors may help explain why Gambians have tended to use government institutions for borrowing more than for saving.

Demissie, Asafa, Lyle Brenneman, and Jeffrey Nash. 1989. "Study of the Operations and Management of The Gambian Cooperative Union." Unpublished report to the Harvard Institute for International Development and the Ministry of Finance and Trade, The Gambia.

Diop, Abdoulaye-Bara. 1981. *La Société Wolof: Tradition et Changement.* Paris: Karthala.

Haswell, Margaret R. 1975. *The Nature of Poverty: A Case-History of the First Quarter-Century After World War II.* New York: St. Martin's Press.

Hopkins, Nicholas S. 1971. "Maninka Social Organization." In Carleton T. Hodge, ed., *Papers on the Manding* pp. 99-128. Bloomington, Indiana: Indiana University.

Linares de Sapir, Olga. 1970. "Agriculture and Diola Society." In Peter F. M. McLoughlin, ed., *African Food Production Systems*, pp. 193-227. Baltimore, Maryland: Johns Hopkins University Press.

March, Kathryn, and Rachelle Taqqu. 1986. *Women's Informal Associations in Developing Countries.* Boulder, Colorado: Westview.

Ousmane, Sembene. 1983. *The Money Order.* London: Heinemann.

Ramamurthy, G.V. 1986. "Agricultural Credit Policy and Structure: The Gambia." Unpublished report to the United Nations Food and Agriculture Organization, Technical Cooperation Program.

Shipton, Parker. 1989b. "How Gambians Save—And What Their Strategies Imply for International Aid." Unpublished working paper. Washington, D.C.: Agriculture and Rural Development Department, The World Bank.

——. 1990. "African Famines and Food Security: Anthropological Perspectives." *Annual Review of Anthropology* 19: 353-394.

——. 1991a. (forthcoming). "Time and Money in the Western Sahel: A Clash of Cultures in Gambian Rural Finance." In Michael Roemer and Christine Jones, eds., *Markets in Developing Countries.* Washington D.C. and San Francisco: ICS Press, for the International Center for Economic Growth.

——. 1991b. (forthcoming). "Borrowers and Lenders in The Gambia." In Lawrence H. White, ed., *African Finance.* Washington, D.C. and San Francisco: ICS Press.

Tuck, Laura. 1983. "Formal and Informal Financial Markets in Rural Senegal." Unpublished report to the U.S. Agency for International Development, Washington, D.C.

Weil, Peter. 1971. "Political Structure and Process among The Gambia Mandinka: The Village Parapolitical System." In Carleton T. Hodge, ed., *Papers on the Manding*, pp. 249-272. Bloomington, Indiana: Indiana University, Research Center for the Language Sciences.

Wing, Michael. 1983. "The Credit System of The Gambia". Unpublished report to the U.S. Agency for International Development, Washington, D.C.

4

Informal Financial Groups in Cameroon

Gertrud R. Schrieder and Carlos E. Cuevas[1]

Cameroon's financial market shows the typical fragmentation observed in most developing economies. The banking system, in serious disarray in the late 1980s, coexists with a strong credit union movement and a wide variety of informal financial intermediaries. Formal financial institutions have failed to effectively mobilize voluntary savings or to provide significant credit services in rural areas. In comparison to Cameroon's banks, the credit union network based in Bamenda (Northwest Province) is widely accepted by the rural as well as the urban population. Although their overall importance in terms of mobilizing savings is not yet significant, credit unions showed an impressive growth rate over the last decade. In addition, they are currently extending into the francophone regions and accepting informal financial groups as members, a significant step in establishing more ties between formal and informal financial intermediaries.

Financial self-help groups (SHGs) can be found in most parts of the world in two basic forms: rotating savings and credit associations (ROSCAs) and nonrotating savings and credit associations (Non-ROSCAs) (Seibel 1986; Miracle and others 1980; Bouman 1977; and Ardener 1964). In Cameroon, ROSCAs were first reported by Meyer in 1940. They are known as djanggis in the anglophone provinces, while the French speaking population calls them tontines.

1. We thank Erhard Kropp and Hubert Rauch of the Deutsche Gesellschaft fur Technische Zusammenarbeit (GTZ) for their support of our field work in Cameroon. Dale Adams and Fritz Bouman contributed useful comments and editorial suggestions.

43

This chapter documents and analyzes the activity of rotating and nonrotating informal financial groups in Cameroon, based on a field survey carried out in the Fall of 1988 (Schrieder 1989). The findings highlight the extensive participation of rural people in informal groups and the dominant role that informal finance plays in the circulation of funds in the country. Informal financial groups appear as the single most important form of financial intermediation in Cameroon, a finding that confirms and extends the results of previous research in this country (DeLancey 1977; and Bouman and Hartweld 1976). A brief conceptual framework is presented in the following section, followed by a description of the methods and data used in the study. The final section reviews the main findings and summarizes the major implications of the study.

Conceptual Framework

An SHG is defined as a "voluntary group valuing personal interactions and mutual aid as means of altering or ameliorating problems perceived as alterable, pressing, and personal by most of its participants" (Smith and Pillheimer 1983, pp. 205-206). Rotating and nonrotating financial groups are SHGs where the group expects to solve financial problems shared by most of the participants. Individual group members contribute their funds on a regular basis and agree on whether a member might benefit from their pooled financial contributions, for example, by borrowing from the group's fund. A summary description of the different group types is shown in Figure 1.

Rotating Savings and Credit Associations

The most comprehensive definition of ROSCAs has been provided by Ardener (1964). She defines a ROSCA as "An association formed upon a core of participants who agree to make regular contributions to a fund which is given in whole or in part to each contributor in rotation" (p. 201). This definition suggests that the regularity of the contributions and the rotation of the fund are main features of a ROSCA. In general, each member of a rotating financial group contributes the same amount. For this reason, each member's contribution and financial take-home are identical. However, there exist groups where the participants may

FIGURE 1. Financial Features of Rotating and Nonrotating Savings and Credit Associations

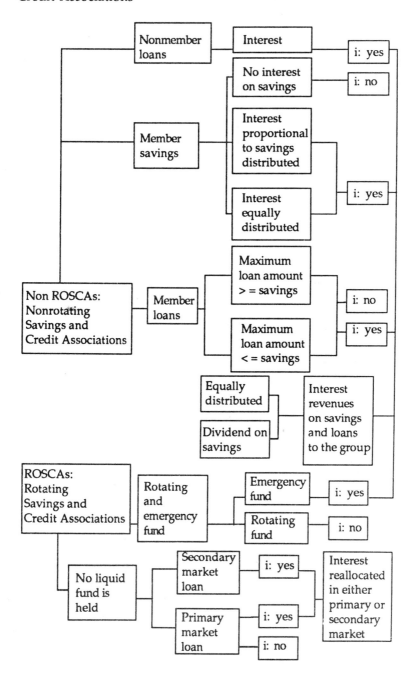

contribute varying amounts per meeting. In this case, the group has to ensure that the contributions from each individual correspond with each member's financial benefit for each cycle (Ardener 1964; and Warmington 1958). Recent literature has extensively discussed the self-help groups that are organized as rotating savings and credit associations (Seibel 1986, 1984; Miracle and others 1980; and Ardener 1964). Nzemen (1988) extended the concept of rotating savings and credit associations by contributing a mathematical framework for their financial transactions. Therefore, rotating financial groups are subdivided into four subtypes according to their specific financial features. The subtypes are defined as: ROSCAs with an interest free primary fund and no emergency fund, ROSCAs with an interest free primary fund and an emergency fund, ROSCAs with interest charged on the primary fund and no emergency fund, and ROSCAs with interest charged on the primary fund and an emergency fund.

Nonrotating Savings and Credit Associations

A nonrotating savings and credit association is defined as an organization wherein participants agree to save regularly on a contractual basis. The savings might be used for member and/or non-member loans on an interest or interest free basis.

Another interesting aspect of a nonrotating savings and credit association is the direct correlation between the subscribed amount, the individual's savings capability, and creditworthiness. Non ROSCAs can be divided into three groups: savings associations, savings and credit associations, and credit associations.

Savings associations are based on regular contributions of fixed or variable amounts from members to the group fund. This fund is either kept by the treasurer at home, deposited in a savings account, or a combination of both. At the end of a specified period, the group members receive their deposits.

Savings and credit associations work exactly like the nonrotating savings associations and, in addition, the group savings fund is also used to allocate loans to members and possibly to nonmembers. An emergency fund might complement the savings fund. Usually, debtors of the emergency fund must pay interest on their loans. Debtors of the main savings fund might or might not have to pay interest. Money that is not lent is kept by the treasurer at home and/or deposited in a savings account. Interest revenues of nonrotating financial associations are either equally distributed among the group participants or in proportion to their accumulated savings according to commercial bank practices.

In contrast to the savings association, in which a time period of operation is specified, the participants in the credit association agree to contribute variable amounts for an unspecified time period. Normally, the group participants subscribe once at the foundation of the group or at their entry, however, individual members might subscribe additional funds to their group share. A money lending group uses its fund exclusively for nonmember loans. Interest is charged in advance and loan terms seldom exceed one month. The interest is reinvested in nonmember loans until the end of the business year. At the end of the business year, the group members receive a dividend out of the interest revenues based on their subscriptions.

Methods and Data

The data analyzed here were obtained from a survey conducted in three Provinces of Cameroon (Northwest, West, and Central) in late 1988. Four questionnaires for different populations provided information on the internal decisionmaking process, control of group conduct, funds management, selection of beneficiaries, mechanisms of social control, the importance of women as group members, and the relative importance of SHGs in the community.

Leaders of 13 financial SHGs and a total of 136 members of 11 of these groups were interviewed. Three-quarters of the total number of the randomly selected members interviewed were women. About 60 percent of the interviews were carried out in the Anglophone Northwest Province, while the Central and West Province, both predominately French-speaking, accounted for 9 percent and 33 percent of the interviews, respectively. The financial self-help groups covered in the survey had a total of 1,057 participants. The principal occupation of the respondents was farming (77 percent of the sample). The category housewife accounted for only about 10 percent.[2] Public and private employees represented 7 percent, merchants 5 percent, and businessmen only 1 percent in the sample.

---

2. Most women in the survey called themselves farmers rather than housewives since they produce food crops and thus contribute to the total income of the family.

Financial Self-Help Groups in Cameroon

We found that the degree of financial intermediation and monetarization increased from the most simple type of ROSCA (those with an interest free rotating fund and no other financial intermediation role) to the ROSCA type where the rotating fund is auctioned among the members to the Non-ROSCA that operates an emergency fund and a mutual aid fund. This indicates that the types of financial SHGs should not be thought of as strictly separated categories but rather as a continuum of group structures and operational modes. Three out of the thirteen groups interviewed were ROSCAs, while 10 were Non-ROSCAs, one group was a moneylending group, and another was an "investment" group that owned a corn mill. The data gathered show that all types of financial SHGs (with the exception of the money lending group) have some features in common:

a) All groups are self-selecting regarding their membership. New members have to pass a period of regular savings before they are eligible for loans.

b) Meetings follow a specific pattern and protocol. Most meetings start with a prayer.

c) Contributions, loan payments, and loan demands are made publicly in front of the groups.

d) Financial sanctions (fines) are assessed to participants who arrive late to a meeting, disturb the meeting, or do not pay their contribution.

e) In addition to the financial sanctions mentioned above, there are social sanctions that apply to defaulters. Defaulters lose their reputation in the community and might never again be accepted in any other informal financial institution, therefore, defaults are rare. During the course of this study, eyewitnesses reported that groups might sell all belongings of a defaulting member to force loan repayment.

Main Features of Informal Groups

A majority of all financial SHGs surveyed were founded by indigenous members of the community (53 percent of the sample). Most of these initiators still participate actively as members in the organization they founded. The remaining groups were brought to life by missionaries, administrative village authorities, and traditional village authorities with 33 and 13 percent, respectively. On average, the groups in the survey had existed for ten years in 1988.

One informal financial institution had an age of 34 years, while the most recent groups were founded two years ago. One-half of the groups showed at least seven years of functioning, and a number of them were founded before independence in 1960. Mutual trust and place of residence were most often reported as the common bond of the financial SHGs (50 percent of the groups), whereas ethnic group and gender appeared to play a less important role as a membership condition than was commonly assumed (21 percent and 14 percent of the groups, respectively).

Women in Cameroon are traditionally food crop producers who sell their surplus in local markets. Due to the recent financial crises in Cameroon and the relatively low prices for cash crops—the traditional domain of the men—the financial standing of farmwomen was better in 1988 than that of male smallholders. Thus, farm women seem to be more active in financial SHGs than were their husbands due to their more substantial and steadier flows of cash income.

The total number of members per group varied between 5 and 350 participants, although the largest group was organized into three sub-groups to reduce geographical dispersion. The size of groups consisting solely of men (4 in the sample) ranged between 5 and 24 participants while women-only groups (also 4 in the sample) totaled a minimum of 26 and a maximum of 200 members. The data indicate that financial SHGs wherein both genders participate are dominated by women. Men in mixed groups serve mostly in the position of secretary since they are more often literate than are women. On the other hand, the position of treasurer is usually occupied by women.

Most financial SHGs are governed by a board of members. This was the case in 86 percent of all groups interviewed. Only two groups reported a single individual leadership structure: a money lending group and a corn mill group. All groups kept records in written form. In about 79 percent of all the groups interviewed, the secretary kept track of the number of members, their contributions, and loan and deposit transactions. It was also found that all financial SHGs had at least a register book to record their financial transactions. A cash and visitor book was used by 21 percent of the groups and a member passbook, loan, and interest book was used by another 14 percent.

Generally, the member who is or was the most recent beneficiary of the rotating fund in a ROSCA provides the group with palm wine and corn beer. In ROSCAs where the rotation is determined in advance, the actual beneficiary supplies the beverages and the food. In groups where the primary fund is allocated by auctioning, the last beneficiary accommodates his fellow members and pays for drinks and food. Understandably, this kind of entertainment was only found in groups with fewer than 100 participants.

Deposits and Contributions

The most common meeting frequency is monthly. This was the case in 43 percent of the groups. Other meetings were weekly, bi-weekly or every three weeks. Members' contributions are normally paid at every meeting, however, in special cases, the members' contributions are paid at once when the group is founded, or when a new member enters the association.

Thirty-six percent of the interviewees reported that their financial SHG pays them interest on their deposits. Not all of them could specify the interest rate since the rate is generally calculated at the end of the cycle. This is because the interest revenues from member loans and/or savings accounts can only be quantified at the end of the savings period. The average return on savings was about 50 percent with a range from 12 percent to 60 percent per annum for the respondents who specified an interest rate on their savings. These rates are higher than those reported by DeLancey (1977) in his earlier sudies of Cameroonian groups (10 percent and 12 percent, respectively).

Six informal financial institutions reported sources of funds other than the members' contributions. One nonrotating savings and credit association had a current FONADER loan and four groups (also Non ROSCAs) had received a loan from FONADER the year before.[3] Two groups had loans in 1987 as well as in 1988 from the Liywontse Association, an umbrella organization of 24 informal financial groups in the Nkar area (Northwest Province). A credit union had granted a loan to the corn mill group in 1987. This group had borrowed from this credit union for the first time 22 years ago. All other groups had obtained their first loan from their creditor institution within the past two years.

---

3. *Fondation National de Développement Rural* (FONADER) is a public development institution that was being replaced by a public agricultural bank.

Uses of Group Funds

About three-fourths of all groups interviewed used their funds primarily for member loans. About 46 percent of these groups also held reserves either at the treasurer's home and/or the bank or the credit union. One group, the money lending group, granted exclusively non-member loans, and another informal financial group invested its funds in a corn mill and accumulated their savings as well as the revenues from the corn mill operations in a nearby credit union. This group remunerated the mill operator, a rotating function among the group members, and paid dividends to members at the end of the year.

The average member loan amount granted was the equivalent of US$490, the smallest loan reported was US$3, while the largest was US$14,060. However, the majority of the member loans reported in the survey ranged between $3 and $63 (see Table 1).

Loan terms in the sample had a mean of 9.5 months. The shortest term was one month, while the longest term was four years and eight months. However, 83 percent of all loan terms found in the survey varied between one month and one year. The interest rates charged by informal financial groups varied widely. The one extreme was an interest rate of 6 percent per year (nonrotating savings and credit association), the other extreme was a 360 percent interest rate per year (money lending group). Three groups did not charge any interest on loans. If one excludes the extreme interest rates indicated above, the average rate charged on loans was the equivalent of 33 percent per year.

TABLE 1. Informal Loan Categories

Amount US$	Frequency	Percent
3 - 31	40	36
32 - 63	30	27
64 -156	18	16
157 - 313	6	5
314 - 3,125	12	11
More than 3,125	5	5
Total Sample	111[a]	100

a. Missing Values: 25.
Source: Schrieder (1989).

The interviews showed that informal financial groups generally do not require guarantees from their borrowing members. This was found to be the case in 83 percent of all groups. Two groups considered the members' savings as sufficient security for their loans and one interest charging ROSCA required a check as guarantee for the contributions not yet subscribed. The money lending group, however, required several loan guarantees. The debtor had to sign a loan contract and a check for the amount of the loan. All member loans are made in front of witnesses. Generally, the whole group acts as a witness (85 percent of all groups), otherwise loans are witnessed by the group board. About 83 percent of all groups give loans only to members who have proved their savings capability. Also important (in 58 percent of the cases) is the regular participation of the members in the group's meetings and other activities.

In the sample, three-fourths of all interviewed ROSCAs allocated their rotating fund through general agreement prior to the beginning of the cycle. However, this order was open to changes by the group board in agreement with the members if a group participant could document an urgent need. If funds in nonrotating savings and lending associations are limited, the member with the most urgent need generally has priority. The need for money by members in ROSCAs is also a strong determinant for the allocation of the group's fund. Seventy-three percent of all rotating and nonrotating groups with loans named a member's need as the determinant of loan allocation. This flexibility in the allocation of funds explains the finding that only two of the 13 groups interviewed operated a mutual aid fund. Emergency funds however, were observed in almost one-half of the groups in the sample. Mutual aid funds reflect a voluntary group service to support members in unforeseen circumstances. Group members are not necessarily obliged to make mutual aid contributions while the assistance by means of the emergency fund is obligatory. This is because mutual aid in cash and/or in kind is considered a non-reimbursable grant while emergency funds have to be repaid. Mutual aid is more commonly observed in health related emergencies, while the emergency loans are associated with loss of property due to theft or other causes.

Relative Importance of Financial SHGs

Local Cameroonian experts in agricultural finance claim that almost everybody in Cameroon belongs to at least one financial SHG. A person who does not participate in any informal lending and savings association might lack money or might have a bad reputation in the community (Lantum 1988).

In this survey, almost 80 percent of all adult family members participated in at least one financial SHG, a proportion somewhat higher than that reported by Warmington (1958) and DeLancey (1977). However, our study includes rotating as well as nonrotating groups while Warmington and DeLancey limited their analysis to rotating self-help groups. About 52 percent of all interviewees belonged to multiple informal financial lending and savings associations. In one-third of the cases, at least one other family member also participated either in the same group as the interviewee or in some other financial SHG. About 42 percent of all interviewees belonged to two financial SHGs, while 52 percent of all respondents belonged to at least two financial SHGs and 10 percent participated in more than two financial SHGs.

Seventy-one percent of all groups interviewed provided their participants with loan services. The exceptions were two pure savings groups, a corn mill group, and the money lending group. Only 8 percent of the sample had loans from formal financial institutions. However, additional loans from other SHGs not included in this survey were found in 17 percent of the cases.

Interviewees held voluntary savings in external formal financial organizations, however, deposits in financial SHGs other than the groups in the data set were reported almost three times as often. Overall, informal savings institutions are far more important than are formal savings organizations. Fifty-nine of the respondents held savings in other informal financial institutions, while only 15 percent had bank or credit union accounts.

The total accumulated amount of informal group deposits by the respondents in the data set was US$105,625 in 1988. This estimate includes savings in the interviewed groups as well as deposits in other informal financial groups. The mean over the total amount of voluntary informal group savings for all respondents was US$777.

Relative National Importance

As stated earlier, 79 percent of all adult household members surveyed participate in at least one financial SHG, however, we assume that about 70 percent of Cameroon's population participates in informal lending and savings associations. Although our findings regarding the participation rate in financial SHGs is higher, a lower figure is preferred in order to avoid overestimating the relative importance of informal groups in the overall economy. This more modest assumption takes into account the fact that informal financial institutions seem to be less popular in the Northern Provinces and other regions not covered by this survey. Also, 70 percent represents a middle value between Warmington's and DeLancey's estimation of 75 percent and 64 percent, respectively. Cameroon's population totalled about 11 million citizens in Autumn 1988 of which the active population is estimated at about 3.5 million. This number has been calculated under the assumption that Cameroon's active population rate is 30 percent of the total population (Ministry of Agriculture 1984).

With the foregoing assumptions, and using the average member loan from the sample data indicated above, it is possible to estimate the total amount of credit granted through informal groups in Cameroon at about US$1.2 billion (US$490 times 0.7 participation rate times 3.5 million active population). This amount is equivalent to 36 percent of all claims on the private sector by Cameroon's commercial banks and its development bank in March 1988. This implies that these indigenous financial groups provide 27 percent of all loan requirements in Cameroon. Bechtel had estimated that more than 50 percent of all short- and medium-term loans are granted by informal savings and lending groups. This is not inconsistent with our findings, given the different loan amounts involved in institutional and non-institutional lending.

The mean over the total amount of voluntary informal savings for all respondents was US$777. Using the same assumptions about participation in informal groups and active population, the total national savings handled by informal financial institutions is $1.9 billion dollars, an amount equivalent to 1.2 times the magnitude of all demand, time, and savings deposits in Cameroon's commercial banks and in its development bank in March 1988. This analysis thus indicates that informal voluntary savings account for about 54 percent of total financial savings in Cameroon.

Concluding Remarks

This chapter has described and analyzed the main features and operational modes of informal financial groups in Cameroon and their relative importance in the country's monetized economy. Two major issues emerge from this analysis. First, informal SHGs appear to be able to adjust their structure and operating principles to a wide variety of circumstances. These groups are capable of responding to widely different demands for financial services, a major advantage over formal financial institutions.

The second issue relates to the striking importance of informal groups in Cameroon's overall monetary circulation. The estimates reported in this chapter suggest that informal groups account for more than one-fourth of total domestic private sector credit, and for more than one-half of total financial savings. These findings emphasize the need to consider the likely effect of policy measures on the functioning and viability of informal financial groups. The current initiative of establishing a public agricultural bank in Cameroon should be evaluated in terms of the effects this institution might have on the motivations and incentives associated with the formation and functioning of informal financial groups.

References

Ardener, Shirley. 1964. "The Comparative Study of Rotating Credit Associations." *The Journal of the Royal Anthropological Institute of Great Britain and Ireland* 94: 201-229.

Bechtel, Heinrich. 1988. "Institutional and Operational Problems and Constraints in External Finance of Informal Savings and Credit Rings." Unpublished paper prepared for the Deutsche Gesellschaft fur Technische Zusammenarbeit (GTZ), Eschborn, Germany.

Bouman, F. J. A. 1977. "Indigenous Savings and Credit Societies in the Third World—Any Message?" *Savings and Development* 1:181-218.

Bouman, F. J. A. and K. Hartweld. 1976. "The Djanggi, a Traditional Form of Saving and Credit in West Cameroon." *Sociologia Ruralis* 16: 103-119.

DeLancey, Mark W. 1977. "Credit for the Common Man in Cameroon." *Journal of Modern African Studies* 15: 316-322

DeLancey, Mark W. and Virginia H. DeLancey. 1975. *A Bibliography of Cameroon*, 4 vols. New York: Africana Publishing Company.

Lantum, Alexander. 1988. "The Liywontse Association of Nkar—A Joint GTZ/FONADER Pilot Project," Unpublished paper. Bamenda, Cameroon.

Ministry of Agriculture. 1984. *Agricultural Census*, vol. 1 Cameroon.

Miracle, Marvin P., Diane S. Miracle and Laurie Cohen. 1980. "Informal Savings Mobilization in Africa." *Economic Development and Cultural Change* 28:701-724.

Nzemen, Moise. 1988. *Théorie de La Pratique des Tontines Au Cameroun.* Yaoundé, Cameroon: Société de presse et d'Editions du Cameroun.

Schrieder, Gertrud R. 1989. "Informal Financial Groups in Cameroon: Motivation, Organization and Linkages," Unpublished M.S. thesis. Columbus, Ohio: Ohio State University.

Seibel, Hans Dieter. 1984. "Savings for Development: A Linkage Model For Informal and Formal Financial Markets," Unpublished paper presented at Yaoundé, Third U.N. Symposium on the Mobilization of Personal Savings in Developing Countries, Dec. 10-15.

———. 1986. "Rural Finance in Africa: The Role of Informal and Formal Financial Institutions." *Development and Cooperation* 6:2-14.

Smith, David Horton and Karl Pillheimer. 1983. "Self-Help Groups as Social Movement Organizations: Social Structure and Social Change." *Research In Social Movements Conflicts And Change* 5:203-233.

Warmington, A.W. 1958. "Savings and Indebtedness among Cameroon Plantation Workers." *Africana* 28:329-343.

5

Rural Finance in Somalia

Virginia DeLancey

Agriculture is the largest sector in Somalia's economy. In 1987, it contributed about two-thirds of Gross Domestic Product and provided a livelihood for 80 percent of the population. Crop production contributed only 14 percent of Gross Domestic Product, and yields are generally low. One reason for the low productivity is limited usage of modern agricultural inputs. Because per capita income is extremely low, approximately US$290 according to World Bank figures, it is generally assumed that farmers do not have savings sufficient to finance all of their investment opportunities or even seasonal input requirements. Thus, access to loans by small-scale farmers as well as large-scale farmers and plantation owners is thought to be essential for increasing production.

When the research for this chapter was conducted in late 1986, the formal sources of credit in Somalia consisted of the Somali Development Bank, the Commercial and Savings Bank of Somalia (CSBS), and several agricultural marketing and service institutions. Many large-scale farmers had access to formal loans from these sources; however, most small-scale farmers did not. The latter depended mainly on sources such as informal loans from shopkeepers, moneylenders, family, friends, or neighboring large-scale farmers. They also resorted to short-term wage employment on neighboring large-scale farms to supplement their funds. Occasionally, they participated in rotating savings and credit associations, or sought assistance from traditional work groups that contributed labor without direct monetary compensation. This distinction between the sources of finance for large-scale and small-scale farmers is important. That is, if poor farmers do not have access to formal loans in Somalia, there is a danger of a growing gap between the wealthy and the poor, unless informal sources are able to provide the necessary financial services.

Methodology

To determine the extent of small-scale farmers' access to credit in Somalia, and the types of informal credit they use, survey research was conducted by members of the Faculty of Economics, Somali National University in 1986. We interviewed farmers in the Afgoi Division of the Lower Shabelle Region, which is located between Somalia's two rivers (the Shabelle and the Juba) in the most important agricultural area of the country. We used stratified, random sampling procedures that enabled us to include farmers who had irrigable land as well as farmers who worked rainfed land, and also small-scale farmers, large-scale farmers, and plantation owners.

In accordance with Ministry of Agriculture practice, we defined small-scale farmers to have less than 30 hectares of land, large-scale farmers to have 30 to 99 hectares of land, and plantation owners to have 100 hectares or more. After selecting the villages, we interviewed a random sample of small-scale farmers who had title to land. Because there were so few of them, we interviewed all large-scale farmers and plantation owners operating in the selected areas. This provided a total of 191 usable interviews, 164 with small-scale farmers, and 27 with large-scale farmers or plantation owners. In our sample, 84 percent of the small-scale farmers had less than 5 hectares of land. The average small-scale farm was 3.7 hectares. The large-scale farmers and plantation owners had farms ranging from 30 to 300 hectares in size; however, two-thirds of them had less than 100 hectares of land.

The interview was a formal one, written in both the English and Somali languages. It was almost always conducted in Somali, but the responses were recorded in English. During the in-depth interviews, the farmers were asked questions about investments in land, use of agricultural inputs, capital, labor, savings, and most importantly, their access to formal as well as informal loans.

Research Findings

Irrigation

In some parts of Somalia, and particularly in the Afgoi Division of the Lower Shabelle, irrigation is an important investment. There was a large difference between investments in irrigation by small-scale compared to large-scale farmers; only half of small-scale farmers had irrigated farms, while all of the large-scale farmers did.

In some countries, the costs of irrigation are borne by the state. However, in Somalia, the cost of irrigating farm land is a heavy burden for farmers. Thus, many of the small-scale farmers find it difficult to pay for digging or maintaining irrigation canals, where necessary, or for the purchase of an irrigation pump without access to loans. Small-scale farmers sometimes bear an additional financial burden. They have more difficulty obtaining access to the best land near the river, land which is easier and less costly to irrigate than more distant land. Irrigation is important not only for purposes of crop production, but also for access to loans. The formal credit institutions and programs often require farmers to have title not only to land, but also to irrigated land, in order to obtain loans. This is true even within the recently-initiated UNDP/FAO supported Seasonal Credit for Small Farmers Program which is lodged in the Commercial and Savings Bank of Somalia.

Tractors and Other Heavy Equipment

There is widespread use of tractors in Afgoi Division, even on small farms. In our sample, 77 percent of small-scale farmers, and 96 percent of large-scale farmers used tractors, especially for preparation of the land for planting. All of the small-scale farmers who used tractors rented the tractor services, often by the hour, either from ONAT, the parastatal organization that owns agricultural machinery and provides such services, or from private farmers who owned tractors. However, 50 percent of the large-scale farmers owned tractors. Most of the small-scale farmers who did not use a tractor could not afford to buy one and believed that they were too expensive to even rent. Other heavy equipment is also used. Many farmers rent the services of bulldozers to clear new fields, and some large-scale farmers own them. More than one of the latter mentioned they had been assisted in their purchase by the U.S. Commodity Import Program. Finally, some farmers either owned or desired a backhoe which is used for digging and maintaining irrigation canals.

Seasonal Inputs

Use of modern agricultural inputs is limited in Somalia, but there are also differences in usage by large-scale and small-scale farmers. Among the individuals interviewed, less than 10 percent of small-scale farmers used any improved seeds, fertilizer, or pesticides. Many more large-scale farmers used at least one of them, but this was still less than one-half. Very few of either group used herbicides or animal feed. The most important reason given for not using improved inputs was that the farmers felt they could not obtain them. The second most important reason was that they did not believe they needed them. Some members of both groups claimed that animal feed and pesticides were too expensive, and nearly 40 percent of small-scale farmers indicated that they had never heard of herbicides.

Educational differences among farmers may be a determining factor in input use; the less-educated small-scale farmers may not be aware of the potential of such inputs, may not put any effort into searching for them, and may thus conclude that they cannot find them. But there may be other reasons for the difference in input usage, as well; there may be differences in ability to access inputs, based upon government policy. For example, agricultural inputs are often an integral part of agricultural extension/credit programs; seasonal loans are often extended in kind for agricultural inputs. When such programs concentrate upon large-scale, "progressive" farmers, then small-scale farmers may have little access to such inputs.

A significant number of farmers used hired labor to work on their farms, although small-scale farmers used it less often than large-scale farmers. In our sample, 58 percent of small-scale farmers, and 85 percent of large-scale farmers used hired labor. Small-scale farmers relied more on family members and traditional work groups, especially the *goob* (28 percent) and also the *barbaar* (82 percent), both of which are described in greater detail below. However, many of the small-scale farmers themselves became hired labor for the large-scale farmers in order to supplement cash incomes.

Savings

We asked each of the farmers interviewed to identify their two priorities for saving money if they were able to do so. Their replies were consistent with the findings above. Top priority for the small-scale farmers was to irrigate their farms (51 percent). This was followed by buying livestock (38 percent), and buying farm machinery (37 percent). There are many reasons why Somali farmers may want to buy livestock, one of them being to hedge against the risks in crop farming. Top priority for large-scale farmers differed. As they had already irrigated most of their land, top priority was for purchasing farm machinery (70 percent), including tractors, bulldozers, and also backhoes. This was followed by irrigation of the remainder of their land not yet irrigated (33 percent).

We also tried to determine the level of actual savings, and the deposit institutions used by farmers. There is an old myth that African farmers cannot or do not save. But, this has been disproved many times in many countries. In our research, over half of the small-scale farmers (57 percent) and nearly all of the large-scale farmers (96 percent) admitted to savings. Of the small-scale farmers who said they had savings, the amount averaged 21,000 So.Sh. (US$140). For the large-scale farmers who saved, the amount averaged 480,000 So.Sh. (US$3,200). Fifty-three percent of small-scale farmers kept savings in their home, averaging 10,900 So.Sh. (US$73). Only 7 percent of the small-scale farmers saved in the bank. But, those who did deposit in banks had an average of 73,000 So.Sh. (US$487) there. In contrast, while large-scale farmers kept some savings in their homes, 85 percent of them also kept savings in the bank, averaging 656,000 So.Sh. (US$4,373).

Farmers also kept savings in the form of loans to others who needed cash. And, to some extent, they also used rotating savings and credit associations (ROSCAs), locally called the *shaloongo* or Italian *aiuto*. However, ROSCAs are more commonly found in urban areas of Somalia, particularly among market traders, wage employees, and even civil servants.

Although the amounts saved by the farmers are considerably more than is commonly believed, they are not sufficient to meet the seasonal liquidity needs for agricultural inputs or for the longer term needs to purchase farm equipment, especially for the small-scale farmers. Some of the farmers interviewed desired additional funds to finance farm investments and modern inputs.

Formal Finance

The Somoli Development Bank (SDB)

At the time of the research, the SDB provided medium- and long-term loans to farmers for the purchase of land and machinery. Fourteen of the 27 large-scale farmers had had at least one loan from the SDB. Of the 14 who had received such loans, four of them had received two loans, and one of them had received three loans. The most common reason for borrowing was to buy a tractor. But, purchase of additional farm land and irrigation equipment were also given as reasons. Loans ranged from 14,000 So.Sh. (US$93) to a 2.5 million So.Sh. (US$16,667) line of credit. The median amount was 100,000 So.Sh. (US$667). Only one of the 15 women in the sample had obtained a loan from the SDB, a 250,000 So.Sh. (US$1,667) loan to buy a tractor.

Of the 13 large-scale farmers who did not receive loans, only 4 had requested a formal loan. Most of the others who had not received a loan maintained, at one extreme, that they had not attempted to get one because the bank does not give loans to poor people or, at the other extreme, that they did not need to borrow from the bank because their own resources were sufficient.

No small-scale farmers received loans, and only 7.5 percent tried to get one. Most (24 percent) did not attempt to get one because they believed that they would not get one if they tried, because the bank, in their mind, did not give loans to poor people or to nomads. Some (20 percent) simply did not know how to deal with a bank. The remainder gave various reasons for not attempting to obtain a loan including:

1. They had no assets, collateral, or bank account;
2. Their farm was not irrigated;
3. They had no guarantor for their loan;
4. The bank gives loans only to large-scale farmers;
5. It is necessary to know someone at the bank;
6. The bureaucracy is too complicated or time-consuming;
7. The bank is too far away, time- or money-wise;
8. They did not want to incur debt because they could not repay it;
9. They were afraid to go to the bank for fear of looking like a thief or of looking too poor;

10. They could not tell the difference between the SDB and the Commercial and Savings Bank of Somolia (CSBS), or (by several) they had never been to Mogadishu, where they believed the banks were located.

Commercial and Savings Bank of Somalia (CSBS)

At the time of the research, the CSBS provided medium-term and seasonal loans for equipment and farm expenses. It also managed a special UNDP/FAO-supported Seasonal Credit for Small Farmers Program. Similar to the findings for the SDB, 8 of the 27 large-scale farmers (30 percent) had received loans from the CSBS in the past. Two of them had had two loans, and four had had continuous lines of credit and/or overdraft facilities. The most common reason given for borrowing was to pay expenses for plowing, renting a tractor, or paying general farm expenses. But, purchase of a tractor and purchase of an irrigation pump were also given as reasons. Loans ranged from 5,000 So.Sh. (US$33) to a 4 million So.Sh. (US$27,000) line of credit, averaging 1,082,000 So.Sh. (US$7,000) with a median of 300,000 So.Sh. (US$2,000).

Also similar to the findings for the SDB, only five of the small-scale farmers said they had obtained a loan from the CSBS, and the loans were small compared to those of the large-scale farmers, ranging in size from 1,000 So.Sh. (US$7) to 4,000 So.Sh. (US$27). Three of the loans were to plow or rent a tractor, and one was to maintain irrigation canals.

Of the 19 large-scale farmers who had not received a loan, only 6 (32 percent) had attempted to get one. The most common reason given by the large-scale farmers for not seeking a loan was that they did not know how to deal with the bank. Of the 157 small-scale farmers who did not receive loans from CSBS, only 13 (8 percent) had requested one. The reasons given by the small-scale farmers for not getting a loan from the CSBS were similar to those they gave for not seeking one from the SDB. The response that they do not know how to deal with the bank could be a generalization to cover up for a wide variety of frustrations and fears about going to the bank. But, the data suggest that a large number of farmers, especially small-scale farmers, do not believe that they personally have access to formal credit facilities, and they do not even think of asking for formal loans.

Informal Finance

Shopkeepers

Shopkeepers have played a role in providing credit for as long as
they have existed in many locations throughout Africa. In some
countries they have been accused of exploiting their customers by tying
them to their services forever with debt. Less attention has been paid
to the positive aspects of loans from such sources. For example, African
shopkeepers have provided loan services, in small amounts, as a source
of last resort for many villagers, particularly small-scale farmers.
While large-scale farmers may find it easier to go to the bank for their
credit needs in Somalia, small-scale farmers usually approach the
local shopkeeper for small loans. For example, while only 30 percent of
the large-scale farmers had taken loans from shopkeepers, 52 percent of
small-scale farmers had. The most common reasons given by large-scale
farmers for taking these loans were to pay farm expenses, labor, or
equipment rental; those of the small-scale farmers were more likely to
be simply for survival purposes: food and clothing. About half of the
informal loans of small-scale farmers were taken in kind, and most of
them were in the form of food. Although large-scale farmers borrowed
less often from shopkeepers, the size of their cash loans was larger
than those of the small-scale farmers. Cash loans to large-scale
farmers ranged from 6,000 So.Sh. (US$40) to 100,000 So.Sh. (US$667),
with a median of 30,000 So.Sh. (US$200). Cash loans to small-scale
farmers ranged from 50 to 25,000 So.Sh. (US$.33 to US$167) with a
median of only 2,000 So.Sh. (US$13).

Moneylenders

Another source of credit in many countries in Africa is the
moneylender. This is a difficult concept to research in Somalia, as
lending with interest is contrary to the principles of Islam.
Moneylenders are not like shopkeepers who may make loans secondary
to their main occupation of selling goods. Moneylenders make their
living by lending money for profit. Because of religious prohibitions,
such activities tend to be covert in Islamic countries. Nevertheless, four
(15 percent) of the large-scale farmers, and 13 percent of the small-scale
farmers admitted to borrowing from moneylenders. Again, these loans

to large-scale farmers were relatively large, averaging 35,000 So.Sh. ($233), while loans to small-scale farmers averaged 9,400 So.Sh. (US$63).

Other Monetary Sources

Beyond the above sources of loans nearly half of the small-scale farmers said that they did not have any other source of finance. Some said that they would "wait up" until they had additional money, and some said that they would go to work on the local plantations for a wage if they needed additional funds. Their next most common reply was to go to their families. About 14 percent of the small-scale farmers said that they would do so, and about 22 percent of the large-scale farmers responded likewise. Ten percent of the small-scale and 15 percent of the large-scale farmers said that they could ask for help from their friends. Seeking help from other farmers was also a possibility (10 percent of small-scale farmers and 7 percent of large-scale farmers said that they could do this). Finally, other sources used by small-scale farmers were to borrow from a neighboring large-scale farmer or an employer, who is often the same large-scale farmer.

Nonmonetary Sources—The Goob and the Barbaar

A *goob* is one of the simplest types of traditional work groups. It is described in the *Socioeconomic Baseline Study of the Bay Region* (University of Wyoming 1984) which refers to research by Mahoney (1961). It is usually formed by a neighbor who needs temporary help in his/her fields. Help is sought from adults or children, for a specific activity such as land preparation, planting, weeding, or harvesting. The goob usually works for no more than a day, although at times it may require several days to complete a specific task. Members of the goob are usually fed a meal of the local staple, for example *soor* (porridge) and milk, on the days they work. There is no monetary pay for the work. Yet, there is also no necessary expectation of reciprocity for the organizer to participate in a goob formed by someone who has formerly worked for him or her.

A University of Wyoming research team found in their study that the goob was the most common type of work group in the Bay Region of Somalia, a region of rainfed agriculture that contrasts with the Lower Shabelle Region where irrigation is important. Over 10 percent of the heads of households they interviewed had used a goob in the last year and 6 percent had participated in another's goob. It is interesting to note, however, that the Wyoming team found that fewer goobs were being formed than in the past. The shortage of rains in the preceding years had depleted the surplus grain that was used to feed the goob, and the Agricultural Development Corporation (ADC), the parastatal organization that fixes the price of certain staple crops, was maintaining a very low official price for sorghum. The farmers apparently had calculated that the marginal benefit of the goob was less than the marginal cost (the cost of feeding the goob), and were thus using this traditional source of assistance less often, even though they needed it to increase their production.

A *barbaar* is a different type of work group. The term barbaar literally means "youth," but it implies that it is composed of "capable" or "tough" ones. The Wyoming team also described this type of work group in the Bay Region (University of Wyoming 1984). They found that a barbaar is often composed of unmarried males, usually between the ages of 15 and the late 20s, although it also may include a few females, some married men, and an occasional older man or woman. Apparently, at some time in the past, it might have been an age-grade unit cutting across kinship groups, but this is no longer true in general. Moreover, because of certain of its social activities, it is not found in all villages, particularly in villages that are tied to a specific religious figure.

The members of the barbaar are loosely organized to take responsibilities for individuals in need. According to the Wyoming team, the members select a leader, an *aaw*, who organizes the barbaar's assistance to those needing help. The aaw also provides the barbaar members a meal of a slaughtered goat for each of three consecutive years, or a single feast of a three-year-old bull. Barbaar members may be asked to work the fields of someone too old or sick to do their own work. They may take a sick person for medical care or return a sick or injured animal to the village, or do any other job that requires a group of physically capable individuals. In some cases, the barbaar members may also work each other's fields, and thus may operate much as a rotating work group, completing the work on each member's farm in turn. In some African countries it is believed that such rotating work groups are the predecessors of the money-based ROSCAs. In Somalia, the traditional work groups are more common in the subsistence agricultural sector, while the ROSCAs are more prevalent in the markets of the cities. In general, a barbaar is held together by an unwritten pact of mutual responsibility to care for those in need, but also by a social bond of friendship. Thus, if a member does not participate in the work of the group, he/she will be fined or excluded from membership unless he/she has an acceptable excuse. Such ostracism would then prevent subsequent participation in associated social activities, such as dancing and singing in the evening.

Our study in the Afgoi Division showed that the farmers used goobs as a substitute for finance. In general, the large-scale farmers used traditional forms of labor assistance less often than did the small-scale farmers. For example, in the Afgoi Division, 28 percent of the small-scale farmers used the goob, but only 15 percent of the large-scale farmers used it. The large-scale farmers, with their greater access to financial resources, especially from formal loans, more commonly paid their farm labor cash wages.

Conclusions

Farmers in Somalia require loans for long-term capital investment and for seasonal inputs to increase agricultural production and productivity. But, our study showed it is difficult in general for farmers to obtain formal credit, and that it is even more difficult for small-scale farmers to access the formal loans. They often must rely on informal sources for loans.

Why do the small-scale farmers have difficulty obtaining loans from the formal institutions? First, there may be an education factor. Education is important not only for understanding new technology and for implementing improved agricultural practices, but it is also important for knowing how to obtain title to land and how to deal with application procedures in formal credit programs. Indeed, the large-scale farmers were more highly educated and also more literate than their poorer neighbors. Fifty-two percent of the large-scale farmers had completed primary school, while only 5 percent of the small-scale farmers had. Furthermore, 85 percent of the large-scale farmers said that they could read and write in the Somali language, while only 41 percent of small-scale farmers said that they could.

But, there are also other factors that make it difficult for small-scale farmers to access credit in the formal programs. For example, they are less likely to have collateral to guarantee their loans, and there are few formal loan schemes that lend without collateral.[1] Although a large percentage of Somali farmers are women, many of them do not

---

1. In particular, in many agricultural credit programs it is necessary to hold title to land in Somalia, and to hold title to irrigated land for use as collateral.

hold title to land and are thus blocked from access to formal loans. In subsequent research among the women in the Lower Shabelle it was confirmed that very few women were able to participate in the CSBS-sponsored Seasonal Credit for Small Farmers Project, because they did not have title to irrigated land, and were not members of a cooperative or a group that qualified for credit (DeLancey and others 1987). Yet, they are some of the most important potential beneficiaries of agricultural credit. Similarly, small-scale farmers are less likely than large-scale farmers to hold title to land, or to irrigated land.

Just as important as the reasons above, small-scale farmers who hold title to land are often geographically distant from the formal sources of credit and they are not known by the credit administrators. Many poor people do not know the procedures for obtaining a bank loan, nor do they have the minimum financial resources to travel to banks or to sustain themselves through the bureaucratic red tape required to negotiate a loan. As a result they turn to informal finance. Alternatively, they try to obtain the necessary resources through wage work on nearby farms, or they simply "wait up" until they find the necessary resources. Unfortunately, although these sources of informal finance are important to small-scale farmers because of their lack of access to formal finance, they do not provide sufficient financial services.

In sum, if credit is necessary for improving agricultural production and productivity, and if the large-scale farmers have greater access to credit than the small-scale farmers, the large-scale farmers will become wealthier, and the small-scale farmers will remain poor. If we see that income is becoming more unequally distributed, then we must become concerned that more equitable development is not occurring. Thus, we must begin to consider how to remedy that situation. How can we improve the distribution of income? One way is to improve the distribution of credit to those who have been denied access to it. This in turn could increase their investment, which could lead to an increase in their production and hence their income. The relevant question for Somalia, then, is how can small-scale farmers be helped to obtain greater access to credit and thus be able to participate in the development process? Answers to this question might be found in more careful analyses of how informal finance services these individuals.

References

Commercial and Savings Bank of Somalia. 1986. "National Input and Credit Committee, Seasonal Credit for Small Farmers Project (United Nations

Capital Fund Project - SOM/82/001)." Report on Agricultural Credit Seminar held on 27 September in the Cooperative Training Centre-Mogadishu, Mogadishu, Somalia.

——— 1987. "Seasonal Credit for Small Farmers - UNCDF Project - SOM/82/001 - Some Basic Facts." Unpublished paper presented at the Branch Managers Seminar on Credit for Developing Agricultural Production, January 25-27, Mogadishu, Somalia.

DeLancey, Virginia, Deborah E. Lindsay, and Anita Spring. 1987. "Somalia: An Assessment of SWDO and of the Social and Economic Status of Women in the Lower Shabelle." Washington, D.C.: Robert R. Nathan Associates, Inc. for the U.S. Agency for International Development.

Food and Agriculture Organization/Ministry of Education. 1983. "Rural Household Survey in the Three Regions of Somalia Among the Agricultural Settled Villages." Unpublished paper Women's Education Department, Ministry of Education, Mogadishu, Somalia.

Haakensen, J. M. 1982. "The Socio-economic Studies of Two Southern Somali Villages: Lama Doonka and Beled Amin." Unpublished report presented to the Community Health Department, Medical Faculty, Somali National University and the Swedish Agency for Research Cooperation (SAREC), Mogadishu.

Jamal, Vali. 1983. "Nomads and Farmers: Incomes and Poverty in Rural Somalia." In Dharam Ghai and Samir Radwan, eds., *Agrarian Policies and Rural Poverty in Africa*, pp. 281-311. Geneva: International Labour Office.

Lewis, I. M. 1981. *Somali Culture, History and Social Institutions: An Introductory Guide to Somali Democratic Republic.* London: The London School of Economics and Political Science.

Mahoney, Frank. 1961. "Problems of Community Development in Somalia: The Pastoral Nomads." Unpublished report prepared for the Agency for International Development, Washington, D.C.

Massey, Garth. 1987. *Subsistence and Change: Lessons of Agropastoralism in Somalia.* Boulder, Colorado: Westview Press.

Tammi, G. 1985. "Agricultural Finance Profile of Somalia." Unpublished report prepared for the U.N. Food and Agriculture Organization and the U.N. Development Programme, Rome, December. FAO/UNDP Project Som 81/006.

University of Wyoming. 1984. *Socioeconomic Baseline Study of the Bay Region,* 2 vols. Laramie, Wyoming: University of Wyoming.

6

Informal Rural Finance in Niger: Lessons for Building Formal Institutions

Douglas H. Graham[1]

The informal sector plays an overwhelming role in supplying financial services to rural people in Africa. Yet research on this topic is limited and policymakers tend to ignore it or to minimize its importance. On the other hand, considerable attention and resources have been devoted to the promotion of supply-leading financial strategies as a vehicle for rural modernization. However, the results in Niger have been meager with formal finance failing to create much viable presence in the countryside. Thus the issue has arisen as to what strategy is most appropriate to reach a rural clientele with a sustained stream of financial services. I here explore this theme by first reporting on the findings of a survey of informal finance in Niger in the mid-1980s. This is followed by a review of the debate that occurred within policy circles concerning the most promising paths to follow to create a broader base of viable rural financial intermediaries in the country. Not surprisingly the results of the survey of informal finance played an important role in influencing this discussion.

1. The author acknowledges the support of the USAID Mission in Niamey and the Office of Rural and Institutional Development of the Bureau of Science and Technology, and the Agency for International Development in Washington. Tom Olsen and Lance Jepson were particularly helpful in Niamey and Sandra Frydman and Eric Chetwynd in Washington. Kifle Negash played an important role in the collection of the data, while Michel Keita of the Institut de Recherches en Science Humaines in Niamey and Sanda Maina of the Ministry of Rural Development - Government of Niger deserve special thanks for their counsel and participation in the fieldwork.

Niger is a drought-prone, sparsely populated, Sahelian country where subsistence agriculture predominates. Large migrant cattle herds are another important agricultural activity, moving across borders into neighboring Burkina Faso, Mali, and Nigeria. Risk and uncertainty is common to their rural environment and informal finance is almost the only source of finance outside the major cities.

Research Design

In 1985 and 1986 a team from Ohio State University surveyed a random sample of approximately 400 farm households in 22 villages in Niger and, subsequently, followed up with a field study of 38 wholesale and 58 retail merchants, 56 Tontine groups (Rotating Savings and Credit Associations) and 39 active moneykeepers in these same villages (Graham and others 1987). These villages were chosen to represent a national sample from five distinct agronomical areas from the irrigated perimeters for rice production along the Niger River through changing rainfall zones that included variable dry land farming environments. Diverse tribal groups were represented including Zarma, Touareg, Hausa and Peul among others. Results of these studies showed the importance of informal finance in the country and the channels through which this intermediation occurs. Each of these informal vehicles merits discussion in any consideration of finding an appropriate path of transition from informal to formal financial activity. First, however, it is useful to clarify the relative importance of formal and informal finance in Niger.

Formal versus Informal Finance

Formal finance in Nigerian villages consisted of loans issued through the Caisse Nationale de Credit Agricole (CNCA), the only formal institution making loans in rural areas. These loans were made up of animal traction, fertilizer, and seed loans. They were always distributed in kind by a parastatal input supply agency with equal amounts allocated to all farmers in a given village. The demand for in-kind loans was estimated by extension agents with all farmers considered eligible. Clientele selection, loan evaluation and differentiated loan rationing adjusted for risk were not operational considerations for CNCA management. This management largely played a wholesale role, retailing their in-kind loans through other field level agencies.

At the time of the household survey in the mid-1980s, the CNCA had practically stopped all lending due to high arrears, no additional donor support, with preliminary audits underway to determine its future. For all practical purposes there was no formal loan activity in rural Niger at this time. Nevertheless, to gain an insight into the relative access between formal and informal sources of credit in the recent past, the random survey documented all formal loans received by rural households in the past five years. The average access to at least one formal loan in the last five years among our 400 rural households came to 22 percent (for both production and seed loans) and only 15 percent (for production loans alone). Only 4 percent of the households had access to a formal loan in all five years.

In contrast, 85 percent of the households had used informal finance. The probability of gaining access to a formal loan in the past five years (i.e. 22 or 15 percent as cited above) multiplied by the average formal loan size documented in the survey, allows one to estimate the typical, representative loan value for all formal borrowers during this period. This total only represented 2.2 percent of the 1985 agricultural income recorded for these families (about 1 percent for production loans). In contrast the total value of informal loans estimated the same way represented 17 percent of the 1985 agricultural income of these same rural households. Thus informal loans were many times more important than formal loans when expressed as a percent of the agricultural income earned by these families. Whether stated in terms of access (people served) or volume, informal borrowing was of overwhelming importance to these rural households when compared to formal borrowing.

Loans from family, friends, and relatives constituted a majority of this activity. These loans carried no interest and were tied to reciprocal labor obligations or to the expectation of reciprocal loans, an important insurance policy for rural households facing the shifting fortunes of the drought-prone Sahel. The remaining informal financial activities were carried out by merchants, tontines, and moneykeepers. While other forms of informal sector groupings exist for various religious and community affairs, merchants, tontines, and moneykeepers constituted the most important financial operators on the informal scene. Each merits separate comment.

Merchant Finance

Wholesale merchants secured credit from urban based banks. In these transactions non-land collateral was highly associated with the amount and the term structure of the loans. These loans were then rechanneled to village retail merchants in the form of a consignment of consumer goods for which cash repayments were expected following the harvest. The retailers, in turn, sold the goods to villagers on credit. Following the harvest the chain of cash repayments worked itself back up through the layered informal network to the wholesale merchant and the bank.

Several conclusions emerge from a study of financial practices by merchants. First, whether formally pledged or not, wholesalers with a large collateral base (usually inventory holdings) clearly secured larger average sized loans and longer-term loans from their urban based banks than those with less collateral. Retailers, by the same token, also secured a larger consignment of goods (an implicit loan to be repaid later) for a longer period of time, the larger their collateral base. Indeterminant terms or open lines of credit were evident between retailers and their village borrowers. These contracts comprised 40 percent of all retail transactions. Interest charges were admitted to by some but not by most wholesalers and retailers. This reticence to admit interest charges is not surprising in an Islamic society. It is likely that implicit interest was built into the prices of the consigned goods that were to be repaid by the villagers following harvest. The same implicit interest was likely for the cash repayment from retailer to wholesalers. These contract features could not be documented well in a short single visit interview.

Tontines

The village level tontines (called Susu or Esusu in other West African countries) represented a wide diversity of groups from housewives and farmers to market vendors, small businessmen, school teachers, and extension agents among others. For the most part each of these rotating savings and credit associations had a common occupational bond although some limited mixing of groups and gender occurred. These occupational bonds were also highly correlated with similar income levels and, to a lesser extent, age groupings. Close proximity was also an important feature of their groupings.

Membership size ranged from 4 to 40 individuals with the frequency of meetings and contributions and loans ranging from five days to one month and the lifecycle of a complete tontine cycle from one month to a year. Generally no payments were reported for the right to move up in the queue for a loan. The sequential order to receive a loan (i.e. the right to draw upon the programmed savings contributions) was flexible with the group responding to special member problems and needs. An informal treasurer operated in the high income tontines, a post that generally received some form of remuneration or a privileged position in the sequential order of loans. Tontine leaders reported some problems with delinquent members, because members migrated after receiving their loan or because they fell into a destitute situation. Finally it was not uncommon for members to be in more than one tontine at the same time. It was not possible to determine the use made of tontine loans since the tontine organizer (rather than the members) was the source for the documented activity.

Two findings stand out from this research on the 56 tontine groups in the 22 villages. First there was a remarkably wide income or wealth differential involved in the average member contribution and average sized loan per tontine. This income differential refers to the different uniform size of contribution (and loan) generated by each tontine. The assumption is made that this is a rough proxy for the relative wealth and income differentials as a whole across the tontine groups. Member contributions for each cycle ranged from a low of 25 cents (in equivalent CFAF currency) in the lowest income tontine to a high of US$70 in the highest income group. Uniform tontine loans ranged from two dollars to US$700 in these villages. The average tontine loan size for all 56 tontines was equivalent to US$111, almost twice the US$65 rural per capita income figure for Niger in 1985. This amount was larger than the average seed loans granted by the CNCA but slightly less than the average production loan. The lowest income tontines were composed of housewives and farmers. The housewives met frequently (every week) and the farmers organized their payments around harvest seasons. The high income tontines consisted of market vendors, businessmen, teachers, and extension agents who met less frequently and for longer periods of time. Cattle herders' informal groups were not included in this survey.

The second major finding underscores the large volume of funds that moves through these groups. The aggregate total for the contributions for the entire life cycle of all 56 tontines (that is, the period of time that allows each member access to a tontine loan) amounted to US$72,000. This highlights the ample base of local savings available for financial intermediation in rural Niger. These findings caught the attention of policymakers and donors alike. However, the existence of a promising potential for rural deposit mobilization is one thing, the appropriate or feasible mechanism that could transform these informal savings into a more efficient formal form of financial intermediation is another thing.

Moneykeepers

Moneykeepers round out this discussion of indigenous financial arrangements in rural Niger. Thirty-nine moneykeepers comprised our sample in the 22 villages (an additional 17 individuals had no current active accounts, but had been moneykeepers in the past). Males predominate in this profession. Merchants are the most commonly chosen persons to undertake these activities. Moneykeepers offer multiple services to their clientele. Not only do they hold deposits, for which they pay no interest, but some also offer pawnbroker and general storage services, especially for textile inventories. A few moneykeepers among the Hausa act as purchasing agents on their trips to Nigeria, bringing back goods for their clientele. Finally, moneykeepers also engage in loan activities with an average loan size of US$144. The term structure on loans was generally shorter than those on deposits suggesting an appropriate rudimentary matching of term structure between assets and liabilities. Explicit interest was admitted to in only a small number of these loans. It was not possible to determine the existence of implicit interest here.

The deposit services cover a wide range of customers. Some moneykeepers have only a handful of deposit accounts. Others handle as many as 150 depositors. The total volume of deposits varied from a low of 30 dollars (in equivalent CFAF) to a high of US$13,000. As in the case of tontines the aggregate level of deposit activity for these 39 moneykeepers was substantial. The volume of deposits for all 39 ranged from US$34,000 during the dry season to US$79,000 in the immediate post-harvest season. Thus there was a sharp seasonal variation, but in the end, a significant flow of funds circulated through these informal channels.

Lessons

The lessons derived from the above findings for these various channels of informal finance are several. First, the scope and magnitude of informal finance are significant in Niger. The scope was wide, the magnitude impressive. Second, despite the rudimentary nature of some of these activities, an embryonic form of financial intermediation was clearly occurring within these informal intermediaries. Third, these activities were generally well organized and business-like. For the most part these mechanisms are generally self-sustaining even in the face of the risky Sahelian environment that causes delinquent clientele from time to time.

A major lesson for formal finance is that any viable financial intermediary at the village level must be prepared to offer the financial services demanded by villagers. This demand emphasizes deposit and savings services, short-term and open lines of credit and nonproduction loans. Informal finance is also marked by constant contact and frequently changing terms and conditions on loan contracts which may transform short- to longer-term loans. Multiple services are widespread with not only deposits and loans but in some cases pawnbroking, inventory, and marketing services built into some of these lenders activities. The implication is clear, credit alone is not the usual focus for local financial intermediaries. Yet it is this focus that predominates in all formal attempts to reach villages with formal finance in Niger. Thus it is not surprising to note widespread failure in these attempts (Graham and others 1987). It is quite likely that formal finance cannot hope to emulate the diversity of services and flexibility of conditions inherent in informal finance at the village level. At best, formal financial institutions might be able to reach a relatively more manageable clientele in larger regional towns rather than in smaller villages.

Informal Finance and the Government

The scope, magnitude, and overwhelming role of informal financial activity in Niger is clear. Furthermore, the positive and beneficial role of this finance in satisfying important and legitimate needs at the village level is also clear. The innovative and flexible adaptations of this informal activity to risks and uncertainties earn it a durable, strategic role in village life that should be drawn upon in any attempt to inculcate or introduce more formal forms of finance at the village level. The issue is how to do this. How does one "cross over" from informal to formal finance or downscale formal finance to emulate the virtues of informal finance and what, if any, should be the role of the government in this transition (Seibel and Marx 1987)?

The government in Niger is similar to most African governments in having devoted its energies to a supply-led financial development strategy in the past. Prior to the mid-1980s there was a strong desire to induce and direct economic growth at a more rapid pace and along more explicit lines than would have occurred naturally. These efforts, as has been widely documented, caused a substantial worsening of the terms of trade for agriculture and export activity, and a large role for government, indeed an overwhelming role for the state emerged with widespread parastatal activity. This created strong bases for political patronage through employment generation in selected regions as well as creating unsupportable fiscal deficits that would eventually drive the economy to stagnation and decline in the 1980s.

Large irrigated and integrated rural development projects were set up in Niger in this vein with the Caisse Nationale de Credit Agricole (CNCA) designed to service the cash flow needed by these projects. The objectives of the CNCA were to service these parastatal entities with liquidity, cover their payroll, and transfer loans to farmer-beneficiaries in these projects. As mentioned earlier, no financial analysis, creditworthiness studies, or risk analysis was undertaken. The ample supply of donor monies lured the CNCA into a policy of quick disbursement and weak loan recovery efforts. In the end the CNCA was a financial wholesaler, dependent upon the goodwill and commitment of other parastatal employees to both disburse as well as to recover its loans. The CNCA was not a serious financial institution carrying out financial intermediation services. It was an administrative conduit to channel funds to previously selected target clientele through other agencies. Thus it is not surprising that the institution became bankrupt and was forced to discontinue its operations in the mid-1980s.

This supply leading financial mind-set, however, still had a strong hold on government officials in the late 1980s. Its origins, in part, are derived from the top-down, state-driven and state-operated administrative machinery inherited from the French. And it is consistent with a strong anti-private sector bias that shapes the thinking of the political elite (Courcelle and de Lattre 1988). At the same time these officials have a highly negative attitude toward the various forms of informal finance in their midst. It was precisely these activities that this modern governmental "elite" was trying to replace.

Traditional trade and village level finance is generally considered backward, perhaps lending itself to colorful folklore for foreign researchers but not useful for much else. At worst any emphasis on researching or dealing with informal financial groups and actors on the part of donors is perceived as a misallocation of resources better spent elsewhere to break the chains of underdevelopment.

With this mind-set still operating in some official circles, imaginative and innovative approaches toward promoting a transition from informal activities to more formal institutions encounter bureaucratic obstacles. Still, some positive factors were operating in Niger. First, from the mid-1980s onward many government officials learned through painful experience the limitations of their parastatal driven paths of development and the deficiencies of the supply-led channels of financial development. Twenty-two public enterprises have been subject to privatization programs in the late 1980s (Nellis and Kikeri). Second, due to the above mentioned field research documenting the nature of informal finance, many officials now appreciate the magnitudes of the reservoirs of savings available in villages.

At this point two approaches to the transition were discussed in Niger. The first directed its attention toward the possible decentralization of a resurrected national agricultural development bank. In this reorganization, local branches would be set up in selected villages with local managers who would enjoy some degree of operational autonomy. These villages would be located within the amply supported integrated rural development (IRD) area where substantial liquidity has been generated through official development projects. Deposit mobilization services would be offered along with credit facilities and credit would not be restricted to production loans. Indeed outside advisers strongly recommended that most loans not be production loans to reduce risk and to promote portfolio diversification. The term structure would be very short as a means to establish creditworthiness since land collateral is inoperative in a land surplus economy like Niger with poorly defined property rights and a problematical legal environment for financial transactions (Bromley 1989). Outside monies were to be restricted (though not eliminated) as local deposits were to form the base of on-lending. This decentralized approach would presumably succeed in bringing a formal institution into these selected villages, acquiring more of a local identity and offering deposit, short-term, nonproduction loans to a cross section of villagers, in short, meeting the demand for the kind of financial services revealed in the village level research on informal finance. It was hoped that this new approach in which a formal institution would emulate the positive properties of informal finance could create the conditions for a viable village level, formal financial intermediary with a healthy loan recovery record in these areas.

However, continued debate revealed a resistance in some circles to scale back the top-down bias characteristic of the past. It was unclear how much delegated authority would in fact be passed on to the local managers of the financial institution, but continued discussion suggested very little. Furthermore, there was a serious question whether the existing cadre of civil servants from the old CNCA or other parastatal agencies had the appropriate skills and attitudes to carry out the delegated managerial responsibilities of a local branch manager. Deposit services were considered of some use but the credit function was clearly the predominant activity envisioned, thereby reducing the relative role of local deposits and the local identification of funding sources. Production loans were also emphasized in these discussions, indeed these loans were often referred to as the spearhead of modernization, and there was a visceral reaction against issuing loans to traders among most government circles. In the end the old supply leading mind-set surfaced in a new guise as the concepts of decentralization, diversification, and multiple service functions were downplayed and the old direct credit bias resurrected. By 1990 nothing had come of efforts to reform the formal financial market in rural Niger. As mentioned earlier, it may be too much to expect even honest and capable branch managers to match the diversity and flexibility common to informal village finance. However, it may be possible to offer valuable financial services with some degree of portfolio diversification for a more established clientele in the larger regional towns in Niger.

A second approach emphasized a bottom-up strategy. This built upon the strengths of informal finance and was more prepared to incorporate these features in a semiformal institution such as a savings and credit cooperative that could act as the catalyst for the transition from informal to semiformal intermediation. Here the emulation ran in the opposite direction with an upscaling of informal groupings into a more formal organization. The subtleties and nuances of financial management documented through participant-observer research might have shed more light on the more feasible avenues for joining together various informal tontines, moneykeepers, and merchants into a village based savings and credit cooperative. In the absence of this research, one had to infer the most appropriate mix from the national survey data.

This would not be a government organized cooperative. The cooperative organizer would logically come from a nongovernmental organization (NGO) or a private voluntary organization (PVO) that would respect the local autonomy and local initiative needed for such ventures. The advantages of such an effort lie in the natural decentralization that is inherent in a village run and village organized operation. The existing set of financial services could be largely replicated in this new group. More importantly this cooperative would bring scale and scope economies to the otherwise disparate and occupationally segmented tontine groupings and create the basis for a wider range of income levels in the membership and a more diversified set of village activities represented in the institution. This would introduce information economies and some degree of portfolio diversification compared to the activities of the currently more segmented groups. Finally, if several neighboring villages successfully launched these initiatives, spatial economies could emerge through a league of savings and credit cooperatives with an associated interlending facility to intermediate among surplus and deficit units and to act as a lender of last resort.

This kind of organization would need substantial bookkeeping and management training. In the end, however, it might prove to be far less expensive to launch an NGO oriented activity of this nature than to establish a wide network of decentralized formal bank branches with all of its associated centralized infrastructure. Moreover, such NGO initiatives could lend themselves to a series of pilot projects that might be altered and reshaped to adapt to changing local circumstances or terminated altogether if the experiment proves to be a failure. This flexibility is less likely in a decentralized development bank. More importantly an NGO initiative could more likely build on the tontine tradition to create the institutional ethos to instill the social solidarity and social sanctions necessary for viability in a village based setting. These are extremely difficult collateral substitutes for any outside institution such as a decentralized development bank to draw upon when they attempt to move into a village with a heavy dose of outside monies. In the end the argument for this bottom-up approach prevailed and a project was designed to implement this through the World Council of Credit Unions (WOCCU). The project was still in its infancy in 1990.

Conclusion

It is clear that informal finance in rural Niger is substantial. Wholesale and retail merchants, village moneykeepers, and tontine groups are the principal agents in this financial activity. It is also clear that these intermediaries offer valuable financial services to villagers. Any attempt to reach this clientele has to recognize the nature of the demand for financial services and the need to create institutions that can meet this demand as efficiently or better than these traditional intermediaries. Important lessons here are to accept the need for short-term loans, frequent adjustments to adapt to changing conditions, consumer loans, and deposit services. In short, multiple services and frequent contact are essential to create information economies, credibility, and a loyal lender-client relationship.

Two approaches to create this transition or crossover were discussed in Niger. The first emphasized the decentralization of an agricultural development bank directed toward emulating the positive properties of informal finance. This would entail autonomous local branches, deposit and savings mobilization services, short-term consumption and trader loans to diversify the portfolio away from medium-term production loans. This approach attracted favorable attention from authorities since it offered them an option to resurrect a recently closed agricultural development bank. Continued discussion, however, underscored resistance to truly effective decentralization and diversification away from the previous supply-led financial strategies. Old habits and attitudes die hard. Conceivably such a decentralizing approach could work elsewhere. It did not appear promising in Niger.

The second approach was designed to build on the strengths of informal finance at the village level. This initiative emphasized the creation of a more formal financial group from the separately segmented tontines, merchant, and moneykeeper networks. Scale and scope economies could be gained through a savings and credit cooperative combining these elements. Spatial economies could eventually be exploited as more villages created their cooperatives and an interlending facility designed to operate among them.

This is typically an NGO or PVO oriented activity. This grass roots initiative would take at a minimum a five-year period to become established, perhaps too long a period to attract donor support. However the pilot project dimensions of this effort allow for mid-course corrections. The major input is technical assistance not loan funds. The principal challenge is to identify the most promising mix of village level intermediaries to draw into this endeavor and the creation of appropriate incentives to motivate their interest and support. Case study approaches documenting the decisionmaking processes at the informal level could make a contribution here. In the end, this low key, low profile approach would likely prove more durable than the decentralized development bank approach for Niger.

References

Bromley, Daniel. 1989."Property Relations and Economic Development: The Other Land Reform." *World Development* 17: 867-877.

Courcelle, Michael, and Anne de Lattre. 1988. *The Private Sector in Niger.* Paris: CILSS-OECD.

Graham, Douglas H. and others. 1987. "Rural Finance in Niger: A Critical Appraisal and Recommendations for Change." Unpublished report submitted to USAID Mission Niamey, Niger, Department of Agricultural Economics and Rural Sociology, Columbus, Ohio: The Ohio State University.

Nellis, John, and Sunita Kikeri. 1989. "Public Enterprise Reform: Privatization and The World Bank." *World Development* 17: 659-672.

Siebel, Hans Dieter, and M.T. Marx. 1987. *Dual Financial Markets in Africa.* Germany, Saarbrucken: Breintenbach.

7

Informal Finance in Sri Lanka

Nimal Sanderatne

In this chapter I describe the array of informal financial arrangements found in Sri Lanka and assess their significance. I also discuss efforts to develop semiformal credit arrangements and outline recent attempts to link formal and informal markets. In the final section I draw lessons from the Sri Lankan experience with informal finance that might be useful in formulating finance policies in other countries.

As in other countries, informal arrangements in Sri Lanka move in diverse ways to perform finance functions. The wide array of arrangements includes direct professional moneylenders, informal credit arrangements tied to land, labor and marketing, informal groups such as voluntary credit societies, and informal savings associations. Informal finance involves a wide range of sources, instruments, agreements, understandings, and contracts. Informal sources have provided essential funds for economic activities in the large cities, towns, and rural areas of the country. Although there has been a progressive expansion in institutional lending, informal lenders still play a significant role in the provision of credit in Sri Lanka.

The next section of this chapter assesses the significance of informal lenders over time. The third section categorizes the wide array of informal credit arrangements and discusses the characteristics that distinguish informal credit arrangements from formal lending. The fourth section reexamines several stereotyped characteristics of informal lenders. The fifth section describes several attempts to develop semiformal institutions (such as rural banks) to remedy the deficiencies of institutional lending and assesses their success. The sixth section discusses recent innovations to link formal and informal markets by commercial banks, particularly the appointing of credit facilitators known as *Praja Naya Niyamakas* (PNN). The last section attempts to distill the policy implications of the experience in formal, informal, and semiformal lending that may have applicability in other countries.

Significance of Informal Finance

Informal lenders in Sri Lanka are sources of finance for a wide range of activities from petty trading to financing large investments of unincorporated firms. In urban areas informal borrowings of both small and large sums of money are a continuous activity that knows no time nor season. A well-known phenomenon in urban areas is the daily borrowing of funds on condition that the borrower repays an additional sum at the end of the day. Such loans are used by retail vendors to purchase the produce they sell and by laborers to hire a cart or wheel barrow. Larger sums are borrowed by proprietary enterprises for purchase of capital items. Traders, in particular, borrow funds to finance their stocks. A large number of small and micro industries are financed by informal sources.

The informal sector, by its very nature, eludes the collection of information on the nature of its activities. Some participants in informal urban money markets are secretive for fear that their activities may be disclosed to authorities who may try to control or tax them. For this reason lenders as well as borrowers may resist giving information and, therefore, there has not been any systematic collection of data on the activities of the informal urban money market in Sri Lanka. Data, however, have been collected on the incidence of borrowing and the character of informal lending in micro studies of particular villages or rural areas in Sri Lanka and in national sample surveys. Even in these rural credit surveys, especially those of national coverage, there are difficulties in obtaining data as borrowers do not want to be characterized as poor, failures, or not having means, while lenders do not wish to be tainted as moneylenders—a derogatory profession that has been characterized as unsocial and exploitative. Therefore, the incidence of informal credit is often greater than disclosed by survey data.

Although efforts to increase institutional lending have succeeded to some extent, surveys of rural credit and indebtedness disclose the continued importance of informal finance (see Table 1). In 1957, informal lenders were responsible for nearly 92 percent of rural lending; in 1969, 75 percent; and in 1975-76 less than one-third of the outstanding debt and 45 percent of the loans taken by paddy farmers during the survey reference period (April 1 1975 to March 31 1976) were from informal traders.

In 1957 the major proportion of formal credit was from cooperatives which accounted for 4 percent of total rural credit. As much as 44 percent of total credit was from relatives and friends; 16 percent was from professional moneylenders; and 12 percent from boutique keepers, traders, and commission agents. Landlords, who as a category of lenders subsequently declined in importance, accounted for 8 percent of total debts (Department of Census and Statistics 1957). It is most significant that professional moneylenders accounted for only a small part of informal lending.

TABLE 1. Distribution of Rural Credit by Sources, Sri Lanka 1957, 1969, 1975-76 (percentage of total borrowing)

Sources	1957	1969	1975-76
Formal Sources:	8	25	55
Government	3	3	6
Cooperatives	4	10	5
Commercial banks	1	7	37
Rural banks	0	0	5
Other financial institutions	0	5	0
Informal Sources:	92	75	45
Moneylenders	16	12	0
Part-time lenders	0	19	0
Boutique keepers	7	14	29
Merchants & commissioned agents	4	2	0
Landlords	8	2	0
Relatives and friends	44	26	12
Others	13	0	4
Total	100	100	100

Notes: In the 1975-76 survey the informal sources were comprised of only three categories: moneylenders, noninterest lenders, and others. Therefore, noninterest lenders have been placed under relatives and friends.

Sources: 1957: Department of Census & Statistics, *Survey of Rural Indebtedness 1957.* 1969: Central Bank of Ceylon, *Survey of Rural Credit and Indebtedness 1969.* 1975-76: Central Bank of Ceylon, *Survey of Credit and Indebtedness Among Paddy Farmers 1976.*

By 1969 the quantum of formal loans to the rural sector had increased substantially through various agricultural credit programs, and grew even more with the formation in 1981 of the People's Bank whose specific objective is to serve the credit needs of the rural sector. Despite these institutional developments informal credit sources still accounted for 75 percent of total debts in 1969. Credit from cooperatives and commercial banks increased significantly and a new category, other financial institutions, accounted for nearly 6 percent of loans. Among informal lenders, relatives and friends continued to dominate but their share of lending declined significantly from that of 1957. Professional moneylenders declined in importance in overall lending from about 16 percent in 1957 to 11 percent, but semiprofessional moneylenders and boutique keepers emerged as important lenders accounting for 18 and 14 percent respectively of total debts. Landlords contributed less than 1 percent of total credit (Central Bank of Ceylon 1971).

The survey of credit conditions among paddy farmers conducted by the central bank in 1975-76 disclosed a continued decline in the relative importance of informal sources of loans. Only 45 percent of the amount of loans borrowed during 1975-76 was from informal lenders. Boutique keepers were the most important informal source and were responsible for 30 percent of the total amount borrowed. Noninterest lenders accounted for 13 percent of the amount of loans taken during the year.

Even if allowance is made for the fact that the sample of this last survey consisted of only paddy farmers, the overall change is indicative of formal sources becoming more significant in the rural credit market. In the last decade prior to the survey, a fairly large amount of credit had been given to paddy farmers and a lesser amount of credit for other food crops. By the end of 1975 there were 338 rural banks that had mobilized more savings than they lent to their customers. The bank network had also expanded to 562 branches.

Since institutional credit volumes have fluctuated quite markedly, it is likely that the relative importance of informal loans has varied from year to year. In an average year of government agricultural lending it is likely that informal lenders are about as important as institutional sources but when a large amount of institutional credit is pumped into the rural sector as in 1967 and 1977-78, the relative importance of informal sources likely declined. Conversely, when there is a contraction of institutional credit, informal sources are likely to be predominant. For instance in 1978-79 institutional credit for paddy cultivation increased substantially from SL Rs107 million in the previous year to SL Rs448 million but declined in subsequent years.

The preceding analysis of several national surveys of rural credit suggest that although the share of institutional credit in the rural sector has increased, informal lenders narrowly defined, account for a very significant proportion of credit. If a more comprehensive definition of informal lenders is accepted, there is little doubt that informal sources predominate. One serious limitation to coming to conclusions on the current situation is that the most recent available national data is from 1975-76 and is drawn from only a segment of the rural sector, albeit an important one.

Types of Informal Finance

The wide array of informal financial arrangements and sources might be grouped into three main categories and subgroups as discussed below.

Direct Money Lending

Direct sources of informal loans might be subdivided into three broad categories: professional moneylenders, part-time moneylenders, and personal (nonprofessional) sources of finance. Professional moneylenders are individuals whose primary occupation is money lending. High rates of interest, the entirety of the transaction being in cash, and their easy access characterize these lenders. Since professional moneylenders combine money lending with other services—such as petty trading, wholesale procuring of produce—or are landlords, it is sometimes difficult to distinguish them from part-time moneylenders. Part-time lenders include an array of persons generally residing in the village or in close proximity to it, who are mainly involved in other activities. Their money lending activity is often secret and they only make loans to persons they know. The third category of moneylenders includes friends, relatives, and landlords who assist persons in times of need. The distinguishing characteristic of this group of lenders is that they may lend free of interest or at a low rate of interest. Money lending could be a reciprocal transaction where the borrower might turn lender at other times or the reciprocity may be in nonfinancial terms. It may also have no reciprocity but merely be a part of the social and kinship relations in the village. A fourth form of credit arrangement is pawning, which is popular in both rural and urban societies. Under this arrangement a loan is obtained by pledging gold or jewelry. While many transactions may be with professional pawnbrokers, the security provided could persuade persons who are not regular moneylenders to lend on such security. Pawning has been institutionalized in Sri Lanka, and since 1963 the People's Bank—a state commercial bank—handles pawning.

Indirect Money Lending

A very common phenomenon in both urban and rural society in Sri Lanka is that a large number of poor households obtain their provisions on credit from boutiques and shops. Often the arrangement is a flexible system of revolving credit. When the consumer obtains provisions, the cost is added to his account by the shopkeeper and when the consumer is able to repay a sum of money this is set off against his debt. The consumer has a great degree of trust in boutique keepers and the accounting is entirely left in hand. Though trade credit of this nature has no apparent interest charge, interest costs are likely to be concealed in the form of higher prices for purchases.

Credit linked to marketing of produce is another well-known phenomenon in Sri Lanka, especially in vegetable cultivation and the purchase of paddy. In these arrangements farmers sell produce to "commission agents" who have earlier given loans. The ample flexibility of these commission agents and the convenience they provide in purchasing the output are among the reasons for preferring to sell produce to and secure loans from them. There is no explicit interest charge for loans, but the prices paid for the produce is usually lower than when the purchase involves only a cash payment.

The third source of this type of credit is landlords who provide inputs for cultivation. Here too there is often no apparent interest charge and the provision of these inputs is part of the land tenure relationship. An implied interest rate is often borne by the tenant as the share rent arrangement is adjusted to a higher rental. In addition to the provision of inputs, landlords often provide finance that is repaid in kind at harvest time and the valuation of the produce often includes an interest charge.

Pledging of standing crops provide another means by which cultivators obtain credit. This is most prevalent in the case of seasonal crops where the standing crop may be pledged in advance for a sum borrowed. In perennial crops, the debtor may agree to give the entire produce of the land until such time as he repays the loan. In such arrangements the crop becomes the interest payment and the period of loan may not be stipulated. Such pledging of crops could involve long periods of time where the sum borrowed is large. There could also be arrangements where the amortization of the loan is included in the produce payment and the loan is liquidated in a stipulated period of time. These arrangements are not generally in the form of legal instruments but are informal agreements.

Voluntary Groups

Voluntary groups are formed in Sri Lanka for specific needs such as meeting expenses for funerals as well as for other diverse purposes. Thrift and credit societies and rotating credit societies or *cheetus* are the most common forms of these groups and are widely prevalent in the country.

Cheetus take different forms, but their essential characteristic is that participants contribute at regular intervals and the pooled sum is distributed as a lump sum on the lottery principle, auction bidding, or a predetermined order of payment. These voluntary credit associations create a motivation and psychological impetus, among low-income participants to save significant amounts (Bouman 1984).

New Perspectives on Informal Lenders[1]

The money-lender is generally characterized as one who lends small sums of money at very high interest rates for short periods without security and mostly for consumption purposes (Sanderatne 1988). The usurious and exploitative nature of interest rates has received ample publicity. There is also the inference that the moneylender's role is parasitic, rather than functional and that society would be better off without them. In fact the role, function, and character of informal lenders vary with changes in financial markets over time and with the diversity of financial conditions in the country.

It is generally assumed that interest rates charged by informal lenders are exorbitant. In fact a wide spectrum of interest rates prevail in Sri Lanka. A study done in 1976 showed that interest rates ranged from 0 to 250 percent or more per annum (Table 2). Of the total volume of

---

1. This section is based on data collected in a nationwide survey of credit and indebtedness among paddy farmers conducted by the central bank in 1976. Although the sample selected for this survey was primarily of paddy (rice) farmers, the general characteristics of informal lenders cannot be expected to be different as paddy farming predominates in the rural sector.

TABLE 2. Interest Rates in Informal Sector (1976, 1978-79 & 1981-82)
(percentage of total)

Interest rate per annum	1976	1978-79	1981-82
0	31.2	72.1	54.1
1-10	4.2	4.1	1.6
11-20	15.8	3.5	13.0
21-50	36.8	3.0	3.0
51-100	6.2	5.4	4.0
Over 100	5.8	11.9	24.3
Total	100.0	100.0	100.0

Sources: 1976: Department of Census & Statistics, *Survey of Rural
Indebtedness 1957.* 1978-79: Central Bank of Ceylon, *Survey of Rural
Credit and Indebtedness 1969.* 1981-82: Central Bank of Ceylon, *Survey
of Credit and Indebtedness Among Paddy Farmers 1979.*

informal lending about one-third (31%) was interest free, about one-
third (34%) was at interest rates of below 25 percent, and about one-
third (36%) was lent at interest rates of over 25 percent per annum
(about 30 percent was between 25 and 100 percent and about 6 percent
above 100 percent per annum). The modal interest rate was 26 to 50
percent per annum (Table 2). Many surveys and village studies in Sri
Lanka have shown that a significant proportion of informal loans are
interest free. Kinship, friendship, patron-client relationships, and
reciprocity are important factors in meeting credit needs especially in
times of emergency.

Interest free loans should be cautiously interpreted as some of them
may have built-in interest. Loans obtained from traders may be
nominally free of interest but farmers' obligation and commitment to
sell their produce to the lender could result in their receiving lower
prices for their products than would occur in a cash deal. Similarly,
boutique keepers may give credit on purchases and charge higher
prices. A more subtle and disguised cost of interest free loans are loans
given to ensure existing tenancy and labor arrangements that are
beneficial to the landlord. Also some loans reported as obtained
without an interest charge may be loans in kind and the timing of
repayment in kind and the different measure used could include an
interest component.

A 1976 study showed that the volume of credit at very high interest
rates was modest, but the number of loans transacted was large. About

19 percent of loan transactions was estimated to be at interest rates above 25 percent, but only 4 percent of the total number of loans transacted was at rates of interest above 100 percent (Fernando 1988).

The general impression is that informal lending is mainly for nonproductive purposes such as ceremonies, household consumption, and fortuitous needs such as sicknesses and deaths and not for the cultivation of crops, business purposes, and capital expenditure. In fact the survey data disclosed that about 50 percent of informal lending was for cultivation, about 10 percent for trade, and 4 percent for house construction. Informal lending for agricultural production was about 65 percent of the amount lent by institutions, and informal lenders lent about five times that of the institutions for industry and trade. There is an interesting difference in the purposes of lending of moneylenders and non-interest lenders. Moneylenders lent more for production purposes than interest free lenders such as friends and relatives.

As far as non-interest lenders are concerned, only about 7 percent of their loans was secured. Moneylenders, on the other hand, secured a fairly large proportion (47 percent) of their loans with immovable assets (19 percent), jewelry and durable consumer goods (16 percent), and machinery and equipment (9 percent). Since the number of secured loans was small, the large number of unsecured transactions gives the impression that security is not a consideration in informal lending. In fact a significant proportion of the larger loans are secured.

Informal loans were in a wide range of sizes. Although the average size of loan was not small, the median and modal sizes were small. The modal size group of informal loans was below SL Rs.250. There was a significant difference in the size of loans of moneylenders and non-interest lenders. While moneylenders extended nearly 9 percent of their credit in big loans (between SL Rs.16,001. and SL Rs.25,000), non-interest lenders lent mostly small sums. While moneylenders did give larger loans, over half of the sums lent by them was in loans of less than SL Rs. 2,000 and over 70 percent of their lendings was below SL Rs. 3,000.

Contrary to the conventional view that informal lenders achieve high rates of recovery, this survey disclosed that loan default was substantial on high interest loans. Therefore the interest rate may include risk premium. High interest lenders may be reconciled to nonrepayment of loans after a certain length of time and borrowers themselves may feel justified in not repaying high interest loans once they have paid interest for a long period time.

The preceding discussion leads to some new perspectives on informal lending. Contrary to popular notions, interest rates of informal lenders may not be as high as is generally supposed, informal lenders do lend for production purposes, and informal lenders secure their larger loans.

Informal loans are varied in size but are generally small. Some high interest rates have created the image of exorbitant charges in the informal market. In an assessment of informal lending, however, it should be borne in mind that informal lenders charge interest on a monthly basis and lend small sums for short periods. Therefore such loans do not necessarily constitute a high cost to the borrower. This is especially true as such lending imposes few transactions costs or other costs on borrowers.

The hypothesis advanced here is that informal lending is demand determined. There is no reason why informal sources should be reluctant to lend for production purposes, if they are willing to lend for consumption. The overall considerations of the informal lender are the rate of return on his funds and the recoverability of his loans. If these two conditions are satisfactorily met, there is no reason for informal lenders to prefer lending for consumption purposes rather than for production. In fact, the informal lender's transactions, unlike many institutional loan schemes which restrict loans for specified purposes, are based on the realistic acceptance of the fungibility of money.

Banking Innovations

The recognition that formal finance has many limitations resulted in several efforts to service the small borrower through adaptations in formal lending. The foremost experiment has been the establishment of cooperative rural banks (CRBs) in 1964 under the auspices of the People's Bank (Kahagalle and Sanderatne 1977). CRBs are not banks but departments of cooperatives that mobilize deposits and lend funds for limited purposes. They are small in size, less impressive than bank branches, and established within the cooperatives, which are a familiar institution in the village. Unsophisticated village clientele find it more comfortable to transact business with their village cooperative society rather than with fully fledged banks whose impressive structures and procedures intimidate them. They are a device for extending limited banking facilities into rural areas.

After the first five years of CRBs operations, their deposits exceeded the volume of loans and in most years since then there have been substantial surpluses. At the end of 1988, CRBs had a surplus of SL Rs.1,068 million with deposits over twice the quantum of advances. In the 25 years of their operation, nearly 1,000 CRBs and similar special branches were established.

While the expansion of CRBs, their distribution in the country and the amount of deposits mobilized by them has been a success, they have had only a limited impact on lending for developmental purposes. The surplus of deposits over total advances (including pawning) implies that they have been mobilizing rural funds for transmission to other areas rather than being a provider of funds for rural and small-scale development. More than one-half of the short-term loans has been for housing, electrification, and water supply and about 20 percent for agricultural production and cottage industry. Loans obtained by pawning, which constituted as much as 30 percent of total funding, were likely to have been used for a variety of purposes, including productive employment (Sanderatne 1988).

It appears that the limited lending was due to excessive prudence with depositor's funds by the cooperative staff. The popularity of pawning perhaps vindicates this hypothesis. Lending based on the viability of projects would have been difficult as most CRB staff do not have the capability nor the time to appraise projects. Therefore, CRBs have turned out to be a limited source of funds for small borrowers. The greater flexibility in the lending procedures has not led to easy access to credit. Expanded access to deposit facilities has been the most important feature of the CRB's activities.

Another more recent innovation is the establishment of Regional Rural Development Banks (RRDBs) in 1985. These unit banks are expected to meet the gap in credit that other commercial banks do not provide. In order to perform this function, RRDBs were given guidelines not to compete with the existing financial institutions, but rather to supplement them by providing loans to small farmers, rural artisans, petty traders, small entrepreneurs, and individuals for personal needs that are not adequately serviced by banks. RRDBs were expected to be a new species of banks that would bring about a new culture in banking. The area of operation of each bank was also limited to make these objectives effective.

In the first three and a half years after commencement of the scheme, 11 RRDBs were established with 80 branches. The security situation has hampered the expansion of the scheme to 14 other districts as well as reduced the pace of branch expansion within each district. RRDBs had mobilized over SL Rs. 100 million in savings at the end of 1988. Unlike CRBs they had lent more than their deposits. About 40 percent of their loans was for agriculture, 21 percent for small industry, and 18 percent for trade and business. They have lent for a wide variety of purposes and many microenterprises have obtained loans from them. High rates of default plague some RRDBs. Although some of the defaults are due to agricultural failures, others are willful defaults created by an attitude that RRDB lending is government lending. There is also evidence that owing to officers in banks being pushed to provide loans they may not have been as prudent as they should have been with depositors' funds.

RRDBs have a high cost structure owing to the tendency of fairly high staff salaries, a disproportionately large number of staff for the small turnover in branches, and costs of servicing large numbers of small loans. The financial margins are also inadequate and consequently most RRDBs are operating at a loss. This would be a unsustainable condition in the long run. Although it was intended initially to transfer the ownership of these banks gradually to shareholders in the community itself, this has not happened.

Linking Formal and Informal Markets

The Praja Naya Niyamaka (PNN) scheme inaugurated by the two state banks in October 1988 is an attempt to link informal credit sources to the institutional banking system. The basic features of the scheme are that the two state banks lend funds to persons of proven creditworthiness, often on the basis of collateral, at an interest rate of 18 percent per annum and expect the PNNs to lend at an interest rate not exceeding 30 percent per annum. The banks give the PNNs guidelines on how to lend but do not require them to provide documentation and other proof of their lending. This scheme is meant to assist small borrowers.

Under this scheme the funds of the banks are expected to supplement the funds of the informal sector to meet the small borrower's credit needs. The increased supply of funds from the PNNs and the consequent increased competition among informal lenders were expected to bring down the cost of borrowing, make credit more readily available for small borrowers, and improve the conditions of borrowing. Since the two banks are expected to appoint about 14,000 PNNs throughout the country, the competition among them and with other informal sources is expected to bring down informal interest rates. The flexibility and convenience in lending, which the banks as institutions could never offer, could be provided by the PNNs with the resources of the banks. The success of the scheme partly depends on the choice of the PNNs. Therefore, the banks are making an effort to choose persons who are not motivated by profit alone, but who also have a social purpose and view the implementation of the scheme as one having a significant impact on improving the productive capacity of the economy, alleviating poverty, and increasing incomes.

In the first ten months of implementing this scheme, the two state banks appointed over 4,000 PNNs and lent about, SL Rs. 160 million to them. It would have been possible to appoint a larger number of PNNs had the security situation in the country been better. In several areas affected by security conditions, the appointment of PNNs has been slow. They have lent for a wide spectrum of purposes, including very small loans for self-employment, petty trade, and various services. However, some of the PNNs have tended to concentrate on relatively large loans.

One of difficulties in this program is the need for the banks to ensure that the informal lender continues to lend unfettered in an informal manner. The banks lend to creditworthy PNNs, ensure recovery of funds lent to them, and give PNNs freedom in the manner they on-lend. The linking with the banks should not result in the introduction of formal procedures. Since the PNN bears the risks of lending, PNNs should be free to lend in any manner they like. Banks should only use moral suasion to achieve the objectives of the scheme, otherwise this linking could be a kiss of death.

Apart from the PNN scheme, several other attempts have been made to link formal and informal finance. One model that was used by banks even prior to the appointment of PNNs and continues today is that of lending to nongovernment organizations (NGO) that in turn lend to groups and individuals on their own terms. The NGO takes the responsibility for monitoring the loans and ensuring recovery. The two state banks made special efforts to expand this model in 1989 as part of the government's program for poverty alleviation.

Some NGOs borrow at market rates and lend at rates that give them a margin to cover risks and build up their own reserves. While the cost of the credit is higher than the direct borrowing rates from the bank, the NGO offers the borrower great flexibility, immediate access to credit, and a minimum of transaction costs. This model of granting loans has reduced the costs of inputs and noticeably improved the prices fetched for the borrower's produce. The latter has been achieved in several ways. Since the marketing is not linked to credit, growers are not restricted to selling their produce to the bulk purchaser of the produce who gave them credit. Therefore farmers are able to obtain the market rate for their produce. Since the borrowers are themselves members of the NGO, they have a sense of responsibility to repay the loans.

There has been an interesting development in the above model, which has enabled its implementation in a more extensive manner. A foreign organization has given guarantees on the bank's lending to NGOs. This has enabled the bank to be more flexible in the granting of the loan as the repayment of the loans are guaranteed. Further, on the basis of this guarantee, the bank is also in a position to lend more than the sum guaranteed on the basis of its own assessment of the recovery rate.

The role of the NGO also varies in the above model. Members of the NGO borrow certain loans directly from the bank and the NGO gives its approval to the bank, supervises the use of the funds, and helps in the recovery, but the bank uses its own lending criteria as it takes the full risks of the lending. In other loans the bank lends to the NGO, which in turn lends to its members, and the NGO takes full responsibility. A third type is where the NGO provides a guarantee but the bank uses its criteria in deciding to make the loan.

There are, however, several difficulties in expanding this model. Many NGOs receive grants from foreign sources for their activities and lend free of interest or at very low rates of interest. Consequently such NGOs cannot easily implement a program with market interest rates. In fact many NGOs are not motivated to borrow at market rates even when banks are willing to lend at minimum market rates owing to their view that if banks are really interested in poverty alleviation they should charge very low rates of interest.

The state banks have also used a government organization—the National Youth Services Council (NYSCO)—to lend to a number of small enterprises employing youth. NYSCO prepares the projects, assists the youth in obtaining skills and inputs, lends part of the needed funds, monitors the projects, helps resolve any difficulties the youth may have, assists in marketing the produce and in ensuring recovery of the funds. This has been one of the most successful schemes both in terms of the extent of the implementation and the recovery of funds. About 3,500 small scale projects have been financed with bank lending of about SL Rs. 25 million. NYSCO has played its role as if it were an NGO.

Lessons

Over the years there have been many efforts to increase formal lending to small borrowers in Sri Lanka. Despite these efforts poor people are ineffectively reached and informal sources meet most needs of small borrowers and savers. The reasons for this are manifold. Small customers find it difficult to complete the necessary forms, get guarantors, provide documentary evidence, and convince the banks of the viability of their projects. Past experience of high rates of default discourage formal lenders from lending to small borrowers. The work load of lending to a large number of small borrowers is greater than in lending to fewer larger borrowers and the supervision of lent funds is difficult.

More recent efforts to increase lending to small borrowers have met with some success though it is still limited in coverage. The reasons for the success lie in the fact that the political leadership has laid down the need to extend such credit. In the two state banks the transformation is like a change of ownership where "new owners" have stipulated new priorities. This has given a new impetus to developing credit schemes for craftsmen, self-employment projects, and particular small enterprises. To some extent these schemes are likely to meet the needs of the small borrower but whether they would themselves have high rates of default and consequently flounder without making a dent in the problem is yet to be seen. Unfortunately, the adaptations of formal institutions to meet the needs of the small borrower has met with limited success. The CRBs have been successful in mobilizing savings but have failed to have a real impact on lending. The RRDBs, on the other hand, have lent more liberally and for a variety of purposes, yet there are indications that their rates of recovery may be low.

A lesson that can be learned from the experience of institutions adapted to serve small borrowers is that they have proved to be more successful in mobilizing deposits than in lending to small enterprises. This suggests that institutions should have the means by which they could reach a large number of persons so as to mobilize deposits. Semi-formal institutions and agents should be commissioned to accept small deposits. Banks can then use these savings through the linkages they adopt to lend to small enterprises. It appears that institutions have a strength in mobilizing savings while informal lenders are more adapted to lending to small borrowers.

What are the lessons of these experiences? Can formal institutions learn from the way informal lenders operate and use those methods in their lending?

The essence of informal finance is the complete flexibility lenders have in decisionmaking. They are responsible only to themselves. They can vary their interest rates and requirements of collateral depending on the nature of each risk. They have a personal relationships with the borrowers, which ensures a minimum of willful defaults. In contrast, formal finance requires internally consistent rules. For instance a bank cannot give some interest free loans and also charge 120-300 percent interest per annum on other loans. Formal lenders cannot use various interest rates to reflect risk or administration costs of loans as informal loans do. Documentation is a necessary part of institutional lending even if such documentation is simplified.

The gist of the above argument is that banks can adapt themselves to suit the clientele to some extent but cannot possibly duplicate all of the features of informal lenders. Banks could be more flexible in their criteria, simplify procedures, reduce form filling, and motivate their officers to lend to small borrowers. Yet they must still retain procedures and require documentation. They will not be able to charge interest rates that reflect the true cost of such lending. Since there are limits to the extent to which banks can act like informal lenders, it is not realistic to expect institutions, however adaptable they may be, to perform extensively the functions of informal lenders. Therefore, new methods must be adopted to meet the requirements of the small borrower. One method is to use an intermediary, preferably an NGO, to perform some of the functions of the bank. The NGO could help in formulating the projects, filling in the forms, negotiating on behalf of the borrower, supervising the projects, and helping in making the investments a success. Another method is for the banks to lend to NGOs, which would perform the functions of on-lending in much the same way as informal lenders. The NGOs could price the loan on the basis of risks and the return to capital. A third method is to lend funds to persons who will take the risks of on-lending to small borrowers. The PNN scheme is such an attempt and provides an effective means of making available adequate finances and increasing competition among informal lenders. The thrust of such a program should be to increase the number of such lenders and amounts rather than control interest rates, purposes of lending, or loan amounts.

References

Bouman, F. J. A. 1984. "Informal Saving and Credit Arrangements in Developing Countries: Observations from Sri Lanka." In Dale W Adams, Douglas H. Graham, and J.D. Von Pischke, eds. *Undermining Rural Development with Cheap Credit*, pp. 232-247. Boulder Colorado: Westview Press.

Central Bank of Ceylon. 1976. "Survey of Credit and Indebtedness among Paddy Farmers." Unpublished study prepared by the Central Bank of Ceylon in Colombo.

————. 1971. "Report on the Survey of Rural Credit and Indebtedness, 1969." Unpublished study prepared by the Central Bank of Ceylon in Colombo.

Department of Census and Statistics. 1959. "Survey of Rural Indebtedness-Ceylon 1957." Monograph No. 12. Colombo, Sri Lanka: Department of Census and Statistics.

Fernando, Nimal. 1988. "The Interest Rate Structure and Factors Affecting Interest Rate Determination in the Informal Rural Credit Market in Sri Lanka." *Savings and Development* (12): 249-269.

Kahagalle, S., and Nimal Sanderatne. 1977. "The Role and Performance of Cooperative Rural Banks in Sri Lanka 1964-1976. " *Staff Studies* 7: 1-44.

Sanderatne, Nimal. 1981. "A Profile of the Informal Rural Credit Market in the Mid Seventies." *Staff Studies*, vol. 11, Colombo: Central Bank of Ceylon.

———. 1988. "Cooperative Rural Banks-A Success Story?" *Economic Review* 14:15-17.

8

Informal Rural Finance in Thailand

Tongroj Onchan

Farm credit has received attention from the Thai government for many years. The first credit cooperative, formed in the 1960s, was aimed at providing cheap credit to farmers who were widely believed to be exploited by moneylenders. The cooperative credit system has undergone many changes since then. In 1969, the Bank of Agriculture and Agricultural Cooperatives (BAAC) replaced the Bank for Cooperatives with the aim of expanding and improving its operations to cover all farmers. The Bank of Thailand also came up with a new policy in 1975 to increase credit supply to agriculture. It required all commercial banks to channel 5 percent of their total outstanding value of lending to farmers, either directly or through the BAAC. In the following years, this loan quota was increased 2 percent annually, up to 13 percent. Since 1976 the quota has been fixed as a proportion of the total deposits of the commercial banks, and this has substantially increased the amount of formal agricultural loans made in the country.

Farm credit policy changed again in 1986 with the Bank of Thailand's new "rural credit" policy. Rural loans are now conceived more broadly than before, covering both farm and nonfarm activities in rural areas. Also, the loan quota for rural lending has been raised to 20 percent of the total deposits of the commercial banks. This has made it easier for banks to meet their minimum targets because loans granted to provincial nonfarm entrepreneurs can also be included to meet the quota. Since the inception of its new credit policy in 1975, BAAC has also greatly expanded its operations. It derived a large part of its loanable funds from deposits by commercial banks that are unable to make small agricultural loans. BAAC lends both to agricultural cooperatives and to individual farmers.

Although there has been a phenomenal expansion of formal credit, the role of informal finance is still very significant in rural areas. A large proportion of Thai farmers still borrow informally. Such loans provide useful and necessary services to farmers, particularly the smaller and poorer ones. However, the Thai government and other concerned people still feel that farmers are being exploited by moneylenders.

This chapter discusses some aspects of the informal credit market in Thailand, particularly its significance, structure, and conduct. Although data on informal credit is usually limited in most low-income countries, a few studies on this topic have been done in Thailand in recent years. I will also refer to the findings of recent research on the role of land collateral for farm credit.

Importance of Informal Finance

It has been observed in Thailand over the past several decades that informal farm finance has declined in relative importance (Onchan 1985). This has been mainly due to the large expansion in institutional loans. However, as shown in Table 1, informal sources continue to provide financial services to many rural people in Thailand. Informal loans are still around 30 percent of total loans in rural areas, and most relatively small and poor farmers rely mainly on informal lenders for their credit needs. (Poapongsakorn and Netayarak 1989). Due to a number of factors, particularly the lack of collateral, poor farmers do not have access to formal loans. Some formal lenders, notably the BAAC, have tried to reach this group by using group guarantees instead of land collateral. Many farmers occupy lands without proper legal documents (Onchan and others 1982). This is another obstacle to obtaining credit from formal sources. Thus, farmers often borrow informally for both production and consumption purposes. Given the slow progress of land reform and land titling programs, informal finance will likely remain important in Thailand for years to come.

Structure and Conduct

The informal rural financial market in Thailand is similar to markets in other developing Asian countries. Credit is available from friends and relatives, moneylenders, traders, landlords, and other

TABLE 1. Importance of Informal Loans in Thailand

	Percentage of Informal Credit	
Year	No. of Borrowers	Value of Loans
Whole Kingdom		
1961/62	92	95
1972/73	72	64
1975/76	N/A	43
1978/79	N/A	36
1986/87	N/A	27
Central Plain		
1956/57	90	94
1961/62	98	97
1967/68	72	75
1978/79	N/A	40
1986/87	N/A	32
Northeast		N/A
1961/62	92	89
1971/72	79	N/A
1972/73	29	17
1975/76	N/A	31
1978/79	N/A	31
1986/87	N/A	17
North		
1961/62	90	90
1971/72	54	39
1978/79	N/A	35
1986/87	N/A	31

Note: N/A means information not available.
Sources: 1957 and 1967/68: Uthis Naksawadi (1958; 1970); 1961/62: Phantum Thisyamondol, Vinrach Arromdee, and M.F. Long (1965); 1971/72: Phantum Thisyamondol; 1972: Phantum Thisyamondol; 1975-76, 1978-79, 1986-87: Office of Agricultural Economics, Ministry of Agriculture and Cooperatives (1977; 1978-79; 1986-87).

farmers. These lenders are often classified as noncommercial (friends and relatives) and commercial (moneylenders, traders). Each of these groups has different behavior patterns in their credit operations. Generally, friends and relatives do not lend to maximize their profits or returns. However, some so-called "noncommercial lenders" charge interest. In fact, they sometimes treat "family" borrowers just like commercial clients (although some leniency may be practiced in regard to loan terms).

There are usually multiple informal commercial lenders in most Thai villages, often five to seven (Poapongsakorn and Netayarak 1989, Dhaiyanonda and others 1988). In addition there are numerous non-commercial lenders who are difficult to identify since anyone may lend small amounts for short periods to relatives or friends. Commercial lenders are more readily identified. The presence of several local lenders does not necessarily mean that the market is completely competitive, however. In many cases, farmer borrowers regularly deal with one particular lender. Switching to or borrowing from other lenders may be frowned upon by one's primary lender (Siamwalla 1988). In fact, borrowing from more than one informal lender is not uncommon, but the borrower usually tries to keep it a secret from his primary lender (Dhaiyanonda and others 1988).

Most informal lending is done by people who live in the same village. Outside lenders, however, also operated in villages with the help of local traders who act as agents. Lenders generally know ample information about the villagers and their clients. Useful information includes ownership and size of land holding, size of family and off-farm employment, and type of farming and personal characteristics. Thai villagers are usually very close—usually related in some way—and are often joined in community development activities. The well-to-do farmers, local traders, and landlords who are lenders are also frequently village leaders. They know most if not all the villagers and can pressure their clients through social sanctions in cases of default.

When considering the importance of different types of informal lenders, relatives and friends have played a dominant role over time, although this has lessened somewhat during the past 20 years (Table 2). Landlords are another significant lending group whose importance has also declined. Other major lenders include rice traders, merchants, and rice millers. Due to their importance in farm credit, relatives and friends deserve special attention if the behavior of informal lenders is to be understood.

In Thailand, as in other countries, savings are the primary source of funds for most informal lending. Some funds for lending, nevertheless, may also be borrowed from formal sources. In the province of Nakhon Ratchasima, in Northeastern Thailand, savings constitute 34 percent of the total loanable funds while money borrowed from formal sources accounts for 22 percent (Poapongsakorn and Netayarak 1989). Informal lenders may even borrow money among themselves to relend to farmers, although the proportion has been found to be rather small, only 6 percent in Nakhon Ratchasima.

TABLE 2. Type of Informal Lenders by Region and Year [a] (Percent)

Region/Year	Relatives and Friends	Farmer	Traders	Rice Merchant	Other	Rice Mill	Landlord
Central Region:							
1957	32.9	N/A	28.4	10.6	6.3	1.9	9.2
1968	21.8	N/A	18.4	16.0	9.6	3.3	5.3
1987	32.9	3.9	0.8 [b]	26.0	10.1	22.1	4.3
Northeast:							
1962	56.0	N/A	6.7	5.8	4.1	N/A	4.6
1987	50.9	16.8	2.1 [b]	27.9	0.7	1.2	0.0

[a] Not every type of lender is included, so the sum in several years is less than 100%

[b] Including professional lenders and salaried employees.

Source: From Poapongsakorn and Netayarak (1989) Table 3.2. Also, data from: 1957: Uthis Naksawadi (1958); 1962: Thisyamodol and others, (1965); 1968: Uthis Naksawadi (1970); 1985: Nipon Ponpongsakorn (1987); 1987: survey of borrowers in 1987.

Most credit is either in cash or of short-term duration, or both. Credit in kind, for example, fertilizer and paddy or rice, is also quite common in some areas. Medium- and long-term credit is rather insignificant. The average amount of informal loans is much smaller than that of formal loans (usually less than half). Although informal credit is generally said to be used mainly for consumption, a recent study indicates that a large proportion (71 percent) is used for production (Poapongsakorn and Netayarak 1989). Significantly, in Thailand, neither the BAAC, which is the most important agricultural credit institution, nor—until recently—commercial banks provided loans for nonfarm activities in rural areas.

With regard to interest rates, formal lenders are usually tightly regulated. They must abide by usury laws that impose low rates of interest. Informal lenders almost always charge higher rates. Although information costs are comparatively low for informal lenders, there are other factors that increase their lending costs (Feder and others 1988). In Thailand, the interest rates on commercial informal loans are usually about two to four times higher than those on formal loans. For example, in 1986/87, BAAC's rate of interest was about 12.5 percent per year, while relatives and lenders were charging 26 percent and 56 percent, respectively (Office of Agricultural Economics various years). Data in Table 3 show the rates of interest charged by different types of informal lenders in various regions over selected years. The rates vary by type of lender and by regions. Relatives usually charge less than other lenders, but the rates are still much higher than those from formal sources of credit. Although it is often claimed that relatives do not charge interest, data from a survey in the Northeast indicate that lending at zero interest rate, even within families, is rare. It does not appear that interest rates on informal loans have declined, even after the expansion of formal credit in 1975. In fact, the data from a study of land titling indicated that the standard rate is about five percent per month, and this rate has prevailed for several years (Dhaiyanonda and others 1988). Data from farm credit surveys done by the Ministry of Agriculture and Cooperatives confirm this trend. The rate of interest charged by formal lenders in Thailand has also been rather stable, around 12 to 14 percent annually, during the past two decades.

Interest rates vary substantially across regions. An analysis of these variations in the informal sector suggest that borrower characteristics (for example, land holdings, ownership of titled lands, and borrower's income), do not account for much of the variation. Characteristics of lenders and contracts (for example, rice mill owners, nonresidency, loan

TABLE 3. The Distribution of Loans, by Source and by Type of Collateral (Percentage of Loans Made)

	Province							
	Lop Buri		Nakhon Ratchasima		Khon Kaen		Chaiyaphum	
Type of Lender/ Type of Collateral	Untitled	Titled	Untitled	Titled	Untitled	Titled	Untitled	Titled
Formal Lenders								
Number of borrowers	86	50	54	50	20	30	49	50
No collateral	14	4	48	14	25	10	0	0
Land	8[a]	78	6[a]	54	10[a]	47	29	56
Group guarantee	77	18	44	32	65	43	158	44
Informal lenders								
Number of borrowers	74	68	22	19	22	15	36	27
No collateral	93	79	86	84	64	87	191	77
Land	7[a]	21	9[a]	11	4[a]	7	4[a]	15
Other	0	0	5	5	32	6	4	8

[a] Some untitled farmers' homes—and the lots on which they are built—are located outside the boundaries of state land and may therefore be offered as collateral. The number of such farmers is small.

Source: Feder, Onchan, Chalamwong and Hongladarom, (1988, Table 11, p. 54).

size, and loan duration) seem to have more bearing (Poapongsakorn and Netayarak 1989).

Loans in kind usually carry higher interest rates than loans in cash. In Buri Ram province, a borrower receives two tang of paddy from the lender, usually a trader or grocery store owner. After harvest, he repays with three tang. The rate of interest depends on the price of paddy and the duration of the loan. When the loan is in the form of fertilizer, repayment is usually in paddy. For example, for a loan of one sack of fertilizer worth 250 baht, repayment is seven or eight tang of paddy in seven months. In both cases, interest rates are high.

Land Pawning

The case of land pawning or usufruct loans, which are common in the Northeast, should be mentioned. Many farmers leave their villages for work in Bangkok or overseas, often going to the Middle East. Instead of borrowing from a commercial bank to finance travel, individuals obtain a loan from someone in his village by surrendering the right to use his land to the lender. The lender can then farm the land until the borrower repays the loan. The interest, in this case, is the lender's net income from farming the land. Because of the increasing scarcity of arable land, such land lending is welcomed by local farmer lenders. Land pawning is generally found in mainly subsistence economies where land values are relatively low and land markets are inactive. The practice is seldom found in other regions such as the Upper North, for example, where the rural economy is generally commercialized and land value is high. In these areas the farmer is better-off borrowing from formal sources.

Land Collateral and Informal Loans

Loan transactions typically involve risk of default. Lenders try to reduce this risk and minimize such losses, often through requiring collateral or guarantees. Collateral increases the lender's expected return and spurs the borrower to avoid intentional default. In developing countries land is the most common collateral in rural areas. Informal lenders are less inclined to accept land as collateral and lenders who do not have links to borrowers in matters other than finance are more likely to use other loan securities. In this section, a brief discussion is presented of the role of collateral and other guarantees in rural credit, particularly informal loans. The data come from samples of borrowing farmers in four provinces of Thailand. The farmers are separated into two groups, namely farmers who have titles to their land, and untitled farmers.

The data show that titled farmers provide land as collateral in 63 percent of the institutional loans sampled. Noninstitutional or informal loans are mostly granted with no collateral or other guarantee. However, for the few informal loans that involve any security, the most common security is land collateral.

The data on the distribution of loans indicate that the importance of traders as a source of credit increases with the degree of commercialization of the area. In Lopburi province, for example, nearly half of all loans and the bulk of informal credit are provided by traders. Lending by relatives and neighbors declines with higher degrees of commercialization, but many of these loans are commercial transactions priced at market rates. Some are intrafamily transactions, however, that carry low or zero rates of interest. Further, the data also show that farmers without land titles (without collateral) depend more on noninstitutional lenders.

The data from the survey also give the mean rate of interest on loans from formal and informal lenders and the composition of lending maturities. Clearly, because formal credit in Thailand is subject to an interest rate ceiling, loans from regulated institutional creditors carry lower interest rates than those from formal loans. Most loans are short-term, twelve months or less. Medium-term and long-term loans are provided by formal lenders more than by informal lenders. Farmers with land titles obtain such loans much more often than do farmers without titles. This is compatible with the observation that farmers without titles lack acceptable land collateral and are thus perceived by formal lenders as potentially high risk clients, other things being equal.

As informal lenders have superior information about borrowers, they are less inclined to require collateral or collateral substitutes. Recent research has shown that an overwhelming majority of informal loans are granted without collateral (Fedu and others 1988). In contrast, the majority of formal loans are covered by collateral or collateral substitutes. In the few instances in which collateral was provided on informal loans, land was the predominant form. Farmers without titles are obliged to provide a collateral substitute, namely a group guarantee, to obtain formal loans. However, group guarantees are less desirable than land as collateral. A group guarantee can, therefore, be expected to result in smaller amounts of credit. Generally, formal loans requiring land as collateral are larger than loans without collateral or loans with group guarantees. As regards the amount of loans provided by informal lenders, the importance of collateral varies among the provinces. With the exception of Lopburi, land collateral seems to offer advantages even in informal lending.

Although land collateral is generally not required by informal lenders, it does help increase access to informal loans. A further insight in this regard may be gained by looking at data from other studies. Information from a survey in Buri Ram, for example, reveals that for a loan of over 5,000 baht, a written contract and some kind of security is required. As the amount of credit gets larger, the need for land collateral also becomes greater (Dhaiyanonda and others 1988) and also from personal interviews with informal lenders). Further, it is not an unusual practice for the lender of a large loan to keep the borrower's land documents. This is to prevent the borrower from obtaining a large loan from another lender. The data from a farm debt survey in 1986/87 also indicate that a large proportion of informal credit requires loan security. Among the informal lenders, the merchants require land collateral more often than other types of lenders (Office of Agricultural Economics, various years).

Clearly, land collateral affects access to credit from both formal and informal sources. It has also been shown that land collateral is required by informal lenders, particularly when the loan amount is large and when medium- and long-term credit is used. Therefore, land ownership security is very important in farm financing and land titling will increase access to rural credit, both formal and informal.

Advantages of Informal Loans

The advantages of borrowing from informal lenders are now well known. Informal credit is more accessible than are formal loans. There is no complicated procedure involved, hence loans can be obtained quickly. In general, less emphasis is placed on collateral than is true of formal loans. Therefore, informal loans are very popular among the small and landless farmers. The terms of credit are also flexible, particularly with regard to the amount, the purpose, the duration, the type and, in some cases, the rate of interest on the loan. As mentioned before, in the informal sector information regarding the borrower plays an important role in credit transactions. The interlinkages between credit and marketing are also very strong in Thailand.

Data on the reasons for borrowing from informal sources indicate that 40 percent of the borrowers from informal sources do so because it saves time and no collateral is needed. Other reasons include: (1) inability to borrow from formal sources as they have not yet paid back previous loans, (2) do not know how to borrow from the formal source, and (3) borrowing for consumption, which is not possible from formal sources.

Another important service of informal lenders is the provision of credit for nonfarm enterprises operated by farm households. Data from a study in Chiang Mai province reveal that about 50 percent of the funds used to finance nonfarm enterprises comes from informal loans, most of the rest comes from savings, and formal loans constitute an insignificant portion. Considering that nonfarm enterprises are very important to rural households in terms of income and employment, informal credit is providing a useful service by supporting these non-farm efforts (Onchan 1989).

There is still a good deal of controversy in Thailand over the issues of the efficiency of informal financial markets and possible exploitation of farmers by informal lenders. Available data on this are not conclusive. While recent research has show a surprisingly large amount of competition in informal lending, some monopolistic practices may still exist that limit the efficiency of informal markets (Siamwalla 1988). This difficult issue of market competitiveness and efficiency will need to be further investigated before any final conclusion is reached.

In this connection, it is of interest to note how borrowers feel about moneylenders. The data from the Chiang Mai survey indicate that about 80 percent of the borrowers were positive about their relationships with informal lenders and over 60 percent felt there was no need to change the lending practices of informal lenders. Some borrowers (16 percent) wished to have more informal lenders and to have some reduction of the interest rate. When asked whom they would borrow from if they had to borrow more than they do now, over 70 percent of the borrowers said they would like to borrow from non-commercial informal lenders (that is, relatives and friends) because the interest rates were low. On the other hand, only 10 percent wanted to borrow from formal sources because of low rates of interest (Onchan 1989).

In a study I conducted several years ago in Buri Ram province, it was clear after talking to many farmers that their attitudes toward informal lenders were generally positive. They can usually rely on these lenders at times when credit is needed. The types of credit offered appeared to accord well with the needs of the farmers. There was ample flexibility regarding the terms of credit such as collateral requirements, forms of contracts, length of time, and repayment schedule. The interest charge was the only negative aspect of informal credit mentioned by many of the farmers I interviewed. However, borrowers seem to accept the rates without much complaint.

Lessons from Informal Finance

Over the past 15 years agricultural credit policy in Thailand has been carried out quite successfully as judged by the phenomenal increase in the supply of formal credit and by the decline in the relative share of informal credit. However, it is difficult to evaluate the economic impact of this credit policy. Over the period, agricultural production has increased at the relatively high rate of 5 percent per annum while the annual growth of total productivity is about 3 percent. Furthermore, agricultural diversification has been achieved and new technology adopted in many areas. The production performance of Thai agriculture has been impressive. Nevertheless, fairness remains an important issue as income distribution is still very unequal in rural areas and also between rural and urban sectors. In this connection, it has often been mentioned that most of the additional cheap credit has gone to relatively large and rich farmers and that the current credit policy has contributed to the worsening of income distribution in Thai agriculture.

Available data on the distribution of formal credit point out clearly that small and landless farmers obtain only small amounts of formal loans. They still depend almost totally on informal sources; the informal financial market is still very active and it is providing useful and acceptable services to these individuals. At the same time, formal lenders, namely the BAAC, are searching for a more effective way to reach small farmers. Starting in 1989, under a directive from the Ministry of Finance, BAAC provided relatively large amounts of loans directly to groups of low-income farmers. This program will continue for five years. The credit is granted to the groups without collateral. As is usually practiced by BAAC, group guarantees are also applied. The results of this policy are not yet known and BAAC may find it difficult to meet the lending targets set by the Ministry. In an attempt to reduce transaction costs, BAAC is considering using farmer leaders, that is, village headmen, to act as its "agents" in the villages. Agents will help BAAC in loan processing by using their knowledge of borrowers. He will be paid by the bank for their services. Through this innovation the BAAC is trying to access information about potential borrowers in the village, which informal lenders already have. As its loan agent, BAAC expects the village leader to help improve the loan processing procedure and the rate of loan recovery. Although agents cannot be informal lenders, they are still respected by farmers. Hence, their personal contacts may help improve the operational efficiency, particularly in regard to the transaction costs of the bank.

The case of BAAC just cited demonstrates an admirable attempt by a formal lender to try to learn from informal lenders. Formal lenders in Thailand understand why informal lenders perform better in providing services to poor farmers. Flexibility is an important aspect of rural financing that most formal lenders must endeavor to emulate. However, it is not possible to be as flexible as the informal lenders, particularly with regard to such aspects as business hours (evenings, Saturdays and Sundays, for example) and readily making loans for consumption and non-farm activities. BAAC has emulated informal finance in its recent attempt to make loans for nonfarm purposes, by becoming more flexible in its loan collateral requirements, by using village loan agents, and by lending to groups.

It may be even more important for the government to learn from informal finance in setting interest rate policies. Providing financial services to poor people in rural areas is expensive and this is a major reason for the relatively high interest rates charged by informal lenders. Without the liberalization of interest rates to reflect the opportunity cost of funds, risk, and the transaction costs of lending, it will be difficult to attain efficiency in operations of formal financial markets.

Conclusions

Informal finance will likely continue to be important in rural Thailand for years to come. Many poor people and individuals without clear title to land will undoubtedly be excluded from formal loans, regardless of what happens in formal financial markets. Contrary to opinions held by some policymakers, many informal lenders appear to provide useful services to Thai farmers. Instead of trying to substitute formal for informal finance, it may be time for policymakers to take a more positive look at informal lenders in an attempt to understand how they are able to provide small, short-term loans to so many people who are not seen as being creditworthy by formal lenders.

A clearer understanding of the strengths and limitations of informal finance will largely depend on additional research. While some very useful analysis of informal finance has been done in Thailand in recent years, the data on important aspects of informal finance are still limited. Documenting rural savings in the informal market is one example. Interlinkages of informal credit with land and labor markets and with product marketing is another area that needs to be carefully investigated. Additional analysis of "usufruct loans" and land pawning might also be fruitful. A case study of informal lenders as credit agents for formal lenders may also lead to some useful policy recommendations. Finally, a clearer understanding of the reasons for the relatively high interest rates in informal finance may encourage policymakers to adopt more flexible interest rate policies for formal lenders. This, in turn, may induce these lenders to expand their services in rural areas.

References

Dhaiyanonda, Charan, Tongroj Onchan and Yongyutm Chalamwong. 1988. "Farm Credit and Land Titles: Case Study of Buri Ram Province" Unpublished study, Center for Applied Economics Research, Kasetsart University.

Feder, Gershon, Tongroj Onchan, Yongyuth Chalamwong, and Chira Hongladarom. 1988. *Land Policies and Farm Productivity in Thailand*, Baltimore, Maryland: John Hopkins University Press.

Naksawadi, Uthis. 1958. "Debt Situations of Farmers and Rice Marketing in the Central Region of Thailand, 1957-1958." Unpublished paper. Office of Agricultural Economics. Ministry of Agriculture & Cooperatives, Bangkok: (In Thai).

───────. 1970. "Research Report on Debt Situation and Paddy Marketing in the Central Region of Thailand, 1967-1968." Bangkok: National Research Council and USOM. Unpublished study. (In Thai).

Office of Agricultural Economics, Ministry of Agriculture and Cooperatives. Various years. "Debt Conditions of Thai Farmers, 1977, 1978-79 and 1986-87." Unpublished report. Bangkok: Ministry of Agriculture, (In Thai).

Onchan, Tongroj. 1985. "Agricultural Credit in Asian Countries: Review of Past Decade." Unpublished paper presented at the Seminar on Farm Credit, Tokyo: Asian Productivity Organization.

───────. 1982. "Land Tenure Security and Farm Productivity in Thailand." Unpublished staff paper, Dept. of Agricultural Economics. Bangkok, Thailand: Kasetsart University.

───────. 1989. "Non-Farm Enterprises, Employment, and Rural Development." Unpublished paper presented at the Symposium on "Measures for Rural Employment Generation," Tokyo: Asian Productivity Organization.

Poapongsakorn, Nipon and Prayong Netayarak. 1989. "Regional Variations in Rural Interest Rates." Unpublished research report submitted to the Asian Development Bank. Bangkok, Thailand: Tammasat University.

Siamwalla, Ammar, (ed.). 1988. "Rural Credit Market in Thailand." Thailand Development Research Institute and Faculty of Economics. Bangkok, Thailand: Tammasat University. (In Thai).

Thisyamondol, Phantum, V. Arromdee, and M. F. Long. 1965. *Agricultural Credit in Thailand: Theory, Data, Policy.* Bankgok: Kasetsart University.

9

Informal Finance in Papua New Guinea: An Overview

Nimal A. Fernando

Financial markets in Papua New Guinea are characterized by duality. This dualism is manifested in two completely different subsectors in the market—the formal and the informal. The dualism is not based on an urban-rural dichotomy. Informal finance is a feature of both urban and rural areas. Thus, the existence of the informal subsector must be explained not in terms of the degree of urbanization but in terms of other factors. Urbanization, however, appears to have a significant bearing on the character of informal finance.

The informal sector consists of a wide array of savings and credit arrangements based, in part, on traditions and operates outside the legal framework. Unfortunately, data and information on the informal subsector are very limited in Papua New Guinea. Except for four or five anthropological studies dealing partially with the subject, informal finance has not been the object of research. As a result, policymakers have little knowledge of this segment of the financial market. Many factors, such as the extraordinarily diverse culture and the highly uneven level of development make generalizations about the informal subsector in Papua New Guinea a difficult task. Yet, the scattered evidence that is available tends to indicate that the informal subsector is probably much more important than the formal sector both in terms of the number of persons served and in the volume of funds handled.

This chapter provides an overview of informal finance in Papua New Guinea with a view to learning from financial arrangements in this subsector in order to throw more light on policies in the formal subsector. The chapter outlines major sources and characteristics of informal savings and credit in the economy.

Sources and Characteristics of Informal Savings and Credit

The informal financial market in Papua New Guinea consists mainly of relatively localized credit and savings transactions of money, real goods and labor services among members of extended families, clans and tribes, friends and relatives, and store owners. Major sources of loans appear to be members of extended families, clans and tribes (*Wantoks*) and store owners.[1]

In addition, loans are extended by informal savings and credit groups generally found among rural women and known as *Wok Meri* (which means women's work in Pidgin or Tok Pisin), and rotating savings and credit associations (ROSCAs). While Wok Meri is almost entirely a rural arrangement of savings and credit, ROSCAs are found in both rural and urban areas. It appears that both Wok Meri and ROSCAs are relatively recent developments, the former dating back to only the early 1960s and the latter with an even shorter history. Village stores are also a new credit institution and have become important only since the early 1960s, partly as a result of the demonstration effect of similar stores operated by religious missions and partly due to the penetration of cash crops into rural areas.

An emerging source of loans in urban areas is the part-time money lender. Although such moneylenders do not yet appear to be operating in rural areas, I observed a growing number of part-time moneylenders combining lending with their usual occupational activities in cities. The part-time moneylenders I have contacted included an officer working in a research institution, an accountant working in a public sector institution, a driver working in a hospital, clerks, typists, and laborers in the formal sector. These moneylenders provide small-, short-term loans mainly for persons who are well known to them.

Since very little is known about informal savings and credit in Papua New Guinea, it is not possible to document the relative importance of different types of arrangements in the sphere of credit and savings. The Wantoks perhaps are a main source of both productive and consumption loans. Stores appear to be a major source of consumption credit in the rural economy while a significant amount of savings takes place within the network of Wok Meri in different parts of the country. Only passing mention has been made about ROSCAs in the rural sector (Burkins 1984; Sexton 1982b; and Skeldon 1980). One study on ROSCAs in a regional urban center was done in 1974 by an anthropologist (Wu 1974). A small-scale survey that I did among 30 public and private sector senior- and

---

1. *Wantok* is the Tok Pisin term used for one who speaks the same language.

middle-level officers revealed that ROSCAs are found in almost all institutions in the city of Port Moresby.

Informal savings and credit arrangements in Papua New Guinea are influenced by a multitude of factors that include culture, the nature of the economy, educational level of the population, and lack of access to institutional sources.

As there is a large subsistence sector in the rural economy, based largely on family labor and to some extent exchange labor use, informal savings and credit take the form of labor and commodity exchanges, in addition to monetary exchanges. Yet, due to the influence of cultural factors some of these transactions are not loans or deposits as generally understood by those terms. Thus, one who contributes a pig to a clan member to pay his "bride-price" may expect a repayment in some form. However, this does not necessarily constitute a well understood obligation on the part of the recipient in terms of interest payment and the quantum and period of repayment. In traditional ceremonial exchange systems, "partners may help each other on a basis of diffuse rather than balanced or calculated reciprocity" (Strathern 1969). In some exchange systems, there is an expectation that interest will operate in transactions. If a man makes a gift to an exchange partner he expects to receive one of greater value in return (Strathern 1969). But, this does not appear to be a widespread phenomenon in rural informal finance. Similarly, within the traditional extended family system, many loans occur in the form of labor provided without cash payment but against future obligations.

Perhaps the most remarkable characteristic of informal savings and credit in Papua New Guinea is the absence of a clear-cut component of interest in most of the transactions. When credit in kind is extended by owners of village stores apparently no attempts are made by the owners to inflate prices. The interest free characteristic can also be observed in loans made by Wok Meri groups to other Wok Meri groups. While the lending group expects repayment of the loans in the future, it does not stipulate or express any concern about receiving interest. These loans are made in cash, unlike the store credit. In many cases the borrowing groups may not have close personal links with the lending group (Sexton 1982a). The rotating savings and credit associations (ROSCAs) found largely among school teachers and relatively low-income groups also provide evidence of interest free loans.

Another salient characteristic of the informal market is the absence of professional and part-time moneylenders in the rural sector. While reference to such moneylenders and loan-sharks is common in most of the other developing countries, their absence is a conspicuous feature of the rural informal market in Papua New Guinea. Perhaps, the precapitalist characteristics of the rural economy coupled with subsistence affluence, communal land tenure systems, and socio-cultural factors, which often tend to measure social status by how much one gives away rather than in terms of how much profit one makes, explain this peculiar feature. Also when people have access to interest free loans from various sources there is no incentive for even part-time moneylenders to emerge.[2]

Another important characteristic of the informal financial market is the absence of the "collateral syndrome." While the formal sector insists on collateral, the informal market generally functions without collateral and transactions are based on personalized relationships between two parties. The mortgaging of assets and pawning of valuables to obtain loans are rare in this market, unlike in many other developing countries in Asia. As a result, money lending operations do not appear to result in a transfer of real assets from borrowers to lenders.

Informal Savings

An analysis of subject catalogues in the libraries of the University of Papua New Guinea and the Institute of Applied Social and Economic Research showed an almost total absence of literature on the subject of informal urban savings. However, a review of literature relating to the rural sector provided some information on informal savings. Interviews with a number of researchers, employees of public and private sector institutions (including banks), and a small-scale survey on informal finance among senior- and middle-level public and private sector officers served as another source of information.

In rural areas, many people, particularly women, hoard money, both coins and currency notes. The villagers receive money from different sources: their cash crop sales, gifts from extended family or clan members, remittances from relatives employed in the formal sector, sales of food crops in village markets, and ceremonial exchanges and bride-price payments (Clark 1985; and Burkins 1984).

Often, despite women's greater role in economic activities in the rural sector, they have limited access to money (Sexton 1982a). Therefore, when they receive some funds, they tend to hoard and keep it a secret from men. This still appears to be a widespread practice

---

2. In a recent study of the cocoa and coconut sectors Livingstone 1989, (p.121) provided data on sources of finance for investment by fermentary owners and transporters. The list did not include professional moneylenders.

among married women. However, hoarding is not a phenomenon confined to rural areas. Even in urban areas, according to some informants, women attempt to reduce the problems arising out of male dominance over money by hoarding. Such practices in the urban sector are, obviously, much more widespread among low-income households. It is women in such households who face greater risks and uncertainty of income and, therefore, who require greater social insurance. Apparently such women view hoarding of money as a method of reducing risks.

An interesting aspect of informal savings in Papua New Guinea is that it is done primarily in the form of money; women do not generally save in jewelry or gold, although one of the country's major exports is gold. The accumulation of gold appears not to have a social value in this society, unlike in India, Sri Lanka, or Malaysia.

Another savings arrangement is through savings groups. These are set up for different purposes and are found both in rural and urban areas. In rural areas such groups involve members of a given tribe, village, clan or subclan. They contribute savings regularly or irregularly to collect money for a given purpose such as payment of church fees, investment in a truck, or construction of a community facility. Generally, savings are handed over to a leader who holds the funds until the need to use the money arises. When small savings groups are set up for specific purposes it is not uncommon for members to work as a group to earn money for contributions. Often people work on farms to earn money for such groups. The savings groups have evolved from traditional arrangements that have been operating for a long time in the rural communities under which groups of people collected various goods to make relatively large payments.

The other rural savings arrangement is the rotating savings and credit association, which is known as *sande* in Tok Pisin (one of the major local languages). No work has been done on the history and various aspects of sandes except one study that deals with sandaying among a minority ethnic group—Chinese—in the urban area of Lae (Wu 1974). However, brief reference has been made to sande groups in several other studies on other subjects. The sandes are found all over Papua New Guinea. They appear to be widespread in the urban and semi-urban areas, among school teachers and plantation laborers, and within relatively low-income groups; they are less common in high-income groups and among businessmen.

Skeldon (1980), writing on regional associations among urban migrants, described the sandes among highland migrant laborers in Lae and Goroka (two regional towns). He writes:

...all highland migrants I interviewed in Lae and Goroka participated in a very simple form of rotating credit system. This is known variously as 'sandaying' or 'fortnighting' and it is a characteristic of the laboring and low income groups from all parts of Papua New Guinea; it is not typical of public servants or other white collar workers. In a sample of 28 working families in Lae, 22 heads of family engaged in 'sandaying' and in a sample of 89 migrant workers around Goroka, 59 sandayed.

According to Skeldon, sandaying is common among students at the teachers' colleges and it "has been well developed among plantation laborers for a considerable time."

Burkins (1984) also makes reference to sande in his work on the Southern Highlands Province. In his household money survey (which covered 24 households) he reported that K122 or 4.5 percent of the total household money income of males, during the reference period, consisted of sande receipts, while sande payments by all males in the sample amounted to K80 or 2.7 percent of the total male household expenditure. It is interesting to note that he reported no sande receipts or payments for females.

While sande is more common among persons with regular and stable incomes it is found among persons with highly unstable sources of incomes as well. In Aroma village in Abau district in the Central Province, six fishing families joined to form a fishing group to earn money for sande contributions. They often went fishing as a group and sold the catch to make each member's weekly contribution of K40 for sande.[3]

It appears that women also take part in sande. Sexton (1982a) made reference to women's sande groups in Watabung in the Eastern Highlands Province. Tolai women in East New Britain also participate in sande.[4] In a small-scale survey undertaken on informal finance involving 30 public and private sector senior- and middle-level officers, four stated that their wives have been sande participants.[5]

Although Skeldon reported that sande is not typical of public servants, I found ample evidence of sande among employees in a number of public sector institutions in the capital city of Port Moresby. These institutions include the Central Bank, Ministry of Finance, the Papua New Guinea Banking Corporation, and the National Research

---

3. I am thankful to Dr. Wari Iamo, an anthropologist at the National Research Institute, Port Moresby for providing me with this information.
4. This was revealed by Jacob Simet of the National Research Institute when I interviewed him in August, 1989.
5. This survey was undertaken by the author in August 1989.

Institute. The survey on informal finance that I carried out showed that sande is common in almost all institutions in Port Moresby.

Evidence I gathered indicates that sande is common among employees with low income, but could be observed among executive personnel as well. The evidence shows that:

- the groups are often small, the most common size being four or five;
- the contribution interval is every two weeks (mainly because salaries and wages are paid every two weeks);
- the members are known to one another; every member contributes a fixed sum in each turn; the recipients are distributed through consensus rather than lottery or other methods; and
- the size of the group is kept small purposely in order to facilitate transactions and to avoid potential defaults.

Often the participants come either from the same occupational group or from those with similar income levels and working in the same institution.

Often the fortnightly contribution is in the range of K20-50. Since the average size of a group is about four or five, total collection per round amounts to about K60-K200 and the cycle is completed within about 2-2.5 months.[6] New members often join only after a series of such cycles is completed by an existing group. At this stage, some of the members may decide to drop out.

The sande participant who I interviewed at the central bank was a member of a group of four persons and his group members were working in other institutions. Each member of his group contributed K50 every two weeks. He had started sande in 1987, stopped in 1988, and rejoined in 1989. His sande receipts have been used to remit money to his extended family members in the village and to buy some electrical items for the household. He has also deposited some money in his passbook savings account with a commercial bank. Another sande participant I interviewed contributed K50 every fortnight and was a member of a group of three persons. He had joined a sande group several years ago and from time to time dropped out and rejoined. He has also in the past used receipts to remit money to parents in the village and to buy a radio, among other things. It appears that many participants have some definite spending goal when joining sande. The evidence

---

6. Skeldon (1980 p. 252) reported that in Goroka there was one group involving 25 workers. In my survey, two respondents reported groups involving 20 and 30 members. These large groups, however, appear to be unusual.

shows that the savings mobilized through sandes are used not only on consumer durables, but also for investment purposes.

The fact that sande is widespread among low-income households tends to indicate that they are eager to save despite low incomes, and that the formal sector schemes do not meet their requirements. The existence of sande among employees of formal financial institutions further confirms this hypothesis, and indicates that informal savings arrangements have advantages over the formal arrangements.

Skeldon noted that some migrant workers participating in sande borrow money from their tribe or seek credit from neighborhood stores to tide them over their "off" period. This supports the view that the poor have the desire and the ability to save and sometimes involve themselves in a finance network in order to save a relatively sizable amount. Given that sande is common both in rural and urban areas and could be found in many institutions in the country, one could assume that significant amounts of funds are saved through this informal mechanism. Unfortunately, it was not possible to give even a rough estimate of the volume of funds involved. But, it appears that more people participate in sande than in savings and credit schemes of formal financial intermediaries.

Another important informal savings arrangement is the Wok Meri groups.[7] According to Sexton, these groups originated in the early 1960s as an effort by women to improve their deteriorating economic status. The women form informal groups consisting of 2 to 35 members to save money earned from selling vegetables, coffee, or, occasionally, their labor. Their activities consist of two distinct phases—a savings phase and an investment phase. After a group has collected money for about five to nine years, they end the savings phase of their activity with a large ceremony.

The organizational unit of Wok Meri is based on a kinship unit. Each Wok Meri group engages in saving under the leadership of one or two "big women." The big woman plays a key role in the group. She organizes groups, establishes and maintains ties with big women from other groups, organizes meetings and ceremonies, and leads the ritual. The big women also encourage their group members to save more money. They themselves often save more than other members.

Mature Wok Meri groups (known as mothers) often promote at least one new group (known as daughters) and encourage the members of that group to save money by giving them small loans to be saved. "Since there is a ban on withdrawing money already deposited in Wok Meri

---

7. This section draws almost entirely on work by Sexton.

accounts, the daughters must quickly save money to repay their mothers." Sexton explains the operational aspects of the groups:

> Wok Meri groups have a savings system they say is similar to banking. Each woman deposits her money into an account and a record is kept in her small notebook, which is labelled her passbook. Her money is kept in her own cloth bundle or mesh bag and all the members' bundles of money are stored together in the leader's house. Money is deposited at meetings in the evening of a market day. So, the women can save some of their money, before they are tempted to spend it or are asked for money by spouses and children. Savings meetings are fairly brief affairs and provide a chance for relaxed conversation among the members before people drift off to their houses to sleep.

Each group has two male representatives, one a bookkeeper and the other a chairman. However, they are not members of the group and do not engage in savings. The members are uneducated, mature women of about 35-40 years in age. Most "big women" are about 50 years or older.[8] Each member saves according to her ability, but with a sense of competition with others. Each group also tries to save more than other groups. Generally, each member deposits about K1-2 at each meeting. They meet once a week in the early stages, more often during the harvesting season of cash crops such as coffee and occasionally at later stages. However, there are no fixed schedules for meetings.

It is not known how many such groups exist in Papua New Guinea. According to Sexton (1982a) the movement is most prevalent in Goroka District in Eastern Highlands Province and in Chuave District, in Chimbu Province. However, according to informants, the groups operate in other districts as well.

The groups utilize the money they save and mobilize through loans for different purposes. In the early stages most of them have been used for group investments in "trucks" and "stores" (Sexton 1982a; and Munster 1975). Later they have shown a greater preference to keep the savings and loans individually, perhaps due to the failure of investments made by groups (Sexton 1982a).

---

8. In rural Papua New Guinea, older married women have relatively greater autonomy and access to money than do younger women. This explains the high average age of Wok Meri members.

Informal Loans

A multiplicity of informal credit arrangements exists in Papua New Guinea. One such important arrangement in both rural and urban areas is the credit extended by Wantoks. In general, these loans do not carry any interest. People rely on credit from wantoks for many different uses including business purposes. The business leaders in rural as well as urban areas have made use of the tradition of combining resources of clan members to obtain credit for starting up businesses.[9] In the early periods such credits have taken mainly the form of labor services but later cash loans became more common. In certain instances business leaders in different parts of the country have been able to finance considerable investments through such funds mobilized from a large number of clansmen (Finney 1968)[10]. Often these loans are made interest free and with open-ended repayment arrangements. However, lenders expect repayment in some form.

The Wok Meri groups explained earlier also make loans in addition to their savings functions. These groups have intergroup credit transactions (Sexton 1982a; and Munster 1975). When a particular group holds the finishing "washing hands" ceremony, other groups may extend loans to the group holding the ceremony. According to Sexton (1982a) these:

> ...small loans are apportioned among the group members, according to their willingness to accept debts and their ability to repay. Each member takes on the responsibility to repay each of her small loans when the creditor's group 'washes hands.' These debts are individualized, but they are not personalized. The two women know only the names of each other's villages, but the lender will also keep her own records of which ceremonies she attended, and the repayment will make its way back to her when her group 'washes hands.'

The group members continue to attend "washing hands" until they repay in full their loans. Since the intergroup credit arrangements are as important as savings arrangements, the Wok Meri groups may be considered another type of savings and credit association with distinct characteristics.

---

9. Known as "big fellow man belong business" in Tok Pisin.
10. Finney (1968 p. 403) reported that one business leader raised over Australian $3,000 from 784 persons scattered over 19 villages.

There are indications that women in some areas, after going through the Wok Meri savings phase, tend to prefer less complicated, short-term involvements in ROSCAs (Sexton 1982a). Perhaps, when women become more familiar with ROSCAs and have greater access to steady money income there may be a tendency for them to shift to ROSCAs.

As noted earlier, part-time moneylenders are emerging as a new class in informal urban markets in Papua New Guinea. These moneylenders are not necessarily rich persons. Some have started their operations with a small amount of money and increased over time the funds available for lending. Some lenders continue to operate with a small amount of money. The most interesting observation, perhaps, is that they could be found in private as well as public sector commercial banks. The moneylenders in these banks were providing loans mainly to their fellow employees, indicating that some bank employees also find that the informal sector has advantages over the formal sector for loans.

Moneylenders deal with persons who are well known to them and their operational zones are small. Some lend to their office mates only while some lend to people in their neighborhood. Loans are almost always for short periods. Unlike other types of informal lenders they specify repayment periods and interest rates. Interest rates, according to the limited information I was able to gather, apparently vary across borrowers, partly on the basis of perceived risks. The rates vary from 10 percent to 20 percent per two weeks. In several cases, the rate was as high as 40 percent for two weeks. Thus, annualized interest rates are very high. As the loans are for very small amounts and for very short periods the borrowers do not seem to consider the terms exorbitant or exploitive. In the absence of institutional sources to rely on for such quick service, they appear to consider these moneylenders as a group providing a valuable service to the community.[11]

Contrary to the popular presumption that informal moneylenders somehow always recover their loans in full, I observed that the part-time moneylenders in urban areas experience default and are sometimes unable to recover their loans in full. Perhaps this may explain in part the existence of very high interest rates in this market. In addition to risks, limited supplies of funds also appear to have a bearing on the high interest rates. It is less likely for a monopoly element to be significant for a long period. The data on 23 moneylenders showed that

---

11. In the survey I conducted, 14 of the 30 officers who provided information were of the view that these moneylenders provide a useful service to the community particularly in situations where banks were not willing to provide small loans. Only three respondents stated that the lenders do something bad by charging high interest rates.

six of them belong to the low-income category of laborers, mailboys and casual drivers; another five were clerks. Only one could be categorized as a businessman. Thus, the entry into the market appears to be easy, and substantial monopoly profits probably cannot exist over long periods of time.

Operators of stores also play a major role in the informal credit market, both in rural and urban areas, by providing consumption loans. During the last two decades, the number of tradestores in Papua New Guinea has increased dramatically. According to the Population Census of 1980 about 10 percent of the households in rural and urban areas derived money income from tradestores. Evidence indicates that many tradestores have, at early stages, adopted a liberal policy of consumption credit and encountered problems (Clark 1985; Burkins 1984; and Finney 1973). However, many store owners, perhaps learning from the past mistakes, now apply restrictive rules in giving loans. Such rules include giving loans only to wage earners and giving credit to a maximum of K2 per two weeks. Some store owners also send reminder notices after one month (Newton 1985). On the whole, owners of stores appear to provide a substantial amount of consumption loans and thereby play a significant role in the informal financial market both in terms of the number of persons served and in the value of loans extended.

Concluding Remarks

Although reliable data and information on the informal finance in Papua New Guinea are very limited, fragmentary evidence indicates that a large informal financial market exists. As is evident from the foregoing discussion it is clear that many people in both rural and urban areas participate in the informal financial market. While formal sources exclude many potential borrowers, informal sources continue to serve them, showing that informal finance enjoys strong cost advantages over the formal sources, particularly when lending small amounts. The existence of formal financial institutions that focus only on lending and do not mobilize deposits indicates that policymakers have failed to learn from the informal sector even the most basic lessons. The assumption that poor people are unable to save is no longer realistic. The limited evidence on informal finance in Papua New Guinea shows that poor households have an ability and willingness to save, and when put together, the amounts they save are substantial.

As there is a serious lack of information on informal finance, it is important to focus future research work on various facets of the informal sector. Such research is likely to throw more light on operational and qualitative aspects of the market, and the knowledge so gained could be useful in formulating policies to serve a wider section of the community in both rural and urban areas.

References

Burkins, D. 1984. "Waiting for Company: Development on the Periphery of the Periphery in the Southern Highlands Province, Papua New Guinea." Unpublished Ph.D. thesis, Philadelphia, Pennsylvania: Temple University.

Clark, J. L. 1985. "From Cults to Christianity: Continuity and Change in Takuru." Unpublished Ph.D. thesis, Adelaide, Australia: University of Adelaide.

Finney, B. R. 1968. "Bigfellow Man Belong Business in New Guinea." *Enthnology* 7: 394-410.

———. 1973. *Big Men and Business.* Canberra: Australian National University.

Livingstone, I. 1989. "The Marketing of Cocoa and Copra in Papua New Guinea." Unpublished discussion paper No. 37. Port Moresby, Papua New Guinea: Institute of National Affairs.

Lucas, J. 1972. "Lae - A Town in Transition." *Oceania* 42: 260-275.

Munster, J. 1975. "A Ban of Hope, Wok Meri." *Point* 2:132-146.

Newton, J. 1985. "Orokaiva Production and Change." The Pacific Research Monograph, No. 11, Canberra, Australia: Australian National University.

Sexton, L.D. 1982a. "Customary and Corporation Models for Women's Development Organizations." IASER Discussion Paper No. 41. Port Moresby, Papua New Guinea: IASER.

_____ . 1982b. "Wok Meri: A Women's Savings and Exchange System in Highland Papua New Guinea." *Oceania* 52:167-198.

Skeldon, R. 1980. "Regional Associations Among Urban Migrants in Papua New Guinea." *Oceania* 50: 248-272.

Strathern, A. 1969. "Finance and Production: Two Strategies in New Guinea Highlands Exchange Systems." *Oceania* 40: 42-67.

Wu, David T. H. 1974. "To Kill Three Birds with One Stone: The Rotating Credit Associations of the Papua New Guinea Chinese." *American Ethnologist* 1:565-584.

10

Informal Finance in the Philippines' Footwear Industry

Mario B. Lamberte

Studies on informal finance in the Philippines abound (Agabin and others 1989; and Lamberte and Lin 1987). They cover a wide range of topics including types of informal finance, interest rate determination, size and structure, interlinkage of informal finance with other markets, and savings mobilization potential, among others. After the liberalization of the financial markets in the early 1980s, an increasing number of people including policymakers began to appreciate the role of informal finance in the domestic economy. In fact, the previous government introduced credit programs that made use of traders/millers/input dealers who are active in lending to farmers as conduits for government funds (Esguerra 1987). The repayment rates in these programs were much better than rates in the conventional types of special credit programs for agriculture wherein soft loans were channeled through formal financial institutions, such as rural banks. The new government has maintained some of these nonconventional types of credit programs. But more importantly, it has officially recognized for the first time in its medium-term development plan the role of informal finance in mobilizing and allocating resources. However, this does not mean that all policymakers have changed their attitude toward informal finance. In fact, many of them still look upon it with disdain.

Most previous studies focused on informal finance in rural areas. This is understandable since this sector, large as it is and vital to the economy, has been relatively poorly served by the formal financial system. The nature of informal finance has been observed by these studies to vary from crop to crop (Geron 1988). For many crops, informal finance makes a lot of difference since it tries to satisfy the requirements of borrowers, such as synchronizing the repayment schedule of farmers to their cash flow patterns with minimal transaction costs.

In contrast, not much is known about informal finance in urban areas. The presumption that the urban sector is adequately serviced by formal financial institutions could be the reason why little attention has been given to urban informal finance. However, a large number of small- and medium-sized manufacturing firms do not have access to formal finance for the same reason that farmers do not have access (Lamberte and others 1989; and Salazar 1985). They are considered by banks not to be creditworthy and lacking in collateral. In addition, their loans are too small for banks to make a reasonable profit given alternative uses of their funds. The fact that these firms have proliferated and have been able to sustain their operations over the years suggest that they are either fully self-financing or have access to external finance other than banks. Thus, it is important to understand the character of informal finance that is supporting the small- and medium-sized manufacturing firms. This is the main focus of this chapter.

The next section presents a descriptive analysis of a segment of informal finance in the urban area, in the footware industry. The last section discusses policy implications.

The Manufacturing Sector and Informal Finance[1]

To fully appreciate informal finance in the manufacturing sector, it is necessary to describe first the processes involved in producing and marketing manufactured goods, because for every real transaction there is an equivalent financial transaction. Since there is a wide variety of industries in the urban sector, it would be virtually impossible to deal with all of them in this chapter. Hence, for the purpose of addressing the objective of this chapter, it is worthwhile to examine in depth one industry. And for this, we have selected the footwear industry located in Marikina, one of the 13 towns and cities comprising Metro Manila. About 70 percent of the total number of footwear firms in the country are located in this town. The information analyzed in this study was obtained from 63 footwear manufacturers randomly selected from a total of 1,219 firms. The average value of the fixed assets of these firms

---

1. This section draws heavily on Lamberte and Jose (1988).

was about US$30,000 U.S. in 1986. Eighty-seven percent of the sample firms are single proprietorship.

Figure 1 outlines in detail the sources of inputs for a typical footwear manufacturer in the Philippines and possible distribution channels for his footwear products. The manufacturer needs material inputs, some of which are locally produced while others are imported. Locally produced material inputs are supplied directly by domestic input suppliers. In the case of imported material inputs, the manufacturer may buy them either directly from foreign suppliers or from domestic traders who import the required material inputs. The choice depends on the manufacturer's financial capacity. Raw material inputs comprise at least 50 to 55 percent of the total cost in footwear manufacture.

The relatively large amounts of funds required to purchase the needed inputs oftentimes strain the capacity of manufacturers. Most affected are the small manufacturers who find it difficult to raise their own working capital internally. Thus, trade credit becomes an attractive arrangement for them. It is also possible that input suppliers who provide trade credit to footwear manufacturers supplement it with cash credit so that the latter can purchase other inputs.

Footwear manufacturers have various distribution channels for their products. Some may have their own domestic retail stores. Others who would like to concentrate in production sell their products to retailers, like department stores and supermarkets, or to wholesalers/traders. The latter, in turn, sell the footwear products to domestic and foreign retailers. One mode is to sell the products directly to foreign buyers. However, only big manufacturers who have direct access to foreign markets have this opportunity. Domestic retailers and wholesalers/traders are the major customers of most of the footwear manufacturers.

It is not easy to capture customers of products whose styles change frequently. Being ahead or at least in step with what is in vogue is necessary for survival of a footwear firm. Thus, it is not enough to simply establish good relations with customers. To stay in business, a footwear manufacturer must be aggressive in marketing his products. Unlike a farmer, he does not just go on producing products in large quantities when the season comes. He starts by sending samples of his products and corresponding price quotation to prospective customers/buyers. Whenever the customers/buyers perceive that there is a sufficient demand for the sample products, they then place an order. Only then will the manufacturer start producing to fulfill the order.

Customers of footwear manufacturers may not immediately pay in cash for the delivered goods. In other words, they obtain trade credits

FIGURE 1. Distribution Channels of Footwear Products and Sources of Inputs

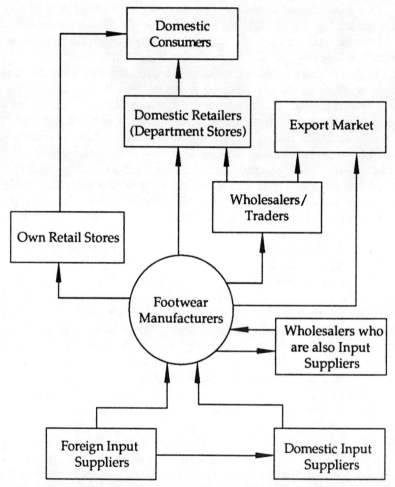

from footwear manufacturers for a term of, say, 30 to 60 days. This is a buyers' market. Thus, to stay competitive, footwear manufacturers must extend trade credits to their customers, especially big department stores and large wholesalers/traders. Here is a case wherein small firms are providing credits to larger firms.

The manufacturer's funds are locked in between the time he delivers the goods to his customers and the time he receives payment. However, he does not stop producing but tries to get new orders to keep his business going. To do this, he needs additional working capital. Such may come solely from internal profits if they are sufficient. The other alternative is to turn around and ask for trade credit from his input suppliers using as security the credit instrument issued to him by his customers who obtained trade credits from him. Thus, we have a case wherein the footwear manufacturer plays a dual role. He provides trade credit to his customers at one end and obtains trade credit from input suppliers at the other end. Synchronizing receipts and payments is crucial in these transactions.

It is likely that the maturity period of the trade credit that the footwear manufacturer obtains from his input suppliers is shorter than the maturity period of the trade credit he gives to his customers. Under such situation, he must look for other sources of funds to pay his obligations to input suppliers. Other sources of loans may include banks, moneylenders, and friends/relatives. These alternative sources of credit may also be tapped by the footwear manufacturer if he does not obtain trade credits from his input suppliers, or if such trade credit is not sufficient for his needs.

The footwear manufacturer may also enter into a "tie-in" arrangement with input suppliers who are also wholesalers/traders. Under this arrangement, the input supplier provides trade credits to the footwear manufacturer on the condition that the latter sells to him the footwear manufactures at a pre-agreed price. The manufacturer's debt is settled once he delivers the goods to the input supplier. This is similar to the trader/miller-farmer "tie-in" or linked credit arrangement prevalent in rural areas (Sacay and others 1985).

Figure 2 summarizes the main points discussed above. In particular, it portrays the flow and kinds of credit provided/obtained by a footwear manufacturer.

Major Findings

This section discusses trade credits granted and obtained by footwear manufacturers, effective interest rates, and other sources of credit.

Trade Credits Granted by Footwear Manufacturers

All the sample footwear manufacturers granted trade credits to their customers (see Table 1). In 1986 alone, the volume of their products sold on credit averaged 82 percent of their total sales. This is

FIGURE 2. Flow and Kinds of Credit

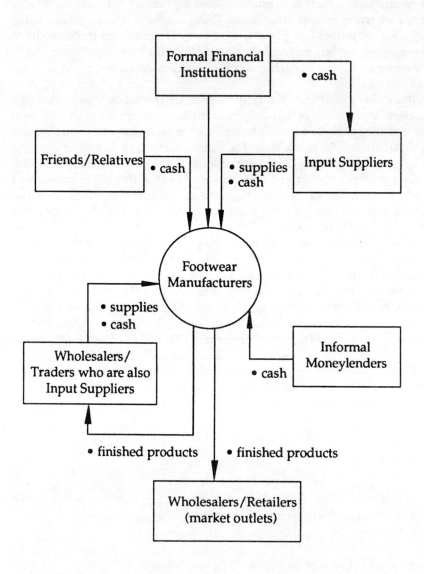

equivalent to about US$70,000 per manufacturer. Retailers, such as department stores and supermarkets, garnered 70 percent of the trade credits granted by footwear manufacturers. About 84 percent of the total

TABLE 1. Proportion and Value of Trade Credits Granted by Footwear Manufacturers to Their Customers

Information	Number Reporting	Percentage Reporting
Number of footwear manufacturers who granted trade credits to their customers	63	100.0
Proportion of trade credits to total sales (in percent)		
Below 50	5	7.9
50 - 75	11	17.5
76 - 95	22	34.9
96 - 100	25	39.9
TOTAL	63	100.0
Mean	83	.
Standard deviation	23	
Median	90	
Value of trade credits (US$)		
Below 4,900	4	6.4
4,901 - 25,000	19	30.2
25,001 - 50,000	15	23.8
Above 50,001	25	39.7
TOTAL	63	100.0
Mean	$68,000	
Standard deviation	$82,000	
Median	$39,000	

Source: Lamberte and Jose 1988.

sample firms granted trade credits to retailers, and roughly 30 percent gave similar arrangements to wholesalers/traders. Except for the individual customers/buyers, the average maturity period of the trade credits ranged from 69 to 72 days, depending on the types of customers.

Since trade credit is term credit, manufacturers usually demand security to ensure payment. The most popular instruments used as security are postdated checks. Implied in the postdated checks is the maturity period of the trade credit.

The postdated check is not a perfectly risk free security instrument. Customers may have closed their bank accounts before the maturity of the check. Delayed payments may also occur. When customers encounter liquidity problems they may persuade the concerned footwear manufacturer not to cash the check upon maturity. Among the different customers of footwear manufacturers, the incidence of delayed payments in 1986 was alarmingly high for retailers and wholesalers/traders (see Table 2).

Respondents were asked whether the prices they charged for their products sold on credit were higher than the prices they charged for the same products sold for cash. Only 22 percent of the total respondents answered the question positively. On the average, the price differential was 7 percent.

TABLE 2. Incidence of Delayed Payments on Trade Credits Granted by Footwear Manufacturers to Their Customers

Market Outlet	Number Reporting	Average Number of Days Delayed	Average Amount Overdue (US$)
Individual buyers	3	6.0 (1.4)	17 (10)
Wholesalers/traders	14	120.2 (165.6)	39 (19,455)
Wholesalers/traders who are also input suppliers	7	13.3 (4.1)	1,250 (1,349)
Retailers (department stores, supermarkets)	29	18.6 (12.4)	1,323 (4,569)

Note: Figures in parentheses are standard deviations.
Source: Lamberte and Jose 1988.

Trade Credits Obtained by Footwear Manufacturers

Since a large proportion of their sales is locked in as trade credits that can be liquidated only after 60 to 90 days, footwear manufacturers must resort to borrowing to continue operating. Ninety (90) percent of the sample respondents admitted that they obtained trade credits from input suppliers in 1986 (see Table 3). Input suppliers and wholesalers/traders who are also input suppliers are their primary sources of credit. About 84 percent of the respondents obtained trade

TABLE 3. Trade Credits Obtained by Footwear Manufacturers from Input Suppliers

Item	Number Reporting	Percentage
Number of manufacturers who bought inputs on credit	57	91
Number of manufacturers who bought inputs on credit from input suppliers	53	84
Number of manufacturers who bought inputs on credit from wholesalers/ traders who are also input suppliers	15	24
Proportion of the value of material inputs bought on credit to total value of the material inputs (in percent)		
Below 51	2	4
51 - 75	15	26
76 - 95	24	42
96 - 100	16	28
TOTAL	57	100
Mean		80
Standard deviation		21

Source: Lamberte and Jose 1988.

credits from input suppliers. Twenty-four percent of them also obtained trade credits from wholesalers/traders who are also input suppliers. On the average, 80 percent of the value of the material inputs was bought on credit. The value of trade credits obtained by footwear manufacturers from input suppliers in 1986 averaged US$23,000. This is only 39 percent of the value of trade credits they granted to their customers in the same year. Of the total trade credits obtained by footwear manufacturers in 1986, 85 percent were contributed by input suppliers while 15 percent came from wholesalers/traders who are also input suppliers (see Table 4). The average maturity period of the trade credit was 48 days for wholesalers/traders who are also input suppliers and 51 days for input suppliers. Note that this is shorter than the maturity period of the trade credits granted by footwear manufacturers to their customers.

There are several credit instruments that may be accepted by input suppliers, but the most popular is the postdated check issued by customers of footwear manufacturers. This is considered the most highly negotiable credit instrument. Interestingly, about 21 percent of the respondents had only verbal agreements with their input suppliers.

TABLE 4. Proportion of the Value of Trade Credit on Inputs Contributed by Each Source and Maturity of Trade Credit

Item	Number Reporting	Average	Standard deviation
Proportion of trade credit on inputs contributed by			
Input suppliers (in percent)	53	85.4	30.0
Wholesalers/traders who are also input suppliers (in percent)	15	14.6	30.0
Maturity period of the trade credit (days)			
Input suppliers	53	51.0	21.2
Wholesalers/traders who are also input suppliers	15	47.5	29.2

Source: Lamberte and Jose 1988

Effective Interest Rates

The effective interest rate on trade credits obtained by footwear manufacturers from input suppliers includes the discount rate on a postdated check, the plain interest rate on trade credit from input suppliers, and the implicit interest rate arising from price differentials of inputs bought on credit and in cash. The components of the effective interest rate on plain trade credit (that is, trade credits obtained from input suppliers) and on tie-in credit (that is, trade credits obtained from wholesalers/traders who are also input suppliers) are shown in Table 5.

The discount for postdated checks is almost the same for plain trade credit and tie-in credit. The same is true of the plain interest rate. However, the implicit interest rate greatly differs between the two sources of trade credit. In particular, the implicit interest rate charged by input suppliers is twice as high as the implicit interest rate charged by wholesalers/traders who are also input suppliers. An explanation of this is in order.

Wholesalers/traders usually have marketing contracts with big retailers or exporters. To assure themselves of a steady supply of

TABLE 5. Components of Effective Interest Rate

Source/Component	Percent per Year	Percent Share
Plain trade credit (Input suppliers)		
Discount rate on postdated checks	33.2	28.5
Plain interest rate	7.4	6.3
Price differential	75.9	65.2
TOTAL	116.4	100.0
Tie-in credit (wholesalers/ traders who are also input suppliers)		
Discount rate on postdated check	31.8	40.7
Plain interest rate	9.6	12.3
Price differential	36.9	47.1
TOTAL	78.3	100.0

Source: Lamberte and Jose 1988.

footwear, they engage in tie-in arrangements with footwear manufacturers. This is the best way for them to reduce business risk arising from nondelivery of goods when they have no control over production. Since footwear manufacturers have alternative outlets for their products as well as alternative sources of inputs, wholesalers/traders are therefore compelled to give footwear manufacturers a better price for their products. The marketing contract also reduces the risk of default on the credit they extend to footwear manufacturers.

This is not the case, however, with input suppliers who are solely supplying inputs. Footwear manufacturers find it necessary to borrow from them since their working capital is tied up with the trade credits they extended to their customers. Thus, input suppliers can exercise some degree of pricing power that is reflected in the greater margins on inputs.

The total effective interest rates charged by input suppliers and wholesalers/traders who are also input suppliers are 116 percent and 78 percent per annum, respectively. These are not substantially different from the rates charged by informal moneylenders, which are discussed below (Lamberte and Bunda 1988).

Alternative Sources of Credit

Aside from input suppliers, footwear manufacturers had other sources of credit to finance their business operations, such as banks, moneylenders, and friends/relatives. Of the 63 respondents, only 6 borrowed from banks in 1986. These are relatively big firms. The average amount borrowed was US$2,700 with a maturity period of one year. The average interest rate was 16.5 percent per annum.

Seventeen respondents borrowed money from moneylenders to finance their business operations in 1986. The maturity period for loans from moneylenders was short, ranging from 30 to 60 days. The interest rate for the loans ranged from 36 to 120 percent per annum. Individuals who presented postdated checks for discounting paid lower interest rates. The average discount rate charged by moneylenders for postdated checks was 36 percent per annum, which was slightly lower than the input suppliers' discount rate for postdated checks. About one-third of the respondents turned to their friends/relatives for additional working capital. These were mostly interest free loans.

There are other types of informal finance operating in urban areas. The most common among them is the "paluwagan," the Philippine version of a rotating savings and credit associations. They can be found in government and private offices as well as in some pockets of low-income communities in urban areas. In one low-income urban community studied by Lamberte and Bunda in 1988, market vendors have formed several paluwagan units. The existence of a variety of paluwagans in this small community offers low-income households opportunities to save and overcome the problem of indivisibilities in investment and consumption that is in accord with their financial capacity. Some paluwagan units have transformed themselves into cooperative credit unions (see Lamberte and Balbosa 1988). In the Philippines, the cooperative credit unions are virtually unregulated, and in that sense, still belong to the informal financial markets. The cooperative credit union of the employees of the Central Bank of the Philippines is one of the largest and fastest growing cooperative credit unions in the country. It offers savings and time deposits to its members and housing and consumption loans. Market vendors' cooperative credit unions are also by no means small.

I have described above the informal financial market in one industry. And even then, only certain aspects of informal finance in this industry have been examined. Nevertheless, the study showed that informal finance is very much alive in the urban, industrial sector. The same character of informal finance can be found as well in other manufacturing industries, such as gifts and housewares, food processing, furniture, and the garment industry.

Policy Implications

Concerned with lack of access to formal credit by small manufacturing enterprises, some lawmakers filed a bill in 1989 requiring banks to allocate a certain proportion of their loanable funds to these firms. At the same time, the Department of Trade and Industry introduced several special credit programs for these firms carrying concessionary rates. Such had been the approach taken in the past to increase the flow of credit to the agricultural sector, but almost all such programs failed, leaving the rural banking system in shambles.

Interestingly, while the special credit programs for the agricultural sector are now being gradually phased out, new ones are being created for the industrial sector. And like the special credit programs for the agricultural sector in the past, the new ones have been designed without taking into account the role and character of informal financial markets in the industrial sector. Policymakers do not know much about the workings of informal finance in the urban, industrial sector. But they cannot entirely be blamed for it because, as pointed out at the beginning of this chapter, there is a dearth of studies on informal finance in urban, industrial areas.

The results of this study offer some useful insights for designing policies that could enhance the efficiency of the urban financial markets, both formal and informal, without necessarily using a special credit program as an intervention instrument. For example, the market for postdated checks recently has attracted the attention of one large commercial bank. In 1986, it set up a Shoe Industry Desk in its Marikina branch. It lends to small footwear manufacturers by discounting postdated checks. Loans can be obtained quickly. It even opens its branch in Marikina on Saturdays to service borrowers. This is one case where a formal lending institution mimicks informal lenders. It competes with input suppliers by offering lower discount rates on postdated checks. Admittedly, its current impact on the market is still limited. The main reason is that it honors only those checks issued by large, well-known retailers and supermakets. In effect, it competes with input suppliers only insofar as the prime postdated checks are concerned. What is important, however, is that it has started an innovative lending program. As it gathers more experience and information about the market, it may expand to non-prime instruments. This is where some intervention is required to accelerate that process by providing more guarantees or sanctions on check writing.

A good information system about the financial health of firms, big and small, which are regularly issuing postdated checks as payments for the goods delivered must be available at a reasonable cost so that banks and input suppliers can make proper assessment of the risk involved. The main reason why the bank mentioned above does not accept postdated checks issued by small retailers is that they have insufficent knowledge about the financial conditions of those firms. On the other hand, input suppliers charge a higher discount rate for postdated checks issued by small firms than those issued by large firms to compensate for the higher perceived risk. Perhaps, the government-owned Credit Information Bureau, Inc. can be strengthened and its coverage expanded to include in its rating program small firms issuing postdated checks. This will hopefully enhance the integrity of postdated checks as a security instrument, approximating the well-established "quedan" (warehouse receipt) system.

References

Agabin, Meliza H., Mario B. Lamberte, Mahar K. Mangahas, and Alcetis Abrera-Mangahas. 1989. "Studies on Informal Credit Markets in the Philippines: An Integrative Report." Manila, Philippines: Philippine Institute for Development Studies Working Paper Series No. 89-14.

Esguerra, Emmanuel F. 1987. "Can the Informal Lenders be Co-Opted into Government Credit Programs?" Manila, Philippines: Philippine Institute for Development Studies Working Paper Series No. 87-03.

Geron, Ma. Piedad. 1988. "Philippine Informal Rural Credit Markets: Efficiency and Equity Issues." Unpublished Ph.D. dissertation. Quezon City, Philippines: University of the Philippines.

Lamberte, Mario B., and Joseph Lim. 1987. "Rural Financial Markets: A Review of Literature." Manila, Philippines: Philippine Institute for Development Studies Staff Paper Series No. 87-02.

Lamberte, Mario B., and Ma Theresa Bunda. 1988. "The Financial Markets in Low-Income Urban Communities: The Case of Sapang Palay." Manila, Philippines: Philippine Institute for Development Studies Working Paper Series No. 88-05.

Lamberte, Mario B., and Joven Z. Balbosa. 1988. "Informal Savings and Credit Institutions in the Urban Areas: The Case of Cooperative Credit Unions." Manila, Philippines: Philippine Institute for Development Studies Working Paper Series No. 88-06.

Lamberte, Mario B., and Anita Abad Jose. 1988. "The Manufacturing Sector and the Informal Credit Markets: The Case of Trade Credits in the Footwear Industry." Manila, Philippines: Philippine Institute for Development Studies Working Paper Series No. 88-07.

Lamberte, Mario B., Rosario G. Manasan, Erlinda M. Medalla, Josef T. Yap, and Teodoro Untalan. 1989. "A Study of the Export Financing System in the Philippines." Manila, Philippines: Philippine Institute for Development Studies Working Paper Series No. 89-07.

Salazar, Bimbo. 1985. "Financial Factors and Small and Medium Enterprises in the Philippines," Unpublished study, Institute of Small Scale Industries. Quezon City, Philippines: University of the Philippines.

Sacay, Orlando, Meliza H. Agabin, and Chita Irene E. Tanchoco. 1985. *Small Farmer Credit Dilemma.* Technical Board on Agricultural Credit, Manila: Government of the Philippines.

11

Collateral Substitutes in Rural Informal Financial Markets in the Philippines

Emmanuel F. Esguerra and Richard L. Meyer[1]

Loan collateral has generally been discussed in the context of formal financial markets in developed economies. Collateral, the asset that a borrower agrees to forfeit in the event of loan default, has been analyzed either as a mechanism to enforce loan repayment (Plaut 1985; Benjamin 1978), or as a screening device to sort borrowers of varying riskiness (Bester 1985). However, collateral, as defined above, is rarely used in the informal rural financial markets of less-developed economies. The reason often given is the inside knowledge the informal lender is presumed to have about borrowers. The legal and insurance environment that influences collateral valuation may also pose difficulties that inhibit collateral. As a result, credit market participants employ a variety of collateral substitutes when the market environment renders most assets less acceptable as collateral or where borrowers possess few collateralizable assets (Binswanger and Rosenzweig 1986). Third party guarantees, threat of loss of future borrowing opportunities, and tied contracts are all common forms of collateral substitutes.

This chapter presents an analysis of the use in informal finance of specific types of collateral substitutes in four villages in Central Luzon,

1. This chapter is based on the senior author's dissertation research. Financial assistance for the field survey and data processing was provided by the Agricultural Credit Policy Council (ACPC) through its Rural Informal Credit Markets (RICM) Research Project. We appreciate the suggestions made by Dale Adams, Douglas Graham, and Mario Lamberte on an earlier draft. The usual disclaimers apply.

Philippines, based on a field survey conducted in 1988. The focus is on farmer-lender and trader-lender loans that have become important in the rural credit market in recent years. These credit arrangements are of fairly recent origin and, while not unique to these geographic areas, appear preponderant where the Green Revolution technology has been widely diffused. Existing credit patterns are explained in light of the material and institutional environment of the study areas that influence the behavior of lenders and borrowers. We show that the use of specific collateral substitutes leads to specialization by lenders in terms of borrower groups.

The next section provides background information about the data used in the analysis. This is followed by a discussion of factor and product markets in the study areas. The fourth section describes some observed features of informal credit contracts, with emphasis on farmer-lender and trader-lender loans, and the collateral substitutes most widely used. Finally, the results of econometric tests supporting a "specialization hypothesis" are presented and discussed.

The Nueva Ecija Data

Four villages from the municipality of Muñoz in the province of Nueva Ecija were selected for the field survey. The survey data cover 171 randomly selected farm, landless agricultural and landless non-agricultural (or nonfarm) households. The data include information on: incomes and transfers received by households from all sources; labor contracts; land tenure and use; quantities, unit prices, and value of farm production; and all labor and non-labor inputs employed in rice production. Information was also gathered on all credit transactions reported by the households during the wet (May-October) and dry (November-April) cropping seasons for 1987/88.

Farm households, comprising about 53 percent of the sample, derive their income from the farm operation regardless of the farm operator's tenurial status. More than half had leasehold contracts and the rest were either owner-cultivators or amortizing owners. The predominance of leases reflects the impact of agrarian reform, which made tenancy illegal in rice areas, thus converting sharecroppers to leaseholders or amortizing owners.

Landless nonagricultural households (17 percent of the total) are engaged primarily in nonfarm activities. Most of the individuals work as blue collar employees at a nearby university; others are self-employed as pedicab operators or are retail store owners. Landless households derive their income primarily from hiring out labor services to farm operators as either casual or permanent laborers. Their responsibilities range from performing specific farm activities (for example, weeding and threshing) to overseeing the entire farming operation for the landowner. Permanent labor contracts typically cover a cropping season, but are renewable based on the worker's performance.

More than half of the landless workers were employed as permanent workers, while the remainder were casual laborers. The latter are paid mostly on a piece-rate basis. Permanent workers, on the other hand, are paid fixed wages in paddy, usually representing 10 percent of output. Unlike the casual laborer who is hired to perform a specifically defined task, the permanent worker, who is hired to assist in managing the farm, usually has considerable scope for decisionmaking regarding input use or labor allocation.

Factor and Product Markets

One of the most far-reaching effects of the yield-increasing rice technology in the Philippines is the commercialization of the rice economy. The greater reliance on commercially produced inputs and the larger marketable surplus have hastened the development of input and output markets. Increased labor requirements along with changes in tenurial arrangements have also contributed to the emergence of a rural wage labor market. These changes have had an impact on rural financial markets.

The evolution of permanent labor contracts has been studied at the International Rice Research Institute (IRRI) (Hayami and Otsuka1989). The *porsyentuhan* (meaning a percentage or sharing rule), became the popular wage contract in Nueva Ecija only within the last decade, and especially in irrigated areas. The popularity of this type of contract, which resembles share-tenancy, owes much to the yield-increasing rice technology introduced in the late sixties, and the outlawing of share-tenancy in the 1970s. The new rice technology increased the income of leaseholders and amortizing owners because the agrarian reform fixed leasehold rents and amortization payments. The income effects have resulted in the withdrawal of some beneficiaries from farming, thus inducing a substitution of hired labor for family labor. At the same time, new technology required the expenditure of quality effort by the laborers, implying greater supervision and higher monitoring cost for the employer. The prohibition against subtenancy, however, precluded using an incentive-compatible contract. As Hayami and Otsuka (1989) conclude: "the semi-tenant permanent labor arrangement plays a role similar to tenancy contracts, while it can easily be disguised as a labor employment contract" (p. 11). The demand for consumption credit by landless workers can be met by their employers who have personal knowledge of them. Casual laborers obtain advances for consumption during slack months from former or potential employers in exchange for labor services during seasons of peak labor demand.

The prospects of higher residual gains accruing to successful farmer-cultivators increased the demand for cultivable land. Increased operating expenses associated with the new rice technology encouraged greater borrowing by farmers. With the demise of subsidized credit programs in the late 1970s and a lack of acceptable collateral, farmer-borrowers had to turn increasingly to the informal credit market. Farmer cultivation rights became an attractive collateral substitute; therefore, land market transactions became closely linked with informal credit market transactions. Credit contracts involving the pawning or mortgaging of cultivation rights became widely used in Nueva Ecija only in the 1980s when access to formal credit became increasingly difficult and farm incomes were falling (Otsuka and Marciano 1988).

The incidence and economics of land pawning contracts are reported in Nagarajan and David (1990) and Rivera and Mangalindan (1987). Otsuka and Marciano (1988) report that, based on their survey of two villages in Muñoz, the parties to a pawning contract are usually small farmers as pawnors, and farmer-moneylenders or trader-lenders as pawnees. In these pawning contracts, the cultivator temporarily gives up cultivation rights in exchange for a specific sum of money obtained from a lender. The loan amount varies depending upon the quality of the land, with the highest amount reported in this study as US$1,000 for roughly a hectare. All farm income earned accrues to the creditor who also assumes all operating expenses for the duration of the loan. Upon repayment, the borrower recovers the cultivation rights.

A farmer may lose his land completely through a pawning contract. In most cases, the temporary surrender of cultivation rights takes place only after a farmer-borrower has accumulated a certain level of debt. By failing to repay previous debts, farmers may obtain additional loans only by turning over their cultivation rights to the lender. An inability to repay over an extended period results in the *de facto* transfer or permanent surrender of tenancy rights. In a regime characterized by land retention limits, restrictions on land sales, and imperfect credit markets, the pawning contract in effect may have become the primary mechanism for transferring land among cultivators and owners.

The increased yields resulting from the modern varieties have necessarily created opportunities for gains in rice marketing. The marketing functions include storing the paddy, milling, and transporting the rice for distribution to end users. Recent studies of the rice marketing system (Umali and Duff 1988; and Umali 1987) show that these functions are carried out by different agents. Traders and commission agents buy paddy (*palay*) directly from producers for resale to millers who store and mill it into rice. Milled rice is then sold to wholesalers and retailers.

Umali reports that palay trader profits, as a percentage of marketing costs, exceed 50 percent and their return on investments range from 100 to 257 percent. Given the small volume of grain handled by most traders and the seasonality of their trading, however, the profitability of buying and selling is confined to a two to three month harvest season. Most owners of grain buying stations report that their profits greatly depend on the volume handled and the rate of turnover. Because of the competition caused by many *palay* buyers, individual paddy traders find it in their interest to maintain regular and secure sources of *palay* during the harvest. Lending to farmers during the cropping season on the condition that they get first claim on the borrowers' harvest helps assure the traders of a stable paddy supply.

Features of Informal Credit Contracts

The survey revealed that 139 of the 171 respondents were borrowers during one or both of the two crop seasons in 1987/88, but only eight borrowed from banks. Of these eight, six also borrowed from informal sources. Table 1 presents some summary statistics on borrowers for the total sample, and by household type.

Loan Characteristics

Cash loans accounted for more than 60 percent of the total reported loan transactions, which numbered about 570. The nonirrigated village reported the fewest loans (59), which is understandable in view of its one crop per year. The average amounts of cash loans, in-kind loans, and land mortgages or pawning transactions per borrowing household are shown in Table 1. These averages may be slightly lower than normal because of the effects of a typoon during the 1987 wet season. Such effects are not expected to be large because most of the harvest was completed before the typhoon. It is unlikely that loan contract terms change drastically in response to adverse weather conditions.

In-kind loans are usually in the form of fertilizer or milled rice for consumption. Each type comprised about 15 percent of the total number

TABLE 1. Means of Selected Variables for Borrower Households in Muñoz, Nueva Ecija by Household Type

	Borrower Households			
Variable	Total Sample	Farm Households	Landless Households	Non-farm Househoids
Observations	139	82	41	16
Household income (P)abc	25,801	32,244	13,123	31,706
Cash loans (P)ab	5,743	8,030	2,022	3,054
In-kind loans (P)ab	2,672	1,659	1,366	882
Pawning contracts (P)ab	16,562	17,500	10,000	0
Total borrowings (P)b	7,676	10,909	2,968	3,165
Average Loan Size (P)b	1,955	2,649	1,013	814
Number of Loans	4.3	4.8	3.4	3.7
Number of Lenders	1.7	1.9	1.3	1.4
Farm Size (ha.)ab		1.65		
Non-farm Income (P)a	20,137	15,981	12,726	30,609

Note: Not applicable where left blank. Standard deviations are in parentheses.

a Number reporting may be less than the number of observations.

b In Philippine pesos. In 1988, 21.07 pesos = US$1.

c The poverty threshold in the Philippines in 1988 has been computed at 32,500 pesos.

Source: Rural Informal Credit Market (RICM) Survey (1988), Agricultural Credit Policy Council (ACPC), Philippines.

of loans. Rice loans were taken mainly by landless workers, confirming the consumptive nature of their borrowings. Practically all in-kind loans required repayment in paddy.

Invariably the loans were of short duration—usually for a cropping season, which lasts anywhere from four to six months. Informal lenders typically disbursed loans only for specific purposes (for example, land preparation, fertilizer and pesticide application, harvesting and post-harvesting), and at specific times during the cropping season to safeguard against excessive borrowing by their clients.

Loan transactions were concentrated in the 0 and 30 percent interest rate per season categories, which respectively accounted for 34 and 35 percent of the total number of loans. Half the number of zero interest loans were in kind. The average implicit rates of interest on rice loans and fertilizer loans amounted to 34 and 112 percent per season, respectively, after considering relative commodity prices. The greater cost of fertilizer loans may be indicative of some imperfections in the fertilizer market.

The relative importance of the various informal loan sources is shown in Table 2. Rice millers lent the largest amount on average, followed by retail store owners. These two sources, however, were less important than farmer-lenders and traders based on number and frequency of transactions. Considering volume of loans, frequency of transactions, and lender class size, traders and farmers constituted the major sources of informal loans and this pattern prevailed even in the nonirrigated village. The information in Table 2 on number of loan transactions per lender type should not, however, be interpreted as the lenders' complete portfolios. Since the information was generated from borrower responses, it reflects loan transactions made by the lenders only to those borrowers residing in the survey villages. It is likely that the lenders' portfolios are much larger than what the information in Table 2 suggests.

The nominal rates of interest charged per season by each lender type are also shown in Table 2. The rates were averaged over all loans granted by each lender type including zero interest loans. Trader credits were generally more expensive than loans from other sources. Perhaps the risk premium attached to these loans is higher considering that traders have less inside knowledge about borrowers. The higher interest cost of trader-lender credit may also reflect the lenders' cost of capital, since some lenders operate on funds borrowed from either formal or informal sources. Alternatively, interest charges may incorporate the implicit price that borrowers pay for the marketing

TABLE 2. Informal Lenders in Muñoz, Nueva Ecija, by Type, Wet and Dry Seasons, 1987/88, Interest Rate Per Season

| | | | | Interest Rate per Season | | |
| | | | | Simple | Maturity Weighted | |
Lender Type	Number	Number of Transactions	Loan Size (P)	Average (percent)	Average (percent)	Maturity (months)
Farmer/ landowner	48	181	1,634	13.8	15.2	3.2
Private moneylender	6	85	1,625	21.2	20.1	3.1
Trader/ middlemen	14	175	1,771	21.3	22.4	3.1
Rice miller	2	7	6,900	17.1	16.0	2.8
Retail store owner	7	51	1,937	13.9	17.7	2.3
Input dealer	4	14	917	22.1	19.5	3.3
Others[a]	34	50	1,285	14.3	17.8	3.1

[a] Includes guarantors, government employees (particularly public school teachers) and other very specific occupations.
Source: Rural Informal Credit Market (RICM) Survey (1988), Agricultural Credit Policy Council (ACPC), Philippines.

services that trader-creditors provide. In contrast, interest rates on loans from farmer-lender and "other" lenders were much lower. It might be hypothesized that the more personal the relation between borrower and lender, the lower the interest rate charged. As commercialization proceeds, however, personal relations become less important in economic exchanges.

Collateral Substitutes

Very few loans involved collateral. In the few cases reported, the assets pledged included farm machinery and animals for which the borrower turns over ownership title to the creditor who retains it until the loan is fully paid. Little evidence was found of land titles being used as collateral, in part because most borrowers do not own land and, in part, because agrarian reform laws prohibit legal ownership transfers except to heirs.

Collateral substitutes are used to enforce repayment in the informal credit market in the absence of collateral. The pawning of cultivation rights is one such collateral substitute. Less than ten pawning contracts were reported in the Nueva Ecija villages, however. This may be attributed to two factors. First, the data include credit transactions entered into by the borrowers only during two cropping seasons. Thus pawning transactions made previous to the survey were not recorded. The second factor may be a recording problem. It is possible that households consciously withheld information about pawning transactions considering the social stigma attached to having to pawn one's assets, let alone having creditors foreclose on them.

Pawning is practiced between farmer-borrowers and lenders interested in cultivating land. When borrowers are unable to repay past loans, they pawn their tenancy rights to the creditor in exchange for a given sum, which together with their outstanding debts constitutes the pawning fee. Alternatively, the creditor may offer to take over the borrower's cultivation rights while extending the period for loan repayment. In this sense, land is still an important consideration for informal lenders even though it is seldom used as collateral. That cultivation rights may be pawned when borrowers are unable to meet their obligations gives the informal lenders a measure of protection against loan losses. Most lenders who enter into pawning contracts are farmers who either cultivate the pawned land directly or hire permanent workers to do it. Sometimes, the permanent workers hired are the original cultivators who pawned their rights.

Another collateral substitute widely used in Muñoz is the required sale of output to trader-lenders. The survey data showed that 106 out of 172 trader-lender loans carried this condition. Under this arrangement, borrowers agree to sell all or part of their paddy to traders at the prevailing market price during harvest time. The trader-lender subtracts the principal and interest due on the loan from the total value of paddy purchased from the farmer-borrower. By providing loans to farmers, traders try to assure themselves of secure rice supplies during harvest. On the other hand, farmers without post harvest facilities—especially storage and transportation—find these tied loans to be beneficial. Most borrowers believe that continual access to loans depends upon establishing their reputation as reliable *palay* suppliers to their trader-lenders.

The informational links that exist between different informal lenders and their borrowers are shown in Table 3. These relations are important because they partly shape the terms of credit contracts. Loans from friends and relatives dominated the informal credit transactions (116 and 135 loans, respectively), while farmer-lenders

TABLE 3. Number of Loan Transactions Classified by Lender Type and Borrower's Relation to Lender

Lender Type	Borrower's Relation to Lender[a]									TOTAL
	1	2	3	4	5	6	7	8	9	
Farmer/landowner	36	4	72	0	0	1	16	37	10	176
Private moneylender	27	0	0	0	8	8	2	6	34	85
Trader/middleman	22	2	29	35	20	25	12	15	13	173
Bank	0	0	0	0	0	0	1	0	20	21
Cooperative/miller	1	0	0	6	0	0	0	0	9	16
Retail store owner	6	0	18	8	0	0	2	0	12	51
Input dealer	8	0	0	1	1	0	0	2	3	14
Others	16	0	16	0	1	2	0	2	13	50
TOTAL	116	6	135	50	29	36	38	62	114	586[b]

[a] Codes: 1- friend; 2 - tenant; 3 - relative; 4 - regular customer in a related business; 5 - friend of a relative; 6 - relative of a friend; 7 - friend/relative of a regular customer; 8 - hired laborer/permanent worker; 9 - other;

[b] Total is less than number of reported transactions because of missing information on either variable in the cross-tabulation.

Source: Rural Informal Credit Market (RICM) Survey (1988), Agricultural Credit Policy Council (ACPC), Philippines.

made 108 loans to friends and relatives. This result is not surprising given the highly personalized nature of credit transactions and village social relations. Loans to tenants were negligible, but loans to hired laborers or permanent workers were quite numerous. These loans came mostly from farmer-lenders, or traders who were simultaneously engaged in farming. The actual numbers of loans to hired laborers could be higher. The problem is that production relations may be hidden under social or familial relations, and therefore are included in the friends and relatives category. It is not unusual for farmers to hire their relatives and friends if it reduces problems associated with labor shirking.

Most impersonal loans were made by private moneylenders, traders, and other sources. In general, these loans were either supported by third party guarantees, as indicated in the relations specified in Table 3, or were backed by some acceptable form of collateral substitute.

Informal Lender Specialization

The use of various forms of collateral substitutes in the informal credit market derives from the fact that the different types of informal lenders lend for diverse reasons. For the farmer-lender who extends consumption loans to landless laborers, the objective may be to elicit the optimal effort from the permanent worker, or to secure casual laborers during periods of peak labor demand. For the trader, acquiring the farmer-borrower's marketable surplus at harvest time is clearly the main motivation for lending. For lenders employing the pawning contract, the objective is to reap the gains from farming that modern technology and tenurial reform have provided. In all cases, collateral substitutes help enforce loan repayment and serve as screening devices through which borrowers are chosen. Lenders tend to specialize in lending to certain borrower classes according to the collateral substitute used.[2]

Another way of explaining informal lender specialization is to view farmers and traders as lenders with different financial technologies. The use of collateral or its substitutes entails a cost to lenders. In designing loan contracts, lenders will accept only those collateral substitutes in which they have a comparative cost advantage. Farmer-

2. Floro reached a similar conclusion in her study of credit relations and market interlinkages. She found that lenders sorted borrowers through the type of market interlinkage employed. Her sample, however, included only farm households.

lenders do not tie credit to paddy sales because they are not involved in trading. But they are engaged in cultivation and employ farm labor so cultivation rights and labor services are acceptable collateral substitutes.

As for borrower preferences, one can postulate a self-selection process. Borrowers are fairly familiar with the terms and conditions associated with the various credit contracts available from informal lenders in the village. They then choose a type of loan contract such that the probability is maximized of receiving a loan from the lender approached.

The likelihood of receiving a loan from a specific type of informal lender is a function of a vector of borrower characteristics and unknown parameters that can be estimated using econometric techniques. More specifically, it is hypothesized that trader-lenders will specialize in lending to farmer-borrowers, while farmer-lenders will be the principal credit source for landless workers. Furthermore, it is expected that the probability of obtaining a loan from either source is positively related to farm size because the borrower may choose to pawn his cultivation rights in the event of loan default.

To test these hypotheses, a single-equation logit model was estimated for trader-lenders and farmer-lenders using the maximum-likelihood method. The dependent variable is dichotomous, taking a value of 1 if the borrower received a loan from lender Y, and 0 otherwise. Explanatory variables are household type (TYPE), size of operating unit (AREA), household size (HHSZ), number of dependents (NODEP), and borrower's relation to lender (REL). TYPE and REL are binary-valued. TYPE is equal to 1 if the borrower is a farm household, and 0 if landless. REL is 1 if the relation between borrower and lender is personal (that is, friends or relatives) and 0 otherwise. Two separate equations were estimated. The first estimates the probability that a borrower receives a loan from a trader-lender; the second from a farmer-lender. Each of the two equations was estimated twice. The first estimation did not include REL as an explanatory variable, and the second did.

The results of the logit estimation are reported in Table 4. In the first set of regressions where REL is excluded (equations 1 and 3), the hypothesis regarding lender specialization toward borrower classes is only partially supported. Although both equations yielded the expected signs for the TYPE variable, the estimate was significant only for the farmer-lender equation. The variable AREA had the expected sign but was significant only for farmer-lenders. This is an interesting result which reinforces the conjecture that only those with a comparative advantage in farming will consider cultivation rights an attractive collateral substitute. In the second set of regressions, which includes REL (equations 2 and 4), the "specialization hypothesis" is generally supported as indicated by the signs and the relevant test statistics for the TYPE variable in both equations. The improvement in the reliability of the coefficient estimates for the TYPE variable when REL is included in both equations underscores the importance of information about borrowers that lenders consider prior to granting a loan. AREA still has the expected positive sign, but the inclusion of REL turns the farm size variable insignificant for the farmer-lender equation (equation 4). This result suggests that when the lender possesses additional information about the borrower, the borrower's ability to repay as reflected in the land area potentially available to be pledged no longer significantly influences the probability of obtaining a loan. Furthermore, the opposite signs for REL in the two sets of equations confirm the importance of personal and familial relations for farmer-lenders, while the relations of traders with their clientele are more commerical with an element of third party guarantee.

TABLE 4. Possibility of Receiving a Loan from Trader-Lenders and Farmer-Lenders Single-Equation Maximum Likelihood Logit Estimates

Variable	Trader-lenders		Farmer-lenders	
	(1)	*(2)*	*(3)*	*(4)*
Constant	0.9426	1.0136	0.41	0.3967
	(0.32)	(0.33)	(0.34)	(0.35)
TYPE	0.2379	0.4063	-0.5253	-0.8745
	(0.14)	(0.15)	(0.15)	(0.17)
AREA	0.0306	0.1680	0.2863	0.0580
	(0.10)	(0.10)	(0.13)	(0.13)
HHSZ	-0.2531	-0.2461	-0.0614	-0.0555
	(0.14)	(0.14)	(0.15)	(0.16)
NODEP	0.3120	0.2942	0.0417	0.0520
	(0.15)	(0.15)	(0.15)	(0.17)
REL	--	-0.4848	--	0.7056
		(0.11)	(0.11)	
Chi-square	286	358	242	277

Notes: Standard errors are in parentheses. -- indicates not calculated
Source: Field Surveys done in 1987-88

Conclusions

We have shown that the use of specific types of collateral substitutes in rural informal financial markets can be traced to the behavior of lenders and borrowers in other factor and product markets. This behavior leads to borrowers being screened according to the type of collateral substitute desired by the lender and offered by borrowers. The econometric results also reveal the importance of personal or family relations as an informational link between farmer-lenders and their borrowers. Moreover, if the rise in importance of trader-lenders is interpreted as indicating increasing commercialization, then the negative sign for the REL coefficient is consistent with the view that commercialization expands exchange relations beyond the circle of family and friends.

The preliminary nature of these estimates must be emphasized. Other variables such as default probability and loan size may influence the probability of getting a loan to the extent that they signal borrower riskiness. These variables were excluded because their inclusion introduces simultaneity issues not dealt with in this chapter. A more complete empirical model would include other explanatory variables that are jointly endogenous with the probability of receiving a loan from a particular source. Two-stage estimation procedures would be more appropriate in this case.

If the "specialization hypothesis" is sustained using more complete empirical specifications, the major implication will be that collateral substitutes lead to segmentation in rural informal financial markets. Segmentation occurs because the "screening technology" available to different lenders effectively determines which borrower types are more likely to be granted loans and, therefore, borrowers through a process of self-selection approach only certain lenders to apply for loans. Borrowers without the requisite collateral substitute demanded by an informal lender may be completely rationed out of loans from that particular source.

Specialization according to collateral substitutes implies that certain types of lenders have an advantage over others in lending to particular types of borrowers. This chapter shows that this advantage derives from the close association between the collateral substitute used and the relationship between informal lender and borrower in related factor and product markets. A farmer-lender who deals with landless households in the rural labor market has an informational advantage over a trader-lender in lending to landless borrowers. Similarly, farmer-lenders not involved in trading cannot use tied output sales as a feature in their credit contracts to attract farmer-borrowers and enforce loan repayment. On this basis, competition among informal lenders is likely to be limited to segments of the informal market in which each lender has access to the same screening technology. The nature of the collateral substitutes analyzed here implies investment in a long-term relation with the borrowing clientele. This investment becomes a potential barrier to entry for new lenders who might contribute to a greater volume of lending and lower interest rates.

Research on loan contracts in rural informal financial markets often is limited to a simple description of contract terms, frequently with an emphasis on interest rates. The research reported here goes beyond this by attempting to analyze the behavior of borrowers and lenders in multiple markets and to test how their behavior influences loan contracts. This type of research is necessary to improve our understanding of informal finance, and to draw implications from it for use in designing financial policies.

References

Benjamin, D. K. 1978. "The Use of Collateral to Enforce Debt Contracts." *Economic Inquiry* 16:333-359.

Bester, H. 1985. "Screening Versus Rationing in Credit Markets with Imperfect Information." *American Economic Review* 75:850-855.

Binswanger, H. P., and M. R. Rosenzweig. 1986. "Behavioral and Material Determinants of Production Relations in Agriculture." *Journal of Development Studies* 22: 504-539.

Floro, S. L. 1987. "Credit Relations and Market Interlinkage in Philippine Agriculture," Unpublished Ph.D. dissertation, Stanford, California: Stanford University.

Hayami, Y., and K. Otsuka. 1989. *Kasugpong in Central Luzon: Indianization of the Philippine Rice Bowl?* Los Baños, Philippines: International Rice Research Institute.

Nagarajan, G., and C. David. 1990. "Land Pawning Contracts: Evidence from Rice Growing Villages in the Philippines." Unpublished paper presented at the Seminar-Workshop on Rural Savings and Informal Credit in the Context of Financial Liberalization. Manila, Philippines: Agricultural Credit Policy Council.

Otsuka, K., and E. Marciano. 1988. "Permanent Labor Contract in Central Luzon: A Study on Tenancy and Labor Contracts Under Land Reform Regulation." Los Baños, Philippines: International Rice Research Institute.

Plaut, S. 1985. "The Theory of Collateral." *Journal of Banking and Finance* 9:401-419.

Rivera, F. T., and M. B. Mangalindan. 1987. *The Structures and Processes of Land Markets and Related Transactions and Arrangements in the Rice Industry.* Nueva Ecija, Philippines: Central Luzon State University.

Umali, D. L., and B. Duff. 1988. *The Rice Marketing System in the Philippines: Implications for Grain Quality Improvements.* Unpublished paper. Los Baños, Philippines: International Rice Research Institute.

Umali, D. L. 1987. *Rice Marketing and the Rice Price Stabilization Program: The Philippine Case.* Los Baños, Philippines: University of the Philippines at Los Baños, Laguna.

12

The Kou in Japan: A Precursor of Modern Finance

Yoichi Izumida[1]

Much of the recent literature about rotating savings and credit associations (ROSCAs) and on other informal savings and credit groups has focused on low income nations, and, as a result, it is increasingly acknowledged that these groups are a common form of financial intermediation in these countries (Bouman 1977). It is less well recognized, however, that these groups also earlier played an important role in nations such as Japan that now have modern financial systems. These groups are called *kou* in Japan and they were a popular form of financial intermediation, especially in rural areas, until the mid-1900s. Although most kous have now disappeared, Japan's experience with them provides interesting lessons for low-income countries that are struggling to modernize their financial systems—the most important lesson being that long and accumulated activities in informal finance can provide a foundation for modern financial development.

The objectives of this chapter are to describe the development of kous in Japan, and to discuss their influence on modern financial institutions, especially the rural credit associations and the urban mujin companies.[2]

1. The Japan Foundation provided support for the research reported in this chapter.
2. Credit associations were predecessors of present day agricultural cooperatives in Japan. In 1900, a cooperative system made up of industrial associations was established. These included rural credit associations and other types of cooperatives such as marketing associations and urban credit associations. Rural credit associations made up the majority of these organizations. It should be noted that the modern financial system created in the late 19th century in Japan was strongly influenced by preceding

The Term "Kou"

Kou is a simplified name for group savings and loan associations in Japan. Sometimes the more comprehensive terms of *tanomoshi-kou* and *mujin-kou* (or simply *mujin*) have been used with only slight differences in their meanings. Tanomoshi-kou connotes mutual help or helping the poor, while mujin-kou suggests money making or finance. In rural areas the term tanomoshi-kou has been more frequently used, while in urban areas the term mujin is more common. The original meaning of *tanomoshi* was reliable, trustworthy, or dependable, while the early meaning of kou was meeting or association for discussion. The origin of the term kou appears to have come from associations of monks who assembled to discuss Buddhism. In Buddhist literature the term mujin means the absolute, unlimited, and inexhaustible world. In ancient India one faction of Buddhism concluded it was not reasonable to waste temple offerings and that these offerings should be used for worthwhile purposes including supporting temples and lending to individuals. This was termed mujin-in-goods and this practice migrated to Japan. Over time, mujin came to be known in Japan as a lending institution of goods or funds. Gradually, securities such as mortgages and other guarantees were required on some types of mujin loans carrying interest (Zenkoku Sogo Ginko Kyokai 1971).

Kou in Japan

The oldest document referring to kou is dated 1275 A.D., suggesting that the kou system was introduced in the 12th or 13th century at the latest (Ikeda 1918). During this period pawnshops, called *mujin-sen* (mujin money), were also common. It is surprising how slight the basic structure of kou has changed from the 13th century to modern times. A kou contract written in 1345 A.D. describes this basic structure (Nippon Sogo Ginko 1967):

---

financial heritage. For example, merchant-landowner-finance groups contributed much to the formation of the modern banking system (Teranishi 1982; Patrick 1967). The early influence of kous on small business finance and agricultural cooperatives is also noteworthy.

1. Members made a written contract at the first meeting and agreed to abide by the rules of the kou.[3]
2. Members had the obligation to pay a certain amount of money at each meeting, except when they received the fund. If a member who had not received a fund did not fulfill all the obligations of being a kou member, he or she lost the right to draw a fund. Members who had received funds, and later defaulted on their obligations, suffered compulsory exclusion from the group and were also punished as criminals.
3. Rotation of the fund was determined by lot.
4. Members who had received a fund had no right to receive additional drawings. To guarantee that they continued to pay into the fund, members were sometimes required to obtain two cosigners who were members of the association.
5. Members met two or three times a year.
6. After all of the members had received a fund, the kou might be disbanded.

These ancient rules are similar to modern kou rules with some important changes. By the 14th or 15th century rotations in some kous were determined by bidding rather than through drawing lots, and kous including property mortgages had appeared. In the Edo Period (1603-1867), kous were common in both rural and urban areas. Some farmers were reported to use kou funds for operating expenses or investments (Mori 1982). While estimates of the total volume of funds moving through kous are not reported, some authors mention funds valued in thousands of units of gold. Especially in kous operated by merchants, the total value of the fund and the frequency of meetings increased during the Edo Period. The number of *oya-nashi-kou* (kou without a parent—those set up not to help a particular individual) was reported to have increased in urban areas.

Kou was also popular in samurai (warrior) society. Some feudal clans attempted to use a form of kou as a fiscal instrument to fund public expenses (Mori 1982). These clans tried to improve their financial position by mobilizing money through kou. Various new forms were also invented during the Edo Period, including arrangements whereby the fund as well as share payments varied in amounts. Also, in this period new methods of transferring rights in kou, buying and selling shares in kou, and kou mortgages were established. These financial innovations laid the foundations for later mujin-companies in urban areas. Still

---

3. Almost all kous had their own contracts, but not all were written. Various case studies suggest that until the Meiji Restoration kous with recorded contracts were rare.

another innovation was the gambling kou called *torinoki-mujin* in which members did not pay further into the mujin after winning a fund. These appeared in many urban areas, especially in conjunction with temples. Later, lotteries were based on these gambling kous.[4]

To illustrate the kou system in the Edo period, it is useful to describe a typical example from a village near Osaka. This kou was formed to help a farmer named *Oya* (the parent). It was started in 1721 and ended in 1732. The kou involved a total of 11 members with one meeting per year. The total value of the fund was one thousand units of money. Oya, who had a urgent need for a relatively large amount of money, received the first fund. After the first meeting the rotation of the fund was determined by bidding. Several early bidders won the fund after offering discounts of nearly 20 percent in the payment required of each member who had not earlier won the fund. In the latter stages of the rotation bidders offered no discount.

Two interesting points stand out in this case. First, the original purpose for organizing the kou was mutual help, but after the first meeting the kou took on the function of intermediating between those who wanted to receive the fund early—borrowers—and individuals who received the fund late—depositors. The ratio of total payments made to the kou by individual members, to funds received, ranged from 0.47 to 1.54. The ratio of the second and third receiver of the fund—who needed funds urgently—were fairly high. On the other hand, the members who received the fund in the 8th through the 11th position— individuals who were effectively depositors in the kou—received relatively high returns on their savings. This kou served two functions: mutual help for an individual (Oya), and financial intermediation for the other ten members.

Kou in the 20th Century

During the Meiji Period several modern financial institutions were formed but informal lenders continued to provide the bulk of the financial services. According to Asakura (1961), the total amount of disbursements from pawnshops alone exceeded those of banks in 1880. Reports from various branches of the Central Bank of Japan described the importance of kou in 1910 as follows: In Kyoto Prefecture, there were 985 registered kous, and members numbered 149 thousand

---

4. Gambling activities created social problems for some individuals who were lottery losers, so the government prohibited them during some periods.

individuals. In Fukushima Prefecture it was reported there were about 4,000 kous, and in Hiroshima 22,376 kous with 3.9 million yen in kou funds (Central Bank of Japan 1961b).

A survey of farm household indebtedness conducted in 1911, uncovered interesting features about kous (Table 1). First, the amount of debt from institutional sources for the average borrower was higher than from informal sources. The average amount of debt from kous and other similar associations was only about 75 yen, which was about one-third of the average debt from formal lenders. This showed that kous were handling relatively small loans and deposits. Second, the study also showed that interest rates on kou loans were generally less than

TABLE 1. Sources of Farm Household Debt in Japan in 1911

Source	Value of Debt (million yen)	Number of Borrowers (1,000)	Average Debt per Borrower (yen)
Formal source	231	945	244
Special financial institution[a]	77	89	861
Other banks	131	495	265
Insurance companies	1	3	213
Industrial associations, etc.[b]	22	358	61
Informal sources	518	6,843	75
Money lenders	151	1,300	116
Pawnshop	10	1,048	9
Merchants	12	284	43
Kou and similar associations	63	1,050	60
Relatives, friends, etc.	270	2,925	92
Other non-institutional sources	12	236	51
TOTAL	749	7,788	96

[a] Government banks: the Japan Hypotec Bank, the Agricultural and Industrial Bank, and the Hokkaido Colonial Bank.
[b] Industrial associations were cooperative type institutions, including credit associations, established in 1900.
Source: Ministry of Finance, *Survey on Farm Household Indebtedness,* 1912. (This survey did not detail debts from landlords. Their role was quite significant until the land reform after World War II.)

those charged by other informal lenders (moneylenders, pawnshops, and merchants), but higher than those charged by formal lenders. Third, unlike most formal lenders, kous and other similar informal institutions in rural areas usually did not use mortgages. The kou relied on mutual trust and informal sanctions to ensure loan repayment.

In 1915 a survey provided nationwide statistics on the mujin. Although this survey was not a census, it did strongly suggest that kous and mujin were important in most parts of the country. Further information on the importance of the kou was provided by a survey of tanomoshi-kou published in 1935 (Table 2). This survey was done by the Ministry of Agriculture through asking city, town, and village officers to report on tanomoshi-kou activities in their units. About 83 percent of these administrative offices reported information for 1934. According to the survey, there was at least one kou operating in almost 75 percent of the cities, towns, or villages. On the average, there were about 40 kous in each unit with an average share value per individual subscription of 20 yen. The proportion of kous designed to help a single individual was higher in towns and villages than in cities, which suggests that mutual help kous were quite important in rural areas. The durations of kous were quite diversified but, judging from the fact that the proportion of kous with duration of more than one year was dominant, showed kous were involved in fairly long-term finance. The fact that 90 percent of the kous were money-kou showed the relatively high degree of monetization in Japan at the time, even in rural areas.

TABLE 2. Characteristics of Japanese Kous in 1934

	Urban	Towns and Villages	Total
Number of Kou	13,320	285,774	299,094
Average number of kou per each unit of administration	162	40	41
Share of kou with parents (%)	36	68	66
Average value of fund for one kou (yen)	n.a.	n.a.	427
Average value of subscription per account (yen)	n.a.	n.a.	20

Note: n.a. means information not available
Source: Ministry of Agriculture, *Survey on Tanomoshi-Kou.* Tokyo, 1935

From this survey the Ministry of Agriculture estimated there were about 350 thousand kous in the country, involving 5 million people. Since this survey was done during the Great Depression and during a time of intense stress in the formal financial system, it may somewhat overstate the importance of informal finance in more normal times.[5]

No information is available on the uses of loans from kou, but some use indication can be drawn from the names applied to various kous (Table 3). Since almost every kou has a name, such as horse-kou, savings-kou, and so on, the name of the fund gives some hints about the motivations for peoples' participation. As can be seen in Table 3, kous were organized for a variety of purposes. Kous were formed not only for economic purpose, but also for recreation, religious, and social purposes.[6] As Geertz (1962) described, the kou is more than a simple economic institution. "It is a mechanism for strengthening the over-all solidarity of the village." (p. 251).

Because of fungibility it is difficult to determine the precise use made of loans even when borrowers explicitly state their reasons for borrowing. Still, as is shown in Table 3, it is likely that kous provided funds mainly for long-term purposes and had less to do with short-term financing or operating expenses. There may be several reasons for this. Originally kous were based on small geographic areas with most of the members living in the same village. As a result, their short-term and seasonal needs for funds were often similar. Thus, it was not possible for kous to adjudicate short-term demand and supply of funds in a small area. Although institutional short-term loans were available in many regions from credit associations, these loans were mainly used by large farmers or landlords. In addition, it was possible for kous in Japan to have a long cycle because there was relatively little inflation in the country from the Meiji Restoration in 1868 to the late 1930s.

In the last several decades most kous in rural areas have disappeared. In the 1950s, several surveys still showed a few kous operating in rural areas, especially in outlying areas such as Okinawa and mountainous villages of Nagano, Yamanashi, and Gifu. However, the importance of the kou in the country diminished so much that the

---

5. According to the Survey on Farm Household Indebtedness done by the Ministry of Finance, the share of kous in total farm household debts was about 8 percent in 1912. Later surveys done by the Ministry of Agriculture showed the share of kous in farm debt growing to 17 and 18 percent in 1935 and 1942, respectively.
6. According to the field survey by Kawashima and Watanabe (1944), the most important reason for participation in traditional kou was to have a feast at the kou meeting. Finance had a secondary meaning for them.

Japanese Farm Household Economy Surveys conducted after 1963 did not collect information on them.

TABLE 3. Classification of Kou and Correspondent Names of Kou

Criterion	Function	Name of Kou
For help or not	For help	Oya Kou (association with parent)
	Not for help	Oya nashi Kou (association without parent)
By purpose	Help, or aid	Insurance-Kou, Mutual-Help-Kou, Relief-Kou, Charity-Kou
	Savings	Savings-Kou, Installment-Savings-Kou
	Finance	Finance-Kou
	Purchase of goods	Fertilizer-Kou, Bedding-Kou, Roof-Kou, House-Kou, Tatami-mat-Kou, Tile-Kou, Shoes-Kou, Umbrella-Kou, Horse-Kou, Bull-Kou
	Public interest	Public-interest-Kou (Construction of well, bridge, etc.)
	For friendship or solidarity	Same-age-Kou, Women's-Kou, Same Area-Kou, Fuji-kou
	Religion	Ise-Kou (Ise is a famous shrine), Kannon-Kou (Kannon is Goddess of Mercy in Buddhism)
Money or in kind	Money	Money-Kou
	In kind	Rice-Kou
Quantity or value of subscription	10-yen-Kou, 20-yen-Kou, 200-yen-Kou	20-Koku-Kou (Koku=150kg. of rice)

Source: Kawashima and Watanabe (1944); Embree (1939); Yamaguchi (1935); Ikeda (1918); Tsuda (1916); and Ministry of Finance (1915).

Strengths and Weaknesses of Kous

Around the turn of this century, researchers and policymakers became concerned about the contribution of kous to development and how they related to modern financial arrangements. Several researchers examined roles and problems of existing financial institutions and the government sponsored various surveys of kous. This resulted in a number of publications during this period on the mujin or tanomoshi-kou that evaluated the reasons for their existence, their roles, and their strengths and weaknesses (Table 4). These publications stressed three particularly important strengths of kou: easy access for farmers, savings promotion, and relatively low interest rates.

Easy access for farmers came from the small size and location of kous close to members. Also, members knew each other through tight social relationships and this made kous reliable and secure. These factors resulted in very low transaction costs for members and few loan defaults. Members generally made every possible effort to pay their subscriptions and rare defaulters even went so far as to flee if they were unable to meet their kou obligations. For people in rural areas it was virtually unthinkable to default intentionally on a kou obligation.

As for promoting savings, it is clear that kous facilitated savings. Further, the system was important in educating people to save by linking savings and borrowing. Many members participated in kous and saved in order to have the opportunity to borrow sometime in the future. Through this process, members learned the important lesson that deposits and loans are closely linked and, therefore the need for discipline.

Interest rates in kou were generally higher than those charged by institutional lenders, but less than those charged by many sources of informal loans. This relatively low rate of interest was supplemented by low transaction costs between borrowers and depositors, incurred through membership in the kou. Interestingly, some kous had rules that set interest rate ceilings or set maximum values on bids for the fund. These ceilings resulted from a feeling that extremely high interest rates were destructive to group solidarity.

While kous have obvious strengths, they also have weaknesses. Their first weakness is size. Because of the small number of individuals involved and the limited geographic area that a kou covers, each kou can only play a very limited role in reallocating resources among surplus and deficit units in a society. Also, it is difficult for kous to provide the high degree of liquidity that many individuals desire for their savings. Finally, many people desire to keep their personal financial transactions private which is difficult in a kou.

TABLE 4. Strengths and Weaknesses of Kous

Strengths	Everybody knows what a kou is because of its long history and popularity
	It is easy to organize a kou
	It is easy for ordinary people to participate
	It encourages savings
	Kou has interest rates that were lower than those charged by pawnshops and moneylenders
	Members can borrow long term with amortization repayment
	Generally borrowers need not offer mortgages
	It makes use of mutual help spirit
	In case of kou, debts are not a shame for fund-receiver
	It helps stimulate speculative spirits
	There are opportunities for all participants to get loans
Weaknesses	Kous are easy to organize, but this sometimes makes them vulnerable in times of economic stress
	Levels of interest rates vary widely, depending on bidding
	Rates of interest are sometimes high
	Members not always able to receive funds at the time of need
	Legal relationships are not well established and disputes are difficult to resolve
	Sometimes an organizer swindles members
	Unexpected receiver of funds may waste the money
	In the complicated forms of kou, it is difficult for members to calculate interest rates

Source: Yui (1935); Ikeda (1918); Tusda (1916); and Ministry of Finance, *Survey on Mujin* (1915).

Formation of Mujin-Companies

While the history of the kou is interesting to study, it is perhaps more important to understand how kous contributed to Japan's current financial system. This contribution can be divided into urban and rural segments. In rural area kous facilitated the development of the highly successful farmers cooperatives. In urban areas the contribution occurred more directly in the form of mujin-companies, which have evolved into modern financial institutions.

Initially, mujin-companies appear to have grown out of arrangements where an individual or merchant was managing, on a commission basis, several associations at one time. One publication during the Edo period describes the selling and buying of kou accounts by these commission agents and also mentions one man who managed 220 kous (Zenkoku Sogo Ginko Kyokai 1971). Obviously, this tended to occur mostly in urban areas where it was possible to organize a number of kou in a relatively small area. In the process of transforming these informal organizations into formal ones, the main problem was how to determine creditworthiness of members and to establish some measure of mutual trust in the groups. Mori (1982) pointed out that some finance-oriented kous had at least one member who was a rich merchant or landlord (usually they also were moneylenders). Participation of important people was regarded as a way to enhance the creditability of the association. In some cases, these prominent people obtained special privileges such as being the first person to receive the kou fund or by receiving a commission. Actually, many merchants became the organizers of mujin-companies and in effect guaranteed the payment of kou members who may have had little or no contact with other members.

It should be noted that many merchants and landlords were involved in other forms of informal finance. Merchants did commodity financing, while landlords make loans to tenant farmers. Lessons learned from these traditional activities were applied in the mujin businesses (Teranishi 1982).

According to the Survey of Mujin in 1915, the first mujin-company was established in Tokyo in 1901 with a capital of 10 thousand yen. By 1912 this company had grown to 27 branches with capital of a million yen. Stimulated by the success of this company, many similar institutions were rapidly formed with the number growing to 1,151 by 1913. There were several reasons for their popularity. First, in those days ordinary people and small businesses lacked access to formal finance. Second, mujin-companies offered clients advantages not found in common kous. In a traditional kou system if a member wanted to withdraw from a kou it was sometimes necessary for the individual to receive permissions from all other members. Occasionally kous collapsed because of the default of one member. In mujin-businesses, other members could still get loans from the companies even when a few members defaulted. Third, their allocative efficiency increased because they could increase the size of transactions. They handled mutual installment loans and savings, and organized a number of accounts into one group. Rotations of loans were determined by lot, by bidding, or by some combination. Their business was not based on mutual trust of participants, but on reputation of the company. One mujin-company could manage multiple associations simultaneously. According to the Survey of Mujin in 1915, one mujin-company handled 17 rotating associations, of which the average number of accounts varied from 50 to 60. Thus the total transactions of one company could be much bigger than was the case in traditional mujin.

Early in their development some of the mujin-companies were not completely responsible. A few companies cheated members by secretly enrolling their staff members in the association. The employee was then scheduled to be the first receiver of the fund. Other companies broke up just after collecting the subscriptions from the first meeting. Still, the fact that this form of informal finance continued to grow strongly suggests that the demand for these services provided by mujin companies was relatively strong.

To reduce chances for abuse, mujin-companies were institutionalized under the Mujin-Business Act in 1915. The main contents of the act were:

1. Mujin-companies were required to obtain a license from the Minister of Finance;
2. Minimum capital requirements were established for these companies;
3. The name of the companies should contain the term of mujin;
4. The companies were prohibited from having any side business;
5. The business area of one company was fixed;
6. The use of mujin funds was limited to loans to members, deposits in banks or post offices, and investments in securities;
7. Employees of the company were prohibited from being members of kous administered by the company;
8. Companies were required to file regular reports with the Ministry;
9. Government audits were imposed on the companies.

In short, the companies were regulated and thus became part of the formal financial system, and the highly personalized features of the traditional kou largely disappeared in urban mujin. Mutual help was no longer a feature of the mujin.

With the Act, many traders sought registration, and about 300 of them formally applied for licenses. Of these applicants only 158 received licenses and the remaining operators of mujin-companies had to liquidate their activities.

Mujin Mutual Loans and Savings Banks, currently found in Japan, are direct decedents of mujin-companies. After the enactment of the Sogo Ginko Law in 1951, mujin-companies were converted into Sogo Ginkos. They have been classified as financial institutions for small business. Nowadays their business is almost the same as ordinary private banks. Recently some of these institutions have attempted to convert themselves into regular banks.

These banks offer a special variant called a mutual installment contract (pseudo-mujin), where no group is organized. Account holders who pay installments for a certain period of time borrow money, or have the use of the funds whenever they want. Presently Sogo Ginkos occupy a normal position in the Japanese financial market with about a 5 percent share in outstanding personal savings. Their number was 69 with 4,279 branches at the end of 1985.

Kous and Rural Credit Associations

Kous also strongly influenced the formation of rural associations that dealt with financial activities. But, unlike the direct evolution of urban kous into mujin-companies, the influence of the rural kous was more subtle and less direct. Prior to the 1940s Japan had three types of institutions providing financial services in rural areas: Private banks, specialized financial institutions, and credit associations. The specialized institutions—mostly established in the 1890s—provided mainly medium- to long-term loans on mortgaged collateral. They received many forms of privileges from the government and their businesses were closely regulated. By and large, tenants and small farmers were unable to borrow from these special banks and were forced to use informal loans.

After a long discussion in the National Diet, the Industrial Association Law was enacted in 1900 that led to the formation of industrial associations, the majority of which were credit associations in rural areas. These associations embodied much of the traditional spirit of mutual help found in the traditional kou, which was also captured in the philosophy of Ninomiya Sontoku (Ishiguro 1987)[7]. Long before this legislation was enacted, widespread and long-term participation in kous had schooled rural people in the value of group activities, cooperation, the benefits of saving, and the need to repay loans long before this legislation was enacted (Yokoi 1909). Through widespread participation in kous, most of the rural people in Japan had learned the discipline that is a prerequisite for successful financial intermediation; the formal cooperative structure simply gave them an opportunity to exercise that discipline in a broader institutional framework.[8]

The performance of these credit associations has been truly remarkable. Over the period of 1905 to 1925 the number of credit cooperatives in the country rose from only about 600 to over 12,000 Over time, most farmers in Japan joined these associations and the deposit and loan activities became the economic foundation of these associations.[9] Other figures on performances of credit associations also show the success of these associations. Currently, the agricultural cooperatives in Japan, which developed from credit associations after the War, have been very successful in providing financial services to farmers, as well as other related activities. The Norinchukin Bank, the apex bank of agricultural cooperatives in Japan, has grown to be one of the largest banks in the world.

Conclusions

The history of informal finance in Japan is long and rich in detail. While the kou has largely disappeared from the hustle and bustle of current day Japan, its influence can still be found in the genes of some of

---

7. It is interesting to note that the formation of credit associations in Japan was heavily influenced by early German experience with Raiffeisen cooperatives.

8. Kato (1985) and Saito (1973) have made interesting observations about the role of landlords in this process. They pointed out that the local landlord was a major factor in helping to set up and manage many of these credit associations. Unlike the experiences in many low income countries, the landlords in Japan did not absorb most of the loans. This may have been due to the fact that interest rates on loans were not concessionary and most of the funds spent were from local deposits rather than from government funds.

9. It should be noted that during the period from 1905 to 1925, interest rates in credit associations were not regulated by government, which seems to be one factor in their early success.

its offspring: the mujin-companies and the agricultural cooperatives. The discipline involved in saving, repaying loans, and making loans on the basis of creditworthiness trace many of its roots to the kou heritage.

The most important feature of the Japanese experience with the kou is how it influenced formal financial institutions that evolved to provide services for the common person. The financial services provided by the credit associations and the mujin-companies were logical extensions of the kou, built on its strengths, and were seen as indigenous rather than alien institutions by common people. In addition, in no point in its history did the Japanese government try to destroy the informal financial system or to create an economic environment in which it could not operate and evolve. Extensive regulation, especially in the form of low interest rates, was never one of the major policy instruments exercised in Japan.

What lesson might be drawn from the Japanese experience with kou that would be timely for policymakers in low-income countries and employees of donor agencies? Perhaps governments and donors ought to take a more careful look at the existing system of informal finance and attempt to build on that system, rather than trying to destroy it.

References

Asakura, Kokichi. 1961. *History of Financial Structure in Japan during the First Half Period of the Meiji Period* (in Japanese), Tokyo: Iwanami-Shoten.

Bouman, F. J. A. 1977. "Indigenous Savings and Credit Societies in the Third World: A Message." *Savings and Development* 1:181-218.

Central Bank of Japan. 1961. "Survey on Mujin-Companies" (in Japanese) reprinted in *Documents of Financial History in Japan*. Vol. 25. Tokyo: Central Bank of Japan.

Embree, John F. 1939. *Suye Mura - A Japanese Village*. New York: Black Star Publishing.

Geertz, Clifford. 1962. "The Rotating Credit Association: A 'Middle Rung' in Development, " *Economic Development and Cultural Change* 3:241-263.

Ikeda, Ryuzou. 1918. *Actual State of Mujin and its Theories* (in Japanese), Tokyo and Osaka: Daisyokaku.

Ishiguro, Tadaatsu, ed. 1987. *Ninomiya Sontoku: His Life and Evening Talks* Tokyo: Kenkyusha.

Kato, Yuzuru. 1985. *Agricultural Development and Programmed Finance* (in Japanese), Tokyo: Gakuyushobo.

Kawashima, Takenori, and Yozou Watanabe. 1944. "Kou Custom and Village Life" *Hogaku Kyokai Zassi* (Journal of Association of Law) 62:5-9 (in Japanese).

Ministry of Agriculture. 1935. *Survey on Tanomoshi-Kou* (in Japanese). Tokyo: Ministry of Agriculture.

Ministry of Finance. 1912. *Survey on Farm Household Indebtedness* (in Japanese). Tokyo: Ministry of Finance.

————. 1961. "Survey on Mujin 1915" (in Japanese). Reprinted in *Documents of Financial History in Japan*, vol. 25, Tokyo: Central Bank of Japan.

Mori, Kahee. 1982. *Dissertation of Financial History of Mujin*, Works of Mori Kahei vol. 2. Tokyo: Hosei University Press (in Japanese).

Nippon Sogo Ginko Nenshi Hensanshitu (Editorial Team for the History of Nippon Sogo Bank). 1967. *History of Nippon Sogo Ginko* (in Japanese). Tokyo: Nippon Sogo Ginko.

Patrick, Hugh T. 1967. "Japan 1868-1914." In Rondo, Cameron, ed. *Banking in the Early Stages of Industrialization*. London: Oxford University Press.

Saito, Hitoshi. 1973. "Japanese Agricultural Cooperatives in the Beginning - with Special Reference to Organizational Aspects," (in Japanese). In Takigawa, Tsutomo, and Saito, eds., *Agricultural Cooperatives in Asia* Hitoshi, Tokyo: Institute of Developing Economy Publisher.

Teranishi, Juro. 1982. *Japanese Eonomic Development and Finance* (in Japanese). Tokyo: Iwanami-Shoten.

Tsuda, Takeo. 1916. "Research on Tanomoshi-Kou (1), (2) and (3)" (in Japanese), *Sangyo Kumiai* (Industrial Association), March, April and May.

Yamaguchi, Asataro, "Research on Tonomoshi-Kou in Iki (1), (2)" (in Japanese), *Syakai-keizai-sigaku (Science of Social and Economic History)*, Vol. 5.

Yokoi, Jikei. 1909. "First Attempt for Credit Associations was Kou of Our Country," (in Japanese). *Sangyo Kumiai* (Industrial Association), January.

Yui, Kennosuke. 1985. *Tanomoshi-Kou and Its Legal Relationship* (in Japanese). Tokyo: Iwanami-shoten.

Zenkoku Sogo Ginko Kyokai (National Association of Mujin of Mutual Loans and Savings Banks). 1971. *History of Mujin of Mutual Loans and Savings Banks* (in Japanese). Zenkoku Sogo Ginko Kyokai.

13

Pawnbroking and Small Loans: Cases from India and Sri Lanka

F. J. A. Bouman and R. Bastiaanssen

Over the past several decades governments and donor agencies have funded numerous credit programs directed at small rural enterprises in low-income countries. Few of these programs, unfortunately, have been successful in providing sustained lending to poor people. In part these programs stumble because they often encounter high costs and loan defaults. Pawnbroking is a form of finance that overcomes these problems and provides small, short-term loans to millions of poor people. A clearer understanding of how pawning operates and the services it offers may provide insights into how to strengthen credit programs that are trying to lend to people operating in penny economies. We attempt to add to this understanding by describing pawning activities in one area of India, Sangli, and in Sri Lanka.

Moneylending in a Penny Economy

Formal lenders face severe challenges in penny economies. Sales in these markets are atomized; bananas and cigarettes are sold singly rather than in bunches or packets, melons and pineapples in slices, sugar in lumps, and fertilizer in baskets or kerosene tins. Houses are built or improved in stages. Money transactions in such economies are equally small, very frequent, and are measured in pennies and dimes rather than in pounds or dollars. Loans associated with these transactions are likewise small and short term; a few rupees may be borrowed in the morning to be repaid with interest in the evening. Such transactions are not attractive for banks because of the prohibitively high costs of collecting enough information on prospective borrowers of small amounts to establish their creditworthiness and to provide a high degree of assurance that loans will be repaid. Most banks are also forced to charge low interest rates on small loans that further discourages them from lending to poor people.

As an example of this, consider the plight of an average Indian rural bank that is directed to give priority to serving the economically weak sector of the economy. The annual fixed costs of such a bank are about Rs 60,000 (US$4,100). This includes office expenses, salaries and allowances for its two loan officers: a teller and a clerk, the minimum staff to handle business. With a spread of four percent as profit margin, which is not unusual in India, this bank needs at least a loan volume of Rs 1.5 million (about US$100,000) to cover fixed costs. This does not allow for any loan defaults. In the mid-1970s loans made by the Regional Rural Banks of India, set up specifically to serve poor people, averaged Rs 835 per account (Shetty 1978 p. 1,443). Even when put at Rs 1,500 (about US$100) per account at present to account for inflation, the two loan officers in a typical rural bank need to process 1,000 loans per year—that is 500 each—to achieve the necessary lending volume of Rs. 1.5 million. To build this kind of loan volume, the loan officers would need to extend credit with only cursory attention to creditworthiness, which, in turn, would exacerbate loan recovery problems that are already chronic in India.

Viable financial intermediation in a penny economy requires techniques that overcome the twin obstacles of small volume and loan recovery risks. Pawnbroking has overcome these obstacles for ages.

Private and Public Pawnhouses

Pawnbroking is probably the oldest method of lending. It is mentioned in the *Old Testament* and existed in ancient Babylon, Athens, and Rome (Melles 1950, p. 2) where one could pledge almost anything, including slaves, women and children, even one's own labor, in exchange for goods or money. Private pawning had a lively and, at times, a turbulent history in Europe between the 13th and 18th century. Pawning has also been a popular form of borrowing in Asia since the dawn of history. Nowadays the most popular form of pawnbroking is by pledging gold, jewels, and precious stones. Pledging land and even trees, however, are still important forms of pawning in many low-income countries.

Particularly in Europe, private pawnbrokers (and moneylenders in general) were pictured as being evil Scrooges, and public-spirited citizens and the clergy in Europe championed public pawnshops run by the state or municipality. The first municipal shop in Europe appeared in Germany in 1198, and in France and Italy in the 14th Century (Schwed 1975, p. 24). In the Netherlands, the City Council of Amsterdam opened the first "Municipal Loan Bank" in 1614 (it is still in operation), followed by Rotterdam in 1635. In 1642 and again in 1650, some of the English crown jewels were pledged at the Rotterdam pawnhouse as surety for a loan. The jewels were never redeemed and eventually the pawnhouse sold them at a loss (Melles 1950, p. 71). The Provident Loan Society, a nonprofit pawnshop in New York, opened its doors much later in 1894. It made history in the 1930s when it was offered the famous Hope diamond to pay for the ransom of the purported kidnapper of Lindbergh's son (Schwed 1975, p. 50).

One of the differences between public and private pawnhouses is that, after the contractual loan period has expired, the public lender must put the unredeemed articles up for public auction. If the auction results in a higher price for the pawn than the original loan sum plus interest and auction cost, the "profit" can later be claimed by the original owner-pledger. Private houses do not normally hold public auctions. To curb the supposed malpractices of pawnbrokers, many countries have enacted legislation to restrain their activities. However, this has seldom resulted in abolishing the private pawnbroking business.

In Europe and North America pawnbroking declined and almost disappeared after the 1940s when consumer credit, personal bank accounts, and overdraft facilities became widely available. But recently there has been a revival in pawning, probably because of the phenomenal increase in the price of gold in the 1970s. The new interest in pawnhouse lending has also sparked a revival of private pawnshops that have become, besides a point of lending, a place for the sale and resale of goods in a number of countries. During a recent stay in Brisbane, Australia, the first author noticed many private pawnshops doing a brisk business. Owners of (sometimes superfluous) commodities seemingly preferred to sell to a pawnshop, probably because they expected a fair price by asking for a loan (that they do not intend to repay), or to avoid unpleasant and embarrassing haggling over the price when selling to dealers in the secondhand market.

Advantages of Pawnbroking

A pawnbroking arrangement is a sale-repurchase arrangement between lenders and borrowers that is attractive to both parties.

No credit relation, in fact, exists in a typical pawn contract. The pledger sells, as it were, his pawn for a certain sum below the going (appraised) market value and retains the right to buy it back within a specified time by returning the original sum borrowed plus interest. If he does not, he will lose his property, but no further debt exists and hence no ever-increasing debt load (Bouman and Houtman: 1988, p. 73).

Pawnbroking is attractive to the lender because lending on pledged sureties reduces risk and transaction costs, the transaction taking only the time necessary to appraise the value of the pawn. There is no need to assess a client's creditworthiness. Pawnbroking, therefore, allows the lender a much larger circle of borrowers and greatly increases his loan volume potential, thus eliminating a stumbling block for lending in a penny economy. Likewise, there are no costly legal procedures such as registration of mortgage deeds to protect against default. Seizure of the pledged item is unnecessary because it is already in the lender's possession. If the borrower does not redeem his pawn, the broker may sell or keep it for himself. These conditions allow the pawnbroker to charge lower interest rates than are usually charged on unsecured informal loans.

Pawnbroking is attractive to the borrower because of speedy processing, low transaction costs, and reasonable interest rates. Borrowers do not need to make repeated visits to a bank to deal with its embarrassing bureaucracy. Neither do they need to bribe an underpaid secretary of a village cooperative to produce a favorable decision on their loan applications. Borrowers also avoid incurring additional obligations such as buying from or selling produce to lenders. The borrower simply sells an item to the pawnbroker on the condition that he will buy it back within a specified time for a higher price.

Popularity of Pawnbroking

In Asia the pledging of gold and other valuables has long been popular among rich and poor people who have saved in valuables and gold.

Unlike the coins and banknotes of an individual country, precious metals and stones have universal worth. They have a high degree of liquidity because they can be sold or pledged almost anywhere...Further, jewelry offers emotional satisfaction and bestows status on the wearer; valuables also function as a hedge against inflation, while bank funds are eroded by it. Gold and stones have a high value in relation to their bulk and are easy to hide, transport and negotiate. This is important in times of natural disaster, war or social unrest. (Bouman 1989 p.72).

Pawnbroking is usually for short periods—one to six months—which suits participants in a penny economy. Peak times in pawnbroking in Sangli District, India, for example, are during the marriage months March through May; at the end of Ramadan, the Muslim fasting period; or at the beginning or near the end of the crop cycle when money is needed to meet farm expenses or to bridge the season of food scarcity.

Curiously, the widespread popularity of informal pawnbroking is not shared by lawmakers, public administrators, development planners, and social workers. Nor has it attracted the attention of many researchers or the banking community. Public opinion on pawnbroking is usually infected by moral indignation. In many countries pawnhouse credit has, therefore, come to be regarded as something that only the government should do and legislation is often enacted to curb and control the activities of the private broker. The negative view of private pawnbroking is in contradiction with customers' preference. Pawnhouse credit is not an expression of poverty in Asia; it is much more accurate to explain it in terms of a continuing and growing popularity of saving in the form of gold. People have a choice of putting their savings into a bank account and subsequently withdrawing them when needed; or to save in gold, jewelry, and other valuables and occasionally pledging these items for loans.

The reasons for such behavior is investigated in the two following case studies of pawnbroking in Sri Lanka and India. Expanded versions of these studies have been published elsewhere (Bouman 1989; Bouman and Houtman 1988; and Bastiaanssen 1986). They show that, despite unfavorable legislation and attempts to curb and control their activities, private pawnbroking is very much alive.

Pawnbroking in Sri Lanka

As in other Asian countries, gold and jewelry in Sri Lanka is a popular form for savings. These objects, in turn, are often pledged to pawnbrokers for a loan. Pawnbroking and moneylending were largely done by private individuals in Sri Lanka. Agricultural smallholders traditionally obtained loans from Indian Chettiars who acted as intermediaries between the colonial commercial banks and rural customers (Bouman and Houtman 1988, p.76). Their prominent role ended after the country gained independence in 1947. Soon after, banks were given access to easy refinance and insurance facilities in order to provide cheap loans to agriculture and other priority sectors.

The results of this cheap loan policy were disastrous. Banks were subjected to immense political pressure by subsequent administrations, each competing for the support of the masses through credit handouts. In 1978, for example, 81 percent of the agricultural loans were not repaid (Bouman and Houtman 1988, p.77), and this forced the government to abandon its policy of cheap credit. As a result, without access to cheap refinancing and guarantees against bad debt losses, bank lending to risk-prone enterprises came to a virtual standstill; formal crop loans fell from Rs 365 million in 1977 to Rs 21 million in 1979/80.

Pawning in the Peoples' Bank

The Peoples' Bank (PB) was the first institution in Sri Lanka to face the challenge of rural mass lending by providing pawning services. Established in 1961 as the main government agent providing rural loans, it had 90 rural banks in its network in 1970 and this expanded to 840 by 1983. As early as 1964, PB branches started to offer pawnbroking facilities to compete with the informal market. In 1970, PB branches processed a total of 28 thousand loans of which 18 thousand or 64 percent were based on gold pledging. By 1983 the PB's 840 rural banks were making 315 thousand pawn loans, which was over 80 percent of the PB's total loans in that year. The average size of these loans was only slightly over Rs. 700 (about US$40).

The PB attempted to distinguish between loans for production and consumption, and kept its loan sizes between Rs 500 and 5,000, with lower limits for consumption loans. In agricultural economies, however, the distinction between production and consumption is blurred; the policy of targeting loans only led to unnecessary bureaucracy, to the annoyance of the public. The very advantages of pawnbroking, its low risk and transaction costs and non-monitoring of loans, are thus reduced. Probing for the use to be made of a loan causes congestion at the bank's windows that compounds the lack of experienced appraisers of valuables among bank staff. A further inconvenience was that banks opened late in the morning and closed early in the afternoon and on weekends. Customers looking for discretion and speedy processing often turn, therefore, to private pawnshops that offered almost round-the-clock service.

Private Pawnbroking in Sri Lanka

Private pawnbroking has a long history in Sri Lanka. Under the Pawn Brokers Ordinance, officially recognized brokers have to register and pay taxes, which for some moneylenders was a reason for going underground. The main effects of the ordinance have been inconvenience to the public. There are now two types of private pawnshops: registered and unregistered. The first pays the required 2 percent Business Turnover Tax (BTT) to the treasury, but passes this tax on to its customers. The second type does not pay taxes, but charges higher interest rates than before to account for the extra risk of operating illegally.

Despite these cost problems, both registered and unregistered pawnshops still draw a large clientele because of their superior service. First, they are more accessible to the public than are banks. They conduct business from early morning to late at night, enabling customers to do their pawning discretely. Most lenders combine pawnbroking with a jewelry shop. This makes them experienced appraisers of valuables and shortens the time to settle a loan transaction.

Second, private pawnbrokers offer loans of up to 50 percent of gold value on pawns and rarely put a limit on loan size, which are more advantageous terms than those offered on pawns by banks in Sri Lanka. Unregistered brokers may even go to as high as 80 percent, and this is especially attractive to borrowers who need a lot of money on short notice. In the relationship between borrower and lender, confidence is the essential element to assure a large loan. New and occasional borrowers rarely receive more than half of the pawn's market value, but this still is twice the rate offered by the PB. Some registered pawnbrokers charge 5 percent interest per month and pay the tax themselves. Most unregistered brokers charge 7 percent per month, while escaping the 2 percent BTT. These rates are much higher than those charged by the PB and are probably the reason why private loans

are redeemed so quickly; 50 percent within two weeks, the other half
within two months. But despite the competition of the rural banks, the
private brokers conduct a brisk business. In two case studies, the loan
volume by private pawnbrokers was 12 to 18 times as large as that of
the average rural bank (Bouman and Houtman 1988, p. 81).

Pawnshop Economy in Sri Lanka

Little information is available on profitability of formal
pawnbroking. Differences in banking policy and procedures determine
performance and loan volume at each bank. According to central bank
statistics, the average rural bank in 1980 had 380 outstanding pawn
loans of Rs 400 each, or an average outstanding balance of Rs 152,000
(Bouman and Houtman, 1988 p. 84). Research carried out by the PB
indicates that about half of PB branches operated at a loss in 1980
(Siriwardena 1981, p. 1). This was mainly due to the high default rates
on other, more conventional agricultural loans. The other half of the
banks managed to make some profit; according to the same report, these
profits originated from the positive financial result of pawnbroking
(Siriwardena 1981, p. 2). There is no better proof of the viability of
pawning facilities. Rumors of alleged huge profits made by private
pawnbrokers persist in Sri Lanka. These rumors were not confirmed in a
study in 1981 of two such pawnshops, one registered, the other
unregistered (Bouman and Houtman, pp. 82-83, 89). The registered
pawnshop in Kandytown had an annual turnover of Rs 3 million and a
32 percent return on capital (assuming the broker worked with owned
funds only). This return is only 10 percent above the 22 percent interest
reward on a two-year savings deposit with the PB.

An unregistered pawnshop-cum-jewelry store in Colombo had an
annual turnover of Rs 2 million. The owner's return on capital of 70
percent is considerably higher. But one should bear in mind the extra
risk involved in illegal pawnbroking and the possibility of closure and
extraction of bribes by officials. Another feature of illegal pawnbroking
is refinancing with a registered pawnbroker, the latter requiring a
commission of 1 to 2 percent for this service. Moreover, this particular
broker, besides working with owned funds, borrowed funds from friend
and banks at 2.5 to 4 percent a month. This access to outside funds
increased his turnover, but also reduced average net returns on lending.

Pawnbroking in Sangli District, Maharahstra, India

Pawnbroking has also been a popular form of lending for centuries in India. In Sangli, a semi-arid region, pawnbroking is generally not seen as a disreputable profession. Like in many other countries, the early moneylenders in the district were outsiders, originating from Rajasthan, Gujarat or still further west. When locals later joined in, a network developed of professional and large moneylenders—locally known as Savkars—refinancing smaller operators. Both categories advanced money against gold, jewelry, and other valuables.

When the cooperative sector (from the 1960s onward) and the commercial banks (from the 1970s onward) started to grow in number and importance, the private moneylenders lost part of their market share and the Savkars gradually left the district. Their function of refinancing small lenders/pawnbrokers was partially taken over by the commercial banks.

Since the 19th century, national and state governments in India have passed laws in an effort to restrict the activities of informal finance. The Bombay Agricultural Debtors Relief Act of 1939 was the first in a series of acts affecting settlement of agricultural debts. Other acts followed. Moneylenders had to register and follow prescribed lending procedures and keep proper records for inspection. The Maharahstra Debt Relief Act of 1975 arbitrarily scaled down farmers' debts with private moneylenders, who in some cases had to return pledged collateral without compensation. This official crusade against private lenders caused a number of them to go out of business, leaving a void in pawnbroking services that was particularly inconvenient for poor people. The Reserve Bank of India attempted to fill the vacuum by allowing cooperative institutions to enter the pawnbroking business. In terms of loan volume, institutional pawnbroking nowadays probably outweighs private pawnbroking.

In general, gold advances are more common in rural than urban banks in India. Banks offer pawn loans from 50 to 70 percent of the market value of gold pledged. Loan size varies between Rs 100 and Rs 50,000; banks usually maintain a minimum loan amount of Rs 100 to 300. Extremely large pawn loans are supplied by commercial banks that serve traders and private moneylenders repledging their own clients' pawns with the bank. Although such refinancing is not authorized by the Reserve Bank of India, it is very profitable for banks.

Prospective pledgers, who turn to a bank that has no trained appraiser, are forwarded to a nearby jeweler-cum-pawnshop for appraisal of the pawn's value. When this same jeweler comes to the bank to repledge his own pawns, the bank can hardly refuse a reciprocal service.

The average common pawn-loan amount in Sangli is estimated between Rs 500 and Rs 3,000 (Bastiaanssen 1986, p. 25). Usual interest rates are between 16 and 18 percent annually for both cooperative and commercial banks. These rates are the main attractions of institutional pawnbroking; private brokers charge higher rates. Generally, pawn loans mature after six months, but are then renewable. Around 25 percent of borrowers repay within three months, 70 to 75 percent within six months, 90 to 95 percent within one year, and 5 to 10 percent of borrowers extend their loans beyond one year.

As in Sri Lanka, many pledgers turn to private pawnbrokers because of superior service, despite the lower interest rates charged by banks. Banks keep inconvenient opening hours from 10:30 a.m. to 3:30 p.m. Further, banks that have no trained appraiser forward borrowers elsewhere to get a valuation report. Thereafter, clients of the bank are faced with an avalanche of forms to fill; up to ten for a single transaction. These procedures take time, patience and result in additional cost. If all charges for valuation fees, costs of forms, insurance, stamp duty, and so on are added, total transaction costs may represent up to 5 percent for a loan of Rs 1,400. This greatly reduces the relative advantage of lower interest rates of the formal sector when only a small loan is needed.

The private registered pawnbrokers employ much less bureaucracy, although they are subject to government inspection and regulation of interest rates. Inspection, however, is only superficial and actual interest rates always exceed the prescribed ones. Most licensed pawnbrokers are gold traders, jewelers or goldsmiths who lend almost exclusively against gold. The typical urban pawnbroker is male, belongs to the middle- or upper-class, and is normally well respected in the community.

Despite the growth of formal banking in the district, Sangli recorded a large increase in the number of registered moneylenders, from 183 in 1965 to 250 in 1974. But the Debt Relief Act of 1975 caused many of them to close shop; in 1985 only 95 moneylenders took a license. Most operate in the urban centers. It is unknown whether the overall scale of private lending has decreased as well.

Even in pawning, the lender-borrower relationship relies on trust. New customers usually need a recommendation from a third party plus proof that their pawns are not stolen. Mediation on behalf of newcomers by middlemen, known to both parties, is still a common practice. Secretaries of village cooperative societies often play the role of mediators. Some urban moneylenders employ agents in the countryside on a commission basis. Regular customers, on the other hand, with a reputation of timely repayment, may eventually become entitled to a personal loan without depositing valuables as security.

Private lenders do their own appraising and advance between 75 and 90 percent of the pawn's gold value, the higher advances applying to reliable and regular borrowers. Interest rates, too, depend on the strength of the relationship between the two parties. The Reserve Bank of India has prescribed a set of rates between 9 and 18 percent but these are very unrealistic when pawnbrokers themselves have to pay 17 percent when repledging with banks, or more when borrowing capital elsewhere. This forces the pawnbrokers to manipulate rules and records. In reality, effective interest rates are 2 to 3 percent a month for a gold advance, small and short-term loans may carry higher rates. These rates are consistent with those observed by other researchers in India as noted by Bouman (1989, p. 91).

Despite the higher interests rates compared to those prevailing in the formal market, private pawn operators attract many customers. As in Sri Lanka, this is largely due to superior service. Compared to the one hour or more spent at a bank to negotiate a pawn loan, while other loans may take days or weeks, in a private pawn loan the transaction is completed in about ten minutes.

Low transaction costs are particularly attractive to borrowers of small sums. The average pawn loan in Sangli varies between Rs 500 and Rs 1,500, but extremes occur on both sides of the scale. Some lenders specialize in large loans, like those who refinance fellow pawnbrokers, while other people may handle loans as small as Rs 50.

The number of licensed moneylenders in Sangli may have decreased after 1975, but a new class of moneylender has emerged: the part-time, small-scale operator, who is refinanced by licensed moneylenders. Civil servants, traders, teachers, and employees of sugar factories have taken up pawnbroking without a license. They have regular incomes and access to banks as well, which enhances their role as lenders. In Sangli, this phenomenon was very marked in Ramenandnagar, a small and new industrial town, where work foremen did lending after factory hours as a sideline. They catered to a limited clientele and accepted articles other than jewelry and gold as pledges.

Type and performance of these informal pawnbrokers vary considerably and are dictated by social factors on the one hand—as with lending to relatives and friends—while others operate on a predominantly commercial basis. Especially in the risk-prone semi-arid zones of the district, where little formal credit is available, there is a great need for informal credit. From the study in Sangli the impression was gained that five to ten informal moneylenders (both male and female) operate in each community that has at least 2,500 villagers. Their numbers appeared to be growing at the time of the study, which may be due to the spectacular rise in gold price in India. Elsewhere in the district, the introduction of irrigated cultivation and improved agricultural technology have stimulated farmers to invest in and profit from new crops and activities: sugarcane since 1960, followed by grapes, betel, rose gardens, and dairy development. This caused a rise in loan demand that was met by pawning previously hoarded gold objects. The resulting boom in the formerly dormant economy started in the irrigated areas, spread outward to other regions and occupations, bringing employment, albeit often part-time, and higher incomes to many people. This, in turn, caused a rising demand for consumer goods, even from poor rural households, and increased borrowing from informal sources.

Unlicensed pawnbrokers tend to serve clientele at the lower end of the income spectrum. The informal moneylender must be very sure of the reliability of the borrower, as his operations are illegal and therefore vulnerable. There is always the danger of confiscation of pawns by police whenever a discontented debtor registers a complaint. Consequently village pawnbrokers restrict their lending to within their own community.

Part-time pawnbrokers not only accept gold, but also silverware, copper and brass pots, clothing, and objects of emotional value. Loan rates depend on the lender-borrower relationship rather than on the market value of pledges, and range from 5 to 10 percent a month. Each transaction has its own particular circumstances that dictate loan terms. In a few cases, some lenders take advantage of borrowers with urgent credit needs.

Unlicensed pawnbroking is both expensive and risky. Loans are small and short term (two to four months only); pawns must be stored and guarded and, other than gold, may lose market value quickly. Finally, the illegal broker faces fines and punishment when caught. A high rate of interest, therefore, is by itself insufficient proof of exploitation.

Pawnshop Economy in Sangli

Data on the profitability of institutional pawnbroking in Sangli are not available. Some banks may accept few pawns and some cooperative institutions accept no pawns at all. Other individuals have turned pawning into a specialization that presumably must be rewarding. We collected data on the profitability of a moderately frequented private, registered pawnshop in the area of study. As in the foregoing two Sri Lankan case studies, figures are partly based on extrapolation. The pawnshop studied had an annual turnover of Rs 390,000 on 300 gold advances. Annual return on capital is calculated at approximately 20 percent. Compared to the 12 percent available on a fixed deposit with a bank; this return was not exceptionally high.

Compared to the two Sri Lankan case studies, the figures are much lower, both on the debit and credit sides. Pawnbroking, however, represents only a part of the moneylending done by the individual pawnbroker studied. He also did personal and mortgage loans. Moreover, for many shops, pawning is only a sideline to its main activity, the regular gold trade.

An estimation of profitability of illegal village pawnbroking was of little use. It is only a part-time activity with low turnovers and there is no uniformity at all in operations. But despite its risks, profits appear sufficiently high to attract new brokers into the market.

Conclusions

Lending to small rural enterprises in developing economies faces two major obstacles: risk and volume. These cannot be overcome by raising interest rates on mini-loans, nor by use of conventional banking procedures. There are simply too many loans required to obtain a lending volume that covers a typical bank's overhead when lending must be largely focused on poor people. Paradoxically, the instrument that satisfies all the conditions of quick and safe procurement of loans has been available since early history, pawnbroking.

Compared to other modes of lending in a penny economy, pawnhouse loans are attractive to both lenders and borrowers because of speedy processing, low transaction costs and interest rates and the fact that they involve no obligations beyond a simple sale-repurchase arrangement. In both Sri Lanka and India, registered as well as unregistered pawnshops are booming. In India, the price of gold behaves independently from the world market and has climbed continuously since 1946. This has made saving in gold—and hence pawnbroking—more attractive. Pawnhouse loans are not an expression of poverty in Asia, but rather indications of the popularity of gold and valuables as a savings device.

In both the formal and informal financial sector pawnbroking was a viable business. In villages and small rural towns there are many new entrants into the market of private pawnbroking. Profit margins appeared to be reasonable and there were few signs of malpractice. We found the negative official opinion of private brokers unfounded in both countries, and antagonistic legislation counterproductive, causing inconvenience for the public.

Formal finance can effectively compete with informal operators only through improved institutional performance. The lessons from our research suggest that banks might consider having separate and discrete pawning windows.

References

Bastiaanssen, R. 1986. "Pawnbroking in Sangli District." Unpublished M.Sc. thesis. Wageningen, Netherlands: Agricultural University of Wageningen.

Bouman, F. J. A. 1989. *Small, Short, and Unsecured: Informal Rural Finance in India*. Dehli: Oxford University Press.

Bouman, F.J.A. and R. Houtman. 1988. "Pawnbroking as an Instrument of Rural Banking in the Third World." *Economic Development and Cultural Change* 37: 69-68.

Melles, J. 1950. *Het Huys van Leeninge, Rotterdam, 1325-1950*. The Hague, Netherlands: Nijhof.

Schwed, P. 1975. *God Bless Pawnbrokers*. New York: Dodd, Mead and Co.

Shetty, S.L. 1978. "Performance of Commercial Banks Since Nationalization of Major Banks; Promise and Reality." *Economic and Political Weekly* Special Number, August: 1407-1451.

Siriwardena, S. A. L. 1981. "Financial Markets in Sri Lanka and the Pawning Service of the People's Bank." Unpublished paper, Colombo: Research Department of the People's Bank.

14

Strengths of Informal Financial Institutions: Examples from India

C. P. S. Nayar

In spite of the phenomenal expansion of a variety of formal financial institutions that are supposed to replace the "outmoded and exploitation-infested" informal financial agencies, the latter's popularity is on the rise in India. Is this due to the operational weaknesses of the formal sector, or to the inherent strength of the informal sector? To answer this question one has to examine the operations of both formal and informal institutions.

At the outset it should be remembered that India's informal financial system is broad in coverage, with an organizational structure that includes both corporate and noncorporate forms. There are many types of financial institutions, formal and informal, in India. I confine my discussion to the major types, namely commercial banks in the formal sector and chit funds (ROSCAs), nidhis, hire-purchase finance institutions, and finance corporations in the informal sector.[1] The data on banks used in this study are from published reports by the Reserve

---

1. The term informal finance requires some clarification in India. Some of the institutions—chit fund companies, nidhis, hire purchase finance companies, leasing companies, loan companies, investment companies, and housing finance companies— that are here termed informal are incorporated under the Companies Act 1956 and also fall under certain rules/regulations of the Reserve Bank of India or are covered by specific acts. In most states, professional moneylenders are also licensed. These institutions are semi formal financial institutions. There are forms of informal finance that do not come under government regulations. Prominent among them are finance corporations, indigenous bankers such as Gujarati shroffs, Multanis, Marwaris, Rastogis and Chettiars, various types of nonprofessional moneylenders who extend commodity credit and tied credit, and relatives and friends.

Bank of India (RBI), and an unpublished evaluation study. Information on informal sector finance came from published and unpublished research done by various researchers. However, when the operational details of the two sectors are compared, one should keep in mind the fact that the operations of commercial banks, including interest rate fixation for both deposits and loans, liquidity requirements, and credit-deposit ratio are controlled by the RBI while those of the informal sector institutions are generally free of any such control, although most of them are covered under different acts of government and rules of RBI. Before examining the loan related operations of the informal sector financial institutions, it is useful to describe the workings of the four informal institutions mentioned above.

Chit Funds (ROSCAs)

Chit funds are conducted by companies, partnerships, and sole proprietorships and they are found throughout India. Of late the accent has been on a company form of organization. The salient features of a chit fund, also known as kuri, or chitty or chit may be summarized as follows. A promoter (foreman) of a chit fund collects a specific periodical (usually monthly) subscription from each of a specified number of subscriber members for a specified period. In each monthly installment, the total subscriptions of all members, called the capital of the chit fund, minus a commission of 5 percent given to the foreman, is given out as the prize amount to one of the members selected by lot or auction in rotation. All members must contribute the period subscription until the end of the specified period. As the number of subscriptions (installments) and the number of members are equal, and one member can take the prize only once during the chit period, each member has a chance to receive the prize amount (For details of working of chit funds, see Nayar 1973, 1984, 1986, and 1987; and Radhakrishnan and others 1975).

Certain aspects of chit funds make them different from other financial institutions. For example, traditionally, a chit fund has been viewed as a poor man's institution for accumulation of savings. The merit of a chit fund is that it encourages the poor households to save for a rainy day. The investment of accumulated bits of savings in gold, jewelry, or household utensils or in a goat or a cow by one household through a chit scheme is a sufficient inducement for a nearby household to join a chit. This is particularly so in the case of women who manage household affairs and the poor people who cannot easily acquire assets through other means.

A unique feature of savings in a chit fund is that there is a mild form of compulsion involved. Deposits in a bank, post office, or other institutions are voluntary. After opening an account in any of them, the account holder is not bound to make deposits regularly, even in a recurring account. A recurring deposit can be discontinued before the stipulated period at the will of depositors who receive back the amount in their account at the time of closure. But the position in a chit fund is different. Once individuals become a member of a fund, they must subscribe the stipulated amount regularly and compulsorily during the entire period of the chit. If they discontinue after a few installments, they will not receive the amount subscribed before the end of the chit period (previously, before the enactment of any legislation, they used to lose it altogether). The obligation to pay the subscriptions is so strong that, at times, subscribers may postpone or even cancel other routine expenditures. Sometimes they may borrow to pay the subscription in time and repay the debts afterwards. Thus, there is a self-imposed obligation on the part of the subscribers of chit funds to save.

Another major attraction of a chit fund is that it allows the subscribers to take the total subscriptions, partly paid and partly yet to be paid, in advance. More than anything else, it is this facility for immediate realization of future savings in a lump sum that induces many people to participate in chit funds.

In an auction or business chit, the eligible (nonprized) members meet at every auction date to take the prize amount if the competition in bidding is relatively small or to raise the discount if the competition is stiff. In either case a competitive discount (or interest) rate emerges. The competition is, however, limited to the members. No outside party or outside action is involved in either boosting the rate or depressing it. The chit fund foreman is neutral in the interest rate fixation. It is the borrower who fixes the rate of interest on the loan. What distinguishes a chit fund from other financial arrangements is that it is the only financial institution that allows a borrower to fix the rate of interest on loans.

Nidhis

An indigenous financial institution commonly found in South India is a nidhi, often called a mutual benefit fund or permanent fund. Nidhis are limited companies incorporated under the Companies Act 1956 and its earlier version. Their objective is to promote the habit of thrift among members and to provide loans to them at reasonable rates of interest against the security of gold, jewelry, house, or other real estate. Services are extended only to the shareholder members. Considering the unique nature of their organization, namely, restriction of business to shareholders only, they are governed by special provisions under section 620 A of the Companies Act. Devised to cater to some specific requirements of people in the middle- and low-income categories, they generally keep the face value of their shares very small, often as small as one-tenth of a U.S. dollar.

Nidhis are managed by a board of directors elected by the shareholders at the annual general body meeting under the principle of one person one vote. After the initial issue of block or bulk shares to the promoters and their relatives and friends, other members generally buy just one share.

As the face value of shares of nidhis is very small, share capital does not represent an important source of funds. The shares are not offered to the public through public issue. People take a share of a nidhi when they want to transact business with it, either as a depositor or borrower. With a single share members can make any number of transactions and they can also transfer their shares to other persons. Thus, even when there are thousands of shareholder members in a nidhi, the total share capital remains a relatively small sum.

The major source of nidhi funds is deposits from members. The deposits include savings, recurring, fixed, and cumulative (cash certificates). Generally, fixed deposits form a major part of total deposits. According to a survey of 12 nidhis, their deposit mix consisted of fixed deposits (67 percent), recurring deposits (13 percent), cumulative and cash certificates (14 percent), and savings deposits (6 percent) (Das-Gupta, Nayar, and Associates 1989). Members are not permitted to have current account deposits with nidhis. Most nidhis transfer a major part of net profits to reserves.

Loans occupy the major item in the use of nidhi funds. The borrowers from nidhis are mostly middle- and lower-middle income people and consist of housewives (25 percent), salaried class (20 percent), businessmen (15 percent), pensioners (25 percent), and others (15 percent) (Das-Gupta, Nayar, and Associates 1989). The purposes of borrowings are personal consumption, renovation/expansion of buildings, purchase of real estate, investment in business, and repayment of other costlier debts.

For various categories of deposits, nidhis offer about 3 to 8 percentage points higher interest rates than the prevailing rates in commercial banks. The interest charges on nidhi loans vary in general from 18 percent for a jewelry loan to 23 percent per annum for a landed property loan. The calculation is on a simple interest basis and applies only on outstandings balances. The effective jewel loan rate of nidhis is slightly lower than the jewel loan rate of commercial banks under private ownership.

Hire-Purchase Finance Institutions

These hire-purchase finance institutions are everywhere in the industrialized and non-industrialized world and they are also common in India. The common form of organization is a company that extends finance for the purchase of goods and vehicles and then recovers the principal and interest in installments over a period of time. The companies have systematized their operations including the calculation of hire charges, which are generally on a flat rate basis. In India, the Hire-Purchase Finance (HPF) companies finance mainly the purchase of commercial and other vehicles of not older than three to five years. Banks also extend finance for new vehicles, but not on a hire-purchase basis. They extend loans on the security of the vehicle that is hypothecated to them.

There is another category of less formal hire-purchase finance institutions in India. These are either partnerships or proprietary concerns. They specialize in financing the purchase of old vehicles with low prices per unit. They are known in different parts of the country as auto finance corporations. Their sources of funds are equity funds, deposits from friends and relatives and to a small extent refinancing from banks. They pay interest to their depositors at 18 to 21 percent per annum, almost double the rate paid by banks.

The hire charges of these institutions are about three to six percentage points higher than those of HPF companies. This is because of the high risk involved in financing very old vehicles that are prone to frequent breakdowns. The present hire charges vary from 15 percent to 20 percent flat rate, giving an effective interest rate of 30 percent to 40 percent per annum, depending on the condition of the vehicle and the reputation of the hirer. As these institutions finance vehicles with no standard quality and low resale value, there is no uniformity in hire charges between different institutions or between different transactions of the same institution.

One distinguishing feature of lending by these auto finance corporations is that the bulk of their finance flows to the poorest category of borrowers among transport operators. The well-off transport operators who can afford to invest a sizeable sum of their own seek credit for the purchase of new vehicles from banks or companies. The credit requirement per new vehicle comes to about US$10,000 or more. Against this, the average credit requirement of a used vehicle comes to US$2,000. Again, in the case of a well-off category, the demand may sometimes be for more than one vehicle at a time. Thus the lender's resources are used by a few relatively rich borrowers. On the contrary, as the per borrower finance of the auto finance corporations does not exceed US$2,000 to US$2,500, they are able to serve about 4 to 5 times more borrowers with the same amount of funds.

A study showed that 90 auto finance corporations in a relatively small town called Namakkal in the State of Tamil Nadu in India had financed 1,080 vehicles involving amounts of more than US$2 million in 1986 (Das Gupta, Nayar and associates 1989). The organized sector comprising banks and HPF companies which also operate in the area was much less important, having financed only 30 vehicles. These auto finance corporations supply a mode of transport for goods mostly in the countryside and provide a means of livelihood for thousands of drivers, helpers, and cleaners.

Finance Corporations

A finance corporation is a financial intermediary set up to make a profit from the business of lending money raised by way of deposits or borrowing (Nayar 1982). It may be a proprietary concern, a partnership firm, or a limited company. The most common form, however, is a partnership firm registered under the Indian Partnership Act, 1932. The initial funds for the operation of a corporation are contributed as share capital by the partners who may or may not be related to each other. Besides this contribution they may deposit their money with it and also solicit other deposits.

In deposit mobilization the corporations offer stiff competition to the commercial banks. They accept current savings, recurring and term deposits, and pay interest at rates almost double, sometimes even triple, the rates offered by banks. The corporations' policy in this regard is governed solely by the supply and demand for funds.

It is in lending that the corporations move ahead of banks through innovations. In constrast to an inflexible pattern of lending by banks, the corporations have introduced novel schemes such as 100-day loans, daily loans, very short period (1-7 days) loans with interest liability only for the actual days of the loan, and loans against very old and used vehicles.

The 100-day loan is a best seller among the variety of loans the finance corporations offer. Generally, they carry the following conditions: interest is collected in advance; the loan period is 100 days; and the loan amount is repaid in 100 installments at the rate of 1 percent per day, the first installment falling on the 2nd day and the last day of the 101st day when the loan is fully repaid.

Corporations currently charge a rate of interest of 10 percent. This is for 100 days and the effective rate on a principal of say US$900 (US$1,000 loan minus advance interest of US$100) works out to 41 percent per annum. But the repayment of loans in equal installments reduces the effective loan period to half and doubles the rate of interest. Under such a situation, the rate of interest in the example cited comes to more than 80 percent per annum. One more point to note is that under this scheme of lending the corporations make many loan transactions with a given deposit amount, by making loans out of loan repayments. In a cycle of 100 days, the sum raised through installments of loans made out of an initial deposit of US$1,000, amounts to US$1,692, and including the initial deposit, the total loan transacted comes to US$2,692. If there are three cycles in a year, the total loan transactions amounts to (US$2,692 x 3) US$8,076, eight times the size of the initial deposit (Nayar 1982).

Another popular loan is extended from one day to a week in which the calculation of interest is on a daily basis. The ruling rate is 0.1 percent. Interest for five days on a loan of say US$5000 comes to US$25. If the same loan were from a commercial bank, the rate of interest would be much lower, say 15 percent per annum. But the bank would charge interest for a minimum period of 15 days and also impose various transaction costs on the borrower. The interest works out to US$31.25 for 15 days. Had the borrower who wanted the loan only for 5 days borrowed from a bank, he would have thus paid US$6.25 (US$31.25 - US$25.0) more, in spite of the fact that the corporation charged a higher rate than the bank. One good effect of charging interest on the exact days of the loan is that the borrower will return the loan amount without keeping it idle even for a day. If it were a bank loan, the borrower may keep funds idle or put them to less productive use for 10 more days, because the borrower's cost is the same for up to 15 days. In effect, he blocks the loan from flowing to the most efficient use for 10 days.

There is also a daily loan system in which small sums up to US$1,000 are lent in the morning and recovered in the evening. These loans are taken by vegetable vendors, fish mongers, flower selling women, and other people and are usually lent on market days, which may be one or two days in a week. The current rate of interest is US$2 to US$5 per US$100 per day, which will work out to 720 percent to 1,800 pecent per annum. Still the borrowers take the loan because the interest cost is less than the return on the investment. From the lenders' point of view such loans are risky and involve high recovery cost. Banks do not extend such loans.

Efficiency in Financial Intermediation

Table 1 presents data on four major informal financial institutions that mobilize deposits from households. Data on chit fund companies, mutual benefit fund companies, and HPF companies are collected in RBI surveys. RBI data also include housing finance companies, loan companies, and investment companies in the category of nonbanking companies. I excluded these three because housing finance companies and loan companies are mostly operated with government funds with little involvement of household savings. Investment companies operate in the formal sector confining their activities to trading and investment of shares, although a few of them handle household deposits.

The growth of deposits in the four major informal institutions does not show much slackening during the 10-year period after 1976. These institutions almost kept pace with the growth in deposits in the formal sector as can be seen in columns 7 and 8 of Table 1. It must be noted that the number of bank branches rose from 18,730 in 1975 to 52,936 in 1986, bank deposits increased from US$9,627 million in 1975 to US$70,310 million in 1986 (650 percent increase), and bank loans increased from US$5,890 million in 1975 to US$43,926 million in 1986 (646 percent increase). It is all the more important to note that a major part of this expansion took place in the rural and semi-urban areas where the informal financial institutions were active. Yet, as the figures in Table 1 show, the banks are not able to dislodge informal finance institutions from their business. In other words, people still want the services provided by informal finance. What is it that fastens customers to these informal financial institutions?

Generally, the efficiency of operations of a financial intermediary is judged, among other things, by (1) the speed with which it transacts business, (2) the distribution of credit to many borrowers rather than a few, (3) by the rate of return offered on borrowed funds, (4) by the rate of interest charged on loans, (5) by the intermediation cost, (6) by the

TABLE 1. Deposits in Selected Informal Financial Institutions in India, 1975-86

	US$ Millions					Percent per Annum	
1	2	3	4	5	6	7	8
Year	Chit Fund Companies (subscription)a	Nidhi	Hire-purchase Finance Companies	Finance Corporations	Total	Annual Growth of Deposits in Informal Sector	Annual Growth of Deposits in Banks
1975	26	16	32	233	307	n.a.	n.a.
1980	117	22	73	522	734	33	18
1986	551	59	223	1,202	2,035	22	18

a The annual turnover in chit funds should be 12 times higher than the figures shown in column 2 because what is given is the stock figure at the end of March.

Notes: Figures are rounded off. Rupee figures are converted to US$ at the 1986 March exchange rate of US$=Rs 12.5; n.a.= Information not available.

Sources: Columns 2, 3, and 4 are from "Growth of Deposits with non-Banking Companies," RBI Bulletin, various issues. Column 5 C.P.S. Nayar (1982); C.P.S. Nayar (1984); and prior to 1979 and from 1984 figures are derived using the growth rate given in a., column 8 (all scheduled bank data) from Report on Currency and Finance, RBI Bulletin, various issues.

rate of loan recovery, (7) by the promptness with which the borrowed funds are returned, and (8) by the package of services offered to clients.

If empirical evidence is any guide, the informal financial institutions are more efficient than the banks in respect to 1, 2, 3, 6, and 8 mentioned above, as efficient as the banks in respects to 4 and 5, and a little less efficient in respect to 7 (7 is only in the case of finance corporations).

The major attraction of all informal financial institutions is their speed in transacting business. Scrutiny of loan application, evaluation of property, and verification of title deeds are completed normally within a week for real estate, and the loan will be released immediately thereafter. A loan against fixed deposit receipts and other movable property will be completed within minutes. The banks, on the other hand, may take about three months to process the application for a loan to buy a vehicle for which immovable property is offered as additional security. Borrowers will be lucky if they get even a jewelry loan within hours of submission of a loan application to a bank.

Survey data on size of loans show that the average loan amounts were as low as US$1,020 in the case of finance corporations, US$1,600 in the case of nidhis, and US$976 (amount per chit) in the case of chit funds. Only in the case of HPF companies was the amount financed higher, at an average rate of about US$8,000. Here again, the finance per vehicle of the noncompany sector was low at around US$3,200.[2] The evidence clearly shows that these institutions help small businesses and small borrowers and depositors (Das-Gupta, Nayar, and Associates 1989).

Data on interest rates paid on borrowed funds and charges on loans by the informal and formal sectors show that the informal financial agencies are at least as efficient as banks (Madhur and Nayar 1987).

I analyzed the earnings and expenses of finance corporations and commercial banks in another study (Nayar 1982) and found that: (1) Administrative expenses form only 1.9 percent of deposits of finance corporations, while they are 3.5 percent of deposits for banks; (2) finance corporations spend as much as 2.2 percent of their deposits on fund raising (whereas the banks get deposits without incurring much financial cost, often through direct and indirect governmental support); (3) profit as a percent of earnings is significantly lower for finance corporations (5.3 pecent) than for banks (9.3 percent). This is because a larger part of earnings of finance corporations is given as interest to the savers. The interest paid on deposits and borrowings as a percentage of

---

2. Exchange rate in March 1986 was rupees 12.5 per U.S. dollar.

earnings of finance corporations was 75 percent against the corresponding percentage of 60 for commercial banks. Broadly speaking, these findings suggest that informal financial institutions are more cost effective in financial intermediation—in mobilizing and deploying funds—than are commercial banks.

Informal financial institutions especially show their superiority over the formal financial institutions in loan recovery. While almost all informal financial institutions have a very high rate of loan recovery, the banks are faced with the chronic problem of overdues, particularly in small loans. A recent study on district credit plans (Nayar 1987) that covers the overdue position of commercial banks in four selected districts of Tamil Nadu and Kerala highlights this point.

> Without exception, all the four districts showed very high overdue percentages (i.e., overdues as percent of principal and interest dues) in each of the four years under review. Among the public sector bank branches in 1985, ten out of 19 branches in Coimbatore District, five out of 8 branches in Pudukottai District, five out of 10 branches in Palghat District and 8 out of 11 branches in Trivandrum District had overdue percentages above 50 percent.

Against this huge overdues position of a representative sample of bank branches in South India, it is interesting to compare the overdues position of the informal financial sector. For chit funds, field data show that "bad debts formed about 7 percent of total chit transactions. However, 25 percent of the institutions did not report any bad debts, although there were overdues in some cases" (Das-Gupta, Nayar, and Associates 1989). For nidhis overdues were practically nil (Ramani 1986; and Nayar 1982, 1984). "None of the selected nidhis has reported any bad debt" (Das-Gupta, Nayar, and Associates 1989). The same source comments on finance corporations. "Data on defaults in repayments by borrowers show that 23 out of 42 corporations had problems of defaults. However, overdues were small and loans taken to courts for recovery were nil. Debts which were written off as completely non-recoverable were negligible." In the case of HPF institutions, because of the many safeguards provided in the hire-purchase agreement and the financier's right to repossess the asset financed in case of default and payment of installment, bad debts are very small in these transactions. There may be some overdues at any point of time; but the arrears are generally collected during the term of the HPF agreement (Das-Gupta, Nayar, and Associates 1989). Thus, on the whole, the recovery performance of the informal financial institutions is far better than that of the formal sector

The question that arises is how the informal financial institutions with less manpower—often with traditional accounting practices and low levels of education, no computers, and an indifferent attitude on the part of governmental agencies—recover most of their dues, when the formal sector banks with modern facilities and highly qualified manpower fail to do so? The answer is that the informal financial institutions adopt two major safeguards: First a proper scrutiny of loan application and collateral and, more importantly, a personal assessment regarding the real worth of the borrower before the release of the loan, and second, timely follow up action, again through personal contact, until the loan is repaid. As a loan is granted not mainly on the strength of documents but on the personal assessment by the lender the informal lender binds borrowers with personal and legal obligations while the banks do so with legal obligations only. Often the borrowers take legal obligations lightly and are sometimes happy to be dragged into a court of law by the lender because in that case they can delay the repayment, plead the court to grant them facility of small installment repayments, and even prove that they deserve special consideration.

The second safeguard adopted by the informal sector, namely follow up action, is neglected by the banks. An interview with 69 branch managers of commercial banks in 1987 corroborates this view when they opined that "if some follow up action is taken by the branch staff or some kind of monitoring is done occasionally to see whether the borrower is actually using the loan amount for the purpose for which it was sanctioned, the overdues can be reduced, if not eliminated" (Nayar 1987). What emerged from the same interviews was that the bank staffs do not attach as much importance to recovery of loan dues as they do to making the loan. In India where about 95 percent of the commercial banks in terms of number and volume of business are under government ownership, this may be due to the fact that the granting of small loans, in many cases, is based on a quota system fixed for the bank by the government. When a bank does not reach a target fixed for it, the staff may be criticized.

Strength of the Informal Sector

The reason why many forms of informal finance continue to thrive despite the penetration of commercial banks in rural areas in India is mainly due to the inherent strength of the former. The demand for the services of informal finance is of two types. One is direct demand from both business and households, and the other is indirect demand emanating from the unsatisfied clients of the formal sector. The direct demand comes from borrowers who have little access to formal finance due to reasons such as failure to offer acceptable collateral and inability to conform to stipulations of credit use. These borrowers also may be at the bottom of the list of priorities in a system of credit rationing by the formal sector. The indirect demand for informal credit comes from borrowers who are not able to get sufficient credit at the required time from banks. Of these two types of demands, the direct demand is due to the inherent strength of the informal sector financial institutions, while the indirect demand is due to the constraints of banks.

Conclusions

The major lesson that the formal sector can learn from informal finance is the promptness with which the latter recovers the amount, however small it may be, that is lent by them. It is useful for banks to examine the methods used by the informal sector for loan recovery.

Another point of interest to the formal sector is the types of services offered by informal finance. Some of these services, such as the 100-day loan, can be tried by the banks. The major beneficiary of such measures will be borrowers who, presently paying an interest rate of about 81 percent per annum for their loans, will get them at 17 percent per annum from banks.

Various studies in India show that the informal sector is both better at serving the sectors neglected by banks small businessmen, traders, poor transport operators, handloom weavers, small farmers, self-employed people, and housewives. They are also better at recovering loans. Therefore, banks might consider adopting a policy of encouraging the informal sector with refinance wherever possible (for example, chit funds, HPF institutions, and nidhis). In respect to nidhis which extend loans only against tangible security, deposit insurance by the Deposit Insurance Corporation of India might be extended. With such refinance and liberal credit facilities to the deserving informal financial institutions, the banks will be helping the poor indirectly without undertaking a direct risk of default.

Informal financial institutions function on commercial lines and under competitive conditions. They raise funds locally without any government support or tax concessions and lend these funds to individuals who really require credit even at a fairly high rate of interest. Through this intermediation, the informal financial agencies not only fill a gap left by the formal banking sector but also support development.

References

Das-Gupta, A., C.P.S. Nayar, and Associates. 1989. "Urban Informal Credit Markets in India." Unpublished report. New Delhi: National Institute of Public Finance and Policy.

Madhur, S., and C.P.S. Nayar. 1987. " Informal Credit Markets in India: Their Size, Structure and Macro Implications," Unpublished paper. Paris: The Organization for Economic Co-Operation and Development .

Nayar, C.P.S. 1973. *Chit Finance*. Bombay: Vora and Company.

Nayar, C.P.S. 1982. *Finance Corporations*. Institute for Financial Management and Research, Madras.

Nayar, C.P.S. 1984. "A Study on Non-Banking Financial Intermediaries", Unpublished report. Madras: Institute for Financial Management and Research.

————. 1986. "Can a Traditional Financial Technology Co-exist with Modern Financial Technologies? The Indian Experience." *Savings and Development* 10:31-58.

————. 1987. "Adequacy of Preparation and Implementation of District Credit Plans," Unpublished report. Madras: Institute for Financial Management and Research.

Radhakrishnan, S., and others. 1975. *Chit Funds*, IFMR. Madras: Institute for Financial Management and Research.

Ramani, S. 1986. "A Case Study of Nidhis in the City of Madras." Unpublished Masters thesis. Madras: University of Madras.

15

Informal Finance in Indonesia

F. J. A. Bouman and H. A. J. Moll

Indonesia is a diverse country with a myriad of informal finanical arrangements that defy simple categorization. The country includes densely populated and fertile Java, blessed by nature and an ancient irrigation system that allows a wide variety of commercial and subsistence crops, a finely-tuned infrastructure that facilitates transport and commerce, and a variety of large and small enterprises. The country also includes a number of isolated and sparsely populated outer islands where the money economy has only begun to penetrate rural areas. It also has Bali with its booming tourist industry; the Moluccan islands with their centuries-old spice trade; and huge Irian Jaya where the one million Papuans have only recently emerged from the stone age. Some islands have a booming mining and forestry industry, a large plantation sector, or smallholders; while on other islands farming techniques have not progressed beyond slash and burn.

Because of this diversity, financial markets in Indonesia—both formal and informal—range from the sophisticated on Java to only rudimentary informal finance largely based on self help and mutual assistance in remote areas. Few of these informal markets have been comprehensively studied, but an increasing number of case studies has been done that describe particular informal financial arrangements, mostly in Java, the most important island where 100 million of Indonesia's 176 million inhabitants are concentrated. But even for Java, the available studies only scratch the surface of ubiquitous informal financial arrangements.

In the discussion that follows, we provide an overview of what is known about some important segments of Java's informal financial markets. The choice of topics is partly based on our own experiences and also on available literature. Elsewhere in this volume the reader will find more elaborate descriptions by McLeod (chapter 18) of finanical activities among Javanese micro-enterprises, Seibel and Parhusip's (chapter 17) description of attempts to enhance the linkeages between formal finance and informal groups in Java and Bali, and a colorful description by Hospes (chapter 16) of informal finance in a village on Ambon.

Since informal and formal financial markets are intertwined, we begin our discussion by covering a few aspects of formal finance in Indonesia that have had a direct influence on informal finance.

Formal Finance

Several heavily subsidized credit programs for farmers (BIMAS) and for small businessmen and craftsmen (KIK/KMKP) have been funded by the government since the 1960s. The KIK (Kredit Investasi Kecil) provides investment loans for small businesses, while the KMKP (Kredit Modal Kerja Permanen) provides loans to these firms for operating expenses. Interest rates were subsidized in these programs, not allowing lending institutions to become self-supporting, nor to establish permanent relationships with village clients. As has been the case with similar programs around the world, loan default rates were substantial, transaction costs for lenders and borrowers were high, and savings mobilization was neglected. Many beneficiaries of cheap credit were not the smallest, but instead the larger operators. In a study of the KIK/KMKP programs in late 1983 we were surprised to find that about 90 percent of the borrowers we interviewed in the Jakarta-Bogor area were hajis—individuals who had made the pilgrimage to Mecca, a costly journey that only the affluent can afford.

While most of these cheap credit programs had few direct effects on poor people, they did have substantial, unanticipated indirect effects through expanding informal finance. Since there is no wall between formal and informal financial markets, funds move back and forth between the two markets and go wherever the return is higher. For example, a BIMAS loan to a large farmer may percolate to his tenants via informal on-lending. There are few barriers to entry into informal financial markets; borrowers from formal institutions today may become lenders in the informal circuit tomorrow and many households participate in both markets. Therefore, it is likely that the government's formal credit programs expanded rather than substituted for informal finance.

Hybrid Institutions

Over time, regional and local authorities in Indonesia have developed unique financial schemes resulting in a large variety of hybrid formal and semiformal financial institutions at the district and village level. Table 1 gives a numerical overview of these hybrid institutions.

Some of the banks in the table have a history dating back to colonial times and had the primary goal of providing rural families with small, short-term loans, usually for trading purposes, with repayments due in weekly installments. Although many of these early banks failed, the surviving units prospered by relying on their own funds and careful management. In 1970, however, the Central Bank issued a number of restrictive regulations including supervision by the Bank Rakyat Indonesia (BRI) that curtailed the growth of local banks.

These regulations induced the provincial governments of West and Central Java to design new, semiformal credit institutions outside the

TABLE 1. Financial Institutions in Indonesia in 1987

Financial Institution	Number
Banks	
Badan Kredit Desa (District Credit Banks)	3,550
Lumbung Desa (Paddy Banks)	2,063
Bank Pasar (Market Banks)	175
Badan Karya Produksi Desa (Village Production Banks)	217
Other banks	26
Semiformal rural financial institutions	
Government owned pawnshops	479
Badan Kredit Kecamatan (district banks, Central Java)	486
Kooperasi Unit Desa (village cooperatives)	3,050
Lembaga Perkreditan Kecamatan (loan agencies West Java)	104
Lumbung Pitik Negara (money associations, West Sumatra)	472

Sources: Statistical Year Book of Indonesia, 1988; and Bank of Indonesia, unpublished records.

aegis of the Central Bank. The Badan Kredit Kecamatan (BKK) in Central Java, which started in 1972, became particularly successful. Kern (1986) argues that BKK is "...one of the most unique rural institutions in the world, being one of the few publicly funded credit programs that actually make a profit from providing very small loans to rural borrowers" (p. 121). Its ingredients for success include effective interest rates of 6 percent a month to cover costs of borrowed funds and administration, inflation, and bad debts; village units operating as close to borrowers as possible to allow careful selection and low borrower transaction costs; making low-risk loans, starting with small sums for three months with gradual increases in loan size based on repayment record; and, repayment in weekly installments (Kern 1986, p. 120-126). The BKK model of Central Java has been copied in other provinces, such as in the Lembaga Perkreditan Kecamatan in West Java, with less success.

Some of these institutional hybrids have blossomed with the help of foreign assistance, such as those established among commercial vegetable growers in the highlands of West Java (Moll 1989). Also, many nongovernmental organizations (NGOs) and the credit union movement started their own savings and credit groups. In the early 1980s it became clear that, on the one hand, subsidized credit programs had not attracted large numbers of new participants to formal financial markets, and, on the other hand, that part of the hybrid institutions blossomed. The need for deregulation of financial markets became clearer.

Deregulation

In 1983 the government began deregulating the financial sector by removing interest rate ceilings and by phasing out the lines of credit provided by the central bank. This resulted in substantial increases in bank deposits as attractive annual interest rates of up to 20 percent were offered. At the same time, nominal lending rates reached 24 to 30 percent, rates that reflected market conditions and kept pace with inflation. In 1984 the government redefined the role of the Bank Rakyat Indonesia's village subbranches, from being an outlet for subsidized and targeted credit under the BIMAS program to mobilizing savings and providing general nonsubsidized credit. In October 1988 the government announced an additional set of banking regulations, usually referred to as PAKTO 27. Under these regulations it became possible to open new banks, either privately owned or owned by regional governments, in urban as well as rural areas. This resulted in a proliferation of private banks and fierce competition to lure experienced staff away from existing banks through substantial salary increases. The deregulation reached a milestone in early 1990 when the subsidized KIK/KMKP program was terminated.

Deregulation also influenced development of NGOs that promote savings and credit activities at the local level. Until recently, the Indonesian government looked askance at the proliferation of NGOs even though these organizations helped to rally poor people behind development programs and emphasized, instead, promoting village cooperatives. PAKTO 27 allowed NGOs to form their own banks. Undoubtedly, this and other elements of the deregulation program has resulted in formal finance reaching an increasing number of people in rural areas.

Informal Finance in Java

Only a few studies of the financial system in Indonesia concentrate on, or even discuss, informal finance. Occasionally, casual assertions are made in reports about most people being largely dependent on informal finance—the tone being this is something that must be endured until the government can eliminate this plague.

Informal finance in Indonesia includes all of the types of informal arrangements mentioned by Adams (chapter 2). While no national estimates of its magnitude are available, fragmentary evidence strongly suggests it services a large proportion of the population. In a survey of several hundred urban and rural households in Jakarta, Central and East Java and Bali, conducted for the Asian Development Bank in 1987, Prabowo reported that 90 percent of the total value of loans used by the individuals interviewed came from informal sources (Prabowo 1989, p. 5).

We begin our overview with self-help groups that handle financial transactions, probably the most important type of informal finance found in Indonesia.

Self-help Organizations

Unlike most government credit programs, deposit mobilization is prominent in self-help organizations. These self-help groups serve a variety of purposes. One is social security, an insurance mechanism against illness, death, accidents, loss of income or harvest. Indonesia's ancient *lumbung desa* (village rice banks) are a form of community insurance to which villagers contribute rice for storage, to be distributed on a loan basis in time of scarcity. A second type of group specializes in saving for a particular occasion: social and religious ceremonies and festivals, rites of passage, or a pilgrimage to Mecca. Demand for loans is traditionally strong prior to big national events such as Independence Day, Lebaran at the end of Ramadan, and, in Bali, festivals in conjunction with the Hindu religion (Prabowo 1989, p. 7). Through group saving, members avoid becoming too heavily indebted to storekeepers, moneylenders, and itinerant traders. A third purpose is community development: improving public facilities such as mosques, temples, churches, and community halls.

Self-help groups in urban areas are often based on occupation, and in rural areas on proximity and gender; however, mixed- and cross-membership also occurs. An urban example of the first type is a society of *becak* drivers (pedicabs) in Yokyakarta. In 1983 the group consisted of 52 drivers, concentrated in only one street that had some 15 small hotels and guest houses. The society formed a fund to which each member contributed a fixed amount daily. These contributions were compulsory; the group also had a second fund for voluntary contributions, both by members—if they had a particularly successful day—and outsiders such as sympathetic tourists or shopkeepers and hotel owners to whom the drivers brought new customers. This second fund was used to buy secondhand pedicabs so that drivers no longer had to hire them. The first and main fund, however, was of the social security type. The bylaws of the society mentioned specific amounts of money to be paid in cases of illness and accidents or death, both by members and their next of kin. Although loans may be extended in all these groups, saving is the predominant function.

A fourth group consists of savings and credit societies *pur sang*: the *arisan, Usaha Bersama* (joint effort) and credit unions. Most NGOs in Indonesia concentrate on this fourth type of self-help societies and further description of self-help groups will be limited to these societies only. They appear to be the most important for urban and rural development and also because of the efforts by NGOs to upgrade them to full banking institutions (see Seibel and Parhusip, chapter 17).

ROSCA

The most ancient and widespread form of group finance in Indonesia is likely the rotating savings and credit associations (ROSCAS), called arisans. Several forms are well described by Geertz (1962). The lottery is the predominant mechanism for rotation of the fund; the auction system, in which members compete with each other by bidding for the fund, is seldom found. Through consensus, the fund may also be taken out of turn by a member in distress. Although men may look down upon the arisan as a female pastime, males frequently participate in them.

Arisans are popular in all strata of society. Regular contributions vary from tiny amounts among poor people, to substantial amounts for people with more income. Meetings may be daily, weekly, monthly, or at other intervals. Arisan funds are usually spent on consumption and household items such as kitchenware, sewing machines, bicycles, or to pay school fees or to settle an outstanding debt. In occupational arisans involving traders, shopkeepers, street vendors, and craftsmen, the funds collected may be used for working capital or investments. In Central Java we even came across a case where eight KUDs (village cooperatives) pooled their annual profits in an arisan to allow each KUD to build a new office in turn.

Arisan membership varies in number from very small, such as one among servants in a family household, to 60 or more individuals. When meetings are weekly or monthly, a large arisan has to cope with inflation because of the diminishing value of the fund over time. The way some ROSCAS cope with this problem is to accept contributions in kind. Rice is a common substitute for money (Moll 1989, p. 93), but in cities and towns women also contribute crockery or other household and kitchenware, so that each member eventually wins a complete dinner or tea set.

Arisans also perform social functions. Wives of government officials in Jakarta combined their monthly arisan meeting with a social activity, such as a demonstration of the latest fashion in cosmetics and hairdressing. Elsewhere, it is combined with a religious function such as singing and praying (Hospes, chapter 16). The government and NGOs have also discovered the value of tying arisans into their educational programs in things like family planning, and mother and child and health care. Women were much more inclined to participate in these programs when they were combined with an arisan.

Usaha Bersama and Credit Unions

Cross fertilization of different types of savings and credit schemes occurs regularly in Indonesia. The Usaha Bersama, for example, is rooted in the arisan tradition, but is also influenced by modern cooperative philosophy (Prabowo 1989, p. 9). Cross fertilization features are also apparent in Hospes' description of the savings and credit societies in Tulehu (chapter 16).

As for credit unions, Table 2 shows a rapid increase in the numbers in the country from 1970 to 1985, after which the growth faltered. Several foreign organizations have assisted in this growth. In early 1990 there were 19 regional chapters providing services such as education and training, interlending, insurance, and management assistance to individual credit unions. The movement has not opted to seek legal status because of fears that this would lead to government interference through regulation. It is, however, linked with other NGOs within the Cooperative Council of Indonesia.

TABLE 2. Credit Unions in Indonesia, 1970 to 1988

Year	Credit Unions (number)	Membership (number)	Loans (number)	Assets (Rp million)
1970	9	739	0	1
1975	197	14,834	85	106
1980	535	56,805	1,267	1,457
1985	1,308	145,563	7,618	8,601
1986	1,313	152,842	10,059	11,316
1987	1,322	155,580	11,296	13,283
1988	1,395	166,950	14,205	16,610

Note: The figures in the Table refer to the situation at the end of the year.
Source: Unpublished reports assembled by the Cooperative Council of Indonesia.

Informal Lenders

Various types of informal lenders are another prominent form of informal finance in Indonesia. They come in at least three types: professional, semiprofessional, and part-time moneylenders. Professional moneylenders are individuals who make their living mostly from lending money and they generally work with their own funds. In cases where they also act as money guards, they may use deposits for their own working capital. On rare occasions they may borrow from formal finance institutions. Some professional moneylenders may start as an agent or broker who works on a commission basis lending another person's money, but over time the agent may evolve into an independent operator.

The part-time moneylender only occasionally extends loans. Generally they are people with a regular income from teaching, the civil service, or employment in a factory. They often also have access to loans from institutional sources. This group is probably growing rapidly at the expense of the full-time lenders, as has been observed elsewhere in Asia (Bouman 1989, p. 89). It is common for both professional and part-time moneylenders to charge interest rates of 10 percent a month on loans, but loans to friends and relatives may carry no interest or only a modest interest charge. In part, these relatively high interest rates are due to the nature of the financial services offered and also due to the characteristics of the borrowers. Many of the loans made by full-time and part-time lenders are small, are made for short periods of time, involve no loan collateral, and are made in a way that imposes few transaction costs on the borrower.

Semiprofessional moneylenders are often more difficult for observers to understand. These individuals include shopkeepers, produce buyers, suppliers of fertilizer and farm machinery, landlords, millers, and craftsmen who may extend loans to their clients to facilitate other exchanges. They do not view themselves as moneylenders, but rather feel they must extend loans to maintain or promote their primary businesses. The term semiprofessional moneylender applies to a female ROSCA organizer in a fruit and vegetables market in Jakarta. Although a trader herself, she is much involved in lending small sums of money daily to her fellow traders. The same is true for some itinerant traders who peddle a variety of consumer goods in relatively remote villages. They also make short-term loans and collect periodic repayments (Prabowo 1989, p. 3).

Professional moneylenders are most prevalent in urban areas. They are concentrated around markets and business centers, serving micro-, and medium-sized entrepreneurs in every conceivable segment of the economy. They usually give loans on personal security but may also demand collateral—thus competing with pawnbrokers. Monthly repayments of loans appear to be the most popular form of handling loans from moneylenders (Prabowo 1989, p. 6).

Moneylenders also operate in rural areas. In his survey of households in Central and East Java, Prabowo found that 35 percent of his sample borrowers in both regions reported loans from professional moneylenders (Prabowo 1989, p. 15). We assume that some of them may act as agents for other urban-based lenders or for public pawnshops. Many of these moneylenders operate on a small scale which Prabowo partly attributes to the fact that their activities are illegal. However, this has been the case in Indonesia for more than half a century and laws have never stopped moneylenders from operating.

In our visits to Java between 1976 and 1986 we heard reports of the ancient phenomenon of the "bank keliling" which is a mobile banker who makes weekly rounds in villages collecting interest and repayment on former loans. When Moll (1989) interviewed 80 vegetable farmers in the highlands of West Java, many commented on these mobile bankers who restricted their services to lending rather than collecting deposits.

An indication of the fierce competition in informal lending is Prabowo's account of a new type of scheme under the name of 'cooperative bank' with an official license to operate. "They gave loans without collateral and no paperwork was required. They operate door-to-door, charged an interest rate of 10 to 20 percent a month, collecting loan repayments daily. In Central Java people refer to these pseudo-cooperatives as the lender that always hunts or tries to locate the borrowers" (Prabowo 1989, p. 4-5).

Pawnbrokers

There are both public and private pawnhouses in Indonesia. None of the private houses are licensed. Pawnbroking was a legal monopoly of the government under the Dutch regime and has remained so until the present day. All private houses, therefore, operate illegally, which has not stopped them from doing a thriving business. As is the case in many other Asian countries, the age-old habit of converting cash savings into gold, jewelry, and other valuables, has been spurred in Indonesia by inflation and devaluations and the spectacular rise in the price of gold.

The growth of pawning in public pawnhouses has been impressive, from a volume of Rp 31 billion in 1975 to Rp 156 billion in 1981 (US$ 124 and 468 million at the time), with an average increase of 32 percent from 1978 to 1981. The redemption rate was almost 100 percent. These pawnhouses, despite having far fewer offices than the state banks, have been effective in providing poor people with access to institutional credit.

Policymakers tend to look down on pawnshops. Considering the popularity of legal as well as illegal pawning in Indonesia, we feel this view should be reevaluated. For example, individuals may choose to deposit funds in a bank with the intent of withdrawing and spending them later. But, is not much the same true for savings in gold, that can be turned into cash through a pawnbroker? While it is true that holders of gold have to forego the interest paid on bank deposits, this may be offset by a rise in the gold price, the erosion of the purchasing power of a bank balance through inflation, and the often cumbersome procedure involved in depositing and withdrawing funds from a bank.

Despite the legal government monopoly, private pawnbroking in Indonesia flourishes and brokers accept almost anything as a pawn. Practically every town at a subdistrict level has its own street where these shops are concentrated. Pawning with the local goldshop has become a matter of routine in many farmers' daily lives. These shops operate on a simple sale-repurchase arrangement, selling gold and buying it back. It may even be arguable to classify such sale-repurchase arrangements as money lending.

Pure money lending on the basis of gold as collateral, however, does occur. Hospes (chapter 16) reported a merchant in Ambon advancing loans to buyers of clove crops against 5 percent interest a month. While the public pawnhouse charges only 3-4 percent, the merchant is preferred because he advances much larger sums against the value of gold. This is consistent with observations in India and Sri Lanka (Bouman and Bastiaansen, chapter 13).

Informal Finance and Trade

Both the collecting and distributive trade in Indonesia involve credit transactions at every point where goods change hands. Informal lending permeates every conceivable sector of both the urban and rural economy and is as much a supply-securing as a purchase-promoting device. Of necessity, we will limit our observations to rural areas, and present a typical case from the trade in vegetables in the highlands of

West Java, where the climate has been conducive to commercial vegetable growing (Moll 1989).

Although self-financing is the rule, most farmers in this area obtain rice and inputs (fertilizer and agro-chemicals) from shopkeepers and traders. Shopkeepers specializing in inputs generally provide loans to the larger farmers with whom they establish permanent relationships. Collateral is not required when a satisfactory repayment track record has been established. There is no specific interest charge on these loans, but inputs obtained on credit are priced higher than cash purchases. Shopkeepers run a certain risk, as the returns from vegetable production are erratic, and because competition among shopkeepers allows farmers a certain freedom to switch from one to another merchant.

Vegetable traders also provide inputs on credit to small and large farmers alike, the standing crop serving as collateral. The returns to the lender from these loans result from elevated prices for the inputs and lower prices for the vegetables sold to the vegetable trader than would prevail if the transaction were strictly on a cash basis. The following is a typical example. A farmer financed most of his expenses from his own resources and obtained from a trader a loan in kind with a market value of Rp 12,000 under the condition of selling his total crop to the trader. After 10 weeks, the harvest was sold to the trader at Rp 130 per kilogram, although the actual market price was Rp 135 per kilogram. The costs to the farmer for this loan of Rp 12,000 were: an extra amount paid for the inputs of Rp 1,500, and returns lost due to lower sales price of Rp 7,350. The total cost of Rp 8,850, expressed as interest, was 74 percent in total, or 30 percent per month. But a proportion of this percentage must be assigned to the guaranteed purchase of the crop by the trader, which is important to farmers in periods of low price.

Another method of obtaining loans from traders is via *tebasan*. Tebasan is the institution traditionally used in Indonesia for implementing effective coordination between harvesting and marketing. In the tebasan system the standing crop is purchased three to ten days before harvest, and thus involves a short-term credit transaction. The harvest is done by a middleman with a team of hired laborers, so as to meet timely requirements in transportation and marketing. Farmers also prefer this system for reasons of convenience; it saves the trouble and cost of monitoring labor for harvesting (Kawagoe and Hayami 1989). Tebasan is used for all types of crops.

Even more than tebasan, the system called *ijon* has been cause of much controversy among observers of informal financial arrangements between farmers and traders. Unlike the tebasan, in a typical ijon arrangement the trader/lender buys the crop green (ijon = green) long before the harvest is due and at a price that might be quite low. Opponents, particularly in government circles, consider ijon disastrous for farmers because it may lead to debt bondage. Moral indignation, however, is mixed with amazement that the system so persistently survives, despite its supposed disadvantages for farmers. Simple comparison of ijon prices with actual market prices after the harvest shows interest payment of 10 to 40 percent a month.

The most important ijon commodity in Central Java is rice (Partadireja 1974, p. 63); in East Java and other islands we found it common in tree crops such as fruits and cloves. In the latter case, crops may even be sold years in advance (see Hospes, chapter 16). Closer examination of ijon explains why it remains so popular with small and large farmers alike. "Under the system, the lender assumes complete responsibility for harvesting and selling the crop" (Prabowo 1989, p. 3). A telling example is given by Partadireja. A farmer with a fruit tree sold the budding crop five months before the harvest. The buyer was responsible for protecting the fruit from pests and thieves and for the costs of baskets, picking, and transporting the fruit. "The ijon transaction not only enabled the farmer to transfer all the price risks and marketing costs to the buyer, but also to escape the burden of social obligations to give part of the crop to neighbours" (Partadireja 1974, p. 64-65). Similar ijon arrangements have been noted in the tobacco industry.

Risk avoidance and convenience are, therefore, essential elements in the farmers' behavior pattern and compelling reasons to prefer ijon to other marketing arrangements with traders.

Suppliers' Credits

In 1989 we traced the role of suppliers' credit in the sale of agricultural machinery such as hand tractors and powered threshers from the few large manufactures on Java to the retail shops in villages. The manufacturers allow dealers to pay two weeks to three months after delivery. The dealers, in turn, provide similar credit facilities to subdealers and this line of credit extends down to the retailers. Credit facilities are not standardized; the financial leeway allowed each individual in the chain is a function of mutual trust and creditworthiness.

Unfortunately, little research has been done on other types of supplier credit systems, but it is likely that similar loan arrangements could be found in most of these systems.

Summary and Conclusions

Individuals in Indonesia can choose from a range of financial services provided by banks and hybrid financial institutions in the formal sector, and through an array of informal financial relationships in the informal sector. Although no comprehensive data for the country are available, the few surveys carried out (Moll 1989; Prabowo 1989) indicate that the majority of the rural and urban population, particularly in the lower income brackets, not only depend on, but prefer informal finance.

Our overview of major types of informal financial arrangements in Java shows heterogenity and versatility. These arrangements have three aspects in common: proximity, small size of transactions, and multiple functions. Proximity means that financial transactions generally take place among a group of persons who know each other. The result is that decisions are swift and that face to face contacts and social control both contribute to honoring obligations. In this environment, the transaction costs in savings and credit arrangements are kept to a minimum, something that is essential as the financial transactions are generally small and of short duration.

Multiple functions in informal finance emerge in many forms. Credit is often intertwined with trade and commerce, where it serves as a supply and marketing-securing mechanism, ensuring both parties against insecurity and risk. The saving arrangements in groups also combine a clear individual economic purpose with social security and community stabilizing aspects. It is precisely this unique combination of proximity and multiple functions that explains informal finance's attractiveness to households with a small financial capacity.

Critics of informal financial arrangements usually assume high trading profits, unsurious lending rates, and the existence of monopoly profits. Such assumptions, however, are seldom substantiated by careful analysis. Our experience in Indonesia has led us to believe that actors in these markets play a positive role in the economy, a role that is well worth paying for. The fact that a variety of informal financial arrangements are found in all urban and rural communities, where research is undertaken, shows that millions of households share this viewpoint.

References

Bouman, F. J. A. 1989. *Small, Short and Unsecured: Informal Rural Finance in India*. Delhi: Oxford University Press.

Geertz, Clifford. 1962. "The Rotating Credit Association: A `Middle Rung' in Development." *Economic Development and Cultural Change* 10:241-263.

Kawagoe, T., and Y. Hayami. 1989. "Farmers and Middlemen in A Transmigration Area in Indonesia." *Bulletin of Indonesian Economic Studies* 25:73-97.

Kern, J. R. 1986. "The Growth of Decentralized Rural Credit Institutions in Indonesia." In C. MacAndrews ed., *Central Government and Local Development in Indonesia*. London: Oxford University Press.

Moll, H. A. J. 1989. "Farmers and Finance, Experience with Insitutional Savings and Credit in Java." Unpublished Ph.D. dissertation. Wageningen, Netherlands: Agricultural University of Wageningen.

Partadireja, A. 1974. "Rural Credit: The Ijon System." *Bulletin of Indonesian Economic Studies* 10:54-71.

Prabowo, D. 1989. "The Role of Informal Financial Intermediation in the Mobilization of Household Savings and Allocations in Indonesia." Unpublished paper prepared for the Asian Development Bank in Manila.

16

Evolving Forms of Informal Finance in an Indonesian Town

Otto Hospes

Like other coastal towns in the Moluccan province of Indonesia, Tulehu has resources that guarantee most inhabitants a minimum living standard; sago palms provide the traditional staple food as well as all necessary materials for traditional house construction, and the sea is a supplier of fish, an integral part of the daily diet. Food production requires neither capital-intensive inputs nor large amounts of labor; in one week a half dozen people can collect enough sago food for the needs of three months. For most of the 12,000 people living in or near the town, traditional farming and fishing are still major activities, but in the past couple of decades the range of economic activities has broadened with more government jobs and the opening of new port facilities. Still, when I asked a fish seller what she would do in case of total lack of money, she responded with *ke hutan saja* (we just go to the forest). The forest, even more than the sea, is perceived as a bank of last resort.

In addition to the forest, however, various informal financial arrangements are also increasingly used by all classes of people in Tulehu to satisfy their economic needs and to insure against risks. In the following discussion I outline some of the arrangements I encountered while doing a study there in 1989. Recent innovations in these arrangements show that informal finance behaves like a chameleon; it offers a colorful palette of financial services to villagers and readily adapts itself to their diverse and changing financial needs.

225

Economic Change

The extent and make up of informal financial arrangements is strongly influenced by overall economic conditions. Gradually, these conditions have been changing in Tulehu, causing substantial changes in the nature of informal finance in the area. Tulehu enjoys a strategic position in regional trade. Products such as fish, cloves, nutmeg, coconut, and fruits pass through the town's port on their way to Ambon city, and consumer goods are shipped via Tulehu to other islands. This strategic position gives the inhabitants opportunities to escape the subsistence oriented sago economy: government employees, fish traders, vegetable sellers, harbor laborers, bus drivers, speedboat crews, petrol vendors, and shopkeepers earn most of their incomes from nonfarm activities. Tulehu's central position in trade and transport networks reduces the dependency of the town's economy on the local clove production: in most years there are clove booms in some parts of the region, whose produce passes through Tulehu.

In 1985-86 the strategic position of Tulehu as a regional trade and transport center was reinforced by the construction of a second harbor. Along side this harbor new shops were opened and new labor groups found employment in loading and unloading ships. Both the informal and formal financial sector expanded as a result of these changes.

The construction of the new harbor facilities also attracted the Bank Rakyat Indonesia (BRI), which opened a unit near the new port in 1987. The saving programs of the unit service a broad spectrum of people. One BRI deposit mobilization program called SIMPEDES attracted more than 700 depositors in less than two years. The interest rates paid on SIMPEDES accounts range up to 13.5 percent per annum. These rates are less than the 15 percent annual rate paid on another, more restricted, deposit program called TABANAS, but still the SIMPEDES program had twice as many depositors as TABANAS. This might be due to the response of SIMPEDES to popular financial needs of depositors, such as simple savings procedures, easy withdrawal procedures, and the possibility to win prizes in a lottery scheme.

Clove Harvesting

Many of the people in Tulehu realize substantial but unpredictable cash incomes from the clove business: every several years, clove trees yield a crop that is sold for a considerable amount of money. Cloves also represent a form of savings. After the harvest, part of the crop is often stored in the home and then sold when money is needed. In the 1970s, when clove prices rose to about US$20 per kilogram, 40 mature clove trees, each yielding 10 kilograms, were enough to pay for large expenditures such as a pilgrimage to Mecca or a new house with concrete walls and a metal roof. In the 1980s, the prices of cloves fell to only about US$2 per kilogram, while the cost of a journey to Mecca and house construction material sharply increased. Economic activities in the town shifted accordingly: in the late 1980s few residents were able to make the trip to Mecca, and families who wanted to build a new house did it in steps, resulting in numerous unfinished houses.

The economic boom of the 1970s caused by high oil prices and attractive prices for other commodities produced in Indonesia did little to upgrade the economic base of Moluccan villages and towns. The large government cash flows into rural areas, partly in the form of subsidized loans, were largely used for consumption and resulted in little economic diversification of agriculture. Instead, it moved farmers closer to monocultural clove cultivation. The Indonesian government contributed to this by offering cheap credit for the intensification of clove production. When prices dropped because of the government promoted increases in clove acreage, the farmers were left with increased consumption needs only.

Migrants to Tulehu, such as the Butonese, do not enjoy the same economic opportunities as do the natives: these newcomers lack traditional ownership or usufructuary rights to land and trees, and therefore concentrate on providing labor or financial services. The Butonese are migrants from Southeast Sulawesi and can be found in nearly all Moluccan villages. They provide substantial amounts of informal loans that support the clove business: they either buy the cloves-on-the-trees at harvest time (*beli buah*), and then do the harvesting themselves, or they lend the owner of the clove trees money by buying the rights, well in advance, to harvest clove trees for one or more good seasons (*sewa pohon*)—good seasons occurring only once in three years on average. The Butonese lender assumes both the price and yield risks of the crop.

The Clove Trade

Besides loans provided by the Butonese, there are four other main categories of organizations and lenders who are involved in the clove trade and associated credit transactions: village cooperatives (KUDs), shopkeepers, private professional traders, and agents for cigarette factories.

The cooperative movement is under the general direction and management of the central government in Jakarta, and the KUDs in the Moluccan province have a monopoly on cloves marketing. They buy cloves directly from the farmers for a fixed price and then PUSKUD, the central cooperative, auctions the cloves collected by the KUDs. Many of the KUDs also provide some loans to individuals who own clove trees.

In practice, the KUDs are not able to buy all of the cloves produced and this leaves room for other agents to become involved in the clove trade. In the remote towns and villages in the Moluccas where shopping alternatives and possibilities to earn money are few, local shopkeepers offer consumer goods on credit and accepts repayment in kind: the debt is recorded in kilograms of cloves and the interest payment is embedded in the price paid for the product. These shopkeepers, in turn, may be receiving loans in kind or cash from professional traders or from KUDs. Relatively large amounts of funds enter villages such as Tulehu in this way. At harvest time the big traders and KUDs collect the cloves at the village shops for loan repayment. Profits and interest rates for parties involved are hidden and depend on future market prices for cloves. Credit is a tying device in this part of the cloves market.

Cloves change hands from private traders to agents of kretek cigarette factories (the private channel) and from KUDs to PUSKUD (the government cooperative channel). These channels often cross: professional private traders and shopkeepers let the KUDs sell their cloves at lucrative prices on auction floor at the PUSKUD. Some KUDs that collect more cloves than can be auctioned at the PUSKUD sell their cloves to, or store them with, cloves wholesalers or other merchants in Ambon city. A number of these transactions involve informal loans whose terms vary widely.

Fishing Business

The decline in the price of cloves in the 1980s made the Butonese more cautious about long-term loan agreements with owners of clove trees. As a result, they shifted part of their investments and lending activities to fishing endeavors. Wrecked ships on the shore near Tulehu are vivid reminders of unsuccessful attempts by the government during the 1970s to promote high-tech investments in fishing. When borrowers could not keep up the maintenance or loan payments on these boats they returned to traditional fishing using low-technology equipment such as wooden canoes, rafts, and small nets. In the late 1980s nearly all the owners of fishing rafts (*bagan*) in Tulehu were Butonese. In the late 1980s the construction of a medium-sized bagan cost about US$2,200 far less than the price of a motorized boat but many times the price of a *proa* (wooden canoe). In some cases the Butonese rented these rafts and also provided informal loans for their operations. Some Butonese fish wholesalers in the nearby city of Ambon also supplied interest free loans to fishermen who agreed to sell them future catches.

Many of the Butonese who finance both clove harvesting and fishing activities, in turn, occasionally obtain loans from government pawnshops located in Ambon. As Bouman and Houtman (1988) found in India, these individuals usually pawn gold coins or ornaments. The maximum periods on these loans are 3 and 6 months with interest rates of 4 and 3 percent per month. Pawnshops are able to fulfill emergency financial needs of the Butonese on the spot—an identity card and a gold item are enough to obtain a loan. Many of these loans are repaid within two months. The pawnshop is the only formal financial institution that is accessible to the "landless" Butonese.

Government Employees

A relatively large number of government employees, including teachers, live in and around Tulehu since it is the administrative capital of a subdistrict. Nearly 350 local residents are on the government payroll and about 85 people enjoy government pension payments. This results in a regular cash flow into many of the 2,000 households located in the Tulehu area. Government jobs are valued because white collar workers enjoy some prestige, a regular income, and pension benefits. Government salaries, nevertheless, are usually not enough to cover daily expenditures that can, in effect, force government employees to work in the forest on free days or to have some other part-time job.

Although the monthly salaries of the government employees are hardly enough to cover most household expenses, many employees are creditworthy in the eyes of both formal and informal financial intermediaries because they have stable sources of income. In a credit program called KUPEDES that is provided by the branch of the Bank Rakyat Indonesia (BRI) in Tulehu, for example, more than 90 percent of the borrowers are government employees. A number of shopkeepers in the town supply consumer goods on credit mainly to government employees. The number of their borrowing customers varies but may be as high as 40 persons per shop. These customers are expected to repay the interest-free loan within several months. The shopkeepers do not perceive it as credit but speak of customers "who have not yet paid" (*belum bayar*).

The extensive amount of street vending activities by women in Tulehu indicate the need for extra income among government employees as well as other people laboring in the private sector. These activities are called *bantu suami* (to help your husband), which in fact refers to all income-generating activities of wives. Women dominate as vendors in the vegetable and fish markets and are, generally speaking, substantially involved in small informal loans as well as informal group savings efforts.

ROSCAs

An interesting development in Tulehu is the increasing popularity of arisans among a variety of inhabitants. These associations are similar in many regards to ROSCAs found by Bouman (1979) and other researchers in many low-income countries. Their growing popularity is an indication of the increasing capacity to save due to the expanded possibilities for people in the area to earn income in government service, as workers, or as entrepreneurs. Individuals who are still mainly traditional farmers or fishermen are seldom members of ROSCAs, apparently because they lack relatively steady cash incomes.

During my research I encountered several dozen ROSCAs. A tabulation of these arisans by member characteristics is given in Table 1. As can be noted, a broad range of economic and social groups are members of arisans. One of the Sumatran restaurant/shopkeepers groups had the longest experience with an arisan in Tulehu: they started their group some 15 years ago, when they were newcomers. Each week they came together to eat and drink and play arisan as a means of strengthening ethnic ties. They had earlier exposure to ROSCAs in Sumatra where they were called *bajulo-julo*. Over time this group gradually commercialized the arisan and discontinued weekly meetings. A predetermined sequence of receivers, instead of the lottery system, now determines the rotation of the fund; all participants bring their contributions each day to the group leader and after ten days, one participant comes to the leader to receive the deposits. The group leader is the first person to take the fund.

TABLE 1. Member Arisans Encountered in Tulehu in 1989

Member Characteristics	Number of Arisans
Sumatran restaurant and shopkeepers	2
Haruku women	1
Banda women	1
Harbor laborers	3
Petrol vendors	1
Fish traders	2
Market women and restaurant managers	4
Praying and singing groups	5
Government employees	5
TOTAL	24

Source: Field survey in 1989.

A government employees' group has the second oldest arisan. They started about 10 years ago when government circulars encouraged the savings habit. In the two women's clubs the arisan functions as a focal point to mobilize and organize members around festivities or specific social issues, such as health care and family planning. Their meetings—like their salaries—are on a monthly basis. The 18 other ROSCAs have been started in the last 5 years and were called arisans, which indicates an external origin of the term and practice.

It may be useful to regroup these arisans by applying five additional criteria:

1. by the gender of members,
2. by the primary purpose of the arisan,
3. by the period of rotation,
4. by the mechanism that determines rotation of the fund, and
5. by the existence of a complementary emergency loan fund.

Gender Groups

As might be expected, there was gender concentration among the arisans surveyed. Two of the groups, the harbor workers and the petrol vendors, were made up of only males. The Sumatran restaurant operator/shopkeepers' arisans, and the fish traders' ROSCA had both male and female members. The remainder of the groups had only female members. In part these gender tendencies show social preferences, but they also mirror the gender make up of the economic group around which the ROSCAs were organized—there are almost no females who fish or sell petrol, for example.

Primary Purpose

Some of the groups appeared to be mainly socializing mechanisms, while other arisans had mainly economic functions. The Sumatran restaurant operator/shopkeepers, the Haruku women, and the Banda women groups were made up almost entirely of ethnic minorities who used an arisan as an instrument to tie together people with common roots. These groups had a flavor of being mutual protection associations. The groups built on praying and singing clubs and those comprised of government employees also appeared to be organized largely around social or religious issues. The remaining arisans had strong economic overtones. The primary functions of these economic units were to mobilize deposits, encourage members to save more, to provide loans to members, and to act as a risk management instrument for members. Many of the members in these economic arisans reported they joined because they felt participation resulted in them saving more than if they were not members.

Rotation Period

A third way to classify arisans is by their period of rotation. These periods strongly correlate with the primary function of the ROSCA; if the arisan is primarily a social organization, funds are collected and distributed at the weekly or monthly meeting of the group. If the arisan primarily satisfies savings needs, the members contribute daily, but the fund is distributed every two, five, or ten days. The collection and distribution of the funds in these types of arisans takes place during working hours in a shop, restaurant, or market stall. Every day, each participant brings his/her contribution to the moneykeeper and at the end of the savings period one participant comes to this person to obtain the fund. The daily saving clubs also offer their members short-term lending facilities and a member may borrow from the keeper of the fund, provided that she/he repays before the end of the savings period. ROSCAs that are more economic in nature collect and distribute funds on a cycle that coincides with the payment of members' salaries or wages.

Determination of Rotation

Arisans can also be classified according to the mechanisms used to determine the rotation of the fund—who receives the fund at any given rotation. These mechanisms are closely related to the primary function of the arisan: if the arisan is mainly a socializing technique, a lottery is standard procedure in Tulehu for determining the order of the rotation. If the arisan is mostly an economic group, a member list is drawn up in which the order of rotation is determined both by lottery and deliberation between the treasurer and members who are in need of the fund. I did not find any arisans that used bids to determine order of rotation, a practice that is common in many other Asian countries.

Complementary Emergency Fund

A final way to classify arisans is by the existence or absence of associated nonrotating emergency funds that complement the arisan. Typically, small contributions are made to these emergency funds by group members each time they pay shares into the ROSCA, but the money in the two funds are kept separately. It is also common for this emergency fund to provide loans or grants to members in case of sickness or death and even for religious purposes. In some cases, funds in the emergency funds may also be lent to individuals who are not members of the group. Fourteen of the ROSCAs studied had emergency funds: both women groups, two of the three harbor laborers groups, the praying and singing clubs, and the government employees groups.

Multiple Funds

One of the harbor labor groups I studied was involved in four distinct funds: one that rotated the distribution of the money collected, and three funds that did not rotate. When work is done, the 25 members of the group meet to divide the team's total daily income. The group's income varies between about US$110 and US$340 per working day. Earlier, the members agreed to participate in an arisan that distributed the equivalent of about US$55 to each member in rotation.

Due to the unpredictability of team incomes, this group designed an innovative way to manage the collection and timing of payments to the ROSCA. They agreed to put all daily group earnings in excess of

US$110 into a ROSCA fund. When the "excess-earnings" fund reached the equivalent of about 55 US$ it was given to one of the members of the group, in rotation, who was selected by lottery. If the excess was less than 55 US$, the rotation was postponed until that amount had been accumulated. If the excess income in one day was worth at least US$110, then two members received their rotations in a single day. On average the group worked about three days per week in the port and were able to complete a entire rotation of the fund in about two months.

In addition to the ROSCA fund, the group also made contributions to another parallel emergency fund. This fund was made up of small amounts of money left over after payment of the regular ROSCA shares and by occasional voluntary contributions by members. This fund could be used for any group or individual emergency, such as paying for damages done to cargo handled by the group.

In mid-1989 two subgroups within this team of laborers decided to contribute to still two other forms of nonrotating funds. One subgroup made small contributions to a fund each work day that was used to help Islamic religious leaders, and to assist poor people. This fund might be labeled a social welfare fund. Another subgroup made similar small contributions to a fund that was allowed to build up, and then appropriate shares were returned to contributing members just before the Islamic fasting month began, when large amounts of food were typically purchased. This fund had many of the features of a contractual savings program aimed at assembling deposits sufficient for some targeted purchase.

An Evolving Group

About 15 years ago four women who were relatives started a praying society that met on Sunday evenings. Each week the members contributed to a nonrotating fund that was used for religious purposes and helping poor people. The funds collected were stored in a box in the home of the organizer. Eventually the society grew to 37 members who decided several years ago to contribute additional small amounts each meeting to an arisan. The arisan funds collected are given out in rotation to society members who were chosen by lot. The woman receiving the distribution, in turn, was expected to host the meeting of the society the following week and to use the arisan money to pay for the expenses incurred in hosting the meeting.

The weekly meetings of the praying arisan society further consolidated the existing family and friendship ties among the members and provided a solid base for other commercial activities by the group. A few months after the start of the arisan, the club opened a cooperative store. The 37 members of the club bought shares in the store that provided starting capital equivalent to approximately US$500. The new store developed commercial relations with a wholesaler who soon began to supply consumer goods on credit to the store. Since then, the store has twice issued a 200 percent stock dividend and also extended consumer credit to about 60 customers.

In 1990 the group decided to open a deposit account in the local branch of the Bank Rakyat Indonesia where they deposited idle social-religious funds and some of the cash generated by the store. The attractive interest rate offered by the bank was the main reason for this decision. The society has not sought a bank loan because they are satisfied with the credit arrangements they have with a Chinese wholesaler who continues to provide them goods on credit efficiently and without charging any explicit interest.

Money Guards

This Chinese wholesaler provides 84 shops in the region with consumer goods on credit. He also holds small deposits made by a group of 11 laborers who frequently work for him or for one of his clients. The laborers receive no explicit payment for these funds but they do informally count on his help in case of financial trouble, and he also occasionally gives them free cigarettes. The laborers believe it is not advisable to keep savings at home because the money is too easily spent. The wholesaler said, "I don't pay them any rent (on their money)" and describes his function as a money guard.

Another shopkeeper who is Javanese also is a money guard. He owns two buses for public transport. His drivers play a pivotal role in his enterprise as they must realize enough daily income to pay for the installments on the loans he used to buy the buses. As an incentive to work hard he pays his drivers 20 percent of the daily gross income they generate. Because of this arrangement and the large size of the buses, both drivers are able to save a substantial part of their income which they leave on account with their boss.

The importance of offering money guarding services was clearly understood by the chairman of the local cooperative (KUD). In October 1988 the innovative chairman started the first daily deposit program in the Moluccan province under KUD sponsorship without direction from higher authorities. He advertised the effort as an educational

savings program for children and their parents who want to assemble
funds for school expenditures. Within three months more than 1,000
parents and children opened deposit accounts at the KUD that paid no
interest. The program offers depositors three benefits: a secure place to
deposit funds, convenient hours for making deposits and withdrawals,
and simple procedures. This daily savings program of the KUD
satisfies an illiquidity preference (the money guarding) and a liquidity
preference (easy withdrawal). The KUD chairman's motives are not
completely altruistic. He deposits the funds mobilized in the local unit
of the Bank Rakyat Indonesia and realizes for the cooperative a 13.5
percent rate of return on the deposits. In a casual way he was providing
the link between informal deposits and formal banking that has been
promoted by Seibel (1985).

Conclusions

Some researchers, such as Geertz (1962), have viewed informal
finance as being a static stepping stone or transitory phase that is left
behind as development occurs. Other people, particularly politicians,
have thought informal finance was a scourge that should be eliminated
as quickly as possible. The impressions I gleaned from my research lead
me to be uneasy with both views. Informal finance in Tulehu is
dynamic, growing, and evolving; it appears to have a highly
complementary relationship with development, in general, and also
with growth in the formal financial system. Informal finance also
provides highly valuable financial services to many poor people, to
individuals who start small businesses, and to marginal social groups.
It is doing for poor people what many formal credit programs fail to do:
providing them sustained financial services.

The chances of improving the performance formal finance programs,
in this regard, may be enhanced if more features of the informal
financial system are grafted onto these programs. These include more
emphasis on deposit mobilization, more attention to pawning, more
attention to insurance, and building more convenience into formal
finance programs.

Deposits

I was impressed by the amount and extent of savings that occurred in informal financial markets in Tulehu. The substantial amounts of deposits made in ROSCAs and in other nonrotating group funds show that people in the area are willing to save. The significant use of money guards as a place to hold deposits is an indication that people have a need to save even when the explicit rewards for doing so are nil. While the formal financial system is gradually offering more formal deposit services in the area, clearly formal deposit mobilization opportunities have not yet been fully exploited.

Pawning

Because of the low transaction costs involved for both lender and borrower, pawning is an inexpensive way to provide small, short-term loans to borrowers who would otherwise not be creditworthy. In Indonesia, pawning services are offered by some banks and it may be desirable to extend these services into other banking facilities. In countries where all pawning is done by the informal market, it may be desirable to formalize at least some of these services.

Insurance

Enhancing mutual trust and building unutilized credit reserves that can be used in times of trouble are major reasons for participating in informal finance. In large measure, many forms of informal finance are substitutes for formal insurance and for dependable access to other formal financial services. Formal financial intermediaries might offer various forms of explicit insurance and also provide more dependable services that emulate these features of informal finance.

Convenience

Three of the most impressive features of informal finance in Tulehu are its flexibility, its proximity, and the fact that it is entirely designed to meet needs of its users. Various systems have been developed to mobilize small amounts of irregular savings, along with systems to provide small loans to people who borrow only occasionally to meet some pressing need or to capitalize on some fleeting opportunity. Participants value this flexibility highly and are willing to pay significant amounts to sustain access to these valuable services. The value, in the eyes of users, of these services is enhanced by the close proximity of informal financial transactions to where users work, live, or do most of their shopping. Formal finance would be more useful if it embodied more of these convenience features.

References

Bouman, F. J. A. 1979. "The ROSCA: Financial Technology of an Informal Savings and Credit Institution in Developing Countries." *Savings and Development* 3:253-276

Bouman, F.J.A. and R. Houtman. 1988. "Pawnbroking as an Instrument of Rural Banking in the Third World." *Economic Development and Cultural Change* 37:69-89.

Geertz, C. 1962. "The Rotating Credit Association: A 'Middle Rung' in Development." *Economic Development and Cultural Change* 10:241-263.

Seibel, H.D. 1985. "Saving for Development: A Linkage Model for Informal and Formal Financial Markets." *Quarterly Journal of International Agriculture* 6:390-398.

17

Linking Formal and Informal Finance: An Indonesian Example

Hans Dieter Seibel and Uben Parhusip

Dissatisfaction with the results of many formal credit programs has stimulated searches for new ways to provide more financial services to poor people. Looking more carefully and positively at the performance of informal finance has been a prominent part of these efforts. Recent research has shown that various forms of informal finance are providing sustained and valuable services to many individuals who are seldom, if ever, reached by conventional credit programs. Research is also showing that self-help groups (SHG) play a significant role in this by mobilizing substantial amounts of savings and by making large numbers of loans to members. These groups range from small informal rotating savings associations (ROSCAs) and various types of savings and credit groups to larger semiformal private voluntary organizations (PVOs).

In this chapter we argue that linking SHGs more closely with the formal financial system can solve the transaction cost problem that is pervasive in rural finance, thereby expanding the quantity and quality of financial services for poor people. Three ways have been suggested for doing this. The first is *downgrading* where the objective is to create an environment that induces formal financial intermediaries to reach out and develop financial arrangements with SHGs. A second approach is *upgrading* where the objective is to assist SHGs to become semiformal or formal financial intermediaries. The third way is by developing more direct *links* between SHGs and formal financial intermediaries. In the discussion that follows we report on a pilot project in Indonesia that was aimed at enhancing the linkages between formal finance and various types of SHGs.

Background on Approach

In the early 1980s the German Agency for Technical Cooperation, Gesellschaft fuer Technische Zusammenarbeit (GTZ), sponsored programs in several African countries that focused on expanding the financial services provided by SHGs.[1] These activities focused on informal finance, especially ROSCAs, and ways of linking them with the formal financial system. The results of these efforts, especially in Cameroon and Nigeria, encouraged the Asian and Pacific Regional Agricultural Credit Association to promote similar efforts in Asia. At a meeting in Nanjing, China in 1986, the Association, with GTZ's assistance, agreed to promote baseline research and to also initiate a few pilot programs built around expanding the linkages between formal financial institutions and SHGs. Leaders in several countries, including Indonesia, Nepal, the Philippines, and Thailand, decided to experiment with programs that attempt to facilitate such linkages (Kropp and others).[2]

While these programs are flexible and tailored to local conditions, they are based on six guiding principles:

1. They only work with and through existing formal and informal financial institutions.
2. They stress deposit mobilization.
3. They involve market rates of interest on both loans and deposits in the program.
4. Lending is tied to deposits: individuals and groups can only borrow if they are able to exercise the discipline needed to save in the form of deposits.
5. Loans made to savings groups are secured by group deposits and also by group repayment guarantees.
6. All institutions involved in the program adopt policies that ensure the sustainability of the institutions involved—program revenues should cover the real costs of the program on a long-term basis. The lending institutions must absorb loan recovery risks and be able to cover these costs from their revenues.

Using these guidelines, a pilot linkage program was begun in Indonesia in 1988.

---

1. A summary of much of this work is presented in Seibel and Marx 1987.
2. Acharya (1990) provides a description of the linking program that was developed in Nepal in the late 1980s.

Background on Indonesia

Because Indonesia is a large country with about 180 million inhabitants, there are a large number—possibly as many as 30 million—small enterprises in the country, including farmers. Only a minute percentage of these have access to the formal financial system, which is made up by five large government owned banks, numerous private banks, a number of regional banks, many cooperatives that extend loans, and numerous other formal, semiformal, or completely informal financial institutions and arrangements (Gonzalez-Vega 1982). In total, there are about 15,000 formal financial institutions in the country.

Dissatisfaction with the results of financial repression and, in particular, with many of the government-sponsored credit programs led to major changes in financial market policies starting in 1983. Deregulation included gradual lifting of many restrictions and regulations previously applied to financial markets: for example, interest rate limits, reserve requirements, chartering of new banks, and concessionary rediscount lines in the Central Bank (Bank Indonesia).[3] The net result of these policy changes has been a major increase in deposit mobilization and much more reliance on market forces to mobilize and allocate funds through financial markets. From 1982 to 1990, M2/GDP, the standard measure of financial deepening, increased from .16 to about .45.

There are several financial innovations in Indonesia which are particularly important in providing financial services at market rates and conditions to poor people. The first is a well-established and successful regional lending program for small businesses (Seibel 1989). Another one is the government owned pawnshops in most parts of Indonesia, which are now losing market shares to commercial banks. A third segment is the highly diverse informal financial market that is found in every nook and cranny of the country. This includes informal loans and deposits, financial transactions between individuals as well as group activities, transactions in urban as well as rural areas, and informal financial activities among poor people as well as among people who are more affluent.

The fourth interesting element is a pair of schemes of the Bank of Rakyat Indonesia (BRI), called KUPEDES and SIMPEDES, the first is

---

3. In early 1990 the Central Bank eliminated 32 of its remaining subsidized lines of credit. At about the same time a new regulation was issued that required all domestic commercial banks to lend at least 20 percent of their individual loan portfolios to small enterprises, poor people, or farmers.

a small loan program and the second is a companion deposit mobilization effort (Snodgrass and Patten 1989). In 1983, at the outset of deregulation, the government gave serious consideration to closing most of the village level institutions that had been used to deliver cheap loans to the countryside. This would have included closing about 3,600 village level dependent branches of BRI and eliminating most of the banking facilities available in rural Indonesia. Instead, BRI, under new management committed to the principles of market economy, decided to promote commercial programs to make these branches self-sufficient. KUPEDES and SIMPEDES were major elements of these efforts and they have transformed these village level branches into viable and self-sustaining units. By December 1990, the KUPEDES program was providing US$725 million in small loans to about 1.9 million borrowers in Indonesia at a long-term loss ratio of 2.64 percent. SIMPEDES and other savings schemes were mobilizing funds at the village level from 5.28 million savers, amounting to 124.3 percent of KUPEDES loans outstanding. BRI, which lost 60 percent of all funds lent on behalf of the government under BIMAS before 1983, is now a highly profitable commercial rural bank (Seibel 1989).

Small rural banks set up by PVOs and SHGs under the new deregulation law of October 1988 (Seibel 1989) are the most recent innovation. Finally, daily savings collection at doorsteps is among the most interesting innovation in domestic resource mobilization and has been spreading among small banks in Indonesia since the beginning of deregulation in 1983. While some elements of the formal financial system in Indonesia are providing quality financial services to an increasing number of poor people in the country, the pace is slow—due to the unresolved transaction cost problem in microfinance. Also, it is unlikely if 10 percent of the businesses in the country had regular access to formal financial services in the late 1980s. At the same time, a large percentage of the population, especially poor people, are members of SHGs, that handle loans and deposits. Cursory research suggests that SGHs contact with formal finance is virtually nonexistent.

The Linking Project in Indonesia

In early 1988 the Central Bank organized a task force with the responsibility of developing a pilot program that would link SHGs with the formal financial system. The BRI, the largest bank with a rural mandate, and Bina Swadaya, a prominent private voluntary organization, were other major participants in the task force. APRACA and GTZ agreed to provide technical assistance.

One of the first decisions made by the Task Force was to commission a study of self-help groups. The study was done by Gadjah Mada University (Mubyarto and others 1987). It found a large variety and number of SHGs throughout Indonesia, numbering possibly more than a million. Many of these SHGs, particularly the rotating savings and credit associations—locally called *arisan*—mobilize funds and make loans. Few of these SHGs or their members, however, were dealing directly with formal financial institutions. As a result, few of these SHGs have access to outside funds for lending, many of them did not have access to bank deposit facilities, and many of them have no access to outside training that might help improve the performance of the group. In addition, the study found a small number of private voluntary institutions (PVOs) that were involved in group formation, personal development, training, or providing financial services to SHGs.

Partly based on the study, the task force then decided to support a pilot project that focused on linking SHGs with banks. The project leadership was housed in Central Bank facilities in Yogyakarta, and field activities were concentrated in three regions of Indonesia: Bali, Central Java, and North Sumatra. Emphasis was placed on developing linking programs that would keep transaction costs low for individuals, the groups, and also financial intermediaries.

Because of the tremendous diversity of conditions found in Indonesia, the task force decided early that no single linkage model would be appropriate throughout the country. Instead, they encouraged participants in the program to define many of their own operating procedures. This might include SHGs receiving loans directly from banks or indirectly through a semiformal PVO that supports SHGs. The banks, in turn, were allowed to use loans from the Central Bank at market rates of interest to fund part of their loans to SHGs. SHGs then only lent to microentrepreneurs who were the ultimate borrowers. The final borrower may be an individual or a group of individuals.

A key feature of the project is that individual and group access to Central Bank funds is strongly influenced by the amounts of deposits they assemble. These deposits provide partial collateral for loans, allow borrowers to establish some working relationship with the lender before asking for a loan, and also inculcate financial discipline. While the ratio of deposits-to-loans may vary, a ratio of 1 unit deposited for each 5 units borrowed was a general guideline in the project.

Another key feature of the project was that Central Bank loans carry interest rates that are approximately equal to the rates paid by banks on three-month fixed deposits, and market rates of interest are applied to participant loans and deposits. Interest rate decisions on loans and deposits are largely determined locally by the participant—not by the project. This results in banks having incentives to stress deposit mobilization, savers having additional incentives to deposit (in addition to having access to loans), and participants having incentives to borrow judiciously. It also results in margins on loans that allow the program to be self-sustaining.

In 1989 the inflation rate in Indonesia was about 6 percent, while the interest payments on deposit accounts in banks ranged from 12 to 17 percent. Time deposits in some banks received as high as 24 percent per annum and the effective costs of borrowing formal loans ranged from 17 percent to whatever the market would bear. Some operators of microenterprises have small loans from banks that carry effective interest charges that run as high as 100 percent.

Inspired by project facilitators, participating banks agreed to lend directly to SHGs at more favorable rates, ranging from 24 to 29 percent per annum. The banks, in turn, are able to borrow money from the Central Bank for about 15 percent. Bank loans made to PVOs carried interest rates ranging from 22 to 24 percent. The end user of the loans effectively pay from 30 to 44 percent or more per annum, the exact rates being decided by the SHGs. The ultimate borrowers pay an interest rate that is significantly lower than they would have to pay if they borrowed from moneylenders, the PVOs and banks earn enough margin on their lending to make them interested in participating, and the Central Bank charges an interest high enough so that deposit mobilization by banks is not discouraged.

Project Implementation

Program implementation activities began in October 1988 when approximately 1,000 members of SHGs received training and information about the project through PVOs that were participating in the program. The first loans were made in late May 1989 and by the end of December 1990, 417 SHGs had received a total of 496 group loans with maturities ranging between 6 and 18 months. These group loans were on-lent to about 7,200 SHG members, about 50 percent of whom were women. The total value of loans made during the first 18 months of the project was equivalent to about US$1.9 million, an average of about US$2,850 per group, and an average of about US$165 per group member.

This is 42 percent of the average KUPEDES loan, thus reaching a lower echelon than BRI.

Most SHGs participating in the pilot program mobilized additional funds in order to make deposits associated with their loans. For example, a group with an arisan may ask members to contribute an additional amount at each rotation that is put in a separate fund to meet the deposit requirements associated with later borrowing from a bank. Thus, the total amount of savings being handled by the participating groups is much larger than the amounts mobilized by banks as a direct result of the pilot project. Nevertheless, the deposits mobilized by banks grew rapidly in the initial phase of the project. By the end of December 1990 borrowing groups had deposited the equivalent of about US$240,000 in participating banks; this amounted to about the equivalent of US$575 per group. The ratio of individual group deposits to loan value ranged from 1:4 to 1:6 for 89 percent of the loans, with the average ratio being around 1:5. This ratio will gradually decline as repayments are made on loans.

A total of 26 banks were participating in the program: 12 private banks, and 14 branches of government owned banks. In addition, 16 PVOs were involved in training, group guidance, or processing of loans. Forty-nine percent of the loan volume was lent by banks directly to SHGs with the remaining funds going through PVOs to SHGs. Up until mid-1990 the Central Bank was the only external source of loan funds. A new regulation in early 1990 required all domestic banks to lend a minimum of 20 percent of their loan portfolios to small business and microenterprises. This encouraged several large government banks to consider offering lines of credit under the project.

While it was yet too early by the end of 1990 to come to final judgments about the sustainability of this program, early signs were promising. With an arrears ratio below 1 percent at the bank level, loan recovery performance was excellent, banks and PVOs were eager to participate, and the subsidies to the program were small, mostly in the form of technical assistance to start the effort. It was particularly heartening that all of the participants in the program were treating borrowing as a serious business: banks and PVOs were very concerned about making loans on the basis of creditworthiness and borrowers were very concerned about incurring debt only for projects that had high probabilities of excellent returns. Surprisingly, only one of the participating banks insisted on credit guarantees by the project. All other lenders agreed to rely on a careful selection process and deposits for their informal guarantees.

Conclusions

Only time can tell if the linking project in Indonesia will reach a large number of poor people and, at the same time, also become a permanent and self-sustaining feature of Indonesia's financial system. In our opinion, its continued success will largely depend on four major factors.

The first factor is continued economic growth in the country. SHG members will have more attractive investment opportunities and incentives to borrow, greater abilities to deposit, and more capacity to repay loans if the overall economy is expanding. A basic assumption on which the linking project is built is that members of SHGs have attractive investment opportunities that exceed their own capacities to save, the residual capacity of the group to save, and the ability of other elements of the informal financial system to supply. This assumption is less likely to be valid in an economy that is moribund or depressed.

The second factor is the policies applied to financial markets in the country. Permission to charge market rates of interest on loans and to pay attractive rates of interest on deposits are vital ingredients in the success of the project. Relatively high rates of interest on funds borrowed from the Central Bank are also an important signal to banks that they should continue to seek voluntary deposits. In the unlikely event that the government decided to again adopt cheap credit policies it would be impossible for banks to provide strong incentives to savers, lenders would find it impossible to cover their costs and risks of making small loans from their revenues, and banks would have no incentive to seek voluntary deposits because of the cheap money offered by the Central Bank. In retrospect, it was fortunate that financial markets in Indonesia were deregulated in the 1980s when the project was started.

The third factor is a more subtle issue and relates to the internal cohesiveness and solidarity of SHGs. The multitude of SHGs in Indonesia persists because they provide group goods or economies in transaction costs that cannot be realized by individuals alone. A group organized around an irrigation system, for example, may be an efficient way of maintaining the system and of rationing water, something an individual alone could not accomplish. Likewise, a ROSCA may provide members with a type of insurance in the form of credit reserves that can be called upon in times of emergency, while other ROSCAs may provide members contractual savings arrangements that enhance incentives to save. Again, these benefits are something individuals cannot realize alone. In a social sense, these groups are glued together by the benefits produced by group actions; they maintain their equilibrium by continuing to provide these group goods. It may be easy to dissolve this glue and upset this equilibrium by inserting outside programs into these groups. Clearly, a program that included subsidized credit could lead to problems as groups became short-term "rent seekers." Special care must be used in providing only outside programs that build on and enhance the intrinsic benefits of these groups.

Bureaucratic behavior is the fourth important factor. In large part, the pilot project in Indonesia worked well because appropriate incentives were built into the system for all major participants. The government and the Central Bank were willing to support the program because it promised to service a target group that had been difficult and costly for the government to reach in the past, and because the program used relatively small amounts of government money. Banks and PVOs were willing to participate because they expected to realize additional revenue from their share of the interest margins, and also because they expected the program to increase their volume of clients. Members of SHGs were willing to participate because the program offered them opportunities to access formal loans and to also receive attractive rates of return on their deposits. Sustaining these incentives will be a vital factor in the long-term success of the project.

The initial promising results of the linking project in Indonesia suggest it may be worthwhile for other countries to consider this technique as a way of expanding the access of poor people to more formal financial services. At the same time, we caution that it is necessary to know a good deal about SHGs and the services they provide before starting such programs. Also, we suggest these programs will be more likely to succeed if they evolve gradually in economies that are growing and under financial market polices that are deregulated.

References

Acharya, Meena. 1990. "Promotion of Linkages Between Banks and Self-Help Groups in Nepal." Unpublished paper. Bangkok, Thailand: Asian and Pacific Regional Agricultural Credit Association.

Gonzalez-Vega, Claudio. 1982. "Indonesia: Financial Services for the Rural Poor." Unpublished report prepared for the Agency for International Development, Department of Agricultural Economics and Rural Sociology. Columbus, Ohio: The Ohio State University.

Kropp, E. and others. 1989. *Linking Self-help Groups and Banks in Developing Countries*. Eschborn: TZ-Verlag.

Mubyarto, Bunawan Sumodiningrat, Loekman Soetrisno & Bambang Isawan. 1987. *Survey of Self-Help Groups in Indonesia*. Jakarta: Bank Indonesia/Yogyakarta.

Seibel H. D., and M. T. Marx. 1987. *Rural Financial Markets in Africa: Case Studies of Linkages Between Informal and Formal Financial Institutions*. Saarbruecken/Fort Lauderdale: Breitenbach Publishers.

Snodgrass, Donald R., and Richard H. Patten. 1989. "Reform of Rural Credit in Indonesia: Inducing Bureaucracies to Behave Competitively." Development Discussion Paper No. 315. Cambridge, Massachusetts: Harvard Institute for International Development, Harvard University.

18

The Financial Evolution of Small Businesses in Indonesia[1]

Ross H. McLeod

An argument often made in the literature is that formal loans are mainly directed to borrowers with established reputations and collateral. Although there is much truth in this argument, it does not necessarily follow that orthodox lending practices of banks and other institutions for small firms are socially non optimal. A major task of this chapter is to present arguments in support of the contrary view. A second popularly accepted notion is that small firms are forced to rely on either limited self-finance or exorbitantly expensive moneylender loans. An important finding of this study is that small firms' financing options steadily widen over time as they build up their assets and their reputation.

Small businesses rely on both formal and informal finance. The former aspect can be studied by looking at the formal lending institutions involved, and to this end the writer interviewed the managers of all the banks operating in Yogyakarta, Indonesia, together with a number of merchant banks and development finance institutions based in the national capital, Jakarta. This approach is not appropriate for the study of informal finance, however, since there is no clearly identifiable set of institutions or individuals that constitute an informal finance sector. Instead, it is necessary to look directly at the firms and individuals involved in informal financial transactions. To do this, interviews were carried out with the owners (or, in a few cases, high level managers) of some 120 businesses in Yogyakarta over a period of about ten months. The largest firm studied had a workforce of

1. Originally published in *Savings and Development* 15(1991): 187-209. Reprinted with permission of the editor of the journal.

about 800 people and a small number employed a few hundred workers, but the majority fell within the ranges of 5 to 19 and 20 to 99 workers, which correspond to the government's "small" and "medium" categories of firm size.

Bank Lending Practices

To any person or organization contemplating making a loan, the possibility of default is of fundamental importance. This risk distinguishes lending transactions from other kinds of transactions, and is central to explaining much of what we observe in financial markets.

Lenders come to terms with uncertainty in two basic ways. First, it can be reduced by requiring the borrower to provide security for the loan, by acquiring information that will allow estimates of the probability of default to be made more confidently, and by monitoring the subsequent activities of the borrower. Second, it can be offset by incorporating an allowance for default risk within the nominal lending rate offered to the intending borrower.

These approaches are not mutually exclusive. All of the uncertainty-reducing measures involve costs, and for this reason there can be trade-offs between them. There is also a tradeoff between these measures as a whole and the uncertainty-offsetting measure. Furthermore, it should be noted that the costs of uncertainty-reducing measures and other administrative costs vary across different lender/borrower combinations. Other things being equal, the lender whose costs are lowest for a given borrower has a competitive advantage over other potential lenders. In particular, banks are not always the lowest cost lenders, as shall be seen below.

Uncertainty-Reducing Measures

Provision of Security

In regard to the relationship between asset endowments and borrowing opportunities, there is no doubt that lenders will be more willing to lend (or to lend at cheaper rates) if the borrower has suitable assets with which to secure the loan. The impression given by many writers is that there is something inefficient or undesirable about lenders requiring this security. It seems all too easily forgotten that all investment projects are risky, and there is no reason why the lender should bear the risk.

The reader can readily imagine the strength of demand for, say, million dollar loans if they could be had at moderate interest rates and without the provision of security. The idea of playing with someone else's money is an appealing one: if the borrower's investment project is successful he gains, but if it fails, someone else loses. By requiring security, the lender encourages the borrower in the most direct way to carefully judge the likely success of his proposed investment. This is highly desirable, for the borrower can usually gather and analyze information regarding an investment within his own field of specialization at lower cost than can the lender.

Contrary to the popular views outlined above, bank insistence on the provision of collateral is consistent with efficient allocation of investible resources. There is most likely a high degree of correlation between (sound) investment opportunities and endowment of assets (and thus, ability to provide collateral). A businessman who is well endowed with assets is likely to have become so by having had a high income in the past and, of course, by having chosen not to dissipate it all in consumption. Clearly, the accumulation of wealth is one of the best indicators of entrepreneurial ability.

There are good reasons, then, for requiring security for loans. It is trivial to point out that some sound investment projects may not be undertaken for want of suitable collateral, because some unsound projects will also be precluded for exactly the same reason. On balance, the latter effect can be expected to dominate (if the foregoing arguments are valid), and it can hardly be argued that society is disadvantaged by a practice that systematically favors implementation of those investment projects with the better chance of success.

Because of the impracticability of physical-possession type security for loans to businesses and the costliness of, and other difficulties with, the legal documentation type, commercial banks in Indonesia must give a good deal of attention to other uncertainty-reducing and offsetting measures. In sharp contrast to the no-questions-asked approach of their village and market bank competitors, and despite the tendency in the literature to ascribe overriding importance to collateral, its availability was in fact no guarantee of obtaining a bank loan among the firms studied; rather, it was merely a prerequisite.

Information Acquisition

The most obvious ways of acquiring uncertainty-reducing information are by interviewing the borrower, inspecting his place of business, and requesting him to submit a variety of data. The extent of information sought depends largely on the size of the intended loan. Indeed, one of the biggest problems in lending to small firms is that their book-keeping is often rudimentary or nonexistent. The owners are usually capable of storing all of the relevant information (about prices, costs, revenues, money owed and owing, and so on) in their heads. In this circumstance, banks in Yogyakarta usually required the prospective borrower to maintain a checking account for three to six months before they would consider making a loan. Cash flows into and out of the account could then be monitored to provide at least some of the information that would otherwise be recorded in the firm's books. This, of course, is a very cheap way of obtaining additional knowledge of the borrower's activities.

Third parties with knowledge of the intending borrower's character and activities were the other major source of information used in loan proposal evaluations. These included the applicant's customers, suppliers, neighbors, other banks, and so on. It is very important for branch managers to maintain a wide range of contacts within the business community to whom they can turn for such assistance.

Monitoring

For some loans, banks supervise the expenditure of loan money (for example, by paying it directly to the supplier of items of plant and equipment, or checking with the supplier's bank to see that payment has been received) and monitor the activity of the firm by visiting its place of business or by requiring regular financial or trading reports to be submitted. Again, these procedures are often too costly for small loans to be worthwhile. Nevertheless, there is always at least some monitoring, even if it amounts to nothing more than checking to see that scheduled loan repayments and interest commitments are being met. The rationale for monitoring is that it gives the bank early warning of potential default.

Offsetting Uncertainty and Administrative Costs

In a freely functioning banking system, banks can be expected to seek an optimal (profit maximizing) combination of efforts devoted to reducing uncertainty, on the one hand, and interest rates sufficient to cover both default losses and administrative costs, on the other. Since bank loan transactions can differ substantially among themselves—in particular, with respect to the credit reputation of the borrower, the quality of collateral offered, and the size of the loan—it can be expected that this optimal combination will likewise differ across different transactions.

At one of the banks in Yogyakarta, for example, lending rates ranged from 19 to 27 percent per annum. The exact rate chosen reflected the nature and value of assets offered as security and the bank's evaluation of the borrower's character and ability, as well as the size of the loan. Furthermore, interest rates tended to be lower for borrowers with long-established businesses and for those who had maintained a sound borrowing relationship for some time.

Banks and Competing Sources of Finance

The extent to which banks can offset anticipated loan losses and administrative costs by raising their lending rates is constrained by the demand conditions under which they operate. Demand curves for bank loans are by no means perfectly inelastic. Potential borrowers faced with higher bank lending rates have several other options available to them. For example, they can reduce expenditure by hiring rather than purchasing expensive items and by purchasing second hand rather than new plant and equipment. They can switch to other sources of funds. And, of course, they can simply postpone or shelve planned consumption or investment spending. These considerations afford a plausible explanation for various characteristics of bank lending. For example, each bank had some lower limit on loan size. One bank manager argued that there was "no demand" for loans smaller than the lower limit. The proper interpretation of this appears to be that there would be no demand for smaller loans if the interest rate attaching to them were set sufficiently high to offset the default probability and cover administrative costs. As another manager put it, his bank could not compete with other lenders such as the village and market banks in the provision of small loans.

At the other extreme, the larger the loan, the more resources can profitably be devoted to loan appraisal. Not only is more information collected and analyzed at the branch level, but also higher levels of bank management become involved in the decision making process when loans exceed specified limits. Although this increases the bank's costs in absolute terms, the lending rate can still be lower than that for smaller loans because costs per rupiah lent are less. Nevertheless, the commercial banks begin to run up against competition from other sources as loan size increases—namely, from development banks, merchant banks, and other nonbank institutions—that specialize in large-scale financing activities.

It seems more meaningful to explain these aspects of lending activities in low-income countries in terms of the basic notion of specialization or division of labor, rather than merely asserting that financial institutions "have borrowed the practices and traditions of those in metropolitan centers abroad" (Bhatia and Khatkhate 1975, p. 136). Likewise, to say that, "...small firms...often lack access to institutional credit" (World Bank, 1978, p.6) is quite misleading. It is more to the point to argue that institutional lenders to some extent lack access to—or cannot compete in the financing of—small firms.

Banks and Small Business

It is broadly true that banks are not concerned with financing beginners in business. They do not lend to persons who have yet to accumulate some minimum amount of assets, or to demonstrate both capability in business and creditworthiness. Nevertheless it would be wrong to infer from this that banks are not interested in small businesses. A customer who can profitably use a large loans is certainly a much more interesting proposition than one who requests a small one, but the fact is that there are relatively few large businesses in countries such as Indonesia. Consequently the banks have little choice but to rely on small firms for a large part of their income. Perhaps more important is the fact that some small firms grow to become large ones; the bank that fails to win the business of firms when they are small may find difficulty in doing so when they grow larger.

One of the important tasks of bank branches, therefore, is to seek out and gain the accounts of small firms with good future prospects. Once a firm has attracted a bank's attention, it is usually only necessary for it to operate a checking account for a short period before it can begin borrowing. In contrast to the significant difficulties involved in obtaining a bank loan for the first time, subsequent loan renewals are largely a formality (provided of course that the borrower meets his commitments); furthermore, it is usual for the loan size to be increased and the interest rate to be reduced over time. It is clear then that the supposed lack of access of small firms to bank finance is greatly exaggerated. Indeed, it is worth noting that in Yogyakarta it was by no means unusual for offers of bank loans to interviewed firms to be rejected, and that a substantial number of small firms did not have any kind of bank account.

Diversity of Financing Options

A partial explanation for the fact that many small firms have no banking relationship is that there are various means by which entrepreneurs can deal with finance problems, of which bank borrowing is only one. To gain an appreciation of the other options, I interviewed a large number of small firms, in a wide range of industries.

The data collected for any one firm do not relate merely to its condition at a point in time. Rather, they represent a case history—in most instances stretching over several years, but in others for more than a generation, since several firms had been handed down by their founders to their children and even their grandchildren. The information collected in the interviews has been presented as a series of some 116 case studies (McLeod 1980, Appendix A). One such is presented later for illustrative purposes. A description of the various financial options described in these cases is provided in the following sections.

Self-Finance

Many of the firms interviewed relied heavily on self-finance for their expansion, and they often did so by choice—not because they were denied outside finance. Nor was reliance on self-finance a brake on rapid growth of businesses. The more capable entrepreneurs operated their enterprises so effectively that the reinvestment of profits was more than adequate to ensure rapid growth. Of course, a firm that generates little profit cannot be expected to grow rapidly by self-financing its investments, nor will it be easy for it to borrow. But it can hardly be argued that this reflects any inefficiency in the capital market.

Self-finance of course always requires that the firm's owner be prepared to forego some present consumption in the expectation that the opportunities for future consumption will be expanded by virtue of the investment being undertaken. Many businesses grow slowly, if at all, simply because their owners are not prepared to make the sacrifices (in terms of current consumption and leisure) that are necessary for rapid growth.

Another aspect of self-finance was the provision of funds by individuals who became shareholders or partners in the firm concerned. Although there are many small, limited liability companies and limited liability partnerships in Indonesia, it should be noted that the number of shareholders or partners in each case is almost invariably small; they are usually relatives or friends of the principal owner-manager. There is almost no trading in such firms' shares nor public issues of debt or equity; often such businesses are legally incorporated simply to enable them to obtain some kind of licence or government concession. Nevertheless, some firms did increase their capital base significantly in this manner.

One other common informal equity-financing method for small businesses was observed. The procedure was for an outsider (often a middleman) to finance working capital requirements in return for a certain share of revenue of the enterprise. The outsider was therefore effectively a shareholder in the business, but took no management role in it. The important difference between this system and that discussed above is that equity is held for a defined period rather than indefinitely. The most obvious example is agriculture; here, the equity period is the time between planting and harvest. Another example was the hiring of small motor vehicles used for carrying passengers or goods; in this case the period was as short as a day.

Sources of External Finance

The various sources of external funds to which firms may have access can now be considered.

Supplier Credit for Capital Items. The suppliers of capital items have an incentive to finance customers' purchases, to boost their own sales. Terms and conditions varied from case to case. The interest charge was sometimes explicit, and was sometimes simply built into the purchase price and agreed payment schedule. Legal documentation of the agreement was sometimes, but not always required, and the time for repayment was often flexible.

Trade Credit. Financial requirements relate to working capital as well as to fixed assets. Much of the working capital requirement can be financed by trade credit. The extent to which this occurs appears to depend largely on industry characteristics: advance payment by the customer is much less likely for a bus line than for a construction company, for example. Note also that in some cases the entrepreneur will find it more to his advantage to finance his suppliers or customers than conversely. That, of course, is simply the opposite side of the same coin.

Again, credit terms varied from case to case. Credit was extended for as little as a day or two and as long as two to three months. Discounts offered for cash payment were as little as 1 or 2 percent and as high as 10 percent, depending on the industry concerned, but a charge of 3 to 5 percent per month for trade credit was typical. Often it was taken for granted that credit would be accepted, and no cash discounts were offered.

Family, Friends, Fellow Business Owners, and Friends-of-Friends. Business owners typically borrowed and lent among their circle of family members, friends, and fellow businessmen. Such transactions sometimes carried an explicit interest charge, but sometimes there was nothing more than an implied obligation to provide similar assistance to the same, or another, member of the group on some future occasion. Lending was also transacted between friends-of-friends. Typically, lending rates in this informal short-term money market were of the order of 3 to 5 percent per month, and most loans would be repaid within a month or two—and often considerably more quickly.

Banks, Moneylenders, and Other Financial Institutions. Certain firms and individuals specialize in the business of providing finance to others. In some cases this involves lending only their own funds, but they may also act as intermediaries for other lenders. The cost of bank loans has already been discussed. Financial institutions dealing in very large loans to highly respected customers were able to lend at somewhat lower rates. Moneylenders' rates in Yogyakarta were often of the order of 5 percent per month, with a range of 3 to 10 percent.

One interesting case was that of the several moneylenders operating in Yogyakarta's main market. It was estimated that about one-third of all the traders there borrowed from moneylenders to finance their stocks. Typically, their debt was of the order of Rp10,000 to Rp50,000, and the interest rate was about 7.5 percent per month. Interest was calculated daily and paid to the moneylender as he made the rounds of his clients. Alternatively, the trader might decide to borrow an additional amount or to reduce the outstanding balance.

The reader may view that this is a usurious rate of interest, but the following rough estimate of the moneylenders costs suggests otherwise. Suppose our "travelling banker" employs someone at a modest salary of Rp250,000 per month or Rp10,000 per day, or notionally pays himself this amount. Assume he services 80 customers per day (equivalent to about 10 per hour, or about 6 minutes per customer). Finally, assume the average loan outstanding is Rp50,000. Then the cost per customer per day is Rp125. Expressed as a percentage of the loan balance this is 0.25 percent per day, or nearly 8 percent per month—roughly equal to the level reported here, before making any allowance for the moneylender's own cost of funds. Evidently, the moneylender's customers are happy to pay this rate; the value of the service provided—obviating the need for costly trips to a bank to deposit or withdraw cash—would appear to outweigh its cost.

Case Study: Yogyakarta Bus Company[2]

The following case study illustrates how one small business in Yogyakarta utilized several of the financing options described above.

The interviewee was Mr. Sutarjo, age 45. His parents were farmers. He had some elementary school education, but this was interrupted by the Japanese invasion and the subsequent struggle for independence against the Dutch. In his teens he had an interest in driving and appears to have had some lessons in Yogyakarta. Later, he went to Surabaya and obtained a job as a driver's assistant, which he held for about four months. During this time he gained experience both in driving and in the repair and maintenance of motor vehicles.

At the age of 22 he married, and at about this time his parents bought him a secondhand truck, enabling him to establish his own trucking business. He drove it himself as well as carrying out any necessary repairs. After about five years he had saved enough to be able to purchase a second used truck, which had to be restored to working order before it could be used. Two years later this was repeated when another truck owner was forced to sell his vehicle due to his inability to do necessary repairs.

After a further five years he decided to change the emphasis of his business and began trading in timber. Apparently he was able to earn a living from this activity, but it was not very profitable and so he sold

---

2. Pseudonyms are used to preserve confidentiality. Where the present tense is used, it reflects the situation as it was at the time of the interview.

one of the three or four trucks he owned by this time and bought a second-hand bus. He drove this himself on the route between Yogyakarta and a small town nearby. Meanwhile he continued to employ other workers to operate the remaining trucks.

During the last 5 years his fleet of buses has increased to 13. Apart from the first four, they have been purchased new. The first two new buses were fully financed by a loan of Rp7.5 million from one of the banks. The loan extended over two and a half years and was repaid on time. Subsequently, Sutarjo has had no further bank loans, and indeed now has no relationship at all with any bank. He has purchased an additional seven new buses (one at a time) from the Ford and Mercedes-Benz dealers in Yogyakarta. Both these firms have provided finance on fairly similar terms: 20 to 30 percent down payment, with 12 to 18 months to repay at about 1.8 percent per month interest. Sutarjo prefers the simplicity of supplier finance to the difficult and time-consuming process of obtaining bank loans—even though the latter are nominally cheaper.

The Process of Financial Evolution

Analyses that stress the supposed lack of access of small firms to external finance are essentially based on snapshots, whereas a much more meaningful perspective is afforded by moving pictures. Such analyses never question why it is that some firms are large and some small, by what process the currently large firms came to be that way, or whether there is any logic in suggesting that small, relatively unproven (or even unsuccessful!) business owners should be able to obtain external finance on the same terms as the owners of larger businesses who have already demonstrated their ability to employ resources effectively.

Since small firms have more limited access to finance than do large firms, and since many large firms were small at the time of their establishment, it follows that access to finance must widen as firms grow—or more generally, as they age. Having discussed the diversity of means of financing the capital requirements of enterprises (both large and small), the next step is to elaborate upon this concept of financial evolution of firms—that is, the notion that the range of financing options tends to broaden over time, resulting in a concomitant reduction in the cost of finance to the firm.

The case studies on which this chapter is based typically show that, after a preestablishment phase during which the prospective business owner obtained some kind of formal or informal preparatory training, he received relatively modest backing from his family, or perhaps from a close friend, to help finance the establishment of his enterprise.[3] Following this he depended very largely on the reinvestment of profits to finance the initial growth of the firm. As time passed the circle of people and firms willing to provide him with finance widened, and eventually came to include banks and perhaps other formal financial institutions.

It is not difficult to explain the process of financial evolution of the business owner. At the time when he takes his first step in business, he has no reputation in the business community. He is unlikely, therefore, to enjoy financial backing from any party outside his immediate family and circle of close friends, because the outside financier has virtually no basis for ascertaining the chances of recouping his funds. In many cases, of course, parents simply hand down control of an already established enterprise after the son or daughter in question has gained sufficient working experience to be able to manage it.

The next stage is a phase of consolidation and learning by doing. It is the period during which the business community evaluates the individual's talent for business—when it discovers whether he has what is necessary to succeed as an independent business owner. In this phase, he is very much restricted to self-finance: his family has fulfilled its obligation by helping him to get started, but the business community does not yet feel well enough informed to provide him with additional funds. Nevertheless, by virtue of the simple fact of a business being in existence, information is constantly generated within the business community about it and its owner. Two kinds of such information can be distinguished—that which concerns the ability of the owner to perceive opportunities for profit and to bring them to fruition, and that which concerns his record in such matters as honesty, reliability, and eschewal of sharp practices.

The people in the best position to acquire information of these kinds are those closest to the business owner—both in terms of physical proximity and in terms of business matters. Information is accumulated by these people and firms, and then filters out to the wider community. The main driving force is the value of knowledge, for one of the most important keys to success in business is to be well informed. Nobody wants to find himself doing business with, owed money by, or in any other way dependent on, an unreliable firm or individual. The new

---

3. This often closely coincided with the time of marriage—which seemed to symbolize the moment at which the son or daughter became independent of the family.

business owner is therefore watched by many people during the period in which he consolidates his position in the business world.

Suppliers of inputs will soon see whether the new firm is successful, by paying attention to growth in the orders it places. If the indications are favorable, they are likely to begin to extend credit on purchases. Likewise the supplier of capital goods is well placed to observe the firm's performance and thus to evaluate the risk that would be involved in financing its purchases of such items. A firm that establishes a good reputation may then find that its customers are prepared to make advance payments on their orders. Besides trade credit, bank finance eventually becomes available.

To summarize: the longer a business continues to operate successfully, the wider the financing options open to its owner. The riskiness of lending to it declines, or is perceived to decline, within the business community of which it is a part, and the price paid to compensate for this risk declines correspondingly. The business owner becomes freer to search for the kind of finance that offers him the most attractive combination of characteristics. Nominal cost is only one of several aspects taken into consideration; he will also be interested in the swiftness with which finance can be arranged, the amount of information disclosure required, security arrangements, and the repayment schedule.

A number of observers have looked at the operation of informal financial markets in countries such as Indonesia and concluded that their operations were imperfect. In other words, if there were some omniscient deity willing to reveal which persons had latent entrepreneurial ability, then capital could be directed to the control of this group; society would obviously benefit. In this sense, there is a market imperfection. To judge the efficiency of markets with respect to this standard, however, does not seem helpful. Complete information is a useful assumption for constructing many economic models, as is the assumption of zero transport costs. But the admission that information gathering and transportation are costly does not, in any meaningful sense, imply that markets are imperfect. The only relevant issues are whether there are available more efficient means of production of information or transport, and whether the optimum amounts are being produced.

It can therefore be conceded that some potentially able entrepreneurs will be constrained by lack of funds, and that others less able will put them to bad use. Until some better way of identifying latent entrepreneurial talent is found, however, there is no basis for arguing that this problem is indicative of market imperfection.

In any case, it should be reemphasized that individuals do not need to have a relatively large amount of capital at their disposal before they can demonstrate their entrepreneurial ability. Consider Ms. Tjan—now the owner of a thriving restaurant—who started out selling *sate* from a roadside stall.[4] Having demonstrated her entrepreneurial ability and also having built up some savings, she was eventually able to borrow from various relatives and friends in order to establish her first small restaurant. Consider Mr. Suseno—now the owner of a huge metal casting and fabricating plant—who began his career producing peanut oil, employing just two workers to pound peanuts by hand and using a rice cooking pot to extract the oil.[5] Consider Mr. Untung—now the owner of a large and rapidly expanding automotive dealership and workshop—whose first venture was the production of receipt books from scrap paper cut to size by hand.[6] These and various other case studies tell the same sort of story: where entrepreneurial talent exists, it will eventually find an outlet for expression.

Of course, it is inherently impossible to disprove that sometimes this does not happen. We have no convincing test of entrepreneurial ability other than evidence of success as an entrepreneur. If such evidence is lacking, the explanation could be lack of ability or lack of access to finance. Those who favor the finance constraint explanation, however, must explain why many new entrepreneurs are able to surmount financing obstacles to their progress while others cannot.

The writer's interpretation of the case study material as a whole is that obtaining finance is just one item in a long list of problems encountered during the attempted exploitation of opportunities for profit. The list also includes understanding available technology, organizing the use of factors of production in accordance with that technology, dealing with all government agencies with an interest in the enterprise, handling industrial relations and public relations, delegating responsibility to managers and supervisors, marketing the product, responding quickly to changing circumstances, and so on. With the exception of having the awareness and imagination to perceive opportunities for profit in the first place, the ability to cope with all these kinds of problems would seem to be the most fundamental component of entrepreneurship. In short, it seems much more plausible to argue that lack of entrepreneurial ability makes access to finance

---

4. McLeod (1980), Case Study 77. *Sate* consists of small pieces of meat, barbecued on a bamboo skewer.
5. McLeod (1980), Case Study 32.
6. McLeod (1980), Case Study 64.

difficult, rather than that lack of access to finance holds back entrepreneurship.

Conclusion

The notion that lack of finance is a major obstacle for small firms is not supported by this study. Indeed, the contention that entrepreneurs' plans for expansion are thwarted by lack of access to credit does not sit well with the observation that a very large proportion of economic activity is organized by small firms in Indonesia, nor with the fact that most of the successful and rapidly growing firms interviewed during the course of fieldwork had extremely modest beginnings. If finance is the problem that it is often made out to be, how is it that many small firms are able to prosper and grow?

Furthermore, although it is true that finance is often considerably more expensive for small, new firms, and that their range of financing options is more limited, there is no compelling reason to believe that these observations reflect imperfections in low-income countries' finance markets. Finance transactions involve uncertainty because of the time element involved. Efforts to reduce uncertainty are costly, and they are subject to economies of scale; uncertainty is greater when the borrower has yet to establish a reputation. For these reasons, it is socially optimal for small, new firms to be faced with higher finance costs.

Finally, the empirical work discussed in this chapter presents a challenge to those who hold the view that the reluctance of banks to lend to small (or, more accurately, new) firms is evidence of imperfection in financial markets. It has shown that there are many competing financing arrangements for such firms—including the supply of bank credit indirectly, through other, often larger firms. I have also argued that banks often find themselves at a competitive disadvantage. If this argument is correct, it follows that empirical attempts to validate the imperfections hypothesis must focus on these competing financing arrangements rather than the banks. To concentrate on the latter—as has largely been the case hitherto—is simply to ignore almost everything relevant to the issue.

References

Bhatia, Rattan J. and Deena R. Khatkhate. 1975. "Financial Intermediation, Savings Mobilization, and Entrepreneurial Development: The African Experience." *IMF Staff Papers* 22 : 132-158

McLeod, R. H. 1980.   "Finance and Entrepreneurship in the Small-Business Sector in Indonesia," Ph.D. dissertation. Sydney, Australian National University.

World Bank. 1978.   "Employment and Development of Small Enterprises." Unpublished report prepared by The World Bank in Washington, D.C.

19

Small-Scale Enterprise Dynamics and the Evolving Role of Informal Finance

Carl Liedholm

This chapter examines the dynamics of small-scale manufacturing enterprises in low-income countries and the evolving role of informal finance in that process.[1] Topics that fall within the purview of firm dynamics include the creation, evolution, and disappearance of firms and how these patterns vary by country, stage of development, industrial sector, and policy environment.

Studies of small firm dynamics are important because they provide insights into the feasible and desirable patterns of growth in manufacturing output and employment. Since small firms dominate the industrial scene in most developing countries, a deeper understanding of how these firms evolve may make it possible to pursue an industrialization path that builds on these enterprises, thereby leading to results that are potentially both more equitable and efficient than alternatives stressing large-scale firms. Such studies can also uncover ways that policies and programs can facilitate, or at least not impede, this evolutionary process. There is increasing evidence that

---

1. Small-scale is defined here in terms of employment and generally refers to those firms with 50 workers or less. The term "microenterprise," which is defined in this chapter as a firm with ten or less workers, is used to depict the lower end of the size spectrum. "Modern" small firms are defined to have more than ten employees. The establishments examined in this study include those specifically engaged in the production and repair of manufactured goods. Excluded are establishments engaged in mining, construction, trading, transport, financial, social and personal services.

informal finance plays an important role in this process.[2] Yet, most scholars have not placed informal finance in a dynamic context. McLeod (1986) is a conspicuous exception.

The dynamic themes for both small enterprises and informal finance will be brought together in this chapter. The next section reviews the macro and micro evidence on small firm dynamics. I then examine the evolving demand for finance on the part of these firms, after which I consider the evolving sources of this finance, particularly informal ones. The policy implications of these findings are then examined in a final section.

Small Enterprise Dynamics

The limited number of dynamic analyses on small enterprises in low-income countries can be usefully classified as either macro studies, that examine aggregate changes in the size, location, and sector of such firms, or micro studies, that focus on the birth, growth, and disappearance (death) of individual firms. The salient findings from the dynamic studies will be briefly reviewed.[3]

The macro studies indicate that the absolute number of micro and small enterprises is increasing in virtually all low-income countries. Growth in numbers of firms appears to be highest in enterprises with 2-9 and 10-49 workers, and lowest in one-person enterprises. In some countries, in fact, the number of one-person firms is declining in absolute terms. In over one-half of the countries for which data are available, employment in small and micro firms is growing more slowly than medium and large firm employment, shifting the relative balance of employment toward somewhat larger enterprises. This is one facet of the structural transformation that normally accompanies increases in per capita income. In particular, there is a secular shift toward somewhat larger firms, based in larger localities, producing more modern products.

Micro studies provide important additional insights into the process through which this transformation is taking place. The vast majority of new firms are microenterprises (ten workers or less). As per capita income grows, these enterprises appear increasingly in larger localities. Disappearance (death) rates are highest for micro firms and lowest for

---

2. See for example Chapter 8 on informal finance in the 1989 *World Development Report* by the World Bank.
3. For details and further elaboration, see Liedholm and Parker (1989).

the largest firms (see Table 1). Moreover, death rates are highest in the initial four years, after which firms have a substantially higher chance of survival. Growth rates for surviving microenterprises are quite high, although a sizeable number do not grow at all, particularly those located in more rural localities. Much of the expansion occurs in growth spurts that tend to be concentrated in years five through ten of the firm's life.

The following picture of the life cycle of a typical microenterprise thus begins to emerge. The firm originates as a tiny enterprise—typically a one-person operation—with four years of struggle, a high probability of failure, and little growth. If it survives these first four years, however, it is likely to experience a spurt of growth, that will typically project it into one of the larger size categories of

TABLE 1. Annual Manufacturing Firm Mortality Rates, by Firm Size (in percent)

Region/Country	Dates	Micro (1-9)	Small (10-49)	Medium (50-199)	Total
Africa					
Sierra Leone	1974-80	10.3	-	-	-
Nigeria	1974-80	10.4	-	-	-
Other					
Colombia[e]	1965-71	-	7.7[a]	3.1[a]	5.0
Philippines	1975	-	5.1[b]	-	-
	1972	-	3.5[c]	1.3[c]	-
United States	1976-82	12.5[d]	-	8.3	10.0

- No information

[a] Small modern = 10-24 workers; medium = 25-49 workers.

[b] Small modern = 5-99 workers.

[c] Small modern = 5-19 workers; medium = 20+ workers.

[d] Micro = 1-19 workers.

[e] Data from Colombia and the Philippines uses crude rather than age-specific death rates, due to their reliance on aggregate rather than firm-specific data. This leads to an underestimation of the mortality rate.

Source: Liedholm and Parker (1989).

microenterprise. Relatively few of these microenterprises, however, ultimately graduate or transform themselves into more complex "modern" small and medium enterprises.

Approached from the other end of the processes, how many of the existing "modern" small and medium firms originated as larger firms rather than emerging out of the huge pool of even smaller microenterprises? A summary of the empirical evidence is presented in Table 2.

One important finding is that in five of the six countries the majority of modern small and medium manufacturing firms did not "graduate" from the micro "seedbed," but rather started with more than ten employees. Moreover, the graduation rates in African countries are

TABLE 2. Origins of Modern Small and Medium Private Manufacturing
Firms (with 11 employees or more)

Region/ Country	Year	Number of Firms	Firm Size (Number of Workers)	Percentage with Micro Origin "Graduated"[a]	Percentage with No Micro Origins[b]
Africa					
Nigeria	1965	64	11-200	44	56
Northern Nigeria	1989	59	11-200	42	58
Sierra Leone	1975	42	11-200	30	70
Botswana	1982	20	11-200	20	80
Rwanda	1987	28	30-870	11	89
Asia					
India	1979	244	11-200	66	34
Philippines	1978	47	11-200	49	51
Latin America					
Colombia[c]	1978	76	11-200	50	50

[a] Started with fewer than 11 employees.
[b] Started with 11 employees or more.
[c] Includes metal working establishments only.
Source: Liedholm and Parker (1989).

substantially smaller than those found in Asia and Latin America. In Asia and Latin America, one-half or more of the modern small and medium firms had expanded through the size structure, while in no African country did even half graduate. The percentage of small and medium firms that originated as micro firms, however, is higher in West than East/Central Africa. An important issue is to what extent inadequate access to finance, informal or formal, may have impeded this graduation process.

Evolving Demand for Finance

The magnitude and composition of the small enterprise's effective demand for finance will typically vary as it evolves. In particular, the relative importance of fixed and working capital as well as the overall magnitude of each will change as the firm ages and grows.

At the inception of the small firm, the overall capital needs would seem, at first glance, to be quite modest. The initial capital requirements reported in most studies of manufacturing enterprises are small, ranging from US$63 in Sierra Leone, US$480 in Haiti, US$792 in Jamaica, and US$839 in Bangladesh (Liedholm and Mead 1987). Yet, in relation to average income, the significance of the initial capital barrier looms large. In Bangladesh, the overall initial capital requirement amounted to almost six times the country's per capita income. Moreover, most surveys report the proprietors themselves typically perceive lack of capital to be their most pressing initial constraint in establishing a small enterprise (Liedholm and Mead). These figures also mask the wide variations by type and initial size of small enterprise. In Jamaica, for example, less than US$100 is required to establish a one-person wood carving activity but over US$3,000 to establish a ten person metal-working firm.

The majority of this initial investment is typically used for fixed rather than working capital. In Jamaica, for example, approximately two-thirds of the initial investment of microenterprises went for fixed assets (primarily machinery and tools), while one-third was for working capital (Fisseha and Davies 1981). A similar pattern was reported in Colombia (Cortes and others 1987). These proportions varied somewhat by size, type, and location of enterprise, but in most instances, the relative significance of fixed capital was maintained.

Once the micro firm begins to produce and eventually expands production, however, the demand for working capital typically increases both absolutely as well as relative to fixed capital. This follows because these initial output increases are accomplished primarily by adding variable inputs, which are largely financed by working capital; there is thus an increased utilization rather than an expansion of the initial fixed capital.

Available empirical evidence indicating that a substantial amount of "excess capacity" exists among small and microenterprises provides support for this view. Excess capacity measures are difficult to quantify precisely and studies in developing countries are particularly sparse.[4] Surveys of micro and small manufacturing firms conducted by Michigan State University and host country researchers in five countries, however, have generated some information on many facets of their operation including excess capacity.[5] On the basis of the responses of entrepreneurs to the question of how many additional hours they would operate their existing firms if there were no demand or materials constraints, the estimates of overall excess capacity ranged from 18 percent in Egypt, 24 percent in Honduras, 35 percent in Jamaica, 37 percent in Sierra Leone, and to 42 percent for rural manufacturing firms in Bangladesh. Excess capacity did vary somewhat between industries and by location in each country, but rarely did it decline below 10 percent; virtually no small firms in these countries operated on more than a single shift.

Additional evidence of the relative importance of working capital during the early stages of a firm's existence can be found in the responses of entrepreneurs to what they perceived their most pressing current constraints to be.[6] For instance, in Jamaica, over 90 percent of the microenterprise's financial difficulties were reported to be related to working capital shortages (Fisseha and Davies 1981). Similarly, "cash shortages" were cited by the majority of Haitian micro proprietors as their most pressing financial problem (Haggblade and others 1979).

---

4. See Pan-Thuy and others (1981) for a discussion of the various studies as well as a treatment of the distinction between excess capacity (that is, how close to its desired, efficient level of output a firm is operating) and "capital utilization" (i.e. the proportion of the total time a productive capital stock is operated).
5. A detailed discussion of these studies can be found in Liedholm and Mead (1987).
6. The true need for finance, particularly working capital, however, is lower than proprietor's perceived demand for it. This is because working capital shortages are often the symptom of some other problem. For instance, a raw material delivery bottleneck may force proprietors to keep their raw material inventories at unduly high levels. Consequently, one must distinguish valid needs for working capital from the specious demands that only serve to sustain temporarily a fatally ill enterprise or reflect some other underlying problem. (Kilby and others 1984).

These studies, however, did not identify whether or not the lack of working capital was a problem when they were growing.

One of the few studies to explicitly identify problems during periods of growth is Chuta's study of 300 micro and small firms in Northern Nigeria. An important finding of that study was that "obtaining adequate working capital" was more frequently cited as a problem for rapidly growing micro firms (41 percent), than for rapidly growing "modern" small firms (23 percent). Indeed, for firms growing with just one or two persons, working capital shortages were the most frequently cited constraint to growth.

Why should the demand for working capital be expected to increase as micro firms expand? First, the quantity of working capital demanded would be expected to vary directly with output or sales, since the principal use of working capital is to finance labor, raw materials, and other purchased inputs that go into goods produced for sale. Strong support for this hypothesis comes from an inventory demand study that used data on small enterprises in Sierra Leone (Kilby, and others 1984). This study found that the relationship between the level of sales—indeed the square root of sales—and inventory was positive and significant at the one percent level.

Second, the quantity of working capital would be expected to increase with the lengthening of the production and marketing period for raw materials and finished goods that frequently accompanies the "transformation" of micro- into small- and medium-scale enterprises. Microenterprises in several industry subsectors, for example, produce to order and thus operate much like a job-shop, where customers may even provide the raw materials. This institutional arrangement keeps the marketing and production periods relatively short, the inventory-sales ratio small, and the corresponding demand for working capital relatively low. If these microenterprises not only expand but transform themselves into small and medium enterprises, however, these periods frequently lengthen as one facet of that transformation. Tailors and carpenters, for example, would no longer produce custom orders, but would begin to operate like a factory in which inventories of finished clothing or furniture would be maintained.

Evidence from enterprise surveys in Honduras and Sierra Leone provide support for the differing production and marketing periods between micro and small enterprises in at least some industry subsectors (see Table 3). In both countries, the inventory-sales ratio of small-scale clothing and furniture enterprises were significantly higher than those of their microenterprise counterparts. Thus, as firms in these industries grew, the demand for working capital increased not just with sales, but grew even more because of the increased inventory-sales ratio. The constancy of the ratio for micro and small baking establishments, however, reminds one that this increase is not ubiquitous and must be examined on an industrial subsector basis.[7]

Other characteristics associated with this enterprise transformation, however, might be expected to reduce somewhat the demand for working capital. First, small and medium firms may be able to realize some economies of material bulk purchases, particularly since the transaction cost of placing a raw material order is fixed irrespective of size (Kilby and others 1984). Second, there is evidence that the capital intensity of small and medium enterprises typically exceed those of microenterprises. (Liedholm and Mead 1987). Since the proportion of working capital demand will vary inversely with the capital intensity of production, this should tend to reduce the relative demand for working capital. These two countervailing factors may help explain why working capital shortages appear to become a less severe constraint for expanding small and medium enterprises, when compared with their micro counterparts.

TABLE 3. Inventory-Sales Ratios for Micro- and Small-Scale Enterprises

	Sierra Leone	*Honduras*
Clothing		
Micro[b]	0.02	0.04
Small-scale	0.10[a]	0.10[a]
Furniture		
Micro	0.05	0.04
Small-scale	0.15[a]	0.10[a]
Bread		
Micro	0.02	0.01
Small-scale	0.02	0.01

[a] Significant difference at 1 percent level (Chi Square).
[b] Micro - 10 persons or less.
  Small - more than 10 persons.
Sources: Sierra Leone: data from Chuta and Liedholm (1985).
Honduras: data collected during 1980 survey of 485 rural micro and small-scale industries.

---

7. The constancy of the inventory-sales ratio for bread is, no doubt, strongly related to the perishability of the commodity.

An abundance of other inputs including fixed capital is also required when a microenterprise is transformed into a more complex, modern small-scale enterprise (Liedholm and Boomgard 1989). Indeed, there is typically a sharp, discontinuous jump in the demand for fixed relative to working capital when the firm reaches this stage in its evolution. Unfortunately, data on the precise magnitude and mix of this demand are still somewhat limited.[8]

Evolving Supply of Finance

The sources of finance available to a micro- or small-scale enterprise also change as it evolves. This evolution affects the relative importance of informal and formal sources of finance.

Indeed, at the inception of the micro firm, neither formal nor informal sources of finance play any significant role. Rather, the initial investment of such a firm is overwhelmingly obtained from internal family sources, primarily personal savings and gifts from relatives or friends. The empirical evidence from Africa, for example, indicates that these sources consistently accounted for over 95 percent of the original capitalization of microenterprises, ranging from 98 percent in Nigeria (Aluko 1972), to 97 percent in both Tanzania (Schadler 1968) and Sierra Leone (Chuta and Liedholm 1985). A remarkably similar pattern emerges from the evidence generated in other parts of the world. Personal financial sources represented 94 percent of the original capitalization of microenterprises in Jamaica (Fisseha and Davies 1981), 91 percent in Haiti (Haggblade and others 1974), and 89 percent in the Philippines (Anderson and Khambata 1981). The paucity of funds obtained from either formal or informal external sources at start-up is striking.

The micro firm's access to outside sources of finance, however, begins to widen as it ages and evolves over time. McLeod (1986) argues that

---

8. Indirect evidence from lenders on the relative importance of fixed capital at this stage can be derived from the recent review of microenterprise support programs by the Agency for International Development (AID). In this review of 32 AID projects, the fixed capital component of loans comprised only 20 percent in microenterprise expansion schemes, but 45 percent in enterprise "transformation" schemes (Boomgard 1989). Yet, small firms often attempt to minimize their demand for fixed capital by renting (leasing) or by buying used equipment (Cortes and others 1987, and Chuta and Liedholm 1985).

these expanded opportunities are directly linked to increases in the reputation and assets of the firm.

What pattern of financial evolution might be expected from our knowledge of microenterprise dynamics? During the typical microenterprise's first few years of struggle and initial growth, its assets and reputation would both be limited and its outside sources of funds meager. Consequently, the firm's internal free cash flow from depreciation and retained profits provides the major source of capital during this period in its lifecycle. Internal sources of finance thus continue to dominate. In Sierra Leone and Bangladesh, for example, 89 percent of the capital for expanding units came from this source, while in Haiti the figure was 81 percent (Liedholm and Mead 1987).

Nevertheless, even during this early period a few external sources of informal finance begin to emerge. The first, and most overlooked of these, is credit from customers. Retail customers frequently supply the entrepreneur with either the raw materials or a cash down payment to purchase the raw materials (Kilby and others 1984).[9] In rural Egypt (Davies and others 1984), for example, 80 percent of the firms indicated that customers made advanced payments, either in cash or in kind. The relative importance of this form of credit varied by subsector, ranging from 100 percent for mat making to 43 percent for metal shops. The extent of this practice is often directly related to the reputation of the producer; consequently as the product quality and delivery performance of the entrepreneur become better known to the consumers over time and as the firm's reputation in their eyes grows, customer prepayment should increase. Advance payments by customers represent a creative response to the obstacles arising in low-income countries with limited financial intermediation. The customer provides resources and in return frequently receives implicit interest in the form of a price discount, which may range from 1 to 10 percent depending on the subsector concerned (McLeod 1986).

Another form of informal consumer credit that also grows as the firm ages is the subcontracting mechanism, in which the customer— typically, a much larger firm—supplies the micro firm with the raw materials required to produce the ordered goods. Subcontracting tends to be limited to a few subsectors, such as clothing, wood, and fabricated metal, and is more widespread in Asia than elsewhere (Mead 1985).

---

9. The credit extended to other customers on delivery must be subtracted from this figure to arrive at the net supply of working capital by customers. In Jamaica, 34 percent of the sample entrepreneurs reported granting loans on sales, while in Haiti, the comparable figure was 71 percent. In Egypt, less than 10 percent of the sales were on credit.

An additional external source of informal finance that becomes increasingly available as the firm evolves is trade credit from, or accounts payable to, suppliers of inputs. This source of credit tends to be less important than credit from final customers for most industries in low income countries. Accounts payable from input suppliers tend to grow in importance, however, as the firm evolves and improves its a reputation. In Egypt, for example, it is the somewhat larger and older of the microenterprises that have the greatest amount of input credit (Davies, and others 1984).

Professional moneylenders are another source of informal finance for microenterprises. Microenterprises, however, typically do not make extensive use of this part of the informal financial market in most low-income countries (Kilby and others 1984; and Anderson 1982). In most cases recourse to moneylenders occurs at infrequent intervals, primarily for small working capital loans, for a few days, at interest rates not infrequently exceeding 100 percent; yet the loans are extended quickly and few transaction costs are involved. The access to moneylenders, however, grows as firms age and evolve. In both Haiti and Jamaica, for example, less than 1 percent of the microenterprises used moneylenders at start-up, but the percentage rose to 1.7 percent in Haiti and 3.9 percent in Sierra Leone when they expanded (Kilby, and others 1984). Once the reputation of the firm is established, it typically remains the client of that moneylender for a long period.

An expanding array of informal sources of finance thus become available to the microenterprise as it evolves. Most of these sources initially provide short-term working capital, for which the microenterprise's effective demand initially tends to be relatively high. It is also this type of finance that the informal market is particularly well suited to provide.

There are two major informal sources of fixed capital: supplier credit and subcontracting. Supplier credit for fixed capital typically becomes available when a micro firm becomes well established and develops a good payment record (Kilby, and others 1984). The supplier has some incentive to offer such credit in order to boost sales and can use equipment as security. Fixed capital is also sometimes provided to microenterprises by the larger parent firm as part of a sub contracting arrangement (Mead 1985).

Finally, at a later stage in their evolution, microenterprises may begin to have access to the formal financial market. This frequently occurs once they have transformed themselves—graduated—into modern small and medium enterprises, although a few microenterprises have been able to obtain credit from regular financial institutions (Chuta and Liedholm 1985). Evidence that formal finance plays a bigger role as firms grow is revealed in enterprise surveys in Colombia (Cortes and others 1987) and the Philippines (Anderson and Khambata 1981). Unfortunately, for most countries, data on the graduation or even the evolution of firms from informal to formal financial sources are sparse and this phenomenon has rarely been examined (Meyer 1988).

Implications for Financial Policy

What financial policy implications emerge from this dynamic perspective on small enterprise? Specifically what lessons are learned from the operation of informal finance that might lead to improvements in both formal and informal finance programs?

One important lesson emerging from the findings is that the magnitude and composition of microenterprise's demand for finance as well as its access to the sources of that finance typically vary significantly over its life cycle. Consequently, one must take careful cognizance of these systematic variations to ensure that the needed types of finance are delivered from the informal or formal sources most appropriate at that particular stage of the firm's life cycle.

Although a surprisingly wide variety of informal sources are available to meet many of the evolving needs of microenterprises, there are a few limitations in these informal financial arrangements. First, each of these sources are independent and generally segregated from one another. Consequently, there is little or no integration of disparate sources and uses of funds over time. There is also little integration within individual units of the needed multiple financial services, such as savings, deposit, and checking account activities. When these services are integrated, additional information is generated for lenders on the entrepreneur's evolving financial management ability—one element that contributes to the entrepreneur's growing reputation.

Second, the success of several innovative microenterprise programs, such as the Grameen Bank in Bangladesh and the BKK project in Indonesia, provide an indication that even the effective working capital needs of evolving micro and small enterprises in these countries had not been adequately met by the existing financial system (see Boomgard 1989; and Meyer 1988). If such schemes are to be successful in other countries with similar financial gaps, however, design and implementation clues will have to be artfully gleaned in many cases from the operating characteristics of the informal lenders themselves, particularly with respect to how they keep transaction costs and risks of default low.

Third, informal financial sources are not particularly well suited to meeting the evolving fixed capital needs of micro firms. As firms grow and perhaps attempt to transform themselves into modern small-scale enterprises, informal lenders become less able or inclined to provide the larger sums for the longer time periods that are now required (World Bank 1989).

Enabling the firm to have access to formal sources of finance as it grows provides one viable alternative for increased funds. The transition, however, is not usually a simple or smooth one as usually an entirely new set of procedures and requirements, such as strict collateral, for obtaining loans must be mastered. Moreover, commercial banks and other formal financial sources are frequently reluctant to deal with unfamiliar small enterprises, because of the higher transaction costs and greater perceived risks of lending to them.

Several approaches have been proposed for facilitating this transition. One is to provide technical assistance to the firms themselves to teach them how to obtain loans from formal financial institutions (Meyer 1988). A second approach is to provide technical assistance instead to the commercial banks and similar financial institutions on how to lend more effectively to small enterprises (Kilby and others 1984). With lenders' accumulation of experience and improved information, the risks of lending to these enterprises should decline. Lessons can also be learned from informal lenders, particularly on how they are able to keep the transaction costs of both lenders and borrowers low (Liedholm 1985). Lending institutions however, are not going to willingly engage in this "learning by doing" process unless its high cost (principally high default rates) can be reduced. A loan-guarantee scheme is one such cost-absorbing mechanism, although the track record of such schemes to date has generally been poor (Levistky and Prasad 1987). Commercial banks would be more willing to provide unsecured short-term loans to rural enterprises if the guaranteed portion of the loan were reasonably high and if all screening costs above those incurred for standard loans could be shifted to the guarantor. To help ensure that the guarantee subsidy is confined to learning, the banks should be given an incentive, such as a declining guarantee, to move new borrowers into a normal commercial relationship. A final approach is to graduate or convert an entire microenterprise program or scheme to a commercial source of financing (Boomgard 1989; and Jackelin 1988). The microenterprise lending program would thus act as a specialized intermediary, retailing funds that had been "wholesaled" to it by a formal, commercial source. These three approaches are not mutually exclusive, however, and indeed all may be needed to ensure that the

financial system does not impede the evolution of small firms in
developing countries.

Conclusions

This examination of small enterprise dynamics in developing
countries has focused attention on the evolving role of informal finance
in that process. At different stages in the life cycle of the typical
micro-enterprise the needs of the firm, including its effective demand
for finance, vary in a rather systematic fashion. A surprisingly large
array of informal sources of finance are available to the firm, but the
relative contribution of these informal arrangements varies as the firm
evolves.

Informal financial arrangements have been shown to be quite
responsive to this evolutionary pattern. Yet, the lack of integration of
these diverse informal sources and services as well as the gaps in the
availability of both short- and long-term funds at certain stages in the
firm's evolution point to deficiencies in the existing informal financial
system. It is only when the informal and formal financial markets
become better integrated and more unfettered that the evolving
financial requirements of small enterprise will be more completely met.

References

Aluko, S. A., O. A. Oguntoye and Y. A. O. Afonja. 1972. *Small-scale Industries:
Western State of Nigeria.* Ile-Ife, Nigeria: Industrial Research Unit,
University of Ife.

Anderson, Dennis. 1982. "Small Industry in Development Countries: A Discussion
of the Issues." *World Development* 10: 913-948.

Anderson, Dennis, and Farida Khambata. 1981. *Small Enterprises and
Development Policy in the Philippines: A Case Study.* World Bank
Working Paper No. 468 Washington, D.C.

Boomgard, James. 1989. "A. I. D. Microenterprise Stock-taking: Synthesis
Report." Unpublished report prepared for the Agency for International
Development in Washington, D.C.

Chuta, Enyinna. 1982. "Employment Growth and Change in Sierra Leone Small-
scale Industry: 1974-1980." *International Labour Review* 121: 101-112.

Chuta, Enyinna, and Carl Liedholm. 1985. *Employment and Growth in Small-
Scale Industry: Empirical Evidence and Policy Assessment from Sierra
Leone.* New York: St. Martin Press.

Cortes, Mariluz, Albert Berry, and Ashfaq Ishaq. 1987. *Success in Small and Medium-Scale Enterprises: The Evidence from Colombia.* New York: Oxford University Press.

Davies, Stephen and others. 1984. "Small Enterprises in Egypt: A Study of Two Governorates," MSU International Development Working Paper No. 16, East Lansing, Michigan: Michigan State University.

Fisseha, Yacob, and Omar Davies. 1981. "The Small-Scale Manufacturing Enterprises in Jamaica: Socioeconomic Characteristics and Constraints." MSU Rural Development Series Working Paper No. 16. East Lansing, Michigan: Michigan State University.

Haggblade, Steve, Jacques Defay, and Bob Pitman. 1979. "Small Manufacturing and Repair Activities in Haiti: Survey Results." MSU Rural Development Working Paper No. 4. East Lansing: Michigan State University.

Jackelin, Henry. 1988. "Banking on the Informal Sector." Unpublished paper Prepared for the World Conference on Support of Microenterprises. Washington, D.C.

Kilby, Peter, Carl Liedholm, and Richard Meyer. 1984. "Working Capital and Nonfarm Rural Enterprises." In Adams, Graham, and Von Pischke, eds., *Undermining Rural Development With Cheap Credit.* Boulder, Colorado: Westview Press.

Levitsky, J., and Ranga Prasad. 1987. "Credit Guarantee Schemes for Small and Medium Enterprises." *Technical Paper* No. 58. Washington, D.C. World Bank.

Liedholm, Carl. 1985. "Small-scale Enterprise Credit Schemes: Administrative Costs and the Role of Inventory Norms." MSU International Development Working Paper No. 25. East Lansing , Michgan: Michigan State University.

_____. 1989. "The Dynamics of Small-scale Industry in Africa and the Role of Policy." Working Paper No. 2. Washington, D.C.: GEMINI.

Liedholm, Carl, and Donald Mead. 1987. "Small-scale Industries in Developing Countries: Empirical Evidence and Policy Implications." MSU International Development Paper No. 9. East Lansing, Michigan: Michigan State University.

Licdholm, Carl, and Joan Parker. 1989. "Small-scale Manufacturing Growth in Africa: Initial Evidence." MSU International Development Working Paper No. 33. East Lansing, Michigan: Michigan State University.

McLeod, Ross. 1986. "Financing Small Business in Indonesia," Unpublished paper presented at Conference on Financial Research in Indonesia. Jakarta.

Mead, Donald. 1985. "Sub-Contracting Systems and Assistance Programs: Opportunities for Intervention." MSU International Working Paper No. 24. East Lansing: Michigan State University.

Meyer, Richard. 1988. "Financial Services for Microenterprises: Programs or Markets?" Unpublished paper prepared for the World Conference on Support of Microenterprises: Washington, D.C., June.

Pan-Thuy, N.R. Betancourt, G. Wintston and M. Kabaj. 1981. *Industrial Capacity and Employment Promotion.* Jants, England: Gower Publishing Co.

Schadler, K. 1968. *Crafts, Small-Scale Industries and Industrial Education in Tanzania.* Munich, Germany: Weltform/Verlay.

World Bank. 1989. *World Development Report-1989*. Washington, D.C.: World
Bank.

20

Formal Credit for Informal Borrowers: Lessons from Informal Lenders

Robert Peck Christen[1]

Among other objectives, most microbusiness credit projects seek to increase incomes and generate employment by providing less expensive alternatives to moneylenders for financing microbusiness activities. Most of these programs fail to replace moneylenders as prime credit sources for microbusinesses and, even more tragically, fail to survive as permanent credit alternatives.

In the following discussion I argue that traditional microenterprise credit projects are too expensive to be successful because they rely on credit methodologies borrowed from formal banking. On the other hand, informal moneylenders have financed small businesses since the beginning of commerce. If micro-credit development programs are to be successful they must base their methodologies on those of informal lenders who have not only survived, but who have prospered by lending to the smallest economic activities.

ACCION International/AITEC has based its highly successful microcredit methodology on lessons learned from informal lenders through its own long project implementation experience in Latin America and through its analysis of both successful and unsuccessful programs around the globe. ACCION provides technical assistance to microbusiness support programs throughout the Americas. Currently, about 25,000 businesses participate in ACCION affiliates in 14 countries. Several ACCION affiliates are among the few microbusiness

---

1. This chapter reflects my views as a practitioner in daily contact with both formal and informal lenders to the smallest of all economic activities, but does not necessarily represent the views of ACCION International.

credit programs in Latin America that have reached operational self-sufficiency, a necessary prerequisite to long-term program sustainability (ACCION 1988).

When ACCION began to work with microbusinesses 18 years ago in Recife, Brazil in Project UNO, it implemented a classical formal credit model within its broader technical assistance and training program. Since that time, ACCION has evolved its credit model based on the way informal credit markets work. ACCION's current methodology has proven so successful in terms of impact on poorest businesses, extremely high recovery rates (99.5 percent), and operational self-sufficiency, that in the past few years several initiatives have begun to move this model from the small NGO implementor to larger, more traditional, formal sector lenders. For example, ACCION and its Bolivian affiliate, PRODEM, are actively pursuing plans to convert PRODEM into a private commercial bank, devoted exclusively to the microbusiness sector. ACCION's Dominican affiliate, ADEMI, is exploring the possibility of converting itself into a specially legislated private bank. ADMIC, ACCION's Mexican affiliate, has just signed an agreement with NANFIN, a major state-managed finance company, to administer a US$4.5 million microbusiness lending program in four northern states. In the late 1980s, representatives from Ecuador's banking sector established a foundation devoted to microbusiness lending, backed by major private bank resources. This list will certainly grow as policymakers continue to look for ways to support the burgeoning informal sectors throughout Latin America.

If we examine the evolution of ACCION's approach, we can identify six critical lessons learned from moneylenders, who are the traditional lenders to the poor and who represent ACCION's only real "competition." In the following chapter, I will identify each of these lessons and illustrate how these lessons have been incorporated into ACCION's credit model. The final section discusses macro policy implications that derive from these same lessons.

Lesson #1: Get to Know Your Borrowers

The key to success in any financial market is accurate information about perspective clients. All lenders must determine whether potential borrowers will be both willing and able to repay their loans. They want to know if potential borrowers are financially solvent, if their income stream is constant and reliable, if they are already burdened with other debt, and finally, whether they are committed to repaying obligations. Excellent borrower selection is more important to overall portfolio quality than most other factors combined. Lenders who carefully select their clients avoid defaults and legal proceedings.

The primary reason that formal lenders do not lend to small borrowers is that traditional information gathering systems are both too costly and too ineffective to guarantee high quality borrower selection. Informal lenders, on the other hand, gather useful information on potential clients at a very low cost, thereby minimizing default risk. The reason that informal lenders can gather this information about perspective clients so cheaply and so well is that they, unlike formal lenders, operate in the same commercial or personal environment as their borrowers. For instance, many microbusinesses cash checks from their buyers at their corner store, paying between a 10 to 20 percent discount. The store owner knows the microbusiness since the microentrepreneur probably also buys his weekly food stocks at the store, most likely on credit.

Often, money lending is a secondary activity. Merchants who supply microbusinesses with raw materials or who purchase its products usually establish some sort of credit relationship as an additional service. This credit may take the form of direct loans, materials on loan, or price adjustments. In all of these cases, before a microbusiness gains access to credit facilities, the manager must first establish a working commercial relationship with his eventual moneylender.

Some moneylenders devote themselves exclusively to money lending. They ensure good borrower selection by lending only to close friends or relatives and persons recommended by this select group. This way they live in close contact with their clients and have ready access to information when they confront credit decisions.

In contrast, formal lenders rarely have the opportunity to establish broader commercial or personal relationships with microbusiness borrowers and must therefore rely on secondhand information to assess credit risk. Formal lenders traditionally require technical analysis, documentation of incomes and cash flows and collateral, none of which microbusinesses can offer. The more distant the formal lender is from the informal borrower, the more secondhand information he requires.

The root cause of the failure of many formal lenders to prosper when they lend to poor borrowers is that, in spite of costly procedures for gathering information about potential clients, this information is often not a trustworthy indicator of credit risk.

ACCION, on the other hand, seeks to establish a direct relationship with borrowers in the same fashion as micro-enterprise suppliers or corner store owners by initially lending small amounts and gradually increasing these amounts as the microentrepreneur builds a credit history with the program. Initial loans do not meet all credit needs, but rather are small enough to test borrower willingness and ability to repay without posing undue risk either to the borrower or the lender. Loan terms are initially kept very short, 8 weeks to 6 months, but within a year the program participants reach loan sizes that allow for significant and sustainable business growth.

Delinquent borrowers are either eliminated from the system or are not given larger loans, depending on the severity of the particular program and the lateness of the repayment. In the late 1980s the delinquency rates on average for ACCION affiliates was less than 7 percent of current portfolios, and the loan loss rate was less than 2 percent of current portfolios. ACCION considers a loan to be delinquent the day a payment is overdue, but considers only the late payment to be delinquent, rather than the entire amount of the loan.

Another feature of most successful ACCION microcredit programs is the solidarity group mechanism. This mechanism transfers the primary responsibility for borrower selection to borrower groups, who by any standard, know potential borrowers far better than the program. This mechanism requires an interested microentrepreneur to bring three to four other interested microentrepreneurs with whom he or she will form a group in order to participate in the program. The program makes one loan to the group, which the group distributes among themselves. Should one member default on a loan, then the others in the group pay the late portion and seek recovery directly from the delinquent member. The group has the option of eliminating the delinquent member from subsequent loans. Should the group fail to repay on time, then the group is eliminated from the program. Since the initial loan amounts are relatively small, and subsequent loan amounts become increasingly large, borrowers have a strong incentive to repay and maintain a good credit history.

This methodology is particularly successful where a large number of microbusinesses are located close together and where business owners know each other through daily contact. The methodology is less successful when businesses do not have regular contact. In that sense, this methodology mirrors the success of informal lenders who have an almost daily contact with their borrowers in commercial or personal dealings. Although many formal lenders require cosigners on small loans to poor borrowers, in an attempt to include into the selection process informed individuals who are close to the borrower, this technique is seldom successful since it requires only one person to believe in the borrower's ability and willingness to repay, rather than the three or four required by the solidarity group mechanism.

Lesson #2: Don't Supervise Loans

A corollary to the "getting to know your borrower lesson" is to not waste resources on credit supervision. Although seemingly paradoxical, lenders should not devote valuable resources attempting to control credit use at the firm level. Formal lenders frequently resort to control mechanisms to supplement their initial lack of firsthand knowledge during the borrower selection phase. They attempt to force businesses to make productive investments with the borrowed funds and control the subsequent productive processes, completely ignoring the fungible nature of the marginal liquidity they have provided.

Informal lenders interest themselves in the activities undertaken with the marginal liquidity only to the extent that these activities affect his initial credit risk calculations. After the loan is made, the moneylender doesn't waste any time trying to control the real end use of the funds he provided. If he suspects that the borrower is using the funds in activities that he considers more risky than those he authorized, then he is most likely to deny credit the next time the borrower seeks it.

The informal lender maintains his close proximity to borrowers not through control but rather by offering complementary services that borrowers need. In fact, lending is frequently a complementary service to other, primary services performed by moneylenders for microbusinesses. These services may include providing raw materials, purchasing final products, lending tools or equipment, rent-free work space, or a patronage relationship. This relationship provides the low cost knowledge necessary for the credit decision, while at the same time fulfilling another, also productive purpose.

ACCION International affiliates have learned this lesson well and specifically look to offer complementary services to credit participants. Most programs offer some sort of technical assistance and/or courses in microbusiness management. Some offer savings plans, life insurance, medical services/insurance or fire insurance. Others offer the possibility of participating in organizations that serve as lobbying forces to better conditions in areas where businesses operate or in their regulatory environment. Others offer participation in fairs and sales events that help small businesses project themselves beyond what they could achieve on their own.

In almost every ACCION affiliate, microbusinesses find more than credit. In most cases, microbusinesses pay the true cost of these complementary services. Program self-sufficiency goals include these services as revenue generators in addition to being cost centers. In some cases these complementary services are more profitable than credit. The underlying assumption most programs operate with is that borrowers will think twice before defaulting on a loan if they will not only lose access to further credit but will also lose access to a series of other important services.

Lesson #3: Take Loans to the Client

Since many informal lenders provide loans in conjunction with other services, their borrowers do not have to make special trips to receive credit. This allows borrowers to transact more than one activity in any given trip. Other moneylenders who do not provide complementary services typically live close to their borrowers, or have other tight-knit relations. This means that although clients may have to make special trips to borrow and repay loans, these trips are few, short, and quick. Moneylenders usually decide immediately whether or not to grant a loan.

Formal lenders, unfortunately, function quite differently. Whether because of credit rationing motivated by subsidized interest rates or because of the need to collect extensive secondhand information, formal lenders almost always have extensive application and approval procedures. These procedures require potential borrowers to invest relatively large amounts of time and money into a process that does not guarantee a positive end result. These transaction costs may exceed the interest costs and for very small loans may even exceed the value of the loan itself.

From borrowers' perspectives, transaction cost differences between informal lenders and formal lenders are one of the keys in their decision as to which credit source they will choose to use. Most microentrepreneurs view the high transaction costs involved in applying for and receiving a formal loan, think about the relatively poor chance they have of actually receiving that loan, and decide not to even try. They prefer to borrow from moneylenders or not to borrow at all.

Most ACCION affiliates are credit driven programs, even though they offer other services to complement these loans. Since microentrepreneurs do not have many other reasons to go to the program offices than to apply for and receive credit, and since programs can not be present in microenterprise neighborhoods in the same fashion as moneylenders, these programs have decided to take the credit to the borrower. This reduces transaction costs while increasing the quality of secondhand information gathered. ACCION credit methodology requires that a major portion of the loan application process take place in the microbusiness or in its neighborhood. Field agents visit interested businesses and do creditworthiness evaluations in the workplace. In the case of solidarity group mechanisms, after the initial application phase, most ongoing work takes place in the field. Applicants come to the office only to participate in the initial orientation sessions, and later, to pick up their check. Loans are usually repaid at local banks, although most programs also receive payments directly. In either case, the borrowers' transaction costs involved in repayment are lower than for most formal lenders.

Subsequent loans require even fewer transaction costs since the borrower has developed a credit history. Usually borrowers must only indicate the amount of their next loan to a field agent during a pre-credit visit made automatically prior to a loan's expiration and the approval process is automatically handled by the program staff. Borrowers go to the office to make their last payment and to receive their next loan, all in one visit.

Although ACCION affiliates certainly impose more transaction costs than their informal competitors, these costs are significantly less than other formal sector lenders. The success of these programs illustrates that by keeping transaction costs low, in addition to other features they offer, formal credit operators can provide an attractive alternative to moneylenders.

Lesson #4: Provide Appropriate Credit

Informal lenders usually provide microbusiness loans that are both opportune and appropriate, in contrast to formal lenders. In addition to delivering credit efficiently (low transaction costs), moneylenders provide loans on a timely basis, and in most cases immediately upon request. When credit is part of a commercial transaction, it is extended immediately. When a microentrepreneur sells a third party check at a discount, the credit is extended immediately. When a microentrepreneur asks for a direct loan, he or she may only have to wait a day or two for the moneylender to cover a check. In most cases, informal credit is obtained immediately upon request if it is granted.

This immediacy allows microentrepreneurs to take advantage of special opportunities, take on large contracts, and compete more effectively against other individuals who don't have sufficient working capital. We frequently hear pleas from program participants to lend them US$300 dollars just for 15 days, even if they have to pay 20 percent interest, so that they can take advantage of an opportunity.

Formal credit operators are both unable and unwilling to do this; unable because bureaucratic processes won't allow it even for well-known clients, and unwilling because of legal and moral restraints on maximum interest rates they can charge.

A related issue to timeliness is the appropriateness of the loan services that lenders offer. Whereas informal lenders typically tie their credit very closely to microbusiness productive or commercial cycles, formal lenders usually give long-term, large loans, independent of these cycles. Formal lenders find it difficult, if not impossible to generate a profit with small, short-term loans, that are tied to business cycles. Formal credit mechanisms make these small loans too expensive for lenders to consider.

ACCION International affiliates again seek a middle ground. Although none of the programs have been able to totally replicate informal lender delivery systems, most base their credit mechanisms on very small, short-term, working capital loans, with frequent amortizations. These loans are repeated one after the other and represent a permanent credit source. They are usually tied to production cycles, although they are viewed more like marginal capital inputs rather than the direct financing of production cycles.

ACCION affiliates emphasize opportune credit delivery. Delays in loan disbursements seldom occur and borrowers almost never waste trips to the office. By approximating informal credit delivery systems both in transaction costs and opportunity costs, these programs have been able to generate a strong demand for their credit service. To lower these costs, ACCION programs have developed administrative systems that are capable of handling large numbers of small loans with a minimum of paperwork and bureaucratic process.

Lesson #5: Charge Commercial Rates of Interest

Moneylenders charge microentrepreneurs relatively high interest rates. As a general rule, the smaller the loan, and the shorter the amortization period, the higher the interest rate charged. This is logical since moneylenders have certain fixed costs to cover for each loan, regardless of the loan size.

The supply of informal loans at any given interest rate is limited by the existence of many alternative, lucrative, small-scale productive or commercial activities available to moneylenders. Since moneylenders seldom lend funds that are not their own, they must charge an interest rate that at least equals the rates of return on similarly sized productive investments in commercial activities. At the level of the small or microbusiness, these rates of return, even after subtracting out the owner's wages, can be as high as 200 to 2,000 percent annually.

If microentrepreneurs who have a net return on capital of 200 percent are willing to pay usury rates of 180 percent (15 percent a month) in order to produce and maintain their economic activities, then they certainly would be willing to pay commercial rates of interest for that same working capital (on the order of 2 to 5 percent a month in real terms throughout most of Latin America). It is also clear that the potential savings to the microbusiness of further interest rate reduction through subsidization are probably not that great, particularly when it is recognized that subsidization of interest rates inevitably leads to an increase in both the transaction and opportunity costs of obtaining loans.

Formal sector lenders, as a rule, subsidize interest rates to microentrepreneurs on the assumption that poor borrowers are unable to pay commercial rates of interest. The reality is that no formal credit methodology yet designed in Latin America allows programs to reach financial self-sufficiency while also charging lower than commercial interest rates. Small, average loan sizes prohibits this.

ACCION International has been a ground breaker throughout Latin America in establishing commercial and even slightly higher than commercial rates of interest for program participants. ACCION prefers to reach self-sufficiency and ensure long-term program sustainability through direct operational income (interest and other fees) rather than depending on subsidies for survival. The approximately 30 percent reduction in interest charges represented by most subsidy programs is not significant for microborrowers whose only real alternative is the moneylender, but realistic interest rates are a key to program viability.

Interestingly, most of the restrictions ACCION programs face as to maximum interest rates they can charge come from within. Ethical and political arguments almost always force interest rates below what sound financial management would dictate as optimal levels. Almost never do program participants pressure interest rates downwards. In fact, most ACCION program participants consider program loans made at commercial rates to be "cheap money."

Lesson #6: Be Tough on Defaulters

The bad public image of moneylenders is a result of the high interest rates they charge and the extremes to which they go to collect bad debts. Abundant literature exists that puts usurious interest rates in perspective. Less exists related to the extremity of sanctions moneylenders employ.

In Latin America, informal lenders to microbusinesses seldom resort to criminal means such as assault, arson, theft, or other such techniques to enforce repayment in spite of what the general public might think. The loan amounts are not large enough to risk the resulting sanctions if caught. As we have already mentioned, the most common form of informal finance used by Latin American microentrepreneurs seem to be selling of third party checks and supplier or purchaser credit, rather than direct money lending backed by collateral guarantees. In either case, informal lenders immediately suspend their entire commercial and financial relations with a defaulting borrower, spread the word around about the default, and pursue loan recovery through informal pressure. In those few instances when microentrepreneurs sign legal documents (checks or promissory notes) backing loans, informal lenders may even have legal recourse.

While these sanctions do not seem too drastic when compared to images of broken legs and bombed businesses, they are probably even more severe. Microbusinesses usually operate within a relatively small market and their commercial relations are few. To risk losing these good relations is to risk bankruptcy and even the possibility of future business opportunities. This means that the defaulter risks his entire economic future, probably a much stronger sanction than losing everything he currently possesses.

Formal lenders are reluctant to enforce sanctions against delinquent borrowers, primarily because of the negative publicity generated by punishing poor borrowers for being too poor to repay. At least that is the standard thinking. ACCION programs, on the other hand, largely avoid this dilemma by structuring their incentives systems similarly to those used by informal lenders.

Most ACCION programs reach the poorest of all businesses with a credit methodology that is not based on real guarantees but rather on the loss of future commercial relationships should borrowers default. The solidarity group mechanism mentioned above is not legally enforceable. Should the program attempt legal proceedings to recover loan losses, they would certainly spend substantially more on the court process and lawyers than it would recover. Rather, the incentive to repay in order to obtain an additional, potentially larger loan and maintain a permanent credit relationship is more powerful than any negative real sanction. If the program offers, in addition to credit, other attractive features such as training, medical attention, or legal services, then the incentive is even stronger.

This incentive is stronger yet if its enforcement comes not from the program, but rather from the other members of the potential defaulter's group. The potential defaulter risks not only the loss of access to a future relationship with the program but also damages his future relationship with other group members and potentially his entire commercial community. Other group members will suffer a tangible financial loss due to his default, and therefore will be much more negative in their future relationships than if they merely heard through third parties that the defaulter had not paid an obligation to a formal institution. In fact, in many countries and cultures there seems to be a sort of perverse status in being able to defraud formal lenders without being caught. This does not happen in a solidarity group program.

Policy Recommendations

If financial sector policymakers continue to deepen formal financial markets and wish to extend their coverage downwards to include most productive and commercial actors in local economies, they must design lending institutions that can make far smaller loans more efficiently than any that currently exist. Large lenders who hope to meet the financial needs of the informal productive and commercial sectors will most certainly need to be a specially created, decentralized, private enterprise. Even though these institutions will need to be private enterprises, the profit motive will not suffice. Microbusiness lending will probably never be tremendously profitable under commercial interest rate regimes and large institutions will have difficulty charging higher rates. Thus it will be necessary for them to offer an attractive array of complementary services in order to compete with informal lenders.

Central banks will have to legislate the creation of specialized banking institutions to fulfill this purpose, again due to the relatively low rates of return on bank assets which would be expected. The challenge will be to create dynamic, publicly supported financial intermediaries that operate under the strictest efficiency parameters of the best private sector companies.

References

ACCION International. 1988. *An Operational Guide for Microenterprise Projects.* Toronto, Ontario: Calmeadow Foundation.

21

Regulatory Avoidance in Informal Financial Markets

Robert C. Vogel and Robert Wieland

Informal financial markets (IFMs) are a category of financial transactions that take place outside the formal, regulated banking system. IFMs are comprised of an extremely varied set of transactions and arrangements, but they have in common the fact that the intermediaries who undertake them are, unlike institutions doing formal finance, not required to meet reserve and other requirements of central banks and other official monetary authorities. In the history of development economics the recognition of the significance of IFMs is a fairly recent event, and an agreed upon taxonomy of these phenomena is yet to be. This chapter seeks to contribute to the development of an improved taxonomy of IFM phenomena by drawing attention to the subset of informal financial arrangements that emerge because of regulations imposed on formal finance.

Much of what is categorized as informal finance is independent of formal sector regulation in that it existed before such regulation was instituted and it is transacted by principals and agents for whom such regulations are irrelevant, either because of their small scale of operations or their physical remoteness from regulators. Lending by friends and relatives, moneylenders, pawnshops, money guards, and rotating savings and credit associations are examples of such "regulatory independent" arrangements. As regulations are promulgated and as the reach of regulatory agencies' enforcement arms are lengthened, these informal arrangements may adapt to minimize their risk of being found in contravention of regulations. But this is a different sort of regulatory avoidance than is the focus of this chapter. Here, our focus is on informal financial arrangements that develop precisely to avoid regulations, either to satisfy demand that is confounded by the regulations, or to mine a loophole that is created by them.

Examples of Regulations that Give Rise to Avoidance

Banking regulation can be divided into two fundamental categories: prudential regulation, which is aimed at maintaining the viability of the banking system in the face of several perverse incentives peculiar to finance; and economic regulation, which is aimed at achieving distributional and economic development goals. Prudential regulations place restrictions on the financial structure of institutions that help to ensure that excessive risks will not be taken by decisionmakers in those institutions. Examples include: licensing; reporting requirements; asset quality and capital adequacy requirements; and limits on portfolio concentration. Economic regulation of the financial sector often aims to redirect financial flows and to extract funds from the sector. Examples include: investment limits (both floors and ceilings) by sector, targeted loan rediscounting, interest rate restrictions, and taxes on financial transactions. In the extreme case, governments simply nationalize the banking sector and run it through their finance ministries to achieve their economic objectives. In practice, of course, things are much less clear-cut than this conceptual dichotomy of prudential and economic regulation implies. Licensing requirements can be used as a means to restrict entry to the financial sector, reserve requirements can be a means for financing government deficits, and the distinction between prudential restrictions on portfolio concentration and sector lending requirements can be confused. However, the convention will be maintained in this chapter that prudential regulation is indeed prudential in intent and that economic regulation is that which is justified by economic welfare arguments.

Both prudential and economic regulation can lead intermediaries to try to avoid regulations. But, as the examples discussed below will reveal, regulatory avoidance is often the result of the repression of financial transactions for which there is considerable demand. Such repression is typically the result of economic regulation of the financial sector. When interest rate restrictions are a binding constraint for intermediaries then there is, by definition, disequilibrium in the financial market. When the difference between supply and demand for financial services becomes great enough, alternative arrangements arise by which these services can be supplied outside the constraint of the regulation. This same argument holds for sector-specific investment quotas. It is often the case that domestic inflation and/or exchange rate instability are the factors that make controlled interest rates insufficient to allow financial markets to clear on the basis of the price of money. But whether the fault for disequilibrium lies with the interest rate restriction or the macro-economic policies that made these restrictions overly onerous for the system is a different issue. The failure of financial markets to equate the supply of finance with demand because of regulations restricting the rate of interest that can be charged on loans or the amount of investment a single institution can place with some specified category of enterprises, often leads to the alternative financial arrangements that are the subject of this chapter.

In the remainder of the chapter, examples of regulatory avoidance from three countries are discussed. Each example provides insight into the ways in which individuals and firms respond to financial repression and financial opportunity. While the solutions that these arrangements provide to financial market disequilibrium are second best outcomes (if smoothly operating financial markets are taken as a feasible option), they do represent useful innovations and increased financial intermediation in the face of a difficult policy environment. Following the discussion of these cases, some similarities in the nature and development of regulatory avoiding arrangements are summarized.

Private Finance Companies in Pakistan

Between 1977 and 1979, there developed in Pakistan a number of private finance companies whose explicit purpose was to create investment funds by tapping the small savings of rural investors (Hamid and Nabi 1986). These institutions appeared in a financial market that included: nationalized formal financial institutions that, due in part to regulations on the pricing of financial services, did not well serve rural savers; a considerable increase in savings capability due to remittances from overseas laborers, and; official indifference to private sector innovations (due largely to a change in government). In addition to these factors, policymakers were publicly debating the establishment of an Islamic banking code that would have banned interest on capital and imposed religious taxes on savings. Because the new private finance companies used alternative instruments to mobilize funds, they could escape these religious banking regulations.

By mid 1979—at the peak of private finance company activity— there were a total of 80 private finance companies operating with combined deposits of over 457 million rupees. These companies together had 1,290 branches and employed 13,867 employees. Branches were overwhelmingly located in rural areas, principally in the Punjab. In their 18 months of operation up to mid-1979 these companies mobilized deposits representing 12 percent of formal sector deposits, and employed one quarter as many people as the nationalized banks. These figures indicate phenomenal growth over a very brief period. The special relevance of this growth to the question of formal versus informal financial arrangements lies in how the growth in deposits was achieved.

Hamid and Nabi (1986) report on two factors that helped the private finance companies achieve their spectacular growth. The first of these was their use of local channels for deposit mobilization. Companies set up shop in rural towns and staffed these new branches with sons of village headmen and notables. In so doing, they achieved immediate legitimacy and benefited from the connections that these agents had with the local community. The second important factor that helped the private finance companies to grow was the gap in services provided by the nationalized banks. The majority of private finance company branches were established in rural towns that were not served by any of the nationalized banks. Private finance companies made financial services more convenient to customers by locating near to them, by working longer hours, and by hiring local staff.

Rates of return on investments (which essentially were interest rates on deposits) were freely determined by market factors and were not subject to the ceilings imposed on formal institutions, but these were only a few percentage points above the formal banking sector rates. Given the higher risk of investing funds with these institutions, this interest rate differential can not account for the finance companies' tremendous success at mobilizing deposits. The fact that they took their services to the villages where business potential existed and that they supplied these services with efficiency and convenience for the client better explains this success. Employees were given direct incentives to mobilize deposits, and the use of local employees in conjunction with an avowed objective to invest funds locally all supported the objective of increased deposit mobilization.

While the private finance companies experienced spectacular growth over a brief period, their collapse was equally spectacular. This collapse came about not because the majority of these institutions were employing unsustainable financial practices, but because they were totally unregulated. The collapse of this market provides an important example of the usefulness of regulations for financial markets and institutions. In the face of unregulated entry and the absence of any sort of prudential controls, anyone wishing to set up a *ponzi* scheme (a scheme by which returns can be paid to existing clients only so long as an increasing number of new clients are being brought on board—that is, by using new liabilities to pay returns on existing claims) under the name of a private finance company was free to do so. When unscrupulous agents entered into this market to partake of the high profits that the private finance companies were enjoying, the need for regulation became clear to the companies themselves. In 1979, this began to happen on an increasing scale and customers, recognizing that they did not really know enough to evaluate any single institution, began to lose trust in the private finance company movement at large.

In mid-1979 the owners of private finance companies petitioned the government to regulate and police them, recommending a comprehensive set of prudential requirements for their companies. This petition was rebuffed. Instead the government undertook an inquiry into irregularities committed by a few of the companies and then declared that they could not maintain deposit accounts with the nationalized banks. The government's actions (and failure to act), together with stories in the press about failure and scandal among a few private finance companies, induced a run on deposits that the companies could not withstand. In October of 1979, the government imposed a total ban on deposits with private finance companies, effectively closing them down. As of 1986, claims on defunct finance companies were still being adjudicated. Financial markets were again controlled exclusively by the nationalized commercial banks operating under the aegis of the Ministry of Finance.

Nonregulated Financial Institutions in Guatemala

Vogel and others (1990) report that in Guatemala, significant financial resources are intermediated by unregulated institutions. These institutions fall outside the banking law—principally on the basis of calling their services by some other term than the one that requires adherence to regulation. They keep a low profile, but they mobilize and invest considerable resources and serve a diverse set of customers. To a large extent, the mechanisms employed by unregulated financial institutions are shaped by their need to avoid regulation. So also are the instruments that they offer. Nonregulated financial institutions originated in Guatemala to provide consumer finance, especially through credit cards and for the purchase of cars and other consumer durables. They have since diversified into leasing, factoring, money market funds, and lending for a wide range of purposes beyond consumer finance. Although much of their business activity is focused in Guatemala City, these nonregulated financial institutions have also penetrated the rural areas where they finance marketing agents and other rural enterprises.

The interest rates offered on funds invested with nonregulated financial institutions were, before liberalization of formal sector interest rates, considerably higher than those offered by banks, but they have since come to be within several percentage points of formal sector deposit rates. As was the case in Pakistan with the private finance companies, this interest premium does not explain the success of these institutions in mobilizing funds, given the higher risk of placing funds with unregulated and uninsured intermediaries. On the other hand, interest rates on money lent by nonregulated financial institutions were considerably higher than interest rates charged on commercial bank loans. These high rates did not stifle demand for loans, however, as is shown by the tremendous growth in the portfolio of many of these intermediaries. The loan portfolios of five of the largest of these companies roughly doubled between 1989 and 1990. The considerable intermediation margin that these companies enjoyed, taken together with their ability to contain administrative and commercial risk costs, translated into high profits. By escaping taxes on financial intermediation these nonregulated institutions further assured themselves of better than average profits, even if their intermediation costs had been as high as those of the formal sector institutions.

Nonregulated institutions' ability to attract investors with only moderate premiums over commercial bank deposit rates and borrowers at interest rates considerably higher than those of regulated institutions derives from the failure of the formal sector to satisfy demand for financial services. Due to the restrictions on loan interest rates (and the consequent low deposit interest rates) and the high levels of inflation that occurred in Guatemala up to 1989, and due to large government deficits that were financed in part by bond issues and high reserve requirements, banks were short on loanable funds and long on demand for loans. Credit, therefore, was not wholly rationed by price in the formal financial market, and demand far exceeded supply. In fact many banks lent principally to related firms during this period, and those firms and individuals who were not represented in the ownership of these institutions had little choice but to make use of alternative sources of finance.

The high profits that many nonregulated financial institutions achieved during the late 1980s seem to have not yet induced unscrupulous operators to enter this market in great enough numbers to undermine confidence in nonregulated institutions. This may be in part because the resource mobilization mechanism employed by these institutions has prevented such operators from gaining a foothold there. Most firms employ promoters who are paid both salaries and commissions and who use personal contacts and their good reputation to attract funds. The requirement that a promoter be credible with his clients and the promise of a paid share of the business that he generates could serve to both filter out unscrupulous operators and to keep practicing ones honest. An additional safeguard on the viability of the market that nonregulated finance companies created in Guatemala in the late 1980s is their practice of having themselves audited regularly by an external auditor. This convention lends credibility to the institutions and helps to assure investors that their funds will be safe with the company.

Nonregulated Financial Institutions in the Dominican Republic

The informal financial market in the Dominican Republic (DR) includes household finance companies, commercial finance companies, small personal loan houses, and pawnshops and moneylenders (Zinser and others 1986). The household finance companies accounted for as much as 20 percent of the total credit in the DR in the mid-1980s, lending primarily for construction, remodeling, and other household related costs. Many of these companies were affiliated with regulated mortgage banks. Commercial finance companies lent primarily to businesses for both working capital and for the purchase of fixed assets. Most of these companies also had connections with formal sector institutions and some even undertook cofinancing arrangements with formal lenders. Small loan companies were less intertwined with formal sector institutions, but many of these institutions were registered with the monetary authorities and were subject to some nominal regulation. The restrictions placed on these institutions included loan size limits and interest rate maximums, but these latter were, at 3 percent per month, well above the formal sector rates.

Almost two-thirds of the funds of the nonregulated companies referenced above derived from individual deposits. The bulk of the remainder was invested capital, although a small percentage was obtained from formal sector loans to these companies. Zinser and others (1986) cite an estimate of these companies' total deposit and fixed interest liabilities that was more than one-third the size of formal sector liabilities. Deposits earned between 1 and 3 percent per month in the early 1980s, depending on the size and term of the deposit. Interest rates on loans from these companies ranged from 2 to 3 percent per month for commercial borrowers to as high as 20 percent per month for personal loans. Loan terms were typically less than one year, though in the case of secured loans they were sometimes as long as three years.

Several factors account for the significant scale of the nonregulated sector in the DR. In terms of deposit mobilization, the nonregulated companies pay more than twice as much for funds than do their regulated counterparts. These higher returns could reasonably be expected to generate transfers of funds out of formal sector deposits. What is perhaps more surprising is that such returns did not induce a larger transfer of funds out of the formal sector. On average, interest rates on loans from the nonregulated institutions were also roughly twice the rates of loans from the formal sector. But there was considerable variation in interest rates both according to loan use and loan size. Small personal loans had the highest interest rates whereas larger loans for preferred commercial customers were competitive with formal sector loans. Borrowers came to the nonregulated institutions because they were not able to satisfy their credit needs in the formal market either because the loan amounts that they required were too small to be of interest to formal lenders or because they could not meet another of the non-price requirements of borrowing in that market.

Conclusions

These three examples of informal financial arrangements that arose in direct response to opportunities stemming from financial sector regulations are not isolated cases. Nayar (1982) reports a similar story for the nonregulated banks in India and Larson (1990) gives a like account of nonregulated finance in Honduras. In all of these cases, tight regulatory control of the financial sector has resulted in truncated supply of financial services by regulated institutions. The India case provides a slightly different twist in that there the nonregulated banks prospered even as the formal sector enjoyed tremendous growth. But, in each case, market demand reared its inexorable head and drew forth additional supply through arrangements and transactions that sidestepped the regulations. To government policymakers who wish to direct financial resources according to a specific vision of optimality, this has been a problem. But even these must recognize that it is not so much the fact that alternative arrangements have arisen that is a problem, but that the regulated market is not able to satisfy demand for finance.

Regulation avoiding informal intermediaries represent an induced segmentation of nations' financial markets. Because they often operate outside, not only the regulations that gave rise to demand for their services, but also outside the prudential regulations that benefit both suppliers and consumers of financial services, there are economic costs inherent in the existence of these arrangements. In the cases cited, the volume of finance and, therefore, economic welfare has been increased through the emergence of regulation avoiding arrangements. But due to the segmentation of the financial market, the increased risk for both the principals and agents who operate in an unregulated financial market, and the additional costs that are sometimes incurred in avoiding regulations, such arrangements can only be a second best response to policy induced constraints.

In the case of Pakistan, where the nonregulated financial sector ultimately collapsed, the potential cost of allowing this sort of market segmentation to proceed is made clear. Hundreds of thousands of relatively poor people lost at least part of their savings in that collapse. But the private finance companies failed not because of institutional weaknesses of the majority of companies. They failed because there was no discrimination in their membership and no substitute for the imperfect information of depositors regarding any single company. Regulation could have provided such a substitute, but this was not forthcoming from a government that enjoyed a monopoly on the financial sector before these companies arose, and who again enjoyed this monopoly once they were gone.

Even in countries where the monetary authorities do not act to undermine the regulation avoiding arrangements, it is important to recognize, as Zinser and others (1986) have, that "although the parallel market serves a function in providing more financial intermediation than would exist in a situation of controlled interest rates and rationing, the levels of private saving and borrowing in the combined regulated and nonregulated markets are necessarily less than would prevail in an open market" (p. 13). Such a view recommends that governments neither take a laissez-faire attitude toward regulatory avoidance in financial markets, nor that they try to eradicate them through tighter regulations and stricter enforcement, but that they attempt to understand what factors are leading to the rationing of finance in the formal sector, (thereby giving rise to regulation avoiding arrangements) and work to remove these. Such a policy would remove demand for regulatory avoidance and reduce the attraction of informal finance. If coupled with an effort to permit informal intermediaries who could make the grade into the formal sector, such an approach could not only expand the volume of finance, but might also improve competition in the financial sector and ensure further increases in intermediation volumes.

References

Hamid, Naved, and Ijaz Nabi. 1986. "Privatizing the Financial Sector in LDCs: Lessons of an Experiment." Unpublished paper done by the Development Research Department. Washington D.C.: World Bank.

Larson, Donald W. 1990. "An Analysis of Informal Markets in Honduras." Unpublished study prepared for the Agency for International Development in Honduras.

Nayar, C. P. S. 1982. "Finance Corporations: An Informal Financial Intermediary in India." *Savings and Development* 6:5-39.

Vogel, Robert C., and others. 1990. "An Analysis of Guatemala's Micro-Enterprise Support Program." Unpublished paper prepared for The Inter-American Development Bank, Project Analysis Department, Washington, D.C.

Zinser, James and others. 1986. *Mercado Financiero No Regulado.* Santo Domingo, Dominican Republic: Centro de Estudios Monetarios y Bancarios.

22

Contract Lending to Small Farmers in the Dominican Republic

Jerry R. Ladman, Jose de la Vina, and Roberto Liz

Many government-sponsored credit programs in low-income countries fail to reach a large number of poor people in rural areas on a sustained basis because of the costs and risks associated with making small loans. If these loans are accompanied by technical assistance and marketing services, the program costs are even higher. The past few years an increasing number of policymakers have sought ways to reduce these costs and risks. Recently, some people have suggested that it may be more efficient and effective to extend additional formal loans to informal intermediaries who, in turn, then make more informal loans to borrowers of small amounts.[1] These firms, in some cases, combine technical assistance and marketing services with their loans.

In this chapter we report on such a program in the Dominican Republic. It involves contract arrangements between small farmers and agribusiness or processing firms who use loans to ensure access to steady supplies of raw materials or products. Many of these lending firms obtain bank loans to fund their lending, thus providing small farmers with indirect access to formal loans. This chapter reports the findings of a study done in 1985 on these contractual arrangements. The possibilities of using this type of scheme for small-farmer credit in other low-income countries is discussed in the final section of the chapter.

---

1. Enhancing the linkages between formal and informal finance has been stressed by Seibel (see chapter 17) and by several other individuals associated with the Germans' foreign assistance agency, Gesellschaft fur Technische Zusammenarbiet (GTZ).

Contract Credit in the Dominican Republic

A number of agribusiness firms in the Dominican Republic sign contracts with small farmers to ensure that these firms will receive an adequate supply of various kinds of products. These contracts often entail credit arrangements that are called bridge loans; the firm serves as a bridge over which bank loans pass in order to eventually finance farmers' production.

In our study we surveyed 44 agribusiness firms. They were all processors or marketers that handled 75 percent or more of the country's total production of one or more of nine major agricultural products: cantaloupe, cocoa, coffee, milk, peanuts, rice, sugarcane, tobacco, and tomatoes. Of these firms, 36 provided contract credit to growers and 27 utilized bank loans to finance these credit. In total, these 27 firms financed 46,452 farmers and the mean number of growers financed per firm was 1,228. A sample of 465 farmers, stratified across the 27 firms and products, were interviewed in order to specify the credit delivery system used by the firms, to measure the transaction costs the borrowers incurred with these loans, and to determine the grower's degree of satisfaction with these arrangements. The aggregate results for the nine products are reported below.

Characteristics of Farmers

Contracting growers were mostly owners of small- to medium-sized family farms who depended on their financed crop as their main source of farm income. Levels of education were low: only 21 percent had completed more than six years of schooling. Contract credit was their main source of financing, but 27 percent of the farmers also had loans from the Agricultural Development Bank, 7 percent borrowed from friends or relatives, and smaller percentages of the farmers used other sources of informal finance. It is noteworthy that two-thirds of the farmers surveyed had been clients, at one time or another, of the Agricultural Development Bank.

The Credit Delivery System

The average size loan per grower was equivalent to about US$3,300 and the term was determined by the growing season, usually less than 12 months. Collateral requirements were minimal; 80 percent of the borrowers reported they only needed to pledge their crop as collateral, while most other borrowers needed a cosigner or were asked to pledge their land title. Annual direct interest charges averaged only 10 percent. Some firms did not charge any interest, and the maximum average interest rate charged on loans for any product was 24 percent.

The credit delivery procedures for both lender and borrower were exceedingly simple. The loan application process, which is usually complicated for bank loans, was handled with dispatch, almost always in an office of the firm. This meant some travel by the grower, but since a branch office was typically nearby, the trips did not consume much time nor involve significant expenses for the borrower. Once there little time was wasted, 70 percent of the borrowers spent 20 minutes or less in the office negotiating the contract and the loan. Fifty-seven percent of the farmers made only one trip to the firm in the application phase and another one-third made two or three trips. Only 35 percent prepared a written credit application, for the others a verbal application sufficed. Loan approval was rapid, 41 percent of the borrowers reported immediate approval, and all but 26 percent were approved within 15 days. Only 56 percent of the farmers were required to sign a formal credit contract.

Loan disbursements were also typically made rapidly at the firm's office, mostly in cash or check. Most borrowers reported there was no disruption of production due to delays in accessing their loans. The number of disbursements ranged from one to eight, with the multiple disbursements coming from those firms that most closely monitored the production process because their products were subject to damage and/or there were high-level quality controls in the final markets. In these cases, disbursements were sometimes made in kind, and the firm closely supervised or advised the farmer to try to ensure the growth of a quality product. Indeed, 43 percent of the growers reported receiving technical assistance from lending firms.

At harvest, the growers typically delivered the product to the firm. Three-fourths of the borrowers were able to settle their debts on the day products were delivered; only 15 percent of the borrowers had to wait as long as 15 days to settle their loan accounts. Because the lending firm was also the major marketing channel for the borrower, loan recovery performance was generally excellent.

Although, there was some variation by firms or products, it was clear that the credit delivery system used for contract credit in the Dominican Republic was straightforward and simple for the borrowers and entailed very modest transaction costs for the lender. The following figures for the borrowers' loan transaction costs support this observation.

Borrower Transaction Costs

In our study we collected time costs and cash outlays incurred by the borrower in each phase of the loan transaction. For example, if the borrower spent an entire day in going to and from the agribusiness firm's office to negotiate a loan, the opportunity cost of his time was tabulated as a loan transaction cost. Likewise, any costs of transportation or paperwork associated with obtaining the loan were likewise tabulated as transaction costs. The results of our tabulations are reported in Table 1.

The average total borrower costs incurred in transacting these contract loans was only equivalent to US$7.21. Of this amount 56 and 44 percent corresponded to imputed time costs (using the minimum daily wage) and cash outlays, respectively. About one-half of the costs were associated with disbursement, almost one-third with repayments, and

TABLE 1. Borrowers' Loan Transaction Costs

Phase of Credit Delivery System	Time Costs[a]		Cash Outlays		Total Costs	
	US$	%	US$	%	US$	%
Application	0.71	17	0.57	18	1.28	18
Implementation	2.25	55	1.42	45	3.67	51
Repayment	1.12	28	1.14	36	2.26	31
Total	4.07	100	3.14	100	7.21	100
Percentage of total	--	56	--	44	--	100

Note: Dollar figures are based on a 1985 rate of exchange of RD$ 3.50 = US $1.00.

[a] Based on 1985 minimum daily wage in rural areas.

Source: Computations based on sample survey.

the remainder involved in the processing of loan applications. The small amount of transaction costs involved in the application phase demonstrates the lack of paperwork associated with obtaining a contract loan, which is usually the most time-consuming and costly part of the credit process. It also shows the lender usually knew a great deal about most applicants who applied for loans.

These costs correspond to only about one-quarter of one percent of the average loan size. When added to the average interest charges, the average total borrowing costs summed to only 10.6 percent per annum.

Monopoly Power

Some people have been concerned that credit arrangements linked to land tenancy or to the purchase or sale of products, inputs, or labor might result in borrowers being exploited by lenders (for an example see Braverman and Stiglitz 1982). The Dominican Republic data, however, do not reinforce this concern as far as the explicit charges on loans are concerned. We found that the explicit interest charges were typically less than those charged by other credit institutions. Moreover, total costs of borrowing, including transaction costs imposed on borrowers, were quite reasonable.

It is possible, however, that there are "hidden" charges in the contractual arrangement that more than compensate the agribusiness firm for low interest charges. For example, farmers might be forced to pay excessively high prices for inputs that were lent to the farmer in kind.

In our study, 28 percent of the farmers received in-kind input loans. Of these, two-thirds thought the prices they paid for these inputs were less than those prevailing in the market.[2] Thus, it does not appear that the farmers were gouged on the prices they paid for many of the inputs they acquired through contract lending.

A second possible avenue for exploitation is through the price paid for the product involved in the contract loan. Although 84 percent of the growers we surveyed reported that the lender set the purchase price, there were 55 percent who said they received the going market price or more for their product. About 30 percent of the growers reported the contracting firm had discounted their price because of impurities, water content, or for other reasons. However, half of these farmers felt

---

2. Most of the borrowers who complained about input prices in our survey were rice producers.

the discount was justifiable. Overall, there were surprisingly few product price complaints by the farmers we surveyed that were directed at the agribusiness firm with which they worked.

A third possibility for exploitation is through cheating on the weight of products delivered to fulfill contracts. Only one-third of the growers interviewed raised concerns about honest weighing of their product. This dissatisfaction was concentrated in three products: cantaloupe, sugar, and tomatoes. The fact that most of these farmers planned to continue working with the same agribusiness firm in the future suggests these abuses were largely imaginary or were not very serious.

In summary, there is no evidence that the firms typically nor systematically exercise monopsonistic powers in their dealings with their contract farmers. Indeed, when growers report being disadvantaged, it may be more perceived than real.

There are at least two reasons why price gouging is not an important problem. First, most farmers have access to several contracting firms and are able to switch firms if one firm treats them unfairly. Also, many of the contract farmers have other crop and enterprise possibilities, besides those produced under contract. If the contracting arrangements were exploitative, many of the participants would likely shift to other activities.

Second, it is in the best interest of contracting firms to treat their growers fairly and thereby establish long-term relationships that ensure a supply of high quality products over time. These firms incur various costs in developing contracting relationships with clients, including teaching farmers how to produce the quality of product required and also collecting enough information about farmers to be able to establish their creditworthiness. These costs are reduced substantially if the firm is able to work with the same farmers year-after-year. In addition, firms that abuse their clients would find it more difficult to recruit new clients and might face adverse selection problems with individuals who did agree to work with them.

The farmers' views about the program were the most compelling evidence that little or no monopoly power was exercised against them. Only about 6 percent of the farmers interviewed said they did not want to contract with the same firm in the future.

Advantages of Contract Lending

Contract lending as practiced in the Dominican Republic appears to have at least seven advantages over many government sponsored small-farmer credit programs.

First, borrowers incur extremely low transaction costs in negotiating, obtaining, and repaying their loans under the contract system. Although data are not available on similar transaction costs on small loans from formal financial intermediaries in the Dominican Republic, information from research in other countries shows these costs are generally substantial and that these costs affect borrower decisions about seeking and repaying loans. Adams and Nehman (1970) for example, reported borrower transaction costs ranging from 5 to 33 percent of loan amounts for small farmers in Bangladesh. In a later study in Bangladesh, Ahmed found loan transaction costs ranging from 16 to 146 percent of loan amounts, depending on loan size. Ladman measured transaction costs for clients of a small-farmer credit Program in Bolivia and found them to be about 4 percent of average loan size.

The procedures involved in contract lending in the Dominican Republic, in contrast, were so simple that borrowers virtually ignored the very modest transaction costs imposed on them. Because the lending procedures were closely tied to other commercial transactions with the borrower, the lending firms felt they realized substantial economies of scope by combining lending with these other activities. These credit transaction costs were viewed by the lender as being minor compared to other more important considerations.

Second, the interest costs incurred by contract borrowers were surprisingly low, averaging only slightly more than 10 percent per annum. At the same time the Agricultural Development Bank was charging interest rates of 14 percent and the commercial banks 20 percent on loans made to small farmers. Clearly, the firms that were making contract loans charged less than the going rate and were less interested in making a profit on their lending than they were in having an assured supply of products.

Third, most of the contract borrowers reported that loans were delivered on time, something that is often not done in formal lending to borrowers of small amounts. In contract credit, lenders have strong incentives to deliver loans on time in order to ensure timely planting and harvesting so that products are delivered on schedule. Formal lenders seldom have such a direct incentive to process loans rapidly.

Fourth, technical assistance often is provided with contract lending to secure high quality products.[3] The firms buying these goods have strong incentives to provide quality technical assistance since their profits largely depend on the quality of goods produced by the borrower and user of the technical assistance. Extension agents and supervised credit agents working for government owned development banks who provide technical assistance to farmers have no similar stake in the final outcome of the production process.

Fifth, contract credit provides borrowers with a secure arrangement for marketing their products. Price and marketing uncertainties are major problems faced by most farmers and contract lending helps them moderate these problems. Indeed, marketing is the driving force for the contract system; the agribusiness firm enters into the contract in order to be assured of a supply of raw material. Without this assurance the lending firms would have little or no incentive to provide loans at or below their costs of acquiring additional funds.

Sixth, the contract lending system is durable and long lasting, in contrast to many government credit programs for small farmers that turn out to be transitory. In the Dominican Republic, farmers can be relatively sure of access to loans in the future, as long as they satisfy the terms of their contracts. Our survey showed that 78 percent of the farmers had had contracts with the same firm for more than 3 years, and 40 percent had contracts for more than 10 years.

Seventh, contract lending provided a large number of borrowers of small amounts in the Dominican Republic indirect access to loans from commercial banks. Because of costs and loan recovery risks most banks in the Dominican Republic are unable to provide sustained lending to the class of farmers serviced by contract lending, but they are willing to make relatively large loans to agribusiness firms that eventually filter down to borrowers of small amounts. Moreover, the numbers served are large. In 1985 more than one-and-a-half times as many farmers in the country received contract loans as were able to obtain loans from the government's Agricultural Development Bank.

---

3. In our study we found little or no technical assistance associated with contract loans to cocoa, coffee, rice, and sugar producers. Apparently, the problems of assuring quality standards in these products were less demanding than was true of other products financed under contract lending.

Conclusions

Contract credit in the Dominican Republic offers growers a package of loans and services at low financial and transaction costs compared to alternative sources. It does not depend on government subsidies; it involves commercial banks in providing funds to small farmers, and loan recovery performance is high. The system reaches large numbers of small- and medium-sized farmers and it is durable. Most importantly, many borrowers of small amounts prefer this arrangement over trying to access formal loans directly. Borrowers in our survey were asked to compare contract credit with their earlier experiences with loans from the agricultural bank: 90 percent responded that contract loans were obtained more quickly, 87 percent said it involved less paperwork, 82 percent felt it required less collateral, 75 percent thought it easier to repay, and 91 percent believed it allowed them access to more secure marketing arrangements.

The possibilities for using contract credit more extensively in the Dominican Republic and in other low-income countries appear to be promising, especially in the production of new products. It must be recognized, however, that the driving force in the arrangement is the agribusiness firm that is producing for a certain market. Thus, development programs should emphasize promoting markets and agribusiness operations, and then helping these firms to gain more access to formal loans. Formal loans extended to an agribusiness firm that, in turn, finances its clients may be the most efficient way for banks to reach poor people in rural areas. Although our study only dealt with loans made by commercial banks, there is no reason to believe that development banks could not also use bridge lending to efficiently reach larger numbers of their target clientele.

References

Adams, Dale W and Gerald I. Nehman. 1970. "Borrowing Costs and the Demand for Rural Credit." *Journal of Development Studies* 15:165-176.

Ahmed, Zia U. 1989. "Effective Costs of Rural Loans in Bangladesh." *World Development* 17:357-363.

Braverman, Avishay, and Joseph E. Stiglitz. 1982. "Sharecropping and Interlinking of Agrarian Markets." *American Economic Review* 72:675-715.

Ladman, Jerry R. 1984. "Loan-Transactions Costs, Credit Rationing and Market Structure: The Case of Bolivia." In Dale W Adams, Douglas H. Graham, and J.D. Von Pischke, eds., *Undermining Rural Development with Cheap Credit.* pp. 104-119. Boulder, Colorado: Westview Press.

23

Rotating Savings and Credit Associations in Bolivia[1]

Dale W Adams and Marie L. Canavesi

Bolivia is a poor nation whose per capita income is higher than only a couple of countries in the Americas. It was one of the first nations to default on its foreign debts during the 1980s, it has suffered hyperinflation, its major export (cocaine) is illegal, and its traditional primary export (tin) has declined to less than one-quarter of the value it was a few years ago. Despite progress in stabilizing the economy, these severe problems limit the ability of the government to save and to marshall capital for development. This does not mean, however, that individual Bolivians do not save.

In the following discussion we report on research in Bolivia on informal rotating savings and credit associations (ROSCAs)—locally called *pasanakus*. Our results support the thesis that substantial capacities to save voluntarily exist, even in the poorest countries.

Description of Research

Until recently relatively little has been said in the literature about ROSCAs in Latin America, as most studies of these associations focused on Africa or Asia. Studies in Mexico, Peru, and the Caribbean, however, show that ROSCAs are also common in the Americas (for examples, see

---

1. Originally Published in *Savings and Development* 13(1989): 219-236. Reprinted with permission of the editor of the journal.

Velez-Ibanez 1983; Kurtz 1978; Norvell and Wehrly 1969; and Katzin 1959).

During the summer of 1987 we investigated ROSCAs in Bolivia by doing structured interviews with 470 individuals located in five of the largest cities. These individuals provided information on 453 separate pasanakus. In addition, we also interviewed an additional 450 people in lines waiting for buses and customers in central markets about their participation in, or knowledge of, pasanakus.

The genesis of pasanakus is unclear. It is traditional for farmers in Bolivia to exchange labor through *mingas* and to participate in cooperative land tenure relationships. Other traditional forms of lending or bartering in Bolivia include *trueque, ayne*, and *chuk'u*. It is unclear if Bolivia's pasanakus evolved out of these ancient systems of rural cooperation, were imported, or emerged spontaneously.

The fact that ROSCAs are common in some places in the Americas where large numbers of Indians exist, including Bolivia, suggests that pasanakus may have evolved out of traditional systems of cooperation—pooling of labor may have logically led to pooling of money.

In our structured interviewing we tried to uncover as many pasanakus as possible, collect information on the characteristics of pasanakus, assemble reasons for members participating, and also collect information on the motivation and characteristics of organizers. We conducted interviews in most of the major urban occupational groups, in many of the important urban businesses, and we interviewed employees in about 20 formal financial institutions. In addition, we also asked for estimates, from the persons interviewed, on the proportion of all employees in their offices (organizations) who were currently participating in pasanakus.

ROSCAs in Bolivia

We found pasanakus are common in urban areas. They appear to be equally popular in all five cities studied. As can be seen in Table 1, in the organizations where we did interviews, 8 to 24 percent of the employees were known by the person interviewed to participate in at least one ROSCA within the office or place of business. These percentages are conservative estimates since some of the individuals who were listed as nonparticipants may have been members of other pasanakus outside the office, or members of other ROSCAs within the organization, but unknown by the person we interviewed. Also, the percentages in Table 1 do not capture all of the employees in an office who occasionally participate in ROSCAs, but who were not members at the time of our interview. In addition, about 10 percent of those interviewed reported they or their spouse were also concurrent members of other pasanakus.

In addition to the 470 structured interviews with pasanaku members, we also did brief random interviews with approximately 450 adults waiting in line for buses and shopping in the central markets. These individuals were asked two questions: Are you currently a member of a pasanaku, and are you familiar with how a pasanaku operates? As can be noted in Table 2, the responses showed that 30 to 40 percent of the individuals interviewed, depending on city, were enrolled in a pasanaku, and an additional 18 to 25 percent were very familiar with the operations of ROSCAs. Only 38 to 50 percent of the people interviewed claimed not to be very familiar with pasanakus.

TABLE 1. Percentage of Employees Participating in Intraoffice Pasanakus in Selected Organizations in Bolivia, 1987

Type of Organization	Percent
Financial institutions	16
Central markets	22
Sales	8
Business offices	15
Government offices	17
Private businesses	10
Labor groups	10
Hotels	10
Laboratories	22
Public administration	10
Private clubs	10
Industrial plants	24
Transportation	16
University	10
Communication businesses	9
Miscellaneous	10

Source: Field surveys in Bolivia, 1987.

TABLE 2. Percentage of People Informally Interviewed Who Participated in Pasanakus[a]

City	Playing	Knew but not playing	Little knowledge
La Paz	35	25	40
Santa Cruz	39	23	38
Cochabamba	32	18	50
Oruro	40	22	38
Sucre and other[b]	30	25	45

[a] Results of brief unstructured interviews with about 450 people who were standing in line waiting for buses or making purchases in central markets in mid-1987.

[b] Includes informal interviews done in towns around La Paz: Viacha, El Alto, and El Lago.

Source: Field surveys in Bolivia, 1987.

This information suggests that a sizable portion of urban Bolivians adults are, or have been, pasanaku members—one-third or more. An even higher percentage of urban households likely have at least one member participating in a ROSCA—perhaps up to one-half. In a few urban locations most adults are members of ROSCAs.

Surprisingly, we also found that pasanakus were common among employees of most banks. This raises interesting questions about the benefits employees realize from participating in pasanakus that they cannot realize from the financial institution in which they work.

General Characteristics of ROSCAs

As can be noted in Table 3, the average size of membership in the pasanakus surveyed was 10 with a range from 5 to 110. On average, 60 percent of the total membership of the pasanakus surveyed were women and nearly 90 percent of the groups were composed largely of friends or fellow workers. Eighty-three percent of all the ROSCAs surveyed collected and distributed only cash. Many of the remaining ROSCAs collected cash and distributed some commodity. Nearly six in ten of all the pasanakus surveyed allowed the organizer to take the first pot.

TABLE 3. Characteristics of 453 Pasanakus in Bolivia

Item	Mean	Median	Standard Deviation	Range
Number of members	10.8	10	6.6	5-110
Number of women	6.4	6	4.2	0-40
Number of shares	10.2	10	3.7	10-40
Share value ($US)	17.8	10	21.9	0.5-250
Percentage of income to ROSCAs	16.6	15	9.8	1-80

Source: Field surveys in Bolivia, 1987.

One of the most surprising findings of the study was the relatively large amounts of money people were putting into pasanakus. In terms of U.S. dollars, the average person contributed nearly US$18 to the pasanakus surveyed at each collection period. For those paying a full share every two weeks this amounted to about US$36 per month.

The range in the length of time between payment of shares was 1 to 50 days, with a median of 15. Shares were collected daily in 15 percent of the pasanakus surveyed, 5 percent assembled shares every week, 14 percent every 10 days, 22 percent every two weeks, and 38 percent each month. We were surprised to find that about two-thirds of the pasanakus surveyed were conducted in U.S. dollars, a creative response to hyperinflation.

The most popular method of determining the rotation of the pots was through the drawing of lots at the time the pasanaku was organized, with nearly 70 percent of the groups choosing this method. Another 15 percent drew lots each time the pots were distributed, about 10 percent assigned the rotation following the order of members joining the group, and a small number of groups did the rotation informally on the basis of need.

Types of Pasanakus

We found three types of pasanakus: simple office groups; more complex groups, often found in central markets, that included an organizer who received a commission; and pasanakus that were used by merchants and banks to promote the sale of goods such as clothing, furniture, food, appliances, automobiles, and mortgages. We label these three types *office, commission,* and *promotional* pasanakus.

The most popular form of ROSCAs in Bolivia is the *office pasanaku;* about three-quarters of the groups we surveyed were of this type. Most offices and businesses in the major cities have at least one pasanaku among its employees. Typically the office pasanaku had 10 members, the majority women, who each contribute the same amount of cash to a pot every 15 or 30 days. The organizer of the group is often informally selected, but may be someone who needs a relatively large amount of cash and solicits coworkers to join a pasanaku. It is more typical for the organizer to be a senior employee who can be trusted to handle the collection and distribution of funds. Sometimes the group organizers are allowed to take the first distribution as compensation for their troubles, but, more typically, the organizer of an office pasanaku receives no special consideration.

The rotation of the pot is usually decided by lot at the time of the organization of the pasanaku, or by lot among the "nonwinners" at the time each pot is collected. In some cases the organizer of the group has an implied obligation to make up for any defaults by members invited to participate, especially if the organizer receives special consideration in the allocation of the pots. It is more typical, however, for all members to share equally in any losses experienced by the office group.

A few of these office pasanakus have a social function and give the members a feeling of togetherness through participation. This includes getting together for lunch or drinks each time a pot is collected and distributed. It is much more common, however, for the organizer to collect money and then pass the pot to the "winner" without interaction among other members of the group.

The next most important form of ROSCA was the *commission pasanaku* found in many of the urban markets where the organizers usually receive payment for their services. About 15 percent of the ROSCAs we surveyed were of this type. In some cases, the organizer may manage several pasanakus at one time, and in other cases they may manage a pasanaku as part of other marketing activities. We found women organizers who were managing up to six pasanakus and who had organized in excess of 100 ROSCAs in their lifetime. These organizers may or may not be people who regularly work in central markets.

The most common commission form is for the organizer to receive a payment out of each pot collected that ranges from 2 to 30 percent, the average being ten percent. The professional organizer may also have the option of taking the first pot and in some cases not having to pay shares. It is also common for professional organizers to have the use of money collected until it is distributed to a winner. In some cases, money is collected daily, but distributions are only made every week or even up to every 50 days. In a few cases the organizer, typically a woman, may live almost exclusively on her earnings from managing pasanakus. It is more typical for organizers' pasanaku earnings to be only part of their total income.

As with office pasanakus, the most common membership size for the commission pasanakus is 10, but we found commission groups that had over 100 members. Many of the collections were made daily, but some of the groups contributed money to a pot every five or ten days. The short time between collections may have given organizers more control than if long periods of time were involved. Also, daily collections may have been an accommodation to inflation. The organizer of the commission ROSCA often has a strong moral obligation to make good any defaults in payment to the pasanaku by individuals she had recruited.

There was even less social interaction among members of commission pasanakus than was found in the office form. In many cases the organizer is the only common connection among members of the group.

The third type of ROSCA, the *promotional pasanaku*, is organized by merchants and even bankers who are attempting to increase their sale of goods or services. Five to 10 percent of the ROSCAs surveyed in Bolivia were of this type. The Banco de la Union in La Paz, for example, asked the Central Bank for permission to organize pasanakus whose members would assemble funds necessary to make downpayments on apartments or houses. Each pasanaku would have 20 members and each winner of the pot would have enough money to make the 25 percent down-payment required by the bank. The bank, in turn, would accept this down payment and then extend a loan for the remaining 75 percent based on a mortgage. Pasanaku payments would be made at the end of each pay period.

Car dealers, furniture stores, appliance stores, merchants selling food items, and even tailors organize pasanakus as a substitute for installment payments to increase sales. We found a number of merchants in the central markets of La Paz, for example, who used pasanakus to promote sales of cans of edible oil, sacks of flour or sugar, and almost any other relatively large food staple. Merchants are interested in pasanakus because they promote sales.

We have heard of promotional ROSCAs in other countries experiencing high rates of inflation: Brazil, Chile, and Mexico. Making sales through ROSCAs is a way for both the seller and the buyer to manage and reduce the risks of inflation. It appears that the interest in promotional pasanakus waned in Bolivia during 1986-87 as the rate of inflation sharply declined.

Members' Responses

It can also be noted in Table 3 that, for the average person interviewed, the pasanaku share payment averaged almost one-sixth of total salary (17 percent). Since about 10 percent of the people interviewed, or their spouses, were members of several pasanakus concurrently, the total portion of salaries going into ROSCAs was somewhat higher than our reported figures.

One of our most important findings was the reason members gave for participating in a pasanaku. Ninety-one percent of the 470 members interviewed said their main reason for joining was to save! Only six of the people interviewed said that getting a loan was their main reason for joining. This is in sharp contrast to the basic assumption behind most government and donor sponsored credit projects: that is, that the primary motivation for most people wanting to deal with a financial system is to borrow.

It was also interesting to find that only 8 percent of the members remembered ever having problems in a pasanaku. This response, combined with the fact that pasanakus continue to be extremely popular in the country, strongly suggests that there is little default in pasanakus and that members feel they are benefiting by participating in them. The loan recovery performance in Bolivian ROSCAs is in marked contrast to the loan default problems suffered by government banks.

Few of the members of ROSCAs interviewed had accounts in formal financial institutions; only 16 percent of those interviewed, or their spouse, had a checking or a savings account in a bank or a credit union. More than three-quarters of the people interviewed felt that ROSCAs provided them with more benefits than banks. About one-third of the individuals interviewed felt that participation in pasanakus had increased with inflation, suggesting that use of formal financial institutions had declined.

Organizers of Pasanakus

We interviewed 46 individuals, mostly women, who were currently organizers or managers of pasanakus. Two-thirds of them received no compensations for their efforts, the remaining one-third received a commission or percentage of the funds they collected for their efforts. Most of them, three-in-four, organized the pasanaku for economic rather than social reasons. Individuals who organized pasanakus for social reasons were all involved in office ROSCAs. In contrast, the organizers of the commission and promotional pasanakus almost always realized material gains for their efforts. The organizer gains directly from the commissions collected and from the use of interest free money between the time money is collected and when pots are distributed. The gains for the promotional pasanaku organizer were the net increases in income realized by additional sales made possible through offering customers the possibilities of making purchases through pasanakus.

A large majority of the office and commission pasanaku organizers are women, in sharp contrast to the very limited number of women found in high-level positions in Bolivian banks. The extensive participation of women, both as organizers and members of pasanakus, may show that women have more difficulties in gaining access to formal financial services than do men and that their opportunity costs of organizing pasanakus is also lower.

Conclusions

We were surprised to find that pasanaku membership was so widespread, that they handled such a large amount of money, and that people were putting such large percentages of their income into them. This extensive participation leads us to the same conclusion that Adam Smith (1937) arrived at over 200 years ago when he said "...the principle which prompts us to save...comes with us from the womb, and never leaves us till we go to the grave" (p. 324).

Widespread pasanaku participation shows that the majority of Bolivians living in urban areas are eager and willing to save in financial forms, even when inflation is nearly overwhelming. While we did not spend much time probing rural savings behavior, it is likely that, while many Bolivian *campesinos* are poor, they still want and need to save. The immense investments made by small coca (cocaine) producers in the Chapare region over the past ten years are vivid reminders that poor farmers in Bolivia will save and invest, given attractive opportunities.

There are at least six reasons for the popularity of pasanakus in Bolivia. First, borrowers' *transactions costs* in pasanakus are almost nil. Second, pasanakus are *flexible* and easily adjusted to the needs of the members. Third, saving in a pasanaku is *tied to*—the mirror image of—building a credit rating and borrowing. Most savers are also interested in receiving a loan and others want to build relationships that allow them to borrow in case of emergency.

Fourth, for many people the *value* of these joined financial services exceeds the value of separate borrowing and deposit services. This helps explain the lack of failures among pasanakus in Bolivia. Fifth, transactions costs in pasanakus are low because of numerous *innovations*. Sixth, Bolivians enjoy playing pasanakus because of the gambling aspect and because it is an attractive form of "forced savings."

Pasanakus are popular because they are providing the financial services most often demanded by individuals in Bolivia, while the formal financial intermediaries often do not. We conclude that the failure to mobilize more savings via deposits in the formal financial system is due to faulty policy rather than defective individual savings propensities.

In contrast to the formal financial system in Bolivia, which is severely stressed, withered, and lacking in innovations, the informal financial system—as seen through the pasanakus—was alive and well in 1987. The recent expansion in the informal financial system has allowed a large number of people and firms in the country to survive tremendous economic turmoil. Much can be learned from studying this informal system about the types of financial services that people prefer, as well as learning how to reconstruct the formal financial system on more efficient and equitable lines.

References

Katzin, Margaret F. 1959. "Partners: An Informal Savings Institution in Jamaica." *Social and Economic Studies* 8:436-440.

Kurtz, Donald F. 1978. "The Tanda: A Rotating Credit Association in Mexico." *Ethnology* 17:65-71.

Norvell, Douglass G. and James S. Wehrly. 1969. "A Rotating Credit Association in the Dominican Republic." *Caribbean Studies* 9:45-52.

Smith, Adam. 1937. *The Wealth of Nations*. New York: The Modern Library.

Velez-Ibanez, Carlos G. 1983. *Bonds of Mutual Trust: The Cultural Systems of Rotating Credit Associations Among Urban Mexicans and Chicanos.* New Brunswick, New Jersey: Rutgers University Press.

24

ROSCAs: State-of-the-Art Financial Intermediation

J. D. Von Pischke

"...traditional forms...set standards against which new forms must be compared." Goran Ohlin (1985, p. 81)

A fundamental justification for government and donor-supported intervention in finance is to correct deficiencies in the performance of financial markets. Intervention can occur directly only through the formal financial sector because that is the part of the market that government controls. Many times, however, the alleged deficiencies that are cited as justification for intervention are thought not to rest within the formal segment of the financial market, but to lie beyond the frontier of formal finance. Hence, changes in the configuration of the formal market are expected to overcome what interveners consider to be the problems of informal finance. These include high rates of interest on loans, presumed exploitive relationships between debtors and creditors, alleged incapacity to mobilize savings, an expected inability to handle large amounts of funds, fraudulent practices and insensitivity to government priorities exhibited by a failure to target credit use.

Experience has shown overwhelmingly that direct intervention to displace informal finance, to limit its alleged abuses, or to overcome its presumed shortcomings has a pathology of its own. This pathology has two features. First is a generalized and terribly costly failure to establish viable formal financial institutions to intermediate among large numbers of individuals who most often use informal finance. Second is a failure to create systems that are capable of protecting themselves from flagrant rent-seeking abuses by individuals exercising political and administrative power.

Part of the reason for this substantial financial and institutional fiasco is that the paraphernalia of formal finance is used as the starting point for the design of intervention. This is necessitated by reliance on the formal sector as the channel for intervention. Commercial bankers are made to do what they have purposely avoided, which is to undertake what to them is the high-cost business of dealing with borrowers and depositors of small amounts. Specialized lenders are established to move into areas that the regulated market has shunned, such as agricultural finance, small-scale industrial lending and housing. Such clients generally cannot be accommodated within the cost structures of the formal credit system and the chilling effects of interest rate regulations or government ownership of financial institutions.

The ROSCA Benchmark

An alternative approach to the problem of creating sustained financial services for those beyond the frontier of formal finance consists of attempting to learn from informal models and using these rather than formal models as a platform for innovation. While the retail commercial bank or specialized term lender in developed countries is the model for designing intervention, working from the formal to the informal, the most important model for working from the informal to the formal is the rotating savings and credit association, or ROSCA.[1]

The suitability of the ROSCA as the credit or financial sector project design benchmark arises from three important features. One is its *ubiquity*, as suggested by the variety of its local names, which signifies its general viability and applicability in most parts of the developing world. Second, it unambiguously *intermediates*. Third, it is a *collective* activity, signifying popular, voluntary acceptance and congruity with the norms and expectations of the diverse cultures in which it operates. Other informal financial arrangements appear not to combine these

---

1. There are numerous accounts of ROSCAs in the literature. The most recent ROSCA researcher and analyst is F. J. A. Bouman (1977). His publications along with books by Velez-Ibanez (1983) and Nayar (1973) offer interested readers an introduction to this fascinating topic.

three characteristics in the high degree and profound form exhibited by the ROSCA.

The qualifications of the ROSCA as a standard for project design are demonstrated by a review of the functions and operations of the most simple or classic form of ROSCA. The classic ROSCA consists of not more than several dozen members who know each other, usually as a result of social, employment, or locational bonds; who have little or no access to formal finance; and who agree to contribute a fixed sum periodically to a pool or "hand" that is assembled and distributed by lot at meetings on agreed dates. One member receives the hand at each meeting. When each member has received a hand the cycle is completed, and the ROSCA disbands or reorganizes. Classic ROSCAs are typically established by an organizer who presides over meetings and takes the first hand. More complex forms of ROSCAs, sampled at the end of this chapter, only serve to emphasize ROSCAs' advantages, including flexibility.

ROSCAs meet three key tests of financial performance in a stunningly simple and elegant way: they economize transaction costs, they lengthen term structures, and they manage risks effectively. Even more exciting is their ability to do so within diverse social contexts by creating incentives for good performance and responsible behavior, which accounts for their continued popularity and existence in millions of places in developing countries. Finally, they are essentially private and voluntary and enjoy high levels of immunity from rent-seeking behavior by nonmembers.

ROSCAs Economize Transaction Costs

Deposits and lending often involve high transaction costs for poor people. Deposits may be difficult to make and maintain, for example, because of pressing uses for funds among the relatively large but intimate social groups into which their society is organized, such as extended families, age groups, and villages. Most members of the group are aware of each others' income and wealth, and asking for and giving assistance are normal parts of daily life. Within the group, at least one person may be sick or need help at any time, there are lots of children to be clothed and educated, and rites of passage require gifts and other expressions of participation. Reciprocity is important, and implies transaction costs.

Borrowing also requires transaction costs. Where no one is particularly wealthy, obtaining funds for a major purchase requires soliciting a number of people. Each loan acquired bears its own terms and conditions, some of which may not be specified in detail but constitute relatively open-ended obligations. These types of obligations involve risks, and soliciting assistance may subject the applicant to gossip and speculation concerning motives and behavior.

ROSCAs create pools of funds that are usually difficult for each member to assemble individually, which is an incentive to become a member. ROSCAs permit accumulation because of the contractual nature of membership. Some individuals who might not be disciplined savers on their own will make regular deposits in a supportive social environment, swelling the stock and flow of intermediated funds. Membership is generally taken very seriously: to default on a payment is a stigma. Reported cases of ROSCA failure are infrequent, and suicides by defaulters have been recorded. Accordingly, accumulating funds to meet ROSCA obligations is recognized as important by the community. This gives the ROSCA a senior claim over the myriad of other purposes that enable kin, friends, and neighbors to dip into each others' meager savings. Information about who has how much money and when, which otherwise tends to deplete and possibly even discourage individual and communal savings through social pressure, is transformed through ROSCAs into a means to accumulate funds and protect members.

ROSCAs are organized so that transaction costs are minimized. No one except the organizer has to visit a number of people in order to form a group. Terms and conditions are relatively few, straightforward, and applied consistently. Everyone's share can be equal, preserving social balance. The hand is assembled and awarded in full view of all members, making written records unnecessary. Each hand is distributed in the meeting at which it is gathered, leaving no group assets requiring management or offering temptations between meetings. This makes the ROSCA perfectly matched, as inflows and outflows are precisely synchronized. Perfect matching also permits ROSCAs to operate without any permanent capital. Distributions of the hand by lot, among nonprized members, those who have not yet received a hand, greatly economizes an organizationally difficult and hence, potentially costly, aspect of ROSCA transactions, which is determination of the order of rotation.

The frequency of meetings is fixed with reference to members' cash flows. Shoeshine boys in Addis Ababa have daily *ekub* meetings because they receive cash daily. Office workers paid monthly in the Philippines have monthly meetings. Market ladies in West Africa have *tontine* or *esusu* meetings when markets are held, often on 4, 7, or

14 day cycles depending on locations and goods traded. Meeting times and locations obviously have to be convenient for members.

Speculation about members' motives or behavior can be muted by giving the ROSCA a specific purpose shared by participants. A Society for Iron Sheets, for example, enables members to obtain funds to put roofs on their houses in Kenya; a rice chitty enables each woman member to accumulate a special stock of rice for bad times in Sri Lanka; and a *hui* in Taiwan, a *pasanaku* in Bolivia, or a *susu* in Trinidad enables shopkeepers and stallholders to replenish their inventories periodically.

ROSCAs Intermediate

ROSCAs perform the intermediary functions of transforming future payments into immediate hands and accumulating small payments into larger pools. The number of members is identical to the number of hands, and each member receives one hand during the life of the classic ROSCA. At any point before the final hand, members who have not received hands are net savers, while those who have received a hand are net borrowers. Some members typically want early hands and may be called "borrowers," while "savers" seek later hands. As the ROSCA moves through its cycle, these savings and borrowing positions rotate.

ROSCAs Lengthen Term Structures

ROSCAs' basic financial feature is that they accelerate access to funds—all members except the recipient of the final hand receive the cumulative contractual amount of their contributions in the form of a hand before they could have accumulated it by acting alone, by saving the amount of their contribution each period. This results in more long-term financial behavior by more people. Some who might not bother to make regular deposits for a year, for example, are willing to do so if they can obtain the end result, a lump sum withdrawal equal to their years' deposits, in less than a year. This mechanism equates each member's debt capacity and deposit or saving capacity, which amounts to the sum of a member's periodic contributions.

ROSCA Incentives Reduce Risk

The major credit risk is that a winner of an early hand may fail to make subsequent contributions. Accordingly, an interesting aspect of the ROSCA is how it sustains members' incentives to complete the cycle. While debt capacity equals deposit capacity, at no point before the last hand does any member's net position equal either. A nonprized member's net position is the sum of his or her contributions, while the amount of the hand minus contributions made equals the net position of a prized member. At the outset all members other than the organizer are net savers. In a ROSCA in which 10 members contribute 100 at each meeting, for example, the organizer obtains a hand of 1,000 against a payment of 100, yielding a net position of 900 borrowed. The member who receives the second hand has deposited 200 and receives a hand of 1,000, giving a net position of 800, and so on through the final member who receives 1,000 after having contributed 1,000.

In the first half of the cycle the majority of members have an incentive to continue contributing so that they can obtain a hand. At this early stage the burden of the obligation to contribute is highest; as periodic payments are made the obligation to make future payments lightens. In the latter half of the cycle winning members have an incentive to continue contributing because the people who could be hurt by their not doing so, the minority of nonprized members and the organizer, are a diminishing number who are increasingly identifiable. During this phase members' burdens in the form of promised future payments become relatively small; most of their obligations to contribute have already been met, making it easier to contemplate continued participation. Also, the claims of members on each other are by then quite complex, creating a solidarity that fosters continued payment.

ROSCA credit is clearly saving-based, within a closed system of intermediation funded entirely by members' contributions. This closed circular structure helps maintain clarity among members regarding their organization's objectives and their personal responsibilities, and creates solidarity that makes the ROSCA immune from intervention by outsiders.

The juxtaposition of tension and resolution illustrated by ROSCA relationships is common to successful financial contracts. In this respect the ROSCA is intricate, yet fundamentally simple and elegant. It is state-of-the-art intermediation, as well designed to finance as a Bach fugue is to classical European music or as the Golden Gate Bridge is to the capacities of civil engineering at the time of its construction.

Risk Management and Transaction Costs

ROSCAs' risk management strategies are applied first in organization. Who should belong? How large should each member's contribution be? How many members should the ROSCA contain, or how long should the cycle be? These are financial decisions that require information about the character, motives, and financial performance of prospective members. Members will be especially interested in the stature and reputation of the organizer. In return for this trust, the organizer has control over who is admitted, and may even be expected to make good on any defaults arising from the failure of other members to make contributions in full and on time. Organizational transaction costs and risk are borne most heavily by the organizer. For this service the organizer usually receives the first hand, which constitutes an interest free loan repaid over the life of the ROSCA.

The fixed cycle or term of ROSCAs permits exclusion of poor credit risks from future cycles. This simple exit mechanism is balanced by easy entry: anyone with some friends who has congenial cash flows can form a ROSCA. ROSCAs require no tangible collateral and are purely cash flow lending operations that do not require supervision of members' use of the hands they receive. ROSCAs work entirely on promise, trust, and consent, before other members as witnesses having intimate knowledge of each other. They create or confirm relationships among members that permit the application of certain sanctions. Participants clearly recognize that their relations with other members are the basis for transactions, and that their worth in the eyes of others depends significantly upon their performance under their shared promise.

The member receiving the hand is often responsible for refreshments at the meeting at which the hand is received, especially where ROSCAs meet in restaurants or bars. This transaction cost helps maintain group cohesiveness through eating or drinking together, and impresses on members the importance of continued loyalty to each other. Members can observe each others' health and moods, and gain indications of each others' current financial status. While many transaction costs are an annoyance to those who pay them, the obligation to provide hospitality for one's friends at ROSCA meetings is usually regarded as an honor or as an opportunity for fun, something to be enjoyed.

Flexibility and Modification

The classic ROSCA formula is flexible, and modified forms to accommodate members' priorities and the environment are numerous. In more complex forms of ROSCA, for example, the hand may be distributed by predetermined order, but with arrangements for interruption to assist a member in need. Parallel funds for special purposes may also be subscribed to by ROSCA members at their periodic meetings. Nonprized members may also privately arrange to borrow the hand from the member receiving it. Inflation of course skews the benefits of ROSCAs when the hand consists of a fixed amount of currency. This may be accommodated by distributing the hand by auction, by shortening the life of the ROSCA, by specifying that ROSCA payments be made in kind, by requiring payment in dollars, or by reversing the order of rotation in subsequent cycles.

Auction ROSCAs also respond to commercial considerations. Bids are quoted as a premium (1,100 bid for a hand of 1,000, for example) or as a discount (900 bid for a hand of 1,000), with the difference between the winning bid and the amount of the hand being distributed to nonprized members. An interesting wrinkle in auction ROSCAs in commercial societies, such as in Hong Kong, is the importance of keeping interest rates competitive, which requires active bidding. Some organizers, who receive a double share of interest over the life of the ROSCA as well as the first hand, exclude from subsequent ROSCAs the member who takes the final hand. This member need not bid seriously, as there is no competition for the final hand, and pays no interest while collecting interest from all other hands following the first. (It may be assumed that prospective members with a savings motive may bargain with the organizer for a double stake in order to receive two hands, one through bidding and the other at the end of the cycle.) In fixed order ROSCAs, by contrast, new members, who constitute the largest credit risk, are assigned the last hands.

ROSCAs may have very long lives, providing tremendous term structures. In parts of Asia, for example, chit funds have produced 20-year savings programs combined with 20-year loans. These typically consist of 20 members who contribute to the fund at an appointed time each year. The annual contribution is often assembled through participation in funds having an annual or shorter life, such as monthly chitties of 12 rounds or weekly chitties running for 50 or 52 weeks. Interestingly, the Reserve Bank of India has outlawed chitties having cycles in excess of seven years, presumably to protect nonprized members from the effects of inflation, from the risk of failure of the chit fund organizer (who is often a professional who runs chit funds for a living), or from disputes among members that could disrupt the fund, and possibly to reduce competition with the nationalized life insurance industry.

ROSCAs, such as one formed by staff members of the International Monetary Fund, often include people who have access to formal finance but who prefer the social ambience the ROSCA offers. They may also compete with high cost or lethargic commercial banks or handle transactions that banks regard as too risky. *Tanomoshii* associations of businessmen of Japanese ancestry in Hawaii are reported to put up relatively large sums to finance construction of buildings. This kind of financing is characterized by relatively high risks of cost overruns and by the thin capitalization of contractors. In Africa some ROSCAs intermediate large sums. For example, *tontines* with a hand equivalent to US$1 million are reported in Cameroon (New York Times 1987), where these informal groups greatly economize transaction costs for people active in large-scale modern sector activities. Many have written rules and procedures, and information systems that exclude those who defaulted on earlier or other *tontines*. Of course, ROSCAs may also be ideal means of intermediating private money beyond the reach of the predatory state.

The Winning Formula

But to return to the classic ROSCA and its winning formula: How do the poor prefer to conduct their financial affairs? What sort of intermediation do they regard as useful and friendly? ROSCA operations provide valuable insights into these important questions. The lessons or principles they suggest may be summarized as follows.

First, ROSCAs offer insights into institutional features that are attractive to, and work successfully for, the poor. These include voluntary participation and organizational autonomy and self-sufficiency. These features enable members to include and exclude whomever they wish, and permit anyone to attempt to form a ROSCA. Each group can organize and manage its own affairs, following its own rules. Intervention is not needed or welcome when institutions are devised that the poor can manage themselves.

Second, ROSCAs are modes of financial service delivery attractive to the poor. Savings and credit are provided at transaction costs that are low in the eyes of the participants, or perceived as hardly being costs at all. Services are available at times and places clearly convenient to their users, and in a format that offers scope for flexibility through negotiation among the parties concerned.

Third, ROSCAs provide the terms and conditions governing access to and use of financial services that attract participation by the poor. Savings-based credit requires a commitment from the saver-borrower, which is made voluntarily. Saving and other behavior supporting group objectives are encouraged by the prospect of credit access. Information is used as a basis for managing credit risk. Service delivery mechanisms tap and construct information systems to ensure member satisfaction and organization survival. Where inflation is a problem and where a ROSCA performs more than primarily a social function, ways are devised to maintain equilibrium and a sense of fair treatment between savers and borrowers, offsetting hidden transfers created by inflation.

Fourth, ROSCAs demonstrate types of relationships between users and providers of financial services that are acceptable to and supported by the poor. Credit relationships are built on bonds, behavioral norms and sanctions that prevail outside the ROSCA. These provide the trust and confidence that underlie all successful financial relationships.

Discipline is also essential. It is provided by periodicity and by contracts. Commitments are made that have to be honored on time and in the amount agreed in advance. Accountability is required routinely of all parties concerned and is incorporated into the operations of the organization. Accountability is assisted by face-to-face relationships among individuals who are equal and by procedures understood by all concerned. For the system to work, bad risks must be excluded, which requires enforceable exit mechanisms. The ROSCA as a provider of financial services establishes and enforces senior claims on members. Yet, members are not accountable to the ROSCA for the use of the funds they obtain when they win a hand.

Finally, the ROSCA affirms financial strategies found in successful financial markets generally. One is the matching of flows as a risk and liquidity management tool. Matching is demonstrated by the determination of debt capacity by savings capacity in the form of periodic deposits and loan repayments. A second strategy is conservation of capital and liquidity. The ROSCA does not require capital and liquidity separate from that of its members to manage risk. Capital and liquidity separate from that of members could create rather than reduce risk, yet more complex informal financial arrangements include simultaneous participation in both ROSCAs and fixed funds. This demonstrates another feature of successful financial structures, which is the capacity to innovate spontaneously. A third strategy, characteristic of auction ROSCAs, is reliance on market processes to determine interest rates. Auction ROSCA rates are determined by bidding among members, and there is no evidence that bids are often rigged.

Free bidding is a powerful signal, as is the voluntary and democratic operation of ROSCAs generally. These features permit individual expression, as in the free use of hands and in bidding, mutual accommodation in the form of acceptable group norms and enforceable sanction. The essentially liberal principles of ROSCAs enable participants to empower and protect their relationships collectively and themselves individually.

As benchmarks, ROSCAs challenge developers who attempt to assist poor people through credit projects. ROSCAs provide valuable, efficient, and sustained financial services to large numbers of low-income people around the world, while formal credit projects often do not. Careful examinations of ROSCAs show conditions and the high levels of precision and balance that are required for financial institutions to be successful in serving large numbers of poor people. Insights gleaned from studying ROSCAs may force would-be interveners to recognize the demanding conditions that have to be met for successful, sustainable interventions at the small end of financial transactions in low-income countries.

ROSCAs provide a new perspective on the seemingly intractable conditions that so often stand in the way of success and sustainability for donor-supported initiatives in financial markets. This may lead to diminished enthusiasm for credit programs and a heightened search for alternative means of addressing poverty problems.

References

Bouman, F. J. A. 1977. "Indigenous Savings and Credit Societies in the Third World: A Message." *Savings and Development* 1: 181-214.

———. 1989. *Small Short and Unsecured: Informal Credit in India.* New Dehli: Oxford University Press.

Nayar, C. P. S. 1973. *Chit Finance.* Bombay: Vora & Co.

Ohlin, Goran. 1985. "A New Case for Personal Savings in Development Policy?" In Denis Kessler and Pierre-Antoine eds. *Savings and Development.* Paris: Economica.

The New York Times. 1987. "Informal Capitalism Grows in Cameroon: Grass Roots Credit System." November 30, p. D8.

Velez-Ibanez, Carlos G. 1983. *Bonds of Mutual Trust: Cultural Systems of Rotating Credit Associations Among Urban Mexicans and Chicanos.* New Brunswick, New Jersey: Rutgers University Press.

25

What Have We Learned About Informal Finance in Three Decades?

U Tun Wai

When I began working for the International Monetary Fund in the 1950s only fragmentary information was available about informal finance. At the time stereotypical opinion held that professional moneylenders and landlords dominated nonbank lending, that they regularly charged usurious interest rates, that informal finance was concentrated in rural areas, that informal lenders provided most of the loans in low-income countries, and that informal finance shrunk as formal finance expanded. At the time, only a few economic studies and surveys were available to substantiate these views, and most of them focused on rural areas in South Asia.

As part of a larger study on interest rates, I published an article in 1957 that surveyed much of this information while focusing on five issues:

1. the nature of informal finance,
2. the structure and pattern of interest rates in informal markets,
3. explanations for the high interest rates in these markets,
4. the extent of linkages between formal and informal finance, and
5. the effectiveness of government attempts to reduce informal interest rates.

On the basis of this survey, I concluded that informal finance did indeed provide a majority of the rural loans in the countries where information was available, and that average interest rates on informal loans were substantially higher than on formal loans. I argued, however, that high opportunity costs and shortages of funds—rather than monopoly powers—were the main explanations for these high interest rates. I also concluded that the linkages between formal and informal finance were modest, but were likely to expand with the growth of the formal financial system. My survey of government attempts to regulate interest rates on informal loans showed mostly failures, and I went on to argue that these rates would naturally decline as the supply of formal credit increased.

Fortunately, by the late 1980s the number of surveys and case studies of informal finance had mushroomed. Increasing interest in the private sector, concern about the continued lack of financial services for poor people, and disappointment with the results of many government sponsored credit spurred this research. As a result, there was a much clearer picture of the nature of informal finance in many low-income countries in the late 1980s than there was in the late 1950s. In the following pages I revisit informal finance and summarize some of the major findings that have emerged over the past three decades and contrast this with my earlier impressions.

Changes in Terminology

Recent research has shown informal finance is more complicated and heterogeneous than was thought to be the case 30 years ago. It also shows that informal finance makes a larger and more positive contribution to development than many of us thought. This has led to changes in terminology. Several decades ago various terms were used to describe formal and informal finance such as organized/unorganized and institutional/noninstitutional. Over time the terms "formal" and "informal" have replaced these earlier terms. Research has increasingly shown that many forms of informal finance are well organized and that some of these forms are deeply entrenched social institutions. Increasingly, the application of the terms formal and informal have hinged on regulation by some central monetary authority. If the financial transaction was subject to regulation, the term formal was applied. All other financial transactions were called informal.

But, recent research is showing a significant gray area between these two forms of finance. In some countries, for example, pawnshops may be part of the formal financial system due to close regulation by the central bank, in other countries they fall in a gray area because they only need obtain a government license to operate, and in still other countries pawnshops operate without government regulation or license and are clearly informal. Various types of finance companies, private voluntary organizations, indigenous banks, credit unions, and credit cooperatives present the same definitional problem. Seibel (chapter 17) has suggested the useful term "semiformal" as a label for these gray financial operations that are not regulated by a central monetary authority but which do have a government sanction to operate.

Location, Participants, and Size

While a majority of research done on informal finance continues to focus on rural areas, recent studies sponsored by the Asian Development Bank (1990) in India, Bangladesh, and the Philippines show informal finance is also widespread in urban areas. In some cases, such as the film industry in India, most of the financing for an industry may be informal. In other cases, such as the shoe industry in the Philippines, a mixture of formal and informal loans may be used at various stages of production and sales. It increasingly appears that informal financial arrangements can be found almost everywhere there are market transactions and cash incomes.

Recent publications are also showing that informal finance occurs among and between all economic classes—it is not just rich individuals lending to poor people. Small firms and operators of small farms may be providing larger firms with goods on consignment, which are effectively loans that are repaid when producers receive payment for their goods. At the same time, other large firms may be providing small firms with loans in the form of production inputs that are later repaid in the form of finished goods. Likewise, various forms of group savings and credit activities can be found among the very poorest people in a country, among the middle class, and even among people who have substantial amounts of assets. A number of studies are showing that many informal lenders are people of modest means— particularly single women—who supplement their meager incomes with earnings from informal finance. Nevertheless, most studies show that poor people are more dependent on informal finance than are people who are well-to-do.

Over the years policymakers, especially in South Asia, have been concerned about measuring the relative importance of informal finance. Rural studies in India, Sri Lanka, Taiwan, and Thailand show that, as predicted earlier, informal loans decline in relative importance as the formal financial system expands. Instead of comprising up to three-quarters or more of the total volume of rural lending, informal loans now make up less than half this amount in a number of low-income countries in Asia and Latin America. Information is less complete for urban areas and for Africa. Recent research on microenterprises suggests that informal sources continue to be a primary source of finance for poor people in urban areas. The stressed conditions found in formal finance in many African countries implies that informal finance continues to be very important there.

Two important caveats should be noted, nevertheless, in this general pattern. First, in several countries such as Bolivia, the Philippines, and also Sri Lanka informal finance grew in relative importance during periods when formal financial markets were severely repressed. For example, in the Philippines trader credits filled part of the void left in many areas of the country when numerous rural private banks became insolvent during the late 1970s and early 1980s. Second, in retrospect, too much emphasis may have been placed on relative importance and too little attention given to changes in the absolute size of informal finance. While time series information on changes in absolute size are not available, recent research in Taiwan, Thailand, and India strongly suggest that the absolute size of informal financial markets may increase with development, although at a slower rate of growth than occurs in formal finance. In some cases it appears that formal finance substitutes for some forms of informal finance as the financial system expands. In other cases the relationship between formal and informal finance appears to be more symbiotic and complementary.

Characteristics

Overall, new literature is bringing into sharp relief the differences in the characteristics of formal and informal finance. On average, informal finance is comprised of small and short-term transactions that are based on personal relationships. These arrangements are flexible, adapt to economic change, are often innovative, involve low transaction costs for both lender and borrower, and result in high loan recovery rates. Most informal loans are based on creditworthiness and some elements of the informal system also process substantial amounts of savings. Perhaps most importantly, informal transactions usually occur close to where clients live, shop, or work.

In contrast, formal finance usually handles larger and longer-term transactions that are often quite impersonal. Banking procedures are usually quite inflexible, change slowly, require substantial amounts of paperwork, impose sizeable transaction costs on borrowers, and are sometimes associated with loan recovery problems. At least in the case of government-sponsored credit programs, formal loans are often made largely on the basis of loan targets and "credit needs," and deposit mobilization may be largely ignored. In most cases, formal finance is transacted in the office of the financial intermediary, which imposes additional transaction costs on clients.

Interest Rates

Controversy continues to surround discussions of interest rates in informal finance with some people arguing high rates are economically justified, while other observers argue they are signs of exploitation. One thing that is increasingly clear, however, is it that a broad range of interest rates are typically found in most informal financial markets. Many informal loans are made among friends and relatives that carry no interest obligations. Numerous loans are also made by merchants or traders without explicit interest charges, although some implicit loan charges may be imbedded in the prices paid or charged on goods associated with some of these loans. Many loans are also made among members of informal financial groups without explicit interest charges. On the deposit side, a number of people, particularly in rural areas of Africa, are reported to deposit funds with trusted money guards who pay no interest.

A large number of informal loans are made at moderate rates of interest that may be similar to the total costs of borrowing from a bank, when the borrower's transactions costs are included. Several authors in this volume report revolving loan funds associated with informal financial groups that carry interest charges of 3 to 4 percent per month. Since the members of the group determine the rates of interest charged, it can hardly be argued these rates are a sign of exploitation.

Still, many small, short-term, and unsecured loans in low-income countries—especially those made to poor people—carry relatively high interest rates when converted to an annual basis, and it is this segment of the informal financial market that attracts political concern. Academics, rightly or wrongly, have become generally more positive about informal finance than have politicians. Instead of focusing exclusively on the interest rates charged on informal loans, recent analysis has looked at the characteristics of the people borrowing funds and tried to view interest rates through the eyes of the borrower rather than through the eyes of a moralist.

This research is showing that some borrowers cannot obtain funds from inexpensive sources such as friends, relatives, and merchants—

they are forced to pay high rates of interest because of their precarious economic situation. Other individuals are willing to pay high rates of interest for short-term loans because they expect to realize even higher rates of return on their investments. Ease of access and flexibility of terms may be more important than interest rates to some individuals who occasionally borrow to capitalize on economic opportunities.

The causes of high interest rates are important for policymakers. If rates are high mainly because of the opportunity costs of funds, then a program of promoting economic growth, raising incomes, and increasing savings would help to lower rates. If they are due to monopoly profit, then more competition from formal lenders would be appropriate. While a complete explanation of interest rates in informal finance awaits further analysis, evidence is increasingly tilting the scales against monopoly profits and in favor of inflation expectations, loan recovery risks, opportunity costs of funds, and loan transaction costs as major reasons for high interest rates on some informal loans.

Controversy will likely continue to swirl around how to moderate these interest charges. On the basis of the experience of the past 30 years, it is apparent that whatever approach is adopted it will succeed only slowly, if at all. One may have to conclude that not much can be done to help many informal borrowers, and that high interest rates are a fact of economic life for poor borrowers in low-income countries.

Interlocked Markets

Numerous studies over the past couple of decades have reported merchants and traders who link loans to the purchase or sale of various commodities. This type of lending appears to be far more important than it seemed in the 1950s. Lenders who operate in several markets are seldom professional moneylenders but are rather firms that expand their volume of business by offering credit. Linked credit has been found in such diverse activities in urban areas as the leather products industry; small engineering and metal fabrication; construction; handloom and small textiles; and goldsmiths/gold merchants. In rural areas, credit is often associated with labor arrangements, with various types of land tenure, with purchase of farm inputs, and with household consumption.

Some observers have viewed this interlocking as a way of exerting more monopoly power (for example, Bardhan 1980). Other authors, such as Bell conclude that interlinked transactions allow lenders to reduce their costs through scope economies. Whether exploitation exists is an empirical question. If it does, then it must be due to imperfections in one or more linked markets. A research challenge is to measure these imperfections and identify which, if any, market is monopolistic.

Groups Savings and Credit

Widespread group savings and credit arrangements are one of the most surprising findings about informal finance during the past three decades. A most exciting discovery has been that these informal groups mobilize substantial amounts of savings among poor people. It is much easier to list the low-income countries that do not have large numbers of these groups—for example, Costa Rica and Ecuador—than it is to list those that do.

As Bouman (1979) has so ably pointed out, one prominent type of these groups, the rotating savings and credit associations (ROSCAs), are found in most low-income countries. Scattered research on this topic is showing that large numbers of people participate in these groups and that the amounts of funds handled are often sizable. The way in which ROSCAs have evolved and the variants in different countries are testimony to the kinds of innovations taking place in informal markets. The relatively large proportion of their incomes that many participants place in ROSCAs is an indication of the untapped savings capacities that exist in many low-income countries.

In addition to ROSCAs, recent research is uncovering large numbers of nonrotating savings groups, especially in Africa, that mobilize sizable amounts of money for various types of purposes, including the formation of emergency loan funds. In many cases these savings groups deposit their joint funds in banks, thus reducing the banking costs of mobilizing small individual deposits. Recent efforts by the German development agency, Gesellschaft fur Technische Zusammenarbeit (GTZ) to link more of these groups to the formal financial system capitalizes on the advantages offered by group financial activities.

Resource Allocation

Thirty years ago it was commonly assumed that most formal finance supported productive activities while informal finance mainly promoted consumption and social ceremonies. In part, regulation of informal finance was justified as a way of reducing these so-called wasteful informal loans. Information collected since then suggests the distinction between "production loans" and "consumption loans" was over drawn. The blurring of the lines between production and consumption stem from two factors: the definition of consumption and the fungibility of financial instruments.

It is not at all clear, for example, if the effect of an informal loan made to a farm worker to buy food to bridge his family's consumption needs between jobs is any different from a formal loan extended to a farmer who uses the borrowed funds to employ the same farm worker. In both cases the borrowed money provides funds for the worker to sustain himself and family. The logic of labeling the first case consumption, while the other is productive, is tenuous at best. Likewise, it is unclear how an informal loan that is used to buy gold given to a daughter as part of a dowry has any different impact than a formal loan that is used to buy the same gold. In both cases the bride receives an intergenerational transfer of wealth that may make her creditworthy in times of emergency. Splitting hairs over what is and what is not consumption has little relationship to the marginal changes in borrower behavior caused by access to borrowed funds, regardless of their source.

The assumptions that formal loans could be "tied" to productive uses, while informal lenders largely ignored the ultimate uses made of their loans, reinforced the notion that a distinction could be made between the impact of loans by source. This view of financial instruments ignores their fundamental feature: fungibility or interchangeability. Pesos borrowed from a bank, borrowed from an informal lender, or owned by a borrower are completely interchangeable. For example, funds borrowed from a bank—ostensively to fund productive activities—can substitute for the borrower's own funds that would otherwise have been allocated to production, but instead are used to increase so-called consumption. The final arbitrator of how marginal liquidity is used—regardless of its source—is the marginal returns or utility expected by the borrower from various expenditures, not the justification given for a loan. Government credit planners and bank employees have only a weak influence, if any, over the marginal uses of borrowed funds.

While the arguments that informal finance misallocates resources by boosting consumption appear to be flawed, it is also clear that informal finance alone cannot achieve an efficient allocation of resources in a growing economy. Formal finance has definite advantages over informal finance in making large and long-term loans, in intermediating over substantial distances, and in deposit mobilization.

Informal finance is mainly effective in helping to reallocate resources more efficiently among individuals who have eye-to-eye contact. If a concentration of individuals in one area has excess funds, while individuals in another distant area have too few funds to capitalize on attractive investment alternatives, formal finance must be used to bridge these substantial distances and effect more efficient allocation of resources.

Savings Mobilization

Thirty years ago informal finance was virtually synonymous with money lending. Only in the past few years has savings been associated with informal finance. Recent literature is showing that at least five manifestations of savings occur in informal markets. First, and most importantly, the large volume of informal loans reported in a number of low-income countries is the mirror image of an identical large volume of savings. When informal lenders utilize their own funds they are merely channeling their savings into informal finance. Second, some informal lenders accept deposits and relend funds and thus act as financial intermediaries. Most informal lenders use only their own savings, but studies over the past 30 years indicate that many of them are increasingly becoming financial intermediaries by also seeking and accepting deposits. In India, certain types of professional money lenders such as chettiars and multanies have always accepted deposits from friends and customers.

Third, the popularity of various types of informal savings groups around the world are further manifestations of informal savings. Rotating and nonrotating savings and credit associations are a mechanism for mobilizing funds that are first saved and then collected before they are lent to members. Fourth, savings also emerges when individuals such as merchants, notaries, lawyers, solicitors, or doctors accept money for safekeeping or for investment on behalf of clients. If they relend these funds they become financial intermediaries, if they only hold the funds they are moneykeepers. Fifth, substantial growth in deposits collected by semiformal organizations such as credit unions are further indication of the latent savings capacity that is being tapped outside formal financial markets.

Contact Between Informal and Formal Finance

The adage "East is East and West is West and never the twain shall meet" was probably largely true of formal and informal finance at one time as the paucity of formal financial institutions, particularly in rural areas, in many low-income countries sharply limited access to formal finance. Over the past three decades a large number of banking facilities have been built in these countries that provide much more widespread access to formal financial services.

The weak and indirect links between formal and informal finance that I first encountered 30 plus years ago have been substantially expanded and strengthened. Many recent studies report numerous formal borrowers who are also informal lenders. A number of these studies are also showing contacts between formal and informal finance through deposits. Savings groups may deposit their surplus funds in banks or credit unions, and individuals who receive their rotation of funds in a ROSCA may deposit all or part of these funds in a formal financial institution such as postal savings facilities.

A number of authors have underscored the benefits of closer links between the two markets and suggestions have been made on how to do this (Christen, chapter 20; and Seibel and Parshusip, chapter 17). Two general strategies have been proposed: One is a "top-down" strategy that attempts to increase the access of self-help groups or informal lenders to banks. The program in Indonesia discussed by Seibel and Parhusip (chapter 17) is an example of linking to self-help groups. The possibility of banks lending to moneylenders was suggested in the 1950s by Moore (1953) and also by Mahabal (1954). Several countries including Malaysia and Sri Lanka have had sizeable credit programs that did this linking. In some countries extending loans to informal lenders may not be feasible because of the political sensitivities about moneylenders.

A second strategy is a "bottoms-up" approach based on helping large informal groups to assemble sufficient funds so they might form banks. This type of evolution has occurred naturally in the Cameroon and is also reported to have occurred early in this century in Japan by Izumida (chapter 12).

While it is still too early to judge the success of the various schemes mentioned above, it is apparent that each market has its own comparative advantage. The informal market will always be able to handle small loan transactions more efficiently and expeditiously while the formal market is better at handling large transactions.

Conclusions

Many things have changed since I first looked at informal finance more than three decades ago. This includes sharp increases in the amounts of information available about this topic, changes in perceptions about informal finance, and changes in informal finance itself. While, on average, informal finance has declined in relative importance over the past 30 years, it has likely continued to grow in absolute size and complexity. There is little doubt that a large majority of rural people, women, poor individuals, minority groups, and operators of microenterprises continue to rely heavily on various forms of informal finance.

While some interest rates on informal loans are substantially higher than those on bank credit, informality, low transaction costs, flexibility, and innovativeness continue to appeal to numerous people who patronize informal finance. Most borrowers, when asked, do not feel they are being exploited by informal lenders, and their generally high loan repayment rates strongly suggest they desire to continue a relationship with their lenders. The persistence of informal finance is evidence that it provides valuable services to large numbers of people.

There continues to be controversy over the morality of high interest rates and the possible negative effects of credit transactions linked to other market transactions. Increasingly, however, new literature on informal finance has stressed positive aspects of these activities. The sustainability of informal finance, the types of people it serves, the low transaction costs it imposes on clients, excellent loan recovery rates, extensive successful group performance, and substantial amounts of savings mobilization are features that are often cited.

What action to take regarding informal finance is a key question for policy makers. Thirty years ago the answer was almost unanimously to regulate or eliminate informal finance. Increasingly, this approach has been challenged and alternative and more positive strategies have been suggested and tested. Whatever strategies policymakers decide to follow regarding informal finance, controversy and additional research will likely be closely associated with these decisions. I hope that the additions to knowledge about informal finance over the next 30 years are as interesting and revealing as the past 30 years have been for me.

References

Asian Development Bank. 1990. "Informal Finance in Asia." In *Asian Development Outlook 1990*, pp. 187-215. Manila: Asian Development Bank.

Bardhan, Pranab K. 1980. "Interlocking Factor Markets and Agrarian Development: A Review of Issues." *Oxford Economic Papers* 32:82-93.

Bell, Clive. 1988. "Credit Markets and Interlinked Transactions." In H. Chenery and T. N. Srinivasan, eds., *Handbook of Development Economics* pp. 764-826. Volume I. Amsterdam: Elsevier Science Publishers B.V.

Bouman, F. J. A. 1979. "The ROSCA: Financial Technology of an Informal Savings and Credit Institution in Developing Economies." *Savings and Development* 4:253-276.

Mahabel, S. B. 1954. "Institutionalizing the Moneylender." *Indian Journal of Agricultural Economics* 9:175-178.

Moore, Frank J. 1953. "Moneylenders and Co-operators in India." *Economic Development and Cultural Change* 2:139-159.

Wai, U Tun. 1957. "Interest Rates Outside the Organized Money Markets of Underdeveloped Countries." *International Monetary Fund Staff Papers* 6:80-142.

26

Where to From Here in Informal Finance?

Dale W Adams and P. B. Ghate

Authors of the previous chapters describe a welter of informal financial arrangements in a variety of geographic, political, economic, and cultural settings. They report informal finance is flourishing and providing sustained services to many individuals in low-income countries. The authors strongly intimate more should be known about this important, yet poorly understood, topic. A number of the authors suggest this information might be useful to policymakers, especially those who want to support private enterprise or to reach poor people.

As Wai (chapter 25) points out, there has been a substantial increase in research on informal finance over the past three decades. Much of this analysis is in the form of case studies that have limited generalizability or expensive surveys that provide limited details on the warp and woof of informal arrangements. Informal finance is difficult and costly to study because of its heterogeneity, its dispersed nature, its small transactions, its ties with marketing arrangements, and lack of written records.

Individuals analyzing informal finance encounter many of the same difficulties faced by a collection of blind persons who each feel a single, but different, part of an elephant and then describe the animal: some researchers focus on the high rates of interest charged by a few segments of the informal market, but ignore the low rates charged by many other segments. Other researchers stress the social aspects of group forms of informal finance while overlooking the major economic functions of these same groups. Still other individuals focus on the "badness" of lenders who occasionally seize mortgaged land in times of economic stress, but ignore the much more common and valuable services provided by informal loans that do not involve alienation of assets. It is little wonder that policymakers are confused as they deal with informal finance issues when the descriptions of the "animal" are so fragmented, partial, and laced with value judgements.

While the authors in this volume have not painted a final picture of the "elephant," they have outlined major parts that were not well understood previously and clarified some of the confusion that surrounds informal finance. In the following discussion we summarize major findings and go on to outline segments of the picture that might receive research attention in the future. We conclude with a list of policy suggestions.

Major Findings

For us, at least, three major findings stand out in the preceeding chapters: many of the authors challenged popular stereotypes of informal lenders, a number of the authors argued informal finance was more important than many policymakers have heretofore thought, and various authors identified strengths that help explain the persistence and popularity of informal finance.

Challenged Stereotypes

Much of the traditional thinking about informal finance emphasizes negative aspects: usury, monopoly profits, labor bonding through lending, and loan defaults leading to collateral seizure by lenders. Most of this thinking has been stereotypical and concentrated on the supposedly evil moneylender who takes advantage of poor people. It has also been commonly thought that informal finance should be eliminated—at least tightly controlled—and that overall formal financial development would cause these activities to wither.

This traditional thinking about informal finance is challenged by the presentations in this volume; authors did little verbal flogging of informal lenders. Instead, they report a kaleidoscope of heterogeneous informal financial arrangements, only a small portion of which was done by full-time professional moneylenders. Most of the chapters concentrated on the positive aspects of informal finance, how it contributes to the well-being of the poor, how it supports development, and useful lessons that can be learned from it. While informal sources provide most of the financial services for poor people—particularly for women—several authors pointed out that many relatively large firms and well-off people also regularly use informal finance. In some cases, poor individuals or small firms may be providing loans to individuals or firms that are relatively well-off. Virtually anyone can be an informal lender or borrower.

Several authors showed that the relative importance of informal loans has declined over the past several decades, but went on to stress that this is largely due to rapid growth in formal lending. It was suggested that informal finance normally expands in absolute terms with the growth of formal finance and the economy in general, and that informal sources usually continue to provide most financial services to the poor, regardless of growth in formal finance. Several authors also reported on cases where recent contractions in formal financial markets resulted in an increase in the relative importance of informal finance. The absolute expansion in these activities was partly explained by the rapid growth in the informal sector and partly by the advantages it has in providing certain services.

Importance of Informal Savings

Most of the traditional discussions of informal finance stress only debts or loans. Because it is often assumed poor people cannot or will not save and that most of them have a "credit need" that translates into a social entitlement, there has been relatively little discussion of informal savings. The difficulties of collecting information about confidential saving behavior reinforces this assumption and influences the terminology used to describe activities in informal finance: for example, "informal credit markets," "rotating credit associations," and "credit groups."

In contrast, a number of the previous chapters reported on sizeable deposit and savings activities taking place in informal financial markets. Many of the authors were optimistic about the willingness and ability of even poor people to save in low-income countries. Several authors also argued that savings-deposits were an important element in developing sustainable financial intermediation. In a fundamental sense, large amounts of informal loans are the mirror image of part of the informal savings that emerge in financial form. Someone postpones consumption—saves—in order to accumulate every unit of money lent in informal markets.

A number of the authors focused on various aspects of group savings and deposits. These presentations showed that large amounts of deposits are mobilized through various forms of informal groups, and that savings are a major motivation for people to join groups. In some cases the volume of informal savings flowing through informal markets may be larger than the volume of deposits in banks. The large volume of voluntary savings moving through informal markets also suggests that formal financial markets often fail to offer attractive deposit services, especially to poor people. The widespread use of money guards as a place to deposit interest free funds is a vivid indication of this failure.

The gender issue is particularly important in informal savings. Many of the individuals who are involved in informal savings activities are women. This shows that they have relatively high savings propensities and also experience more difficulty in accessing formal financial services than do men. It also shows they are often sophisticated in handling financial affairs.

Strengths of Informal Finance

Virtually all of the authors mentioned strengths or advantages found in informal finance. Some of these are well known such as flexibility, convenience, low information costs for the lender, and high loan recovery rates. Other advantages mentioned are less well known. For example, several presentations focused on how informal lenders resolve the difficult and sometimes costly loan collateral problems. In some cases the ancient practice of pawning assets is used to reduce the costs of lenders securing loan guarantees. In other cases, informal lenders specialize in accepting certain types of collateral substitutes such as marketing agreements, labor arrangements, or some form of reciprocity.

Another important advantage is that many forms of informal finance provide services at the residence of the client, at a convenient marketplace, or where clients work. Most informal finance is client oriented, while formal intermediaries are often more concerned about their regulators: central banks, government officials, and donor agencies. Intermediaries with a client orientation substantially reduce the transaction costs for customers and make their service attractive even though explicit or implicit interest charges are relatively high. In contrast, many formal intermediaries focus on keeping their transaction costs low, charge relatively low interest rates, but often impose procedures on lenders and depositors that substantially increase the users' transaction costs to the point where total costs of effecting the financial transaction may be higher than if they were done in informal markets.

Still another attractive feature of some types of informal finance, especially those involving groups, is that loans and deposits are often tied. Individuals can increase their access to loans or credit reserves by proving themselves through deposit performance. This includes building bonds of mutual trust that assure future access to loans through reciprocity. In many cases, informal finance allows participants to gradually enhance their creditworthiness, first through savings, then through borrowing and repaying small loans, and only later gaining access to relatively large loans. This process is particularly important for individuals and firms that start small: women, microenterprises, and poor people.

The rich variety of types of informal finance and the fact that these activities can be found in virtually every nook and cranny of an economy demonstrates the innovative and dynamic nature of at least some parts of the informal financial system. It also demonstrates that informal finance is usually more resilient in the face of adversities that affect the overall economy than is generally true of formal finance, in part, because informal finance is unregulated. In some cases, a few forms of informal finance may exist to avoid regulation or taxes and provide services that are similar to those provided by regulated intermediaries.

Several authors also noted the inherent weaknesses of informal finance. It is more awkward for informal intermediaries to provide large and long-term loans than it is for formal lenders, and it is also more difficult for informal arrangements to provide the liquidity and security that formal intermediaries ought to be able to furnish to depositors.

Research Priorities

Much of the research on informal finance in low-income countries describes types of informal finance, often through case studies. The bulk of this research has been done by anthropologists and sociologists. Lesser amounts of economic research have stressed documenting the relative importance of informal finance, changes over time in its importance, interest rates charged in informal markets, and the extent of exploitation. A recent study of informal finance in five Asian countries, sponsored by the Asian Development Bank, also probed the effects of informal finance on resource allocation, aggregate savings, and monetary management (Asian Development Bank 1990; Ghate and others, 1990).

In our opinion, at least six new research topics emerge from a careful reading of the preceding chapters:

1. methodological problems;
2. looking for generalizations that cut across countries;
3. identifying desirable services provided by informal finance;
4. studying the practices and techniques used in informal finance to reduce transaction costs;
5. broadening the analysis of borrowing costs from just interest charges to include expenses associated with providing collateral, transaction costs, and quality of financial services; and
6. studying the interaction between formal and informal financial markets.

Research Methods Problems

Because of heterogeneity, small transactions, legality questions, and dispersion of informal finance, it is extremely costly to do the large surveys necessary to answer statistically significant questions about the relative importance of informal finance for an entire economy. Unless policymakers are skeptical about the importance of informal finance in their country, these large studies probably do not yield information worth their costs. Does it really matter if informal finance provides 40 or 70 percent of the total value of loans in an economy, or whether poor people obtain 50 or 90 percent of their loans from informal sources? It may be sufficient to show that informal finance is important in a few representative industries and within groups that are of policy concern. A more important issue might be understanding how informal finance works and the services it provides. Studies of representative cases may be a less costly way of assembling this information than doing surveys. At least initially, in many countries, research will have to address the concerns policymakers have about informal finance, no matter how unfounded they may seem.

A related practical problem is how to do a rapid diagnosis of informal finance in a country where little systematic analysis of this topic has been done before. Many governments and most large donor agencies do periodic assessments of formal financial markets. If an assessment of informal finance becomes a regular part of these broader assessments, how can researchers contribute insights without doing costly surveys whose results may not be available for several years? Should these assessments have as their unit of analysis the type of informal finance (for example, pawning), an industry (for example, the textile industry), a target group (for example, microenterprises), a geographic area (for example, a central market), or some combinations of these units?

Look for Generalizations

Descriptive studies are a critical first step in science and are indispensable in understanding phenomena as complex as informal finance. It would be possible, however, for the small number of researchers who are working on informal finance to spend all of their time only in describing and detailing the multitude of nuances found within a country and in various regions of the world in just rotating savings credit associations (ROSCAs). There is a seemingly endless and evolving variety of these savings and credit groups. While additional descriptive studies of interesting and innovative forms of informal finance are clearly useful, it would be even more useful if research on this topic increasingly focused on deriving generalizations that hold across types of informal finance and countries. Research that uncovers generalization, in turn, would be more useful to policymakers than is purely descriptive research.

Identifying Desirable Services

Informal finance is popular and persists largely because it provides valuable services to its clients, the vast majority of whom are acting voluntarily. A clearer understanding of the nature and desirability of these services would allow policymakers to design formal finance projects that provide at least some of these services, thereby making formal finance more attractive to individuals and firms currently using informal finance.

Practices and Techniques

Expense-reducing innovations, low transaction costs, and creative ways of handling loan guarantees are hallmarks of informal finance. In contrast, formal finance is often characterized by innovations that are directed at regulation avoidance, result in excessive transaction costs, and involve inflexible loan collateral requirements. The hallmarks of informal finance largely explain why it is successful in providing financial services to the poor, while markedly different characteristics of the formal financial system help explain why poor people remain beyond its reach. Research on informal finance may uncover practices and techniques that could be grafted onto formal finance activities and also suggest policy changes that might allow formal intermediaries to expand the formal financial frontier to encompass more low-income individuals and firms.

Borrowing Costs

A good deal of the research on informal finance has been based on two important assumptions: interest payments were the only cost of borrowing, and a unit of financial service provided via informal finance was identical to a unit provided by a formal intermediary. A number of authors in this volume suggest these assumptions are misleading and should be further tested.

Particularly for borrowers and depositors of small amounts, transaction costs may weigh more heavily in their decisions than do interest payments. Likewise, the costs of providing acceptable loan guarantees to the lender may influence borrowers more forcefully than do interest charges.

Risk considerations should also be included in analyses of borrowing and depositing. For example, a borrower may accept a loan tied to a commodity sales agreement, even though the price paid on the commodity is relatively low, because the lender assumes the risks of changes in commodity prices. Likewise, depositors may prefer to leave their money, interest free, with trusted money guards rather than in interest bearing accounts at a government bank whose practices do not appear to be businesslike.

Too many studies compare interest rates on informal loans with those levied on formal loans without carefully considering the differences in the services purchased. Occasional borrowers of small amounts, for example, may be willing to pay relatively high rates of interest on their loans from dependable informal lenders because doing so may assure them of future access to emergency loans—essentially a line of credit. The relationship may also commit the lender to intercede for a borrower in vital matters such as minor legal and administrative hassles in a village. These same borrowers may ignore formal loans that carry lower interest rates because additional services are absent or because the formal lender is viewed as being transitory. Additional research on these important issues would clarify the subtle services in informal finance that enhance attractiveness and possibly provide important lessons for formal intermediaries.

Interaction Between Informal and Formal Finance

Much of the traditional discussion of informal finance has depicted it as operating largely in isolation from formal finance, partly because of the extensive use of interest rate differentials to measure market segmentation. This has led to some discussion of how to increase connections between formal and informal markets. Increasingly, however, research is showing that formal and informal finance are substantially connected, that economies of specialization explain some apparent market segmentation, and that many people use both formal and informal finance. Connections include group savings that are deposited in banks and formal borrowers who make informal loans.

The interactions between formal and informal finance go beyond simply the movement of funds. In some cases informal forms of finance evolve into formal forms (for example, Cameroon, India, and Japan). In other cases severe repression of formal finance may result in banks converting some of their activities into informal arrangements. There are also a number of cases where formal and semi-formal forms of finance—ACCION in Latin America, for example—have borrowed a number of ideas from informal finance.

Additional research that clarifies the extent and desirability of interactions between formal and formal finance could be valuable to policymakers who are designing programs to enhance connections within financial markets.

Policy Implications

At least five policy strategies for dealing with informal finance were touched upon in the preceding chapters.

Abolish, Regulate, or Reduce

There is virtually no support among the authors of this volume for shrinking or abolishing informal finance. Most of the discussion focused on the positive contributions informal finance makes to development and the well being of the poor. Many of the authors were more in favor of enhancing the performance of informal finance, or at least learning from it, rather than trying to abolish it. At the same time, Vogel and Wieland (chapter 21) stress the importance of prudential regulation when informal intermediaries become large and are handling substantial amounts of deposits.

Benign Neglect

Many of the authors of the preceding chapters favor leaving informal finance alone. Under this strategy the main consideration is to avoid policies that inadvertently and unfairly hinder informal finance, as intervention in financial markets has often done.

Link Formal with Informal

Several of the authors, especially those representing donor or nongovernmental agencies, supported using informal finance as conduits for formal loans (Seibel and Parhusip, chapter 17; Christen, chapter 20). They argued that augmenting the supply of funds available for informal lending may be the only efficient way to effectively lend to poor people. Perhaps other authors, if asked, would argue that infusions of external funds would undermine basic elements that result in success in informal finance. For example, outside funds may lessen the incentive for informal groups to save, increase transaction costs, introduce political decisions into lending, and lessen the incentives to repay loans. An unanswered question is how much outside funds can be absorbed by informal lenders or groups before the elements that nurture their success are altered adversely?

Convert Informal to Formal

Some authors mention the possibilities of helping informal groups evolve into semiformal or formal finance (Seibel and Parhusip, chapter 17). Experimental programs sponsored by the West German's Gesellschaft fur Technische Zusammenarbeit (GTZ) in Cameroon and in Indonesia are providing valuable insights into the possibilities of assisting this evolution. It will be useful for researchers to monitor these efforts over the next few years in order to carefully documents results.

Emulate Informal Finance

A final strategy involves learning from informal finance but not attempting to alter its activities through outside interventions. This would largely involve doing research on informal finance to clarify the types of services it provides and the techniques and practices used to provide financial services to the poor. This should include analyses of informal financial activities as part of financial sector assessments as well as more specific analysis of particular forms of informal finance. Useful ideas from these studies might then be grafted onto formal finance programs so that their design more closely emulates informal finance.

As Wai points out in chapter 25, there has been a substantial increase in the understanding of informal financial markets over the past three decades. We hope our suggestions for researchers and for policymakers will result in an even better understanding of this fascinating topic over the next three decades.

References

Asian Development Bank. 1990. *Asian Development Outlook 1990*. Manila, Philippines: Asian Development Bank.

Ghate, P. B. and others. 1990. "Informal Finance: Some Findings from Asia." Unpublished manuscript prepared by the Economics and Development Resource Center, Asian Development Bank, Manila, Philippines.

About the Contributors

Dale W Adams is professor of agricultural economics at The Ohio State University. Since the mid-1960s he has done research and consulting on financial market problems in low income countries. He has studied informal finance in Bolivia, Guatemala, and the Philippines.

R. Bastiaanssen is a sociologist who did his graduate studies at the Wageningen Agricultural University in the Netherlands. His field research was done in India on informal finance.

F. J. A. Bouman is a retired professor of sociology from the Wageningen Agricultural University in the Netherlands. For many years he and his students did research on informal finance in various countries in Africa and Asia, with particular emphasis on group savings and credit activities and pawnbroking.

Marie L. Canavesi is an anthropologist who taught at the Catholic University in La Paz, Bolivia. Born in Uruguay, she has studied informal finance in Bolivia.

Robert P. Christen has worked for ACCION International in several Latin American countries, the most recent being Chile. He administers and promotes credit programs for operators of microenterprises. Aspects of ACCION's credit programs emulate features found in informal finance.

Carlos Cuevas is assistant professor of agricultural economics at The Ohio State University. Known for his early work on transaction costs in financial markets, he has also done research on informal finance in Cameroon, El Salvador, Honduras, Niger, and Zaire.

Virginia DeLancey is an economist teaching at the American University in Cairo, Egypt. Her work on informal finance has been focused in Cameroon and in Somalia with particular attention to the role of women in these activities.

Jose de la Vina is an economist with the Economic Policy Analysis Unit (UDAPE) in La Paz, Bolivia. He holds an M.S. degree in economics from Arizona State University.

Emmanuel Esguerra is an economist who did his graduate work at the Ohio State University. He was born in the Philippines and has conducted research on both formal and informal finance in that country.

Nimal A. Fernando is a senior researcher in the Papua New Guinea Institute of Applied Social and Economic Research. For many years he worked in the Research and Rural Credit Departments of the Central

Bank of Ceylon. He has written on the topics of informal finance in Sri Lanka and Papua New Guinea.

Del Fitchett is a senior economist with the Economic Development Institute of the World Bank. He has worked extensively in Latin America, the Middle East, and Africa.

P. B. Ghate was born in India. He was a senior economist with the Asian Development Bank where he supervised a large study during the late 1980s of informal finance in Bangladesh, India, Indonesia, the Philippines, and Thailand.

Douglas H. Graham is professor of agricultural economics at the Ohio State University. He has worked on informal finance topics in several Central American countries, in Jamaica, in Mozambique, in Niger, and in the Philippines.

Otto Hospes is a rural sociologist at the Wageningen Agricultural University in the Netherlands. He is a lecturer on rural finance and cooperatives in low-income countries at the Department of Agrarian Law. His work on informal finance has focused on Indonesia.

Yoichi Izumida is associate professor of agricultural economics at the University of Utsunomiya in Japan. His specialty is agricultural finance in Asia, but he also studies rural financial development, including various forms of informal finance in Japan.

Jerry R. Ladman is professor of agricultural economics at The Ohio State University. He and his students have worked on informal finance for a number of years in Latin America, particularly in Bolivia, the Dominican Republic, El Salvador, and Mexico

Mario B. Lamberte is Vice-President of the Philippine Institute for Development Studies. He is an economist who has analyzed a variety of forms of informal finance in the Philippines.

Carl E. Liedholm is professor of economics at Michigan State University. For a number of years he and his students have studied microenterprises in many low income countries in Africa, the Caribbean, and Asia. This includes collecting information on how these small businesses relate to informal finance.

Roberto Liz is executive director of the APEC Foundation for Educational Credit (FUNDAPEC) in Santo Domingo, the Dominican Republic. Formerly, he was sub-manager for development in the Central Bank of the Dominican Republic. He holds an M.S. degree in economics from Manchester University.

Ross H. McLeod is an economist who works for an economics and banking consulting firm in Australia. Most of his work on informal finance has been in Indonesia.

Richard L. Meyer is professor of agricultural economics at The Ohio State University. For many years he has worked on problems of rural finance in Latin America and Asia. His work on informal finance has focused on Bangladesh, Ecuador, the Philippines, and Thailand.

Henk A. J. Moll is lecturer in the Department of Development Economics at the Wageningen Agricultural University in the Netherlands, where he also did his graduate degrees. He has done extensive research on rural finance in various countries in Africa and Asia.

C. P. S. Nayar is an economist who has for many years studied various forms of informal finance in India. Since doing this research he has become the managing director of an informal financial institution in Kerala State, India.

Tongroj Onchan is professor of agricultural economics at Kasetsart University in Thailand. He and his students have for many years analyzed various aspects of formal and informal finance, especially in rural areas of Thailand.

Uben Parhusip is an economist for Bank Indonesia. He is involved in a project that links formal and informal finance in Indonesia.

Nimal Sanderatne is Senior Research Fellow in the Institute of Policy Studies, Colombo, Sri Lanka. He was formerly Chairman, Bank of Ceylon and filled a number of positions at the Central Bank of Sri Lanka, including those of Director of Economic Research and Director of Statistics. He has conducted several studies on informal finance in Sri Lanka and published a number of articles in books and journals.

Hans Dieter Seibel is a professor of sociology at the University of Cologne in Germany. He and his students have done research on informal finance in Congo, Ghana, Ivory Coast, Liberia, Togo, Indonesia, Nepal, Philippines, and Thailand. He has also been involved in action programs to link formal and informal forms of finance in several countries.

Gertrud Schrieder is an agricultural economist who was born in Germany. She did her graduate research at The Ohio State University on the topic of informal finance in Cameroon, and then began a doctoral program at the University of Hohenheim in Germany

Parker Shipton is an anthropologist who has worked on various forms of informal finance in Kenya, the Gambia, and several other African countries. He is an institute associate at the Harvard Institute for International Development and also teaches in the Department of Anthropology at Harvard University.

Robert C. Vogel is Executive Director of IMCC, a consulting firm specializing in financial sector analysis in low income countries, and he is also Director of the World Banking and Finance Program at the Economics Institute in Boulder, Colorado. His work on informal finance has focused on Latin America.

J. D. Von Pischke is a senior financial analyst with the World Bank. He began working on rural finance in Kenya and joined the World Bank in 1975. He has studied finance problems in numerous countries and has written a number of books and articles on financial development.

U Tun Wai is an economist who retired from the International Monetary Fund. Born in Burma, he was early exposed to informal finance through the activities of relatives. He was one of the first economists to write about informal finance.

Robert Wieland is an economist and consultant who has worked worldwide on informal and small agent finance.

Index

(Page numbers in italics indicate material in tables or figures.)